World Wisdom
The Library of Perennial Philosophy

The Library of Perennial Philosophy is dedicated to the exposition of the timeless Truth underlying the diverse religions. This Truth, often referred to as the *Sophia Perennis*—or Perennial Wisdom—finds its expression in the revealed Scriptures as well as the writings of the great sages and the artistic creations of the traditional worlds.

The Mystery of Individuality appears as one of our selections in the Perennial Philosophy series.

The Perennial Philosophy Series

In the beginning of the twentieth century, a school of thought arose which has focused on the enunciation and explanation of the Perennial Philosophy. Deeply rooted in the sense of the sacred, the writings of its leading exponents establish an indispensable foundation for understanding the timeless Truth and spiritual practices which live in the heart of all religions. Some of these titles are companion volumes to the Treasures of the World's Religions series, which allows a comparison of the writings of the great sages of the past with the perennialist authors of our time.

T0307050

The Mystery
of Individuality

Grandeur and Delusion of the Human Condition

Mark Perry

Foreword by
William Stoddart

World Wisdom

The Mystery of Individuality:
Grandeur and Delusion of the Human Condition
© 2012 World Wisdom, Inc.

Cover photograph © Keren Su

Library of Congress Cataloging-in-Publication Data

Perry, Mark, 1951-
The mystery of individuality : grandeur and delusion of the human condi-
tion / Mark Perry ; foreword by William Stoddart.
    p. cm. -- (The perennial philosophy series)
    Includes bibliographical references (p.   ) and index.
    ISBN 978-1-936597-13-0 (pbk. : alk. paper) 1. Theological anthropology. 2.
Philosophical anthropology. 3. Human beings. 4. Individuality. I. Title.
    BL256.P46 2012
    202'.2--dc23

                                                              2012013982

Printed on acid-free paper in the United States of America

For information address World Wisdom, Inc.
P.O. Box 2682, Bloomington, Indiana 47402-2682
www.worldwisdom.com

Nû bite ich iuch, daz ir alsô sît, daz ir verstât dise rede; wan ich sage iu in der êwigen wârheit: ir ensît denne glîch dirre wârheit, von der wir nû sprechen wellen, sô enmuget ir mich niht verstân.

"Now I beg you to be That, that you might understand this speech. I say to you in the eternal truth that if you are not equal to this truth, of which we are now speaking, you cannot understand me."

Meister Eckhart, Sermon 52

CONTENTS

Foreword *by William Stoddart*   *ix*

Preface   *xi*

Introduction   1

1   The Wound of Duality   19

2   Who Am I?   39

3   The Iconic Figure   61

4   Kingdoms and Nations   83

5   Individuality Is Not Individualism   103

6   Beyond Good and Evil   127

7   Satan Is Not an Atheist   149

8   Capital Punishment   177

9   On Authority   197

10   Primacy of Character   219

11   The Forbidden Door   245

12   *Hieros Gamos* or the Sacred Marriage   273

Glossary of Terms   299

Index   307

Biographical Notes   313

FOREWORD

In this wise and insightful book, the author defines what a human being is according to his perennial archetype *in divinis* while, at the same time, situating him in the context of the spiritual wasteland of the contemporary world, which he contrasts with what an integrally sacred tradition is meant to be. His writing exhibits an unusual succinctness and clarity, coupled with a profound compassion. The author's viewpoint is based on the ideas of the "perennialist school", of which the exponent par excellence was Frithjof Schuon.

The term "perennialist school" (also known as the "traditionalist" or "esoterist" school) calls for some explanation. It was first used by the American Academy of Religion in the 1980s. The founders of this current of intellectuality and spirituality were the French philosopher and orientalist René Guénon (1886-1951) and the German philosopher, poet, and artist Frithjof Schuon (1907-1998). It was further expounded by Ananda Coomaraswamy (1877-1947) and Titus Burckhardt (1908-1984). The principal characteristics of this school include the fundamental and essential principles of metaphysics (with its cosmological and anthropological ramifications), intellectual intuition, orthodoxy, tradition, universality, the science of symbolism; spirituality in the broadest sense; intrinsic morals and esthetics; and the meaning and importance of sacred art. A very important characteristic is a deep-reaching critique of the modern world, on the basis of strictly traditional principles. "Universality" means what Schuon has called "the transcendent unity of the religions", and these words became the title of his first book. Universality thus signifies the Supreme Truth that underlies each of the great religious revelations.

It is this supra-formal truth that constitutes the *religio perennis*. This term, which does not imply a rejection of the similar terms *philosophia perennis* and *sophia perennis*, nevertheless contains a hint of an additional dimension which is unfailingly present in Schuon's writings, and this is that intellectual understanding entails a spiritual responsibility, that intelligence requires to be complemented by sincerity and faith, and that "seeing" (in height) implies "believing" (in depth). In other words, the greater our perception of essential and saving truth, the greater our obligation towards an effort of inward or spiritual "realization". The *religio perennis*, by its very nature, is something "secret"; it is a "still small voice", a hidden presence, sought out and found only by those with a hunger and thirst for it, and known only to those with eyes to see and ears to hear. Like Pythagoras and Plato, Guénon and Schuon derive their doctrinal expositions directly from *intellectus purus*—a process which lends to these expositions an unsurpassable lucidity, not to say infallibility.

It is from this intellectual and spiritual current that Perry derives his inspiration. Schuon's *intellectual* teachings have already been the subject of many studies, but I know of no other author who expounds and reflects the specifically *spiritual* teachings of Frithjof Schuon as intimately and authentically as does Mark Perry, who, all his life, had the advantage of being a close associate of Schuon. The reader will enjoy Perry's rich vocabulary and eloquent and evocative prose and, at the same time, will receive powerful spiritual encouragement.

William Stoddart

PREFACE

No book is written in a void: there is always a mentor, or several. In my case I owe a special debt to René Guénon, who was the first to help me situate the fallacy of the "modern world" for what it is, while providing me with its antidote: namely, a respect as lucid as it is profound for the notion of sacred tradition and orthodoxy, compared to which our civilization can only be an anti-tradition since, in essence, it is founded on the repudiation of sacred tradition, whether intentional or not. Guénon's *Crisis of the Modern World* rent, in a moment of piercing clarity, the veil shrouding the eye of my heart; this experience led me to my next mentor.

I owe the philosopher and sage Frithjof Schuon my sense of the Absolute for, before I encountered his works and despite my better instincts, I was not immune to the insidious disease of relativism. And I subsequently owe him my sense of Truth and of the sacred, as well as, on the personal plane, the insight into what a true man of God is. His knowledge of First Principles is unparalleled and his gnosis has been the manna of my existence; I cannot imagine meeting his like on earth again.

Nor can I leave Titus Burckhardt unmentioned, whose book *Alchemy* offered a decisive turning point for me at a time when I was struggling fruitlessly in high school with chemistry; this book freed me from the totalitarian hold of modern science, helping me grasp that the natural world surrounding us is the scripture of a sacred cosmos.

Not least, both of my parents, Whitall and Barbara Perry, in leaving behind the Western world in search of a spiritual master they fancied would be in the Himalayas, embarked in the late 1940s for Cairo, Egypt, on a journey of no insignificant daring, cutting their secular moorings with Boston *bienséance*; their initiative to leap upstream, as it were, was seeded deep into my soul, for which I owe them special consideration.

And how could I leave out William Stoddart, this indefatigable champion of orthodoxy, whose treasure house of wisdom and erudition I have been plundering for counsel decade after decade; his acumen and incisive insights have brought discipline and depth to my own mind.

Finally, I am also deeply indebted to Huston Smith for having written the Preface to my first book; were it not for his enthusiastic appreciation of that book, I might not have written this new book which, alas, came too late for him to read, although upon learning about it he was gracious enough to write to me: "I cannot imagine that anything you write is not important."

By way of brief personal comment, I could say this: I was born a conservative with an innate thirst for spirituality. This requires a brief explanation. I refer to the term "conservative", not in a political or even ideological sense, but in the fundamental sense of "conserving sacred tradition" as well as of "remaining true to the origin". This origin—the origin of all men—is the Eternal, just as, by the same logic, It is the end. By that criterion, the duty of the prototypical conservative ("the one who conserves")[1] must then be to preserve, defend, and uphold real tradition inasmuch as tradition is defined as a cultural crystallization of our sacred origin *sub specie aeternitatis*[2] ("from the perspective of eternity") and not "tradition" as an ossified and often comfortably convenient, when not hypocritical, conventionalism. Moreover, by the nature of things, this bond is under permanent assault from the law of entropy or what amounts to the ruin of time, not to mention the depredations due to human ignorance, for all on earth is subject to inertia and destruction; and this means that unless tirelessly upheld—or unless providentially renewed by Heaven—this bond with our divine origin is subject to inexorable deterioration with the complicit participation of the flood of humanity; whence, the exhortation "be not conformed to this world" (Rom. 12:2).

Not least, this is not a book on "human potential"—anything but! The essence of human individuality derives from man being created in the image of God, namely in the image of a supreme model, or the *Purushottama*, the "Supreme Personality of Godhead", as Krishna mentions in the *Bhagavad Gita* (15:18). This means, by moral implication, that ruin and perdition awaits them who forget they are fashioned in the Divine. Yet, ruin and perdition awaits also them who presume to be divine. What the question comes down to is one of balance: remembering our divine essence, on the one hand, without forgetting our human nothingness, on the other. Noble radiation and humble effacement.

---

1 "Conserve" from the Latin *conservare*, "to keep, preserve, guard" or "to keep watch, maintain". The prefix "*con-*" (or "*co-*") has the function either as an intensive, or means "with" or "together with", in which case the meaning becomes "to preserve together with"; in other words a duty that man cannot perform alone, so help us God.

2 Readers are referred to the Glossary of Terms at the end of book for translations and explanations of all foreign terms.

INTRODUCTION

The personhood of man proves, totally and irrefutably, the idea of a creator God who is Will, Intelligence, and Love, otherwise how would man be endowed with these very same faculties? These faculties are ideally defined in the wisdom of Vedanta as Being, Consciousness, and Beatitude or *Sat, Chit, Ananda*. Now, when defined in depth, the essence of Being (*Sat*) becomes pure strength or Will; that of Consciousness (*Chit*) pure wisdom or Intelligence; and that of Beatitude (*Ananda*) pure Love; and this triad amounts to as essential and universal a name given to God as can be formulated in human language: *Satchitananda*. In turn, these three attributes constitute the essence of man's faculties; and since they cannot emerge from nothing, least of all from matter, they can only be proof of a Supreme Being that possesses them originally in His very nature and hence can bestow them. And this is where our definition of individuality must begin, because to overlook the Divine and to seek the meaning of individuality on a purely psychological plane would be an abortive quest.

It has been said that in order to know man we must know God; however, to know God we need to know man for, to quote Saint Augustine, "when I know myself I shall know Thee",[1] which echoes the Socratic "Know thyself"—our root identity merging with the one Self. Seen from the outside, however, this sounds like an unsolvable riddle, all the more given that our divine essence is heavily overlaid with our passionate individuality, our appetitive soul. Now this begs the question how light could be entombed in darkness, or knowledge in ignorance? Yet, if we consider that even though earthly man is by definition ignorant of God—the vast majority of people live utterly unaware of the Divine, even if they have faith!—the very reason for being of man on earth is his cosmic role as a "bridge" (*pontifex*) between Heaven and earth; therefore his ignorance of the Divine can only be an accidental infirmity, not an essential limitation. Indeed, the very fact that man is aware of the Divine at all proves his potential capacity to know God, much as a flower "knows" the sun even when imbedded as a tiny seed

---

1 "*Noverim me, noverim te*" (*Soliloquies* X, 1:1). The fuller quotation is: "Let me know Thee, Thou who knowest me, so that I may know Thee as I am known." This reciprocity of knowledge between God and his servant is the essence of spiritual awakening, for, unbeknownst, we can only know ourselves through God's knowledge of us, just as in turn God's knowledge of us is the foundation of our knowledge of ourselves, for only God is truly self-knowing. Thus, to know is essentially to partake of Godhead in some veiled degree.

underneath the sod, its outward fate condemned, it would seem, to be all darkness and cold and insignificance.

Hence, short of knowing God directly, we must start "from where we are" and this point of departure is the chasm separating man from the Divine, a bewildering chasm that tempts many—especially in our secular modern culture—to define man in the absence of God, in other words to explain man as an end in himself; or to see man as something concrete and God as an abstraction. A favorite option then is to explain man through psychology when what is really needed is a pneumatology or a "science of the Spirit", without which psychology—or the study of the soul—can only amount to the blind leading the blind because no matter how erudite or subtle our analysis will be we cannot escape the conundrum of the mortal attempting to define the Immortal; we cannot escape by our own means the narrow labyrinth of human observations and speculations unless we can appeal to a higher principle. Or put differently, we might say it is possible to describe via psychology what man is outwardly but not to explain what he is in depth; the problem, in other words, is not the science of psychology, which is obviously legitimate on its plane (as opposed to psychologism), but to reduce man to a creature that can be defined only in psychological terms when what characterizes him is—to echo our opening statement—firstly an intelligence capable of knowing the True, then a free-will capable of choosing this Sovereign Good, and finally a soul capable of loving the Beautiful. Our three faculties, in other words, find their integral fulfillment in uniting with these three sacred ends; indeed, our faculties were fashioned for them because they emanate from the True, the Sovereign Good, and the Beautiful in the first place, the instrument proving the vocation.

To speak of man is to speak of an immortal soul, and this soul, however busy and absorbed man is with his daily pursuits, seeks release finally in something permanent and blissful that no earthly achievements can satisfy to a lasting degree. Turned away from its true end, our immortal soul gets trapped in futilities, all the more seductive if pleasurable, and as a result the soul risks finally becoming identified with the accidental and ephemeral instead of the essential and eternal. Or, it can be drawn to love creatures and objects outside of God, that is to say to idolize man in some degree, be it unintentionally, when the ideal is "to see all things in God and God in all things", to borrow a formulation from Schuon.[2] Not least, also, is the

2 Frithjof Schuon was the foremost exponent in our epoch of the *Philosophia Perennis*, or the "universal doctrine" underlying all religions and cultures. This doctrine is inherent in all true traditions, and is not a separate cult or practice—although one can posit that men of the *Satya Yuga*, or "Golden Age" practiced religion naturally, in a non-confessional form.

temptation of mistaking the social and cultural world we happen to live in as reality—or as a valid norm in its own right—instead of understanding that it is a shadow of the Real and, in the case of our modern civilization, an actual inversion of this Real as shall be detailed later. Virgin nature, on the other hand and by contrast with modern civilization, overflows with symbols of Eternity, all of which offer a word to the wise or rather an image to the contemplative. But to have "eyes to see" we must have a spiritual wanderer's sensitivity, an intuition of a wondrous land from which we have been exiled on earth—as many an olden fairy tale intimates. Thus, "starting from where we are" means the ability to recognize that the modern civilization we find ourselves in cannot in itself, given its Prometheanism, be a reflection of a sacred prototype—unless, that is, we think machines and the like are to be found in Paradise, a nightmarish prospect. As a result, and if we are spiritual beings, we will find ourselves in exile in the modern wasteland. Now, the very sense of an exile, when acute, can be the guiding urge that leads us to seek a solution to our fate in something greater than ourselves, and this "greater" can in the end only be the Divine or the Absolute. In turn, the Divine will reveal itself to us in direct measure as our need is deep because in its depths this quenchless need is none other than the Divine yearning—in mysterious disguise—to reclaim us to Itself, to its holy impartible Self.

The promptings of the Divine we obscurely sense may however fall on deaf ears, for man is stiff-necked and prone to resisting the Spirit, even capable of setting himself up against It in an act of ultimate defiance—a defiance born, very paradoxically, from the very divineness in man himself when misunderstood or falsely appropriated by the ego in the pride of his God-given existential and intellectual powers. The paradox is further sharpened by the fact that man has no choice, he cannot sidestep the Divine no matter what he does: either he submits to God or else he will himself play God—and never more so than when rejecting God—but he cannot just be man without reference to God, try as he may. In other words he can never be neutral or average: either he endeavors to become a saint, *Dei gratia* ("with the grace of God"), or he risks becoming a devil; but he can never aspire to some lazy comfortable middle ground in which he can expect to lead a life of banal non-commitment regarding the life and death issues facing him; his immortal substance makes it such, and the goad of eternity sets the standard he cannot eschew. This means that man, unlike animals, is aware of his individuality as a human being, and

Consequently, this *philosophia* was his *religio*, and vice-versa, the division between mind and heart characteristic of later stages of humanity having not yet occurred.

with this awareness comes an intuitive sense that he can never cease "to exist", even in cold death which finally is only a threshold; indeed, this instinct for immortality, even when denied, is at the heart of everything man does, for better or worse. And finally, in never ceasing to be, man bears tribute to God—whether grateful or grudging—because his immortality is another proof of his being made in the image of a Supreme Being. "Man is condemned to the Absolute", as Schuon has remarked; this is his glorious destiny or else his dire fate; and what choice he makes with regard to the Absolute is his alone, for this is the signal privilege of his divine freedom.

*   *   *

To know man we must know God, we mentioned. However, man will counter, "God is invisible and even unknowable" therefore how can we ever know man if we can only do so by knowing God who is both invisible and unknowable, the *Deus absconditus* of Aquinas? Now if it is true that God—as Godhead[3]—is inherently unknowable by man inasmuch as he is but fallible ego, we will add that God is not just ineffable mystery but glorious manifestation too, *Deus revelatus*; therefore, we may approach Him through that part of His nature He makes visible in creation everywhere, from the loftiest mountains to the tiniest flower, or in all the heavenly qualities we encounter on earth, a doctrine that Saint Dionysius the Areopagite richly developed.[4] Moreover, He has revealed Himself to man through the great religions and their traditions. In that sense "It is easy to know God, but hard to be a human being", as one sage put it,[5] and this is the truth of the situation.

Finally, God dwells in man himself by virtue of his theomorphism, and by virtue of his conscience (of good and evil). And He dwells most profoundly in man's innermost core in the form of the heart-intellect, which is the spark of the Holy Spirit, namely that supra-human faculty of Consciousness-Intelligence-Love mentioned above, without which man could not exist because to do so would amount to existing without God or outside of God, a cosmic impossibility. Not least, we can learn to know God through virtue, which is to imitate God and thus to partake of his Be-

3 By "Godhead", we mean the ineffable God or Supra Being, in contrast to the creator God who is also the personal God of theology.

4 The Areopagite's doctrine on the Names of God and on the Celestial Hierarchy are a kind of Christianized Neoplatonism describing the radiation of the Supreme Principle—as the Sovereign Good—from the essence out to the very ends of creation.

5 We quote from memory only.

ing; at every moment man can choose the noble over the ignoble, the good over the bad, the generous over the petty, and so on, each positive decision leading to a reawakening of his consciousness as he is converted from self-ishness to wisdom and compassion because each correct choice places man on a divine axis, as it were, stretching from earth all the way to Heaven, so that the nethermost point of that axis—or point of earthly contact—reso-nates with the same essence of divinity as the Supreme Principle itself.

As we pause here, it must be acknowledged that it is possible to define man on several levels. Thus if one seeks to define man through psychology one might say he is first a constellation of faculties (reason, emotion, feel-ing, and so on) or that he has a personality with its qualities and shortcom-ings, and also with its complexes and possible traumas, as well as hopes and disillusions, ambitions and passions; but these definitions cannot account for man's immortality. Another way of defining man would be to do so by listing his qualities, for instance to observe that he is intelligent or stupid, courageous or cowardly, generous or selfish; but these attributes still would not account for his integral nature. However, to say that man is intelli-gence, love, and free-will, and to add that being intelligence he is therefore meant to know the Truth, and being love he is meant to unite with the Good, and having free-will he is therefore obligated, by ontological duty, to choose true over false, right over wrong, and good over evil, then we have captured the essential traits that explain not just man but, by extension, all of civilization as well. Yet this still would not be sufficient for if man has intelligence, love, and free-will it is because His Creator has endowed him with His own Divine Nature, and this from the very beginning of creation, in other words even before his human birth; now, God is pure intelligence because He is perfect consciousness, pure love because He is totality, and pure freedom because He is limited by nothing. And it is this connaturality of essence between the Divine and man's heart-intellect that constitutes the basis for man's vocation of *theosis*, that is to say, of divinization or spiritual realization which, if thwarted, explains then his misery. This fundamental assessment goes beyond psychology, and can rightfully be termed pneu-matology, or a science of the Spirit, namely that which makes of man a spiritual being by natural essence and vocation.

To be more precise, a pneumatology of man results from the fact that he can be defined as spirit, soul, and body, and in that hierarchical order. In other words, the soul derives everything from the spirit, and the body de-rives everything from the spirit as well as from the soul, whereas the spirit is derived from neither of those two while determining both. However, if it is clear that the soul is determined by the spirit, it is not immediately as obvious that it can be accidentally determined by the body as well and this despite being hierarchically superior to it; this happens when the soul, though of an "igneous" essence (by contrast to the body's "clay") stoops to the body by allowing carnal appetites to rule it. That said, it is important to specify that the physical body in itself is totally innocent and, in fact, a materialization of the spirit in fleshly form, and therefore not the evil cause of the soul's darkening; that cause has its root solely in the soul itself.

Because the human soul can attain to the highest as well as stoop to the lowest, or even do so concurrently,[6] there is a tendency to see man purely as soul or else to reduce the spirit to the soul, namely to speak of the spirit in psychic terms. But it is essential not to mistake soul and spirit, difficult as this may be for people who equate anything supernatural—no matter how ambiguous—with the spiritual, when in fact the spiritual transcends the psychic. Not in extra-sensory experiences but only in holy virtue is the soul united to the spirit, and so it is really the saint and not the gifted medium, or even the seer, that should be the measure of man. And, in turn, it is the prophet—in Hinduism the *avatara*—that is the measure of the saint, just as God is the measure of the prophet. In Buddhist terms, one would say that the *bodhisattva* is the measure of the saint (*arhat*) just as the Buddha, or rather the *Adi-Buddha*, is the measure of the *bodhisattva*. To heed this hierarchy of spirit, soul, and body—or rather of God, spirit, soul, and body—is the key for understanding man; to omit one of these poles or to confuse one of them with one or more of the others leads to all kinds of mischief and heresy.

*   *   *

Pneumatology in the broadest sense encompasses a temporal dimension and a spatial one. Starting with the temporal, it is easy to look at man as the product of his past, his heritage and upbringing, but for "immortal man", that is to say for "man standing in nakedness before God", the past is not this or that experience or this or that success or failure: the past is his divine origin, just as the future is his meeting in Eternity with his Maker. These two points in sacred time—absolute beginning and absolute end—are decisive, and therefore mundane events of past and future either vanish before these like mist or, if qualitative, are transfigured into their

---

6 Some distinguish in the soul a rational faculty and an irrational one, thus dividing the soul into two parts, i.e. the higher soul which, we assume, would correspond to the reflection of the Spirit in the soul, guiding it through reason (*logos*), and the lower or animalistic soul, driven by passions. Plato, in his *Phaedrus*, explains this twofold nature in referring to the Logos faculty of the soul, on the one hand, which guides its two steeds, *thumos* (passions) and *eros* (appetites), on the other hand.

archetypal significance. Moreover, when understood in their full qualitative significance, these reference points of past and future lie at the root of man's integral happiness in the sense that loyalty on earth to a divine origin, just as faith in a saving mercy at the end, constitute the underpinnings of his felicity while providing him with the fortitude to face earthly trials. Conversely, if those two stations are neglected—namely, the honoring of one's divine origin and the preparation for surrendering one's life to God at the end—man has no enduring chance at happiness no matter how fortunate he may be in his earthly affairs; it is a question of hierarchical perspective and priorities, around which all other commitments are to be subordinated. Needless to say, it takes both real faith and real imagination to break free from the grip of our personal past, crowded as it is with the emotional vividness of our experiences, in order to identify with a dimension of our true self that precedes—or transcends—our accidental personality fashioned as it is, for most men, more by circumstances than by principles. And it takes also true intelligence to be able to properly situate what amounts finally to the accidentality of our human fate, surroundings, and experiences. At the very least, one would not want to invest more of our vital energy in undertakings that are but ripples in time than in the eternal stakes of our existence.

As for the "spatial" dimension of pneumatology, man has a non-geographic divine or supra-personal center, transcending time and form. The reflection of this divine center in man's character grants him the serenity stemming from the capacity for dispassionate objectivity. In concrete terms, this means that an individual, when able to stand in his divine center—even if only conceptually or wishfully[7]—can raise himself high above himself, as it were, and thus renounce himself sacrificially because objectivity is the capacity to see oneself outside of oneself, free from bias, passions, and self-interest. Therefore, the giving up of oneself is the basis for—or the result of—noble detachment; this nobility comes from seeing things impartially and behaving in a manner in which our individuality becomes a vessel for God's "Selfhood". Not least, this nobility brings us also to discover how our individuality and that of our fellow man's are one and the same by virtue of our common celestial birthright, and not just through the solidarity of sharing the misery of existence on earth. It is, in other words, to discover a deeper "self-interest", or one in which individual self-interest shares a solidarity with the universal Self, namely of rediscov-

---

7 We stand in our "divine center" through virtue, immortal by definition, as well as by situating ourselves, intellectually, at the vantage point of the pure observer; each man has access to his conscience, and an aspect of this conscience is the capacity to be a disengaged or impartial viewer. Virtue and intelligence.

ering the archetypal model of man, as embodied by the great prophets; it is therefore to put the interests of the divine Self first in all things, while simultaneously recognizing the stamp of this "Self" in the selfhood of other individuals. However, such an awareness should not blind us to the deviations of individualism, both in ourselves and in others; that is to say, to recognize the "Self" in oneself and in others entails that we recognize at the very same time all that is not in harmony with this divine Self, otherwise we risk pulling God reductively down to our idiosyncratic level while, in a counter-parallel reflex, improperly exalting ourselves.

*   *   *

In pneumatology, the ideas of Origin, Center, Goal, and Objectivity—understood in their archetypal or principial significance—constitute the sacred structural framework of reference for understanding man's essential psychology. Put differently, a psychology that ignores these dimensions in their divine scope cannot truly explain man; it will in fact miss everything that makes it worth being a human being, man's very raison d'être on earth.

In pragmatic terms, when attempting to solve a psychological problem, what matters first is to understand the extra-social and therefore the extra-individual premises of our personal existence. And this means—with respect to the "temporal" aspect of pneumatology—that a child and later the adult needs to learn about his divine Origin as well as to grasp that his life tends ultimately and ineluctably to a meeting one day with his Creator, which macrocosmically is "Judgment Day" and microcosmically the moment when, in death, the individual soul meets the heart-intellect in a moment of absolute discernment;[8] such a knowledge, or such a conviction, will guide all of this person's attitudes and behavior in a profoundly meaningful way. Moreover—with respect now to the "spatial" aspect of pneumatology—this person also needs to learn to see himself as a person like he sees other persons, that is to say to see himself from the impersonal outside and not just from the personal inside, to see himself namely as God sees him; this is an education in humility. And finally, he needs to understand that he is at all times connected to a divine Center which, no matter what he does, he cannot disavow; indeed, his very existence derives both its vital and conscious energy from this Center.

---

8 In eschatological terms, death entails both a microcosmic meeting, when the soul *post mortem* must answer to the heart-intellect, and later a macrocosmic meeting, namely the resurrection of the dead at the "end of the world". However, in esoteric spirituality this "meeting" can occur while an individual is still alive on earth since the meaning of spiritual initiation is to bring about spiritual death. "Die before ye die", said Muhammad.

Thus, to the extent that an individual can grow up with a sufficient understanding of these cosmic dimensions—of the three referential points of Origin, Center, and End—and learn to order his life with reference to them, he will not live in vain and will be in a position to fulfill his human vocation. No true solution to his needs can be found outside of them; his earthly life will be over all too soon, but his immortal soul continues and it is this soul that needs to be helped, and not just the temporal person that psychology examines so expertly.

In short, our awareness of a divine Origin serves to remind us of our essence and guides us therefore to not live beneath ourselves; the sense of our divine Origin gives us the model to live by. Likewise, our awareness of a divine End guides us in truthfulness and sincerity as well as in generosity, for if we are going to meet God we must be prepared to give up all of ourselves— mind, body, and soul; the sense of a divine End calls us to the most rigorous of accounts while at the same time inducing hope in God's mercy. And finally our awareness of a divine Center, both permanent and ubiquitous, means we can live partially outside the world and outside of time, and, as it were, with one foot in paradise. No earthly trial can enslave the individual who is rooted in these three certainties.[9]

*   *   *

It may not be readily obvious that man's relationship with his fellow men depends ultimately on his relationship with God, but this relationship determines everything. Thus, if God is the supreme standard by which all human attitudes and behavior are to be measured, then any lack of faith in God, transposed to our earthly existence, will be reflected in a lack of faith in our fellow men or, to be exact, in a lack of faith in "all men of goodwill"; this will affect issues involving trust, dedication, and commitment, to mention but these, and a deficit here will in turn compromise our relationship with God for if to trust God is to trust "men of goodwill" then to trust them is also a manner of trusting in God. Indeed, a lack of faith in "men of goodwill" has its roots, however obscurely, in a lack of faith in God. And likewise: loyalty to God is reflected in loyalty to others; but if we are faithless before

---

9 Schuon summarizes this state: "Most men believe they are 'now' in this street, then in this house, and so on and so forth, and they believe in any case that they are on earth among an indefinite number of phenomena and situations; but the spiritual man dwells in the Divine Name, which binds him to 'God's Rope', and around him there is only the wheel of the *samsara*. The spiritual man is not completely here, nor completely there, he is neither before nor afterwards, he is always in the Center and in the blessed Now of God" (from a letter dated November 7, 1965).

God, who of our fellow men could expect us to keep our word, because if we take our bearings from fallible beings like ourselves, none of us can be truly good or reliable. More deeply yet, truly spiritual people will treat their fellow men as if they were dealing with God himself, and the respect owed the neighbor will be premised on the idea that a person's divine essence is not only of immediate relevance, but is potentially the realest aspect of who they are, or at least aspire to be. Without this basis in a divine reference point, it becomes impossible to respect another human being in depth and, conversely, it is precisely because of this divine basis, and not because of his accidental personality, that another human being is worthy of respect to begin with.

Selfishness or selflessness? This is the crux of the matter, and all selfhood, when cultivated outside of the Self, cannot attain to blessed selflessness, for "God alone is good". To elaborate: all human problems stem, in the last analysis, from our separation from God. Now the most general mark of this separation is seen in the "hardness of heart" mentioned in both the Biblical and Koranic scriptures, the most immediate manifestation of which is seen in an indifference to Heaven if not actual disbelief in God, or at least in a lack of sufficient faith; and it manifests also in a lack of compassion which can take on many forms, even in something as seemingly peripheral as a lack of thoughtfulness in dealing with another person. Such a core indifference—or infirmity—is enough to affect everything in a person's life, just as curing it, namely to achieve a melting of the heart, opens every imaginable door both to Heaven and to our fellow men. Hence, returning to the distinction between psychology and pneumatology, a psychological issue cannot be dealt with effectively if it is not seen as deriving in essence from a spiritual problem; this is going to the root of things.[10] We would in fact be tempted to say that man cannot be helped lastingly until he is restored virtually if not effectively to his prototype *in divinis*; the terms "wholeness" and "holiness" have the same root and, finally, it is wholeness that heals all divisions and cures all lacks.

If one last point regarding psychological issues and their possible solutions may be allowed: psychology—or rather psychotherapy—tends to want to remedy every grief, or all unhappinesses, by training us to find contentment on a plane that is finally too superficial and therefore beneath the dignity of man. Indeed, psychology, in its obsession with removing suffering, is inclined to miss the fact that not all suffering is a problem and can in fact be a blessing because, when properly understood, it can

---

10 Hence Ma Anandamayi: "Whatever you do without the thought of God is useless" (cited in Ram Alexander, *Death Must Die* [New Delhi: Indica Books, 2006], p. 235).

be the providential goad for a soul's ascent to Godhead. For example, to take the issue of fear: psychotherapy will try to reassure a patient that he or she really has nothing to fear and will work therefore to help that person overcome their fears, when in fact that person, especially if he is not leading a virtuous life, may have every objective ground to fear for the posthumous fate of his soul or to fear displeasing God here and now. One of the strangest disproportions encountered—in profane modern man especially—is that an individual can have paralyzing fears that interfere painfully with his ability to face life, and yet have utterly no fear of God or of posthumous existence;[11] that disproportion goes unnoticed by most people, when in fact the lack of fear of God is proof of implicit pride, however much it is masked by superficial virtues such as "niceness"—the favorite accolade of the heedless. If psychology cannot grasp this imbalance, then of what worth is it?

*   *   *

Now before entering into the substance of this book, mention should be made that when faced with writing about a subject touching upon the Divine, one is tempted to be quiet, because who would dare speak about God who has not found Him? And he that has found Him, it is said, remains silent; how could anyone share the ineffable? Wisdom is, by essence, holy silence. Yet, if those who love God never spoke—even if their only knowledge of Him came from a combination of faith and metaphysical speculation, as opposed to enlightenment—this would be to cede the arena to all those who ignore Him, let alone reject Him—an unthinkable alternative, in fact dishonorable because who would not support a "noble friend" under attack? That said, in wanting to defend God—partly in the fashion of a theodicy—we are conscious that we are tracing a rather lonely furrow for we do so as a Traditionalist rejecting not only secular ideologies, but also criticizing sclerotic religious conventions, not to mention the exalted subjectivism and myriad eccentricities of so-called New Age spirituality. Our quarrel, in other words, is not just with disbelief, but also with false belief, as well as with flawed or degenerate belief.

If we are sometimes forced to criticize religion—but always in the name of Revelation or of orthodoxy—, or what passes for spirituality, we do so partly by singling out believers who do not recognize the conflict between the modern world and religion—and sacred tradition—and therefore who

---

11 Or as Saint Teresa of Avila put it: "How is it, Lord, we are cowards in everything save in opposing Thee?"

enroll religion to bless their version of social progress. Meanwhile, the New Agers, in their idealism for resurrecting ancient beliefs or of returning to nature, rightly perceive some of the dangers of the machine and computer age; yet at the same time many of them have a rhapsodic notion of blending the unmixable: sacred tradition with modern science and evolutionism, while celebrating the fallacious notion of the dawning of an age of "evolved consciousness", a doctrine charismatically peddled through a hodge-podge of pseudo-esoteric borrowings that is finally misguided because wedded to the extravagant, and finally Luciferian, notion of mankind's collective spiritual progress. What, indeed, are we to make of a new dawn of religion in which man is evolving into a god and who, quite unaccountably and also due to the closing of the cycle of prophecy, has suddenly become fully capable of adjudicating right and wrong all by himself, namely in a manner that allows him to dispense de facto with God, because he has discovered somehow that, for all practical purposes, "he is God"? Heaven forfend! And, moreover, a "god" who has determined that to bring Heaven on earth is, after all, a real human possibility, no matter the scriptures and common sense. This socialized spirituality promotes a new age that defies the cosmological doctrine of the apocatastasis (*maha pralaya* in the Vedantic teachings) foretelling the final dissolution of time and form. It has become difficult psychologically for modern man to dwell on an apocalyptic scenario, a doctrine that, for his ancestors, was the essence of spiritual common sense. Hence, no wonder that this chimera of a "better future" comes, for many, at the costly expense of depreciating the past while, for others, it comes with the aberration of transposing an eschatological doctrine of moral improvement obtained through salvation into a materialistic utopia of secular collective progress.

Be that as it may, people today have, depending on their perspective, either the cyclic misfortune or the immense privilege of living in an age where ideas and writings are swirling around in a profusion utterly unimaginable in previous ages; treasures of ancient wisdom mingle alongside brilliant secular knowledge and eccentric New Age mumbo jumbo. Sorting through all this to find Ariadne's thread to lead them out of the labyrinth of the wheel of existence (*samsara*) is harder than ever before, because of the bewildering embarrassment of choices and yet easier if one can find the few ideas that really matter, for these have become eloquently available. But without self-knowledge, and without knowledge of the Truth, any knowledge is likely to lead into a treacherous maze. Moreover, the difference between spiritual enlightenment and dizzying mental gyrations can hinge on the smallest miscue of self-perception: humility or hubris, and life is won or lost. The mystery of individuality is to be sought between both of these poles: paradox of the profane individualist and mystery of the sancti-fied individual.

Man, depending on how one looks at him, is either nothing before the Absolute or, at the same time, everything because of the very Absolute, precisely.[12] Therefore as the author of this book, and "girding our loins with truth" (Eph. 6:14) and plucking from our own immortal substance—which of course we share in common with all of mankind—we shall explore both the nothingness and the everythingness of man, borrowing from some old ideas, while dusting off in the process an ancient wisdom that has lost much of its luster in our gleaming technocratic age. In so doing, our only claim to "originality" will be to live up to the root meaning of that word which is to "return to the Origin". If the reader can stay with us through the various chapters of this book, a clear pattern and a new *weltanschau-ung* will emerge—outlandish as it may strike some at first, for we live in an age where the abnormal has become normal, and one in which, more and more, evil is now seen as good and vice-versa.[13] No doubt, to reverse established assumptions held by "everyone" requires some work. But this "clear pattern" may help the reader become "re-minded", and thus able to seize what "the mystery of individuality" means in its timeless and essen-tial context. Man, in his essence, is Wisdom, Love, and Strength, and their blessed synthesis is sanctity.

*   *   *

To digress a bit now, if questions are raised about the frequent references to terms belonging to a variety of religious traditions, the reason is really quite simple: although the subject matter of this book deals with man created in the image of God, we are not speaking in the name of a single religion, or of a single spiritual credo, but in that of the *philosophia spiritualis* which is timeless gnosis. Moreover, some of the concepts are better expressed in the terminology of other traditions than in that of the Judeo-Christian one familiar to most readers, a tradition which, needless to say, we revere be-yond words. Not least, the subject discussed is man as such, namely trans-historical—and trans-cultural—man as an incarnation of what is known in

---

12 Eckhart formulates this truth thus: "In created things nothing shines except their ideas" (cited in Michael A. Sells, *Mystical Languages of Unsaying* [Chicago: University of Chicago Press, 1994], p. 156)—these "ideas" being the archetypes.

13 "Woe unto them that call evil good, and good evil; that put darkness for light, and light for darkness; that put bitter for sweet, and sweet for bitter!" (Is. 5:20). This reversal is more especially noticeable in the arts and existential customs, including modes of dress and pas-times, and not least in modern forms of dance.

Sufism as the *fitrah*, or the "primordial norm", for this is the core paradigm defining the entire mystery of individuation.

We might also add: nothing attracts more reverence and at the same time more odium than the word "God" because no word is more important and therefore more easily abused. Thus, for many, this word conjures less a notion of the Divine than of a puritanical figure of oppression. Or sometimes this word, if hyper-masculinized, has become automatically synonymous with a culture founded on misogynist prejudice. Thus, it is sometimes helpful to borrow other terms for the Godhead, such as *Atma* or *Brahma* (Hinduism), or to refer to the different levels of Buddhahood; in fact, part of the premise of Buddhism—and why it is sometimes mistaken for an atheism—is precisely that the idea of God cannot fit into a word, whence its doctrine of *Shunyata*, or the Sacred Void. At this juncture, we would in fact be tempted to pray with Meister Eckhart: "Therefore pray God that we may be free of god." But we cannot do so for reasons we intend to clarify later.

On a more intimate note, we would like to mention this too: as stated previously, one would ideally like to avoid having to try to explain—if not over-explain—things spiritual in essence, but in this instance we want to do so to avoid the risk of discussing sacred things in too cerebral a manner, for in so doing there is a risk of *thinking* about the Truth instead of *being* the Truth. And yet for man to think, and especially to reflect and to meditate, is normally the only path to regain being; without a conscious mental effort it may be difficult or impossible to spark spiritual, or cardiac, intuition. Thus we have to write, while keeping in mind that to write about essential matters, and to present ideas, is no more than to propose an approach to Reality; in other words, a dialectical approach can never be a means of exhausting that Reality, because words can never be realer than the objects they connote or the realities they describe; however, it is worth remembering that there is nonetheless a real connection between a word and the reality it depicts, and therefore words do have their magic, to say the least.

There is also a reciprocity between mind and heart, such that a truth which is perforce conceptual at the start must become vital if it is ever to be realized, *Dei gratia*; the mind must rejoin the heart,[14] what is mental must become cardiac. And vice-versa: the hardness of the heart must melt so that the mind can shine. Too often, we find that the mind is cheaply denigrated while the heart is extolled, which is a simplistic but favorite

---

14 Or as Saint Anselm of Canterbury declared: *intellego ut credam*, "I think that I may believe"; the corollary of this is his most famous maxim, *credo ut intelligam*, "I believe that I may know". The reversibility of this equation proves the interdependence of heart and mind.

reflex of spiritual subjectivists and mystical hucksters who either treat the mind with suspicion or do not wish to exert themselves intellectually, or who deem that thinking and contemplation are somehow mutually exclusive, to say nothing of dangling such dialectics before the nose of the easy prey constituted by anti-intellectual bohemian seekers that are looking for a shortcut to *samadhi* that might save them from logic. In actuality, however, both poles need to be converted: in fallen man, the heart is harder than a stone, as mentioned in scripture, while the mind is the opposite: it is fickle and scattered; to reverse this and thus to restore the natural state of man, the congealed heart must become liquefied and the diffuse mind crystallized. The intellectual effort required preliminarily for attaining the primacy of pure being could be compared to focusing a glass lens to sharpen sunlight so as to kindle the soul: when the lucid mind has grasped a real idea perfectly, the heart can catch on fire of a sudden. Logic, or what the Scholastics termed *recta ratio*, is a sacred science in that its function is meant to express the Truth; and the Truth, when formulated correctly, can then be understood, and this understanding in turn can enlighten being.

That said, learning how to think correctly about the Truth often involves a laborious cerebral effort, so much so that sometimes, and all things being equal, it would be tempting to put our pen down and to sit at sunset near a fountain on a terrace somewhere overlooking pastoral vales, in one of those fragrant gardens adorned with sentinel cypresses parted by pebbled alleys, and to disencumber ourselves from all mental constructs; it would be tempting to luxuriate in the simplicity and emptiness of what Zen terms *"mu"* or the primal oneness of being coursing through all of creation, and for an infinite moment just to be—to be without premeditation, without the slightest mental effort, to live in the pure blissful spontaneity of the eternal now. It would be tempting to contemplate perhaps a crescent moon adorning the evening sky while a chorus of crickets intoned their timeless litanies. And, why not, we could sit down with Omar Khayyam's proverbial jug of wine and a loaf of bread, "and Thou". But such emptiness—and such fullness—cannot be conjured forthwith, out of thin air, even with the sincerest of longing. Because, for man, to live without mental constructs requires first a mental act of conceptual awareness and this applies even to him who has had a flash of existential insight into the original nature of being. To sustain and nurture that flash afterwards, in other words, to save it from being no sooner dissipated as it manifests, or to be scattered before the relentless assault of the world's thousand importunities, requires an effort of the mind to enshrine its echo. In turn, true insight, to be sustained or not dissipated, requires virtue to have its vibration re-sowed, as it were, in order to take permanent root in our character; we cannot, in other words, permanently sustain a lucid state of consciousness without translating divine awareness into virtue. All true cognition is finally a re-cognition, and recognition is rooted in what we are and not just what we know.[15]

Ideally, a human being would be imbued with such spontaneous objectivity, such profound nobility, and such guileless childlikeness that the eventide scene evoked would involve no conceptualizing or sentimental reverie. Again, in the scene evoked, the person's soul beholding this moment would, in a kind of consanguinity of the spirit, be transfigured into nature's Eucharistic essence: the deepening vales and the swelling hills and the beholder's physical body would be one in the same beneficent geographic strength and bounty; the fragrant garden would reflect his own soul fragrant with the sacredness of being; the crescent moon would be the emblem of his wisdom; the crickets invocation would echo his heart's reverence; and the draught of wine would be a renewed occasion of devout communion. Landscape and individual would be embraced in the same union of love and wisdom. Such imagery, of course, is but a metaphor suggesting that to proceed from here to there—namely, from commonplace "here" to sacred "There"—entails a temporary abolishment of previous assumptions, mental as well as sentimental, in an act of metamorphosis implying a complete translation from "the same to the Same"—O rare precious paradox!—but now a "Same" understood in its theophanic depth; this is the transfiguration of the two-dimensional circle into the three-dimensional Platonic sphere.[16]

To pursue the idea of epiphany described above, there is a revealing passage in the Koran which says: "Lo! We have placed all that is on the

---

15 Even though knowledge (or doctrine) is the indispensable complement to being, there are spiritual paths premised on a purely non-conceptual approach, such as the Chan school of Chinese Buddhism and Japanese Zen Buddhism, which make a point of avoiding doctrinal reflection in favor of a meditation centered on the irruptive realization of pure Buddhahood. But such an approach presupposes firstly a homogeneous psychic substance and this is partly a question of heredity, and secondly a traditional or naturally esthetic setting providing the harmonious and indispensable framework for this kind of meditation. It cannot, in other words, be done impromptu in a modern living room dressed in trivial attire by someone with an untrained modern mind neglectful of the sacred; respect for Heaven presupposes correctness of both human attitude and formal setting, as well as intelligence of purpose. This "intelligence of purpose" is, for its part, a form of doctrine, for doctrine (the mind element) has to be present in one form or another in a spiritual perspective that purports to be complete. A physical body is made up of both a heart and a head; so too the soul, *mutatis mutandis*.

16 This recalls an anonymous Zen saying, culled from now forgotten readings, describing the path: "At first, I saw mountains as mountains and rivers as rivers. Then, I saw mountains were not mountains and rivers were not rivers. Finally, I see mountains again as mountains and rivers again as rivers."

THE MYSTERY OF INDIVIDUALITY

earth as an ornament thereof that We may try them: which of them is best in conduct" ("The Cave", 18:7). The implication of this verse is that the celestial preciousness of the earth's gifts—which are "signs" (*ayat* in Arabic)—becomes a measure of our spirituality. And this comment leads us to the following perspective: every man stands on the earth before fields, plains, hills, lakes, mountains, rivers, forests, in a universe that before the advent of the machine was a landscape of infinite immensity bounded by legends. This landscape was teeming with symbols that mirrored man's own inner spiritual landscape, such as the birth of spring betokening the miracle of the resurrection, or mountains as the symbols of truth and of fidelity, streams pouring forth and teaching blessed spontaneity and generosity, or tall trees teaching him dignity and magnanimity. Industrialism has run roughshod over this landscape, blunting in the process the symbolism that was so spectacularly open to ancient man, while offering erstwhile undreamt-of civilized comforts. And whereas the physical struggle for survival and hardships prevented pre-modern man from succumbing completely to the appeal of the world, the civilized comfort modern man has gained is too often obtained at the price of an anguish[17] that all is not well despite his titanic achievements. Be that as it may, whether we are modern or ancient, the choice between this world and the Hereafter has remained the same across the ages because man's fundamental substance is the same, just as his fundamental cosmic situation before Heaven can never change. And nature, in her perennial majesty, reflects this timelessness: civilizations are born, flourish, and then disappear; only the man who is most like nature in her primordial wisdom will endure, the man who embodies the strength of her mountains and the generosity of her plains, the freshness of her streams and the mystery of her woodlands, as well as the primordial sanctity of her being, for nothing impure or trivial can long defile her. In nature, man becomes a priest again; and in nature, or rather in a non-artificial lifestyle modeled on nature, man is reborn in his primordial innocence, strength, and nobility.

---

17 This is exactly the "anguish" psychology wishes to cure man of, and that young people want to be free of when they tell each other to "take it easy", and other such trivial modes of greeting or parting—really the worst possible exhortation for a soul drifting through the *samsara*. Contrast that with the mode of interaction encountered in traditional societies where God and Heaven and faith are part of everyday expressions in greetings and attitudes. Their naturalness and gestural eloquence is hard to convey through words, but let us picture the scene of two elderly men, of aristocratic dignity, crossing each other in the street of a Moroccan medina: as they brush by, one of them points heavenward and murmurs "*al-iman*" (faith), while the other nods in radiant assent and utters a blessing, and they pass on absorbed in their solitary invocation, mysterious exemplars of their Prophet's injunction when he said: "Be in this world as a stranger and reckon yourself among the dead."

CHAPTER 1

The Wound of Duality

Duo sunt in homine.
("There are two [natures] in man.")
(Saint Thomas Aquinas, *Summa Theologica* II.2, q. 26, art. 4)

We are attracted to what resembles us most: this is the foundation of the spiritual path; the essence of our return to God is the idea of the divine in man returning to the Divine, or, to quote Plotinus, "the return of the one to the One". Hence ideally, we are attracted to the Good and to Truth like a flower's seed beneath the sod is attracted to the sun to bloom and thus to realize its celestial essence. The whole basis of spiritual realization is the doctrine of identity, of like being attracted to Like, or of the Divine One and All repossessing Itself of that which It really never lost. This is the vertical and essential perspective, that of pure ontology, or that of our supra-individual core. However, seen from the perspective of the individual, it is also true—though not equally so—that we are attracted to what is opposite to us because the individual is a fragment and therefore seeks completion in his missing portion, so to speak, a classic example of this being the love between a man and a woman. However what is much less obvious is that, owing to the Fall, far from being attracted we can also be repelled by what most corresponds to us archetypally, as the medieval motif of the "loathsome bride" illustrates, or the drama of the soul, unwilling to give up its illusory freedom, fleeing the Spirit. And finally, and fatefully, as unenlightened beings we are often attracted, to what is most harmful to us, whether out of perversity or pride—though these are really two sides of the same coin. Indeed, realism obliges us to note that if we are attracted to what resembles us, this qualification—"resembles us"—can mean many things outside of spiritual union, because until we know who we truly are we may be attracted to what resembles us in our ignorance, passion, individualism, or any other number of spurious selves that we acquire through inheritance—or karma—as well as through our individual choices, the intricacies of human circumstances being endless. This is the doctrine of transmigration of the soul enduring what Hindus and Buddhists term the *samsara* or the unceasing cycle of suffering through births and deaths and rebirths as the ego, heedless of the divine gate to liberation, wanders from deluded attachment to deluded attachment. Thus, before yielding to what attracts us the most, we need vitally to ask what is our true self: is it our idiosyncratic and perishable individuality vainly fretting on the revolving rim of Eternity or is it the immortal Self glowing in the depths of our heart? Discerning between the two is the wager of human existence.

In the wake of the proverbial Fall, man's mind and heart have become separated to the point of operating at cross purposes. In most men, the mental individual, nurtured by passions and the illusion of being real in his own right, usurps the throne of the heart belonging to the Divine Self who, now as a monarch in exile, suppressed or banished from consciousness to the outermost fringes of our daily awareness—when not murdered[1]—, lives in exile in our own soul, treacherously bereft of authority and respect.[2] It is this separation between mind and heart that not only is the wound of our duality but is also the cause of all the mischief of individualism posturing as our true nature; we shall dwell on this, all the more as the solution most often proposed, especially in much of so-called New Age spirituality, is to depreciate the mind in favor of the heart, a fool's errand if there ever was one.

Man is intelligence. And intelligence is the capacity to know the Real—mind, heart, and soul. That notwithstanding, it has become popular to celebrate a return to the heart at the expense of ostracizing the mind, a classic instance of "throwing out the baby with the bath water", because the problem with the mind is not the mind, obviously, but cerebralism or a hyper-mental way of viewing reality. In the West, the roots of this distortion can be traced in part to the legacy of many centuries of encroaching rationalism and scientism. What is needed, however, is not a banishing of the mind—something impossible to do without the risk of fatal damage to intelligence—but rather a profound reforming of the mind so that it can be restored to its legitimate role as the mirror of Truth, by contrast to the heart which is the seat of subjective or innermost being. But spiritual seekers today are often quick to be excited about a spirituality that engages feelings and emotions, and combines this with a kind of hazy "feel-good" kaleidoscope of intuitions about God and mankind in which thinking is rejected as a troublesome interloper. Their slogan might be: "Perish the mind, long live the heart!" Or: "Forget logic, what is needed is love."

Meanwhile, the mind, repudiated in its noble role as a guardian and interpreter of the Truth, leaves the heart—now essentially defenseless—to

1 Strictly speaking, the Self cannot be slain, quite obviously, but the individual ego, in an act of spiritual suicide, can behave in a manner that severs his link to the Self.

2 This is the masterful theme of several of Shakespeare's plays, among which *The Tempest, Hamlet, King Lear, Coriolanus, Julius Caesar.* Also, in several of the plays, there is a faithful servant—the symbol of humility and virtue as well as of wisdom disregarded—who accompanies the ruler in exile and helps save the day for his rightful restoration.

sink into directionless subjectivity,[3] allowing the soul in turn to be exposed to a riot of personalistic impressions that can range from mindlessly sweet to the most eccentric when not Luciferian of individualistic extravagances. In a word, rejecting the mind and relying exclusively on the heart risks exposing us to the most sentimental or arbitrary of subjectivisms—or worse—for it is all too easy to declare ecstatically, "I have embraced my heart, now I can live free from the mind at last" when one has never taken the time to learn how to think; but the unexamined life, as Socrates reminds us, is not worth living. He who wishes to free himself from thinking should at least learn how to think first, so as to grant himself the opportunity of making an intelligent decision grounded in sound logic, as opposed to following eccentric intuitions, no matter how compelling. *Distrust thine own self*, should be a rule of existence for the yet unreformed soul. But what can one say? The thrill of committing impulsively to "love" seems to be a favorite cure-all of those who do not want to think, when in fact it is the "knowing soul" that comes closest to Divinity, for intelligence is the highest attribute of man, but provided it be added that virtue in turn is the truest proof of intelligence because true knowledge always leads to the good and to the beautiful, otherwise it is mere cerebralism, precisely. Indeed, knowledge and being are of one substance: to know is to be and, likewise, to be is to know—mind and heart being the twin poles of divine consciousness. Conversely, the refusal to know,[4] or to mistake our personal feelings and intuitions for knowledge, is to take our own subjectivity as the measure of the universe.

*   *   *

One of the classic traps of New Age spirituality is to confuse the psychic with the spiritual, when the psychic is simply the realm of the non-material

---

3 Saint Ignatius of Loyola, in his "Spiritual Exercises" says that the "evil spirit", when attempting to waylay the soul, avoids the mind—which is made for Truth—to focus on both the imagination and on the senses. The danger the saint (and former soldier knight) has in mind is a classic pitfall for the soul which, flattered by the stimulation of its natural wishes and desires, falls for illusion like a fly in a spider's web. Meanwhile, always according to Ignatius, the "good spirit" addresses conscience and reason, and this gives us an important clue about the psychology of the individual soul in search of the Divine. Schuon refers to this as follows: "The tempter serpent, which is the cosmic genius of this movement [towards exteriorization], cannot act directly on the intelligence and so must seduce the will, Eve" (*Understanding Islam* [Bloomington, IN: World Wisdom, 2011], p. 154). And "Eve" is the soul—or the heart, but the "heart" serving here as the core of our subjectivity, and not the heart-intellect which by definition is infallible since it is situated outside of duality, precisely.

4 However there is also the idea of "unknowing" dear to mystics, an idea resting on poverty of soul; this will be explored in the next chapter.

but not the realm of the Spirit proper. However, so long as the soul is still separated from the Spirit it will go through countless rebirths, or even to hell, because the psychic domain covers all the realms outside of Heaven; therefore to equate the psychic with the spiritual simply because it belongs to the supra-sensible realm is simplistic.[5] However, people who have psychic openings, such as experiencing auras or auditions not to mention dreams or clairvoyance, can be so impressed by the experiences enabled by these fissures in their consciousness that they readily mistake such phenomena for spiritual insights when all they betoken is a type of mediumistic opening, if not a mental disequilibrium, but surely not a faculty superior to intelligence proper; indeed, no medium or spiritualist was made more intelligent by his psychic openings. True spiritual insights, for their part, are always characterized by their clarity, beauty, and simplicity, by their intelligence in fact.[6]

---

5 That said, the spiritual realm can, at its nethermost limit, overlap the psychic realm because Heaven as the abode of the blessed, or of sanctified souls, has different levels; the psychic (the soul) when transfigured by the Divine, becomes then a luminous part of the Divine's radiation, its obscuring tendency having been converted into luminescence and beauty. Borrowing from the Vedantic doctrine of the *gunas*, one could clarify this by saying that the spirit realm is pure *sattva* (light), whereas the psychic is pure *rajas* (heat), but with an ascending dimension that opens onto *sattva* and a descending one that opens onto *tamas* (darkness). The difficulty comes from the fact that the *gunas* interpenetrate each other but without *sattva* (Spirit) ever becoming contaminated by the lower two *gunas* since they derive their essence (or energy) from *sattva*. This is as much as to say that Spirit is *in* everything without being *part* of everything. Strictly speaking, however, some will object that *sattva* is part of *Prakriti* (the realm of manifestation) and therefore that only *Purusha* is spirit, or that the spirit realm is non-manifest. Our response is that such lines of demarcation cannot always be rigidly set; all that one can say is that the spirit realm is clearly different from the psychic, but that the psychic can reflect the spirit since nothing can truly exist outside of the Spirit (capitalized); in that sense, *sattva* is a reflection of the spiritual in the manifest, or the part in manifestation which is identified in substance with the spirit, otherwise there would be no connection between these two realms. Beyond that, God knows best. "Srimati Kunti said: O Krishna, I offer my obeisances unto You because You are the original personality and are unaffected by the qualities of the material world. You are existing both within and without everything, yet You are invisible to all" (*Srimad Bhagavatam* 1.8.18).

6 Moreover, they do not go counter to common sense, unless the recipient is something of a dreamer to start with. Traditionally, the Roman Catholic Church has always been extremely cautious about assessing any such kind of out-of-body experiences, and rightfully so, because they very often are no more than a psychic form of individualism, not to mention the risk of the individual becoming a vessel for psychic powers or forces whose true nature and origin he has no clue of. Moreover, such fissures sometimes are the aftermath caused by a life and death circumstance or a serious accident from which the body has not fully been able to heal. True, sometimes such fissures can serve exceptionally as a breach in our five senses opening onto Heaven; however this is a complex issue about which more will be said in the chapter "The Forbidden Door".

To elaborate: without the objective check that intellectual discernment provides, the pole of the heart can become the source of an exalted subjectivism. Indeed, how do we know, when heeding the popular injunction "Follow thy heart", that we are not merely following our ego? Owing to the inversion of poles in fallen man—which orthodox spiritual conversion is meant to right—the heart has become passive (or frozen and monolithic) and the mind active (or agitated and scattered), whereas in their normal state it is the heart that is active and the mind passive inasmuch as the mind operates as a cooling moon to the heart's radiant sun. As the seat of the divine Intellect, the heart sees because it is, and the mind, in turn, reflects the heart's being; but in fallen man, the heart is captured by the restless and faithless mind and becomes in turn emotionally adulterous, latching on to this or that passion or whim offered ceaselessly by the mind's unstable and roving sense of opportunity when adrift, that is when unmoored from the Truth.

Bending to the rigor of Truth requires, initially, a sacrifice, discipline, and even a measure of heroism, for Truth requires giving up (*kenosis* or "self-emptying") what we think is "our-self" and this can be agony for the ego. What the ego does not (yet) know is that its cherished individuality is only a make-believe self born from the delusion of mistaking the personal world it happens to exist in as reality, or as a *de facto* absolute reality; and this "personal world" can be both outward and inward. The question becomes then: does an individual want the Truth, and consent to the self-domination this presupposes, or does he seek pure experience, and the self-indulgence this presupposes; or, is personal experience for this person the measure of Reality?

For those infatuated with impressions, sensations, imaginings, the summons to knowledge may feel like the death of their existence, because the sobriety that comes with the objectivity of renunciation and self-mortification seems to interfere with the freedom of just existing and without thinking too much. And yet no one is born to the Spirit who has not died first to the goad of the flesh and fled the fairground of the ego. All true spirituality is premised on that alchemy: first the *nigrido*, or blackening or the eliminating—ultimate mortification (*katharsis*)—then the *albedo*, the whitening or the transfigurating (*theoria* or enlightenment). In Sufism, the *qabd* or contraction precedes the *bast* or expansion. However, it is worth specifying that the difficulty stems from the ego's initial unwillingness, or unpreparedness, to see beyond itself, for "ye are not straitened in us, but ye are straitened in your own bowels" (2 Cor. 6:12), namely the contraction is really on man's side, not God's, for there is no narrowness in his Love.

Be that as it may, the approach to the One entails—for man—a denial of self, as well as a certain holy monotony because this aloneness, and emptiness, is a preliminary condition for our solemn choice of the One over the many as symbolized by the world and its multiplicity of temptations. In other words, to choose the One is, at the outset, to give up the illusory richness of the soul or of the world (they are twins). As the Sufi Junayd noted, only an empty glass can be filled; quite simply, we must first become empty for God, the sole Fullness there is. At the same time, to choose the One is also to renounce the false richness of the soul's multiplicity, so that God can then give of His manifold riches; the equation is to sacrifice finite multiplicity for the Infinite. Can such a state of poverty, or aridity, last a lifetime? Possibly, for what matters is the Hereafter and God may require that a soul prove the sincerity of its conviction that the Hereafter is the sole Real; therefore, to do so it may be forced to give up everything it has on earth and to persevere despite this deprivation, all the while feeding only on the oxygen of faith—"lovest thou me more than these?" (John 21:15). Such is the path of *sannyasa* in Hinduism, where the renunciate gives up even his social identity and all legal rights, reckoning himself henceforth of the dead. And yet, who is to say that such a desert, such desolation, is any the less spiritual than the path of ecstasy? While rigor and renunciation normally mark the beginning of the spiritual path, sometimes it is a consequence of a vision born out of an immortal love. "It is not I who have left the world", a Sufi once said, "but the world that has left me."[7] In either case, though, there is renunciation.

* * *

Intelligence is the prerogative of the human individual as created in the image of God, just as wisdom is the prerogative of the sage; so one could say that to be human is to be intelligent, or that one cannot be fully human without being intelligent and, ultimately, wise. More essentially, what defines man is the gift of the heart-intellect, and by the term "Intellect" (*intellectus*) we do not mean just the mind or intellectuality, which is really only its functional aspect, but an actual divine faculty residing in what can be termed the "Holy of Holies" within every individual, which is a godlike essence, or the very trace of Godhead Itself residing in each human being. As such, the Intellect is transpersonal and therefore—reflecting God—is objective, immutable, and deathless, as well as wise; it is like perfect or total consciousness, which is thereby also perfect awareness, perfect wisdom,

7 Quoted from memory.

and perfect love. Most men are not directly aware of this divine faculty except when it surfaces, usually in the form of the promptings of one's conscience. But, when confronted with Truth, the heart-intellect responds with the assent of certitude that, once felt, is undeniable and utterly profound, as well as inherently unerring.[8]

What fervent advocates of the pole "heart" ignore—although in some way correctly sense—is that, in primordial man or man of the Golden Age, the heart as a divine faculty was one before becoming polarized into heart and mind, subsequent to the Fall which occurred with the loss of innocence—derived from the sense of original oneness—coming in the wake of the choice between good and evil; in other words, the choice of evil, which is really the choice of duality and by extension of outwardness, and therefore the choice opening the gate to the possibility of evil, was not available before Adam's consciousness shifted from pure contemplation to discursive reasoning. Before the Fall, man saw things in God; after the Fall he could see them both inside and outside of God—or see them as separate from God—and therefore he could see them as an end in themselves, or as objects of his passionate needs and not just as symbols of the Divine. And he saw himself as separate from God, and this separation culminates in alienation, albeit without ever reaching a point of absolute separation since the Absolute encompasses everything, which brings to mind also the mystery of the *bodhisattva* wishing to save all beings down to the last blade of grass: the *bodhisattva* embodies this very truth of the "Absolute encompassing all".

In itself the polarization between heart and mind means that the heart-intellect has at once a subjective and an objective dimension, non-dividable, which in man corresponds to the twin poles of Truth and Love, really the two poles defining God: Truth = the Absolute and Love = the Infinite. Hence, if God is both Truth and Being, both Light and Warmth, then these dimensions must be mirrored in man inasmuch as he is true image of God. Hence, to dismiss the mind is to risk blinding oneself, because man is born both to know and to love, both to see and to be, and indeed in seeing he becomes, just as in knowing truly he cannot but love; "thou shalt love the Lord thy God with all thy mind", Christ said, blending the duality of love and knowledge, and not just "with all thy heart".[9] The discernment of spirits is as precious a gift as can be imagined, and to disregard it is to forfeit finally everything that makes man a man as true image of the Creator.

---

8 Or, as we heard a Hindu sage say, "It is the guru in us that recognizes the guruness of the guru."

9 Likewise, Saint Peter can say: "Gird up the loins of your mind" (1 Pet. 1:13).

Yet seen from an essential viewpoint, the mind is finally but a projection of the heart itself—the heart having in addition to its dimension of "being" a dimension of "vital knowledge"—whence the temptation to defer exclusively to the heart or to extol the heart's seeming superiority, all the more as it is the seat of intimate bonding or of union, a locus free from all division and separation or of alien otherness. In that sense, the heart can be said to be superior to the mind, that is to say, so long as the heart is not reduced simply to being the seat of emotions and feelings. In man there is an alchemical reciprocity between these two poles of Consciousness-Being so that the jewel-like mind, once enlightened, quickens the heart which is otherwise dormant and (in profane man) hardened in egoic self-centeredness; and conversely: once the mind is cleansed—and centered in Truth—it can reflect the heart's light which, like a sun, is supernally aglow even beneath the layer of ice accrued since the Fall. In a certain sense, heart and mind correspond analogically to man's dimensions of depth and height, or those of immanence and transcendence: ontological depth of being rejoining the Self and transcendent height of detachment from the ego-self (and the world) rejoining God's majestic "otherness" or loftiness.

The oneness of the mind and heart polarity is well captured by the great Rhenish mystic Meister Eckhart's declaring that "height and depth are one", so that through depth man rises or is lifted up to God just as in being lifted up he becomes deeply interiorized, for "the kingdom of Heaven is within you".

*   *   *

What the preciousness, as well as the gravity, of the human state entails is without a doubt the most important question to answer for those who care to lead a purposeful life. When the nature of man is considered nowadays it is too often in a secular light that over-emphasizes his psycho-physical existence while separating him from a true cosmological context which alone can situate why man has the type of all-embracing intelligence he has and the capacity for infinite love. It is of course too easy to focus on man's earthly wellbeing, because this is always a quick way to assess the apparent usefulness of any precepts, psychological or otherwise. But considered in the light of man's immortality, to assign the here-below concrete existential priority over the Hereafter does him a serious injustice because in trying to ensure his earthly well-being man often trades his soul in the bargain. This conflict comes from ignoring in what manner the wound of duality determines that man has both an outward and an inward dimension, which are respectively his temporal nature and his intemporal essence; in other words, there is an outward man and an inward man.

To illustrate an aspect of this conflict, we are told that charity must be action-oriented and socially concrete, and not deal with spiritual abstractions that are not of obvious and immediate material benefit to man; by this terrestrial logic, a good priest should then spend his entire time helping the poor and not waste his energy praying "selfishly" in some hallowed solitude, while shelterless wretches are shivering and starving. This is easy to say and an all too typical human reflex when one has, firstly, no idea of the nature of prayer and its efficacy; secondly, no sense that God is really the author of any meaningful action; thirdly, that man's works are inherently meaningless for God, who wants our hearts and not human achievements; and fourthly, that solving suffering does not necessarily cure the root of impiety, which is precisely a central cause for suffering in the first place.[10] And this is moreover easy to say when one does not understand the nature of *karma*, or that saving a soul is not the same as saving a person from suffering; in fact these two things can be mutually exclusive in the sense that abridging some suffering may also accidentally abort a soul's reflex to seek divine help. But these, finally, are imponderables that man cannot solve offhand except to be mindful of maintaining a balance between social charity and prayerfulness, although never forgetting the primacy of prayer over everything else; and by "prayer", should be meant not just personal prayer, but solemn ritual prayer, and also the prayer of the heart where this applies, or *japa* as is known in Hinduism. Indeed, to understand man is to understand that the relationship between creation and Creator centers on the nature of man as a "bridge" (*pontifex*) between Heaven and earth, and this bridge is not just man's theocratic essence but luminous prayer; clearly other disciplines, which focus on the psychology of an individual, on the sociology of a population, or on the anthropology of a race, deal with secondary issues compared to this supreme dimension. "Religion" (Latin *religere*) means, by implication, to bind Heaven and earth, whence the analogy of man as *pontifex*.

Now, in defining man, it may help to refer to him in a nomadic context, that is to say to describe him in a setting that is free from a whole cultural warp that can obscure the essential stakes facing him as he stands before Eternity. For those convinced of progressivism, it may be difficult to grasp that nomadic man is not progressing, nor ever has, or that he is not even the progenitor of modern man. He is not progressing either socially or

---

10 In *The Way of a Pilgrim* (New York: HarperOne, 1954), the wandering mendicant mentions that "Many people reason quite the wrong way round about prayer, thinking that good actions and all sorts of preliminary measures render us capable of prayer. But quite the reverse is the case; it is prayer which bears fruit in good works and all the virtues" (p. 8). If consciousness is the essence of being, than deep prayer is the most vital of acts.

genetically because, in the face of Eternity and beneath the stars circling him above, he does not need to; in fact, part of the nobility of his character results directly from the very scarcity of resources he must contend with, not in their abundance and even less in their refinement, unless it is through craftsmanship, but not in their utilitarian sophistication.[11] Thus, all things being equal, nomadic man is not inferior—morally and spiritually—to the most technologically advanced city-dweller, often quite to the contrary. Be that as it may, he is still man as such standing before God, his Creator, facing the need not just to survive but to save his soul, and, more importantly, to fulfill his role as Heaven's delegate on earth. Importantly also, when discussing nomadic peoples, the assumption is that they existed in an environment identical to the kind of wild nature we know of today, when in fact there is reason to believe that nature was more transparently spiritual in earlier cycles (what the Hindus refer to as *yugas*), matter not having reached the harsh density we know of today.

To survive, nomadic or intemporal man needs of course to be intelligent and brave and stalwart and generous while being efficient at ensuring his livelihood and that of his tribe; to save his soul, he needs to pray to God and to lead a life of virtue, and for this his earthly tribulations provide exactly the moral lever he needs to transcend himself;[12] and to fulfill his role as Heaven's delegate, he needs to be a contemplative and a sage; these three sets of requirements are enough to create a whole moral culture that calls for no improving if ethics is the ultimate touchstone in such evaluations. No complicated sociology, no complicated psychoanalysis, no complicated

---

11 There are many examples of a primitive tribe given access to more so-called advanced tools which ended up ruining their lifestyle. However, when a natural improvement (as opposed to an artificial one) became available, such as the horse to the Plains Indians, this enhanced the tribe's cultural and religious qualities. That said, we are not celebrating the nomadic lifestyle against that of city dwellers since both have divine archetypes. This point will be addressed more fully in the chapter "Kingdoms and Nations".

12 In referring to nomads, we are far from suggesting that they are always an ideal model of man because there are considerable degrees of quality between different nomadic peoples, and barbarity is always a risk for any human society forced to contend directly with the raw elements. But certainly the Tuaregs (or the Blue Men of the desert), the Masai on the African plains, and the ancient Plains Indians in general rank among some of the nobler human possibilities imaginable and one should be able to acknowledge that they lacked nothing of the integral nobility that defines man at his best, all degeneracy notwithstanding. And one can also picture the elite human quality of Abrahamic nomadism; nor can we forget the grandiose symbiosis of Mongol nomadism's meeting with the ancient Chinese, Hindu, and Islamic civilizations which it revitalized. We will also note that Christianity derived its original spiritual impetus from the Desert Fathers, the "wilderness" spirit of which was periodically renewed in the very midst of Western's civilization's growth, notably with the Cistercian order of monks, as well as with Saint Bruno's Carthusians.

philosophical theories or chemical testings are required to grasp what this man is and what he must do to fulfill the vocation of being a human being. And yet, this man—the nomad—has been subjected to every dissection cerebral "experts" can dream of in trying to assess man's progress from alleged stone-age brutishness to cyber-age brilliance, although these experts do not suspect that far from truly beholding this man, they are finally only examining themselves in a bizarrely inverted mirror-game of projections and assumptions born both from their obsession with material parameters and, correspondingly, from their ignorance of the laws of Heaven, and therefore getting nowhere because they are missing the central point of this nomad as a creature of God standing proudly and simply under the same immemorial sun, living in sacred time and not in historical time.

It should be specified, however, that in speaking of this man, we have prototypically in mind primordial man who, before the advent of the great city cultures, lived in the majestic immensity of space—time being for him a modality of space because sacredly circular and not linear, and centered on the myth of the eternal return of life and on the cycle of the seasons that rotated around a timeless axis set in Eternity.[13] In that sense, time was for him perennially renewed and refreshed and not the cause of permanent change—either up or down—along with the temptation of a linear or promethean opportunity at radical progress, a prospect as extravagant as it is vain. Space was for him a fertile cradle, a womb, as well as a holy tomb, circled by the sun and the stars, and not a collapsible or corruptible framework for both the grandiosity and folly of Western adventurism to come. His life was governed therefore by a sacred center and not by the tantalizing mirage of indefinite progress.

To seize what primordial man was in his spiritual essence, inasmuch as we can do so principially, provides us a means for understanding who we are in our timelessness; for this primordial or timeless man is in principle accessible to all men of all epochs and civilizations once we have stripped the individual of his cultural and temporal constructs. But the leading modern disciplines covering the study of man—in some way this is a contradiction in terms[14]—, such as psychology and anthropology, cannot evaluate this primordial being properly since their methodology is beholden to the educational superstructure men are raised with in the modern world,

13 As Schuon has written: "The whole existence of the peoples of antiquity, and of traditional peoples in general, is dominated by two presiding ideas, the idea of Center and the idea of Origin" (*Light on the Ancient Worlds* [Bloomington, IN: World Wisdom, 2006], p. 1).

14 The study of man arose in proportion to man's loss of normalcy. Yet, at the same time, this loss of normalcy compromises the very premises of such a study.

no matter how hard their proponents try to free themselves from such a bias. And the reason they cannot do so finally comes down to the fact that, firstly, man cannot be appreciated perfectly in the abstract, because the very artificiality of such an approach distorts the process; and, secondly, man cannot be properly appreciated outside of spirituality without dismissing the paradigm of man being made in the likeness of his Creator.

Thus to take an example, again from the nomadic realm: when an American Indian raises the sacred pipe heavenward and invokes the Great Spirit, there is no need to analyze this in complicated detail; what we see him doing is what he is doing. At the same time, the profounder meaning of what amounts in effect to a Eucharistic act is forever hidden from the curiosity of profane eyes; it opens onto the mystery of Godhead and the sacredness of creation, and its mystery will not yield to the most probing scientific analysis or other; but it can reveal itself to a contemplative and pure soul. "And God saw that it was good", we read about the creation in Genesis, and it is that seeing, with the wise heart and not with the virtuosic mind alone, that is called for to appreciate the "good" God mentions. In a word, anthropologists are faced with two realities when examining the example of the ritual of the calumet: on the one hand, there is the outward material fact of the sacred pipe itself as inherited by an ethnic group born to an ancient tradition, and all the other material facts of a ritual celebrated in a particular geographic area with its particular cultural nexus of influences—and this is the field where anthropologists excel[15]—and then, on

15 We would in principle like to admire the brilliant work of a Durkheim or a Lévy-Strauss, who both made an apparently gallant attempt to understand "primitive" man free from civilizational prejudices. However, anthropology itself, by definition, is a civilizational prejudice otherwise there would be no need for such a discipline. Perhaps the most radical handicap in this discipline is the materialistic psychologism which cannot break free from the idea of rituals being encoded in a deterministic manner in the collective brain of primitive peoples, a theory that amounts to inverting reality because no consideration is given instead to the idea of a Heaven-bestowed gift coming either through a godlike race of ancestors or through direct revelation, as in the case of the White Buffalo Woman for the Sioux Indians; in other words, no one seems to be able to ask what caused the brain to be so-called "encoded" in the first place, leaving aside the repelling nature of such organic speculations, to say nothing of the patronizing implications of submitting noble natives to a kind of cultural pathogenic autopsy. Moreover, on a different plane, when Durkheim laudably declares there are no "wrong religions"—with reference to totemist cultures—what he fails to see is that not all ancient cultures are of equal quality either spiritually, esthetically, or culturally speaking, starting with the totemist cultures themselves which as a matter of fact are very far from being representative of archetypal man because they are more animistic (or psychic) than based on the Spirit. For us this is a crucial distinction that cannot be overstated. In other words, a true assessment of a people requires a vertical notion of hierarchy and not just a horizontal or "egalitarian" comparison of similarities and differences; the vertical dimension entails discernment and a scale of values, otherwise we have mere

the other hand, there is the nature of the symbol and of the sacrament themselves and these must be considered independently from the coloring and shaping of the collectivity interpreting them. This is where misunderstandings occur, in the isthmus separating priest and symbol or man and Heaven, or outwardness and inwardness: too often these two dimensions, spiritual and material—namely that of pure vertical spirituality and that of the horizontal projection of the spiritual into a collectivity—are confused; and this confusion, which eventually leads to an over-humanization of the Divine, can only be to the detriment of the essential nature of the sacrament itself or of its fundamental metaphysical and spiritual import, which in itself is free from all social sedimentations or cultural accretions, and therefore can never be defined in purely sociological terms.

The same conjunction—and opposition—between outward (or human) significance and inner (or divine) mystery applies to any meeting between man and God, that for instance of the Catholic priest presiding over the mystery of transubstantiation of the bread and wine into the body and blood of Christ, or that of a Hindu priest presiding over the *agnihotra*, the ancient Vedic fire ritual; all these rituals are done on the basis of an understanding that man's heart is really an altar where the Divine Presence abides. How can this be explained or described to an analytic, let alone, scientific mind? The invisibility of these mysteries to the senses, and to a probing secular mind, do not make them the less real; quite to the contrary, for it is their ineffable essence that gives the outward ritual all of its significance and that ineffability is precisely what eludes a merely profane examination. The root cause for this misunderstanding is always the same: a hyper-cerebralized mind that has lost touch with the wisdom of the heart.

Furthermore, to analyze traditional man—and in fact man as such—whether through an anthropological or psychoanalytical prism or through what could be termed "artificial knowledge", is to forget that psychology, along with other modern constructs such as sociology, economics, demographics, and the like, applies only partially to man's full nature because modern psychology and other such disciplines are born from preoccupations that reflect the accidental predicament of man in the modern world;

horizontal observation which allows for all kinds of analogies to be made between what are in fact very uneven cultures and belief systems, resulting in analogies that may not apply or may even be absurd. But this vertical dimension of intelligence, operating on the basis of a hierarchy, as mentioned, is stigmatized as being judgmental, when it is in fact another victim of the leveling democratism of modern thinking that tries to translate even the most sacred of mysteries into notions explainable to profane man, or reduces them to quasi-pragmatic cults involving issues such as comfort and discomfort, fear and security, and so on to explain what constitutes the extraordinary cosmic or heroic grandeur of a tradition.

or else they are shaped by predominantly modern problems and therefore do not apply to man's intemporal self, or to any trans-historical human norm.[16] They are modern inventions premised on the purported superiority of the modern world. Now, to know, as the Hindus did, that a human being has *chakras* (subtle or etheric energy centers) and *nadis* (or nerve networks), or meridians as Chinese medicine does, is legitimate because it is an objective and hence descriptive knowledge free from artificial mental constructs and presuppositions; and it is legitimate because this knowledge is not divorced from the spiritual cosmos that explains it.

At the extreme, it can be conceded that to gain knowledge of the exact functioning of a physical body's organs—a culminating expertise of modern medicine—is an achievement still lying within the realm of what can be termed "legitimate" knowledge. However, to then extrapolate the material concreteness of this knowledge in a manner that ends up denying the soul, not to mention the Spirit, or simply to reduce man to a physical frame of reference shorn of its symbolistic implications, is to leave out everything that gives meaning to man's human genius. There are in essence two problems here: firstly that of a knowledge that actually ends up obstructing knowledge, due to its hyper-complexity and artificiality, and secondly that of a knowledge exceeding its sensible or epistemological boundaries. Thus, by way of illustration, a science, such as molecular biology, as it gains in complexity, ends up compromising not only human common sense but possibly also useful criteria pertaining to all human beings inasmuch as this new knowledge produces a self-validating view of the world where man is seen increasingly as some kind of cellular machine-like complex and no longer as the embodiment of the Spirit. Were that not enough, the notion of the Spirit itself may become the object of forensic biology's for-

---

16 To illustrate the problem we can take our pick from among any number of indigestible neologisms such as "hypergnosis" (as if "gnosis" did not suffice), "contextualism", "deconstructionism", "protoanalysis", "psychocalisthenics", "psychoalchemy", and so on, hybrid terms born from the blending of modern science with loose strands of ancient wisdom, yielding a twisted amalgam of tortured cerebralism, sometimes with pseudo-esoteric extensions. Not that such novel disciplines do not have their possible insights, but new knowledge, no matter how complex and detailed, cannot begin to exhaust the dimension of Infinity; rather, it can only "thicken the plot". Therefore, man—if wise—ultimately has to rely on symbols to define Reality in lieu of interminable scientific speculations, because a symbol's non-discursive nature has a synthetic completeness about it that can answer all relevant human questions. Hence when creation is defined by symbols such as the spiral, the cross, or the circle, this tells us more about the fundamental nature of Reality than any philosophical treatise or laboratory demonstration, because these symbols capture principial schemes. In the end, it is contemplation, not analysis, that can grasp Reality in its timeless depth, because Reality is Being and therefore man can know it only inasmuch as he resembles it in his own being—body, soul, and spirit.

ays, in which case the notion of the Spirit as a truly supra-material instance loses all meaning. The point of these remarks is to situate in what way man ends up creating the tools that correspond to his mentality, a mentality that, in its increasingly secular state, is determined by increasingly non-essential circumstances, when in fact instead of having Reality serve our non-spiritual preconceptions of the universe it is we who should conform as much as possible to Reality as such, not the other way round; and this was in fact the entire perspective of traditional civilizations.

In practical terms, if one wants to understand the psychology of an American Indian or that of a samurai or of a medieval knight—each of whose ethos was based on prowess, honor, and fearless contempt for death—this endeavor requires, in addition to scholarly documentation, a special brand of nobility and self-transcendence on the part of the modern observer; otherwise, this observer, bred in a humanistic environment, is likely to recoil at the ease with which ancient men could apparently face death or deliver it; and, in recoiling, this observer then jeopardizes whatever real insight he could have had. Needless to say, in pointing this out we are not extolling violence but highlighting an ethos of pure bravery and spirituality without which it becomes impossible to understand ancient man. Too often nowadays objectivity is confused with a kind of sterility of attitude, in which all emotion is excluded, as a pre-condition for all investigation, whereas to understand the cosmos requires an impartial mind in addition to a vivid sense of grandeur. In other words, emotion is not necessarily subjective: to admire what is admirable—provided of course that it is admirable—or to love what is lovable—with the same proviso—is certainly not less "objective" than to analyze it with cerebral indifference; in fact, this "indifference" can be more of an emotional choice than might be suspected because indifference before what is lovable is not objectivity but either hardness of heart or mediocrity of temperament. Objectivity and indifference, in other words, are not synonymous; however, objectivity and impartiality are so, though impartiality need not be indifferent to be impartial. Similarly, lucidity is not just a state of dispassionate awareness, but one of intense awareness coming from both the intelligence and the emotions inasmuch as the latter do not distort the object, because emotion is actually a form of perception in that it amplifies the qualitative implications of the object being examined; what matters is to direct emotion, not to extinguish it. And contemplation is not less important than analysis, to say the least, for nothing can be understood through the mind alone: the heart perceives a sphere where the mind grasps a circle only.

*   *   *

It may now seem bold, if not presumptuous, in an age dependent on mea-surements and statistics, to seek to describe man's inner dimension which eludes all such calibration; while we cannot measure this dimension em-pirically, we can grasp conceptually, if not intuitively, that man is not just the product of his natural environment, but above all the product of his supernatural origin. As alluded to above, man is situated at the intersection of two axes, a horizontal one and a vertical one. The horizontal axis can be equated with everything that constitutes man's outward circumstances as well as his human heredity, whereas the vertical axis not only bisects this horizontal plane—as the warp does the weft in a weaving—but also completely transcends it while engaging everything that constitutes man's immortal or trans-individual essence because the horizontal dimension (or time and space, and the matter they encompass) is not a self-sufficient plane: it requires a vertical dimension situated outside of time and space to hold it together as well as to animate it.[17] What this entails humanly speak-ing is that man's end lies above himself; his vertical station—or erectness of posture—unique to him among all creatures, is like a visible trace of that axis, just as his intelligence is meant to look at reality from on high, unlike that of animals which is basically locked in the plane of reality they happen to be part of.[18] So, by contrast to science's search for the truth in the realm of the visible, the palpable, and the weighable, the challenge for man is that the more invisible a plane of reality is the more important it actually is. Thus, we read in the Koran: "Glory be to Him Who created all the sexual pairs, of that which the earth groweth, and of themselves, and *of that which they know not!*" ("Ya Sin", 36:36) [italics ours].

The paradox in our modern world for anyone accepting the notion of the Divine is that allowance must be made for the influence of the super-natural within the natural and this creates an apparent conflict of a mutual-ly exclusive choice between reason and faith, an absurd dichotomy in itself

17 It may seem like a contradiction to affirm that the horizontal plane requires a dimension *outside* of time and space, because where would this "outside" be? Now, this "outside" is re-ally a figurative way of referring to a dimension—or dimensions—that cannot be expressed in our human space-time constructs. However, one can infer that the "space" we know is but one aspect of the pole Infinity and therefore one can infer other dimensions that are symbolically equivalent to our terrestrial space, these being related to the principle of breadth, or of totality, inherent to the Absolute even if they do not correspond to what we know as geographic space, not to mention interstellar space.

18 In compensation, animals, from the shamanistic perspective, embody pure attributes of the Spirit which operate as their medicine. What they lack is total, comprehensive, and ob-jective intelligence—which, unlike man, prevents them from revolting against their Crea-tor—but not a messenger-like dimension that can serve even the Celestial, allowing them thus to be occasional emissaries of the Great Spirit.

but one that has dogged Western culture, in particular, since the advent of the Renaissance, and one that constitutes another legacy of the wound of duality. Here is the seemingly impossible alternative, that few men know how to reconcile: either one tries to be perfectly "logical"—in the material sense of the term—basing then all of one's thinking on proofs taken from the visible universe around us, leaving all the rest to "superstition" so-called, or else one suspends one's rational logic and believes uncritically in the invisible—uncritically, because for the pietist to think in logical or rational terms about the Divinity is unbefitting of humility and even quasi sacrilegious—but without being able to explain this invisible or to prove anything in terms that a rationalist mind can accept. The problem with the second position, that of blind faith, is that it can foster a sense of helplessness before the Sublime which, it is piously alleged, our human faculties are not meant to grasp; now, for an empirical mind, the perspective of uncritical faith amounts to a forfeiting of our powers of reason which are after all legitimate otherwise why would God have endowed man with intelligence? We sympathize but only up to a point, because reason without faith is like trying to think about ultimate Reality under the lock and key of the five senses.

For the pure rationalist the difference between the supra-rational and the irrational is not at all obvious, all the more when those who resort to the supra-rational (or the miraculous) feel they have license to think irrationally—which in actual fact is not to think at all. It is certainly to be deplored that those who defer with dogmatic awe to the supernatural often dismiss logic and intelligence completely, doing so out of a mistaken notion of humility that prompts them (correctly) to reject the "wisdom of the world"—with which they equate reason—but that also predisposes them (incorrectly) to believe gullibly in almost anything gilded by the notion of Heaven or God, whence their sublimistic inclinations, on the one hand, and their humilitarianism, on the other. As a result, believers are liable to slip into a kind of devotional foolishness that the enemies of religion pounce on as proof of the absurdity of the Divine.[19] Or these enemies conclude,

---

19 One example, among countless, of irrational faith is the phenomenon of speaking in tongues (*glossolalia*), which does real discredit to the dignity and intelligence of the Spirit, as well as being harmful to intelligence as such. This practice has been disavowed by many of the Church's most important saints, among which a Saint John Chrysostom, Saint Augustine, Thomas Aquinas, and Saint Bernard. Although the possibility of this phenomenon existed at the very beginning of the primitive Church, when we are told the separation between the supernatural and the natural was less rigid, it disappeared as a possibility almost immediately; even the Desert Fathers, who could perform miracles, apparently did not practice it. This is not to say that instances of it cannot occur, since it is a possibility, but the overwhelming number of people who claim access to it are fantasizing if not pulling

condescendingly, that believers are people who are inherently "insecure" when faith is actually the only avenue open to man separated from God, leaving aside the fact that in essence faith is a form of veiled "intellection", and therefore "intelligent" in its own way, and certainly more so than a pure rationalism fancying it can solve everything through empirical logic.

Now, it should be easy enough to demonstrate that the mysteries of Being can only yield to rational verification up to a point, beyond which one must appeal to metaphysical logic and to intellective faith, not to mention that our human limitations oblige us ultimately to depend on Divine Grace if we are to understand anything at all. Just as man cannot create life, he cannot produce enlightenment, for the source of both life and enlightenment belong to a transcendent order of reality; no man can approach the Real purely by his own means or purely on his own initiative. It is here, moreover, that a childlike sense of the wonder of the universe can lead to intuitions not accessible to a skeptical mind. Thus to accept certain essential articles of faith, for example those in Christianity requiring belief in the virgin birth of Christ, of his death and resurrection, and of the Blessed Virgin's assumption call for beliefs that seem to defy all earthly logic, but that do not defy the miracle of creation itself which is really the greatest miracle of all, at least in the sense that it is unexplainable without spirituality. Moreover, it is not illogical to believe that the supernatural can enter into the natural since the natural is really but a diminished or darkened or more solidified supernatural, and not vice-versa as New Age evolutionism supposes in positing that the supernatural is somehow born of the natural;[20] in other words, life would not be self-sustaining were it not for the animating principle of the Spirit within it, as should be clear from the fate of decomposition that meets all composed bodies.

To return briefly to the example of the Indian holding the sacred pipe, one will readily grant that studying the actual components of each ritual may be of some cultural interest; but ultimately these rituals cannot be di-

---

the wool over the eyes of the unsuspecting. No wonder, then, that excursions into this kind of verbal prolixity, which is usually gibberish or worse, gives religion a bad name; in fact, gibberish ends up destroying the very notion of the Word itself, the most lucid theophany there is.

20 Thus we find a new theology emphasizing that Christ was not wonderful because of his divineness but because of the perfection of his humanity, Heaven forfend! The next step in this type of fake theology (à la Bishop Shelby Spong's "New Christianity for a New World") is, of course, to divinize man himself, namely to divinize his *earthly* humanity and thus to divinize mankind and earth, as if there were not a cosmically insuperable isthmus separating earth from Heaven principially and forever—but an isthmus that the sanctified heart overcomes because, in fact, this heart is heaven-born to start with.

vorced from their alchemical goal which is the purification of man's heart and—through universal spiritual solidarity—the purification of all of creation; man, as true priest, prays with all of creation—as seen in the Lakota formula, *mitakuye oyasin*, "we are all related". That said, before the advent of the modern world, no one would have thought of analyzing these rituals for the simple reason that to isolate them from their theurgic purpose would not have occurred to anyone; rituals were part of traditional man's daily life, equal or more to sustaining himself with food.[21] The scientific mind, however, tends to break apart what should not be separated, and in so doing, perpetuates the break between Heaven and earth; and what is more, doing it by using artificial frames of reference that do not really apply to the subject matter. Thus, for example, to analyze the Middle Ages or ancient Japan, or any traditional society, through a socio-economic prism, especially one based on some kind of socialistic if not proto-Marxist notion of the affluent and dispossessed, or of oppression and exploitation, while ignoring in the process everything that constitutes a sacred traditional civilization, is an exercise in futility especially considering that affluence was never a factor of man's greatness but only a subsidiary effect.[22]

Examining the question of the modern supremacy of the rational mind and its limitations, it is no coincidence that Heaven chose an "unlettered prophet" for the last great revelation, that of Islam: Muhammad is the *nabi 'l-ummi* (the "unlettered prophet), the "unletteredness" referring to that virginity of soul not burdened with worldly knowledge; there is a direct analogy here with the Blessed Virgin in Christianity: both the Virgin and the Prophet of Islam receive the announcement of their revelation, the divine Child for the former and the divine Word for the latter, from the archangel Gabriel.[23] And likewise in Christianity, with regard to learning, there is the spiritual treatise called *The Cloud of Unknowing* explaining the manner of approaching the Divine through unknowing, a theme at the core of John Scotus Eriugena's *agnosia* and Meister Eckhart's unlearning.

---

21 "In the life of the Indian there was only one inevitable duty—the duty of prayer—the daily recognition of the Unseen and Eternal. His daily devotions were more necessary to him than daily food" (Charles Eastman, *The Soul of the Indian*[Lincoln: University of Nebraska Press, 1980], p. 45). That is to say, for an Indian, praying was like breathing.

22 The founders of the various Caliphate dynasties, for instance, whether Umayyad, Abbasid, or Ottoman, and who brought human civilization to an undreamt of apogee of glory, were born in the austerity of the desert.

23 Or the Logos as man for the one and the Logos as Principle (or Word) for the other. Thus, in a certain special sense, one might say that the Prophet of Islam had a "Marial substance", spiritually speaking, while being a statesman and legislator intellectually. That the Archangel Gabriel appeared to both prophets is far from being a coincidence.

Similarly, the famous alchemical adage declares: "The sum of knowledge is to know nothing" (*summa scientia nihil scire*). Spiritual unlearning, however, cannot be undertaken on the basis of ignorance—this is all too obvious—otherwise fools would be wise men; thus any serious spiritual seeker must first learn what he must unlearn and not just what he must learn; some foundational training in *recta ratio* ("correct reasoning") of the Scholastics is indispensable for this.

However difficult it may be to look at man totally objectively or dispassionately or non-sentimentally, and to do so without projecting one's own subjectivity onto him, or projecting onto him the massive and finally profane assumptions of the secular epoch we happen to live in, we must not forget this: there is a transpersonal and intemporal core in each man, the divine Intellect, or Spirit, that knows everything already and forever because it is the uncreated trace of Godhead in man without which he could not exist even for an instant; and this trace of Godhead in man is like the microcosmic prophet or *avatara*, the divine model every man and woman carries immanently in himself or herself which is radically one with the essence of Reality. To have a personal premonition of this is a calling to sanctity, a calling to union with God. Ultimately, there can be no true knowledge unless founded on the premise of unity, namely on the Oneness of the Real that we can only grasp ontologically. Hence, even if "objective" knowledge necessarily presupposes a duality, this duality is not meant to be a chasm, even less a wound, if understood as being the twin poles of a single axis situated in one Reality. Were it not for this sacred unity, both underlying and transcending all divisions, no duality would exist, even for an instant.

CHAPTER 2

WHO AM I?

Be ye therefore perfect, even as your Father which is in heaven is perfect.
(Matt. 5:48)

One of the greatest of truths, and yet most fatal of illusions, is the notion that man is created in God's image or, in Buddhist terms, that every man has a Buddha nature, or in Vedantic metaphysics, *tat tvam asi*, "thou art That"—the "That" being the unnamable essence of Reality. As much as this truth can be of lofty inspiration for the pure contemplative, it can be seriously misleading for the individualist, depending on how it is understood, as well as on how we "see ourselves": man posturing as a god can be either a buffoon or a fiend. In fact, "to see ourselves" can be the first problem, because there is something obsessive and distorting about the self-centeredness of having to deal with our ego day in and day out until our earthly fading,[1] while at the same time having no choice but to experience its intrusive reality. "To know thyself": this is the ultimate secret of all wisdom. But the riddle is to posit correctly who this "self" is or what this "self" consists of, otherwise we will lose our way in the woods.

To declare "thou art That" has a *koan*-like simplicity that can slice through the individual knot in one stroke, annihilating the ego's self-delusion as otherness. But that is an exceedingly rare case. For most people, this formulation can prove to be a confusing ellipsis whose appealing simplicity may tempt one to forego intelligent discernment; and critical discernment, once foregone, opens wide the gates for the most preposterous assumptions and self-flattering speculations about our personal importance. And yet such a truth (the *tat tvam asi*) must be formulated, even at the risk of attracting flocks of solipsists, credulous about their inherent divineness, a growing fashion of the times it would seem; false gurus are not shy about quoting this *mantra* to devotees yearning for a quick path to enlightenment.[2] Thus, are we to wonder why religions, in order to avert such a deadly misunderstanding, have traditionally debunked man's god-

---

1 "A tale told by an idiot, full of sound and fury, signifying nothing" (Macbeth, Act 5, scene 5).

2 A crude variant of this statement is found in the popular refrain: "God loves you just the way you are". This is a misapplication of the correct idea of God who, being Love in His essence, embraces the whole of creation unconditionally; however, the real meaning of this truth is that the sun shines on both the righteous and the unrighteous impartially, and not that the sun "loves" the unrighteous! We will have an opportunity to return to this question.

like conceit by emphasizing that man is an irremediable sinner (Christianity), an ingrate slave (Islam), or must endure thousands of excruciating rebirths (Hinduism and Buddhism) before attaining enlightenment? Here the esoterist retort might be to ask how man could be saved by denying his divine essence, but both the esoteric and exoteric points of view are legitimate even while being opposites on the plane where man must be defined as "fallen", or as fallible.

In reality, however, to say that man must deny himself—or die to himself, in the manner of Christ's proverbial seed—is not quite the same as to say that he must deny his essence, and confusing the two (or in wishing to prevent such a confusion), religion chooses, quite rightly, the safer alternative which is to give priority of emphasis, *de facto* if not *de jure*, to man's helplessness, ignorance, and existential nothingness. And, indeed, what is man unreformed? A shadow, the breath of a buffalo on a winter morning, as the Plains Indians say. Only the saint is real.[3] It is the willful, or rather ecstatic, disregard for this necessary truth which earned death for the Sufi Al-Hallaj, as well as for the Christian mystic Marguerite Porete, however much we may rue their executions for they were martyrs for esoterism in a world where esoterism has to be hushed—and sometimes crushed—for the safety of all believers.

The truth is that if man as such is a semi-celestial being, the same can hardly be said of the unreformed individual, far from it! Not confusing these two planes—that of prototypical man as such and that of a given individual—is a key to understanding what defining man as *imago Dei* entails; and it is precisely this distinction that is lacking, to a greater or lesser extent, in modern notions of spirituality.[4]

*   *   *

"Who am I?" or, conversely, "Who art thou?" A question asked by many, pursued by few, and realized by almost none—not for lack of capacity, surprisingly, but for lack of wanting. "Ask not for water," Rumi said, "ask for thirst".

---

3 "The just shall live for evermore", we read in *The Book of Wisdom* (5:16, Douay Rheims version).

4 Clearly, though, the breakdown of traditional religion has opened a vast recruiting ground for what can be eclectically defined as "New Age Religionism"; therefore one will want to be careful, and charitable, about making sweeping generalizations about what is finally a cyclical phenomenon that has opened doors to an esoteric wisdom once closed to the non-initiates within formerly traditional religious worlds.

This question lies at the root of self-understanding. In purely social terms, it is typical for an individual to take his personal bearings from other individuals, starting with his own family and immediate relatives in a circle of mutually reinforcing human stereotypes. Yet this need for emulation is far from ideal unless one's kith and kin are truly exemplary human beings. Otherwise, it is difficult to break out from a self-fulfilling circle of social mirroring where everyone ends up being a replica of everyone else, duplicating their peer's attitudes and behavior in a manner that in promoting indispensable stereotypes guaranteeing social survival can at the same time prevent spiritual excellence. That is to say, we and our peers, in supporting the collective average as being an implicit paragon that no one should deviate too much from, exclude the possibility of real transcendence; only an individual of supreme worth, much like a swan's apparition in a barnyard,[5] could break this common spell—the spell being the assumption that averageness is a human norm, and by extension that our modern epoch is a norm. Now, in a still fully operative traditional society, the idea of *satsanga* or of seeking out guidance and inspiration from elite spiritual company—if possible, that of saints—is one of the requirements of a religion such as Hinduism. In the absence of such supreme human models, however, it becomes natural to assume that "other people"—especially people we are attracted to—constitute some kind of a norm that we then seek to emulate and, in turn, whose appreciation and approval we court while it determines our own sense of self. In other words, we measure our success or failure by the relative human standards of other people and not by absolute or prophetic standards, not suspecting that there are (or were) other worlds and universes in which far more is (or was) expected of a man or a woman, standards that determine our posthumous fate.[6]

More broadly, our sense of self is furthermore dictated by religious tradition, and this mold, although a providential compromise and not an absolute ideal, can be enough to ensure salvation. While it is an incomparably better choice than the alternative of mere profane existence, religious conventionalism nonetheless tends over time to become more and more beholden to outward social conventions than to Heaven and thus, para-

---

5 The *Upanishads* tell the story of a tiger cub raised among goats who is convinced he is a goat until he meets a real tiger, and thus rediscovers his true *dharma*. Such is many a gifted spiritual individual's lot, forced to defer to his semi-profane peers unless he discovers his true identity in the Self.

6 This explains in part the meaning of Muhammad's saying that at "the end of time" whosoever accomplishes one tenth of the religion will be saved, because standards deteriorate with the condition of mankind.

doxically, it can end up being a real obstacle to true spiritual realization.[7] Forgotten here is that beyond the heredity of tradition there is in the blood of every individual an even more ancient heredity, and this heredity is that of primordial man who contemplated and befriended God directly. As a direct embodiment of the divine image (*imago Dei*), this human being was originally a priest and a prince, or the Adamic mirror whose undefiled perfection enabled the reflection of God's nature to be projected into the cosmos.[8] And this holy heredity, which predates all other heredities—indeed it precedes time—is in principle accessible to any man or woman. Its main constituent traits, to echo our earlier comments, could perhaps be summarized as wisdom, love, and strength, namely: 1. the direct or lucid knowledge of the Absolute; 2. the profound love of God and hence holiness of character; and 3. invincible strength or perfect integrity of the will; in other words: total wisdom, infinite love, invincible strength.

According to this lofty premise, it is not an exaggeration to say that the individual sense of selfhood cannot find its truest completion save in an understanding of its root identity in the divine Self—"Be ye therefore perfect, even as your Father which is in heaven is perfect", Christ said—all the more given that in pure metaphysical terms there can only be one Self whose imprint is mirrored through myriads of individual selves, like sunlight broken and refracted through thousands of waves.

The existential paradox for the individual ego that both rejoices and suffers is that "I am absolutely real" and yet at the very same time "I am nothing". Or, I am "absolutely real" in the sense both that I cannot cease to be—ever—and in the sense that, so long as I exist separately, all that which lies outside of myself is, to a widening degree, something less palpably real than myself, namely something of an abstraction, including beloved persons; and yet at the same time, "I am nothing" for, precisely, there are countless other selfsame egos everywhere just like myself, just as "absolute" and therefore just as real—or just as unreal, depending on the viewpoint. Of course, the mystery of love, when transfigured into selflessness, brings with it the understanding that others are no less "myself" than I am to myself, thus overcoming the personal alienation just outlined.

The mention of the term "primordial man" above requires a brief explanation: contrary to the materialistic theory of evolution, positing gro-

---

7 For instance, the Confucian ideal of filial piety is intrinsically based on the principle of man's divine ancestorship, but has become transformed into a social cult of family unity and pride; not that the latter version is devoid of merit—social stability depends on it—but to call it truly spiritual, or even meritorious, would be a misuse of terms.

8 Ibn Arabi, in particular, developed this doctrine.

tesquely primitive human ancestors,[9] traditional cultures believed in a divine ancestorship, or of a creation that begins in God, or with deities and divine beings appearing first outside of time. Man always originates from "above", whether his appearance on earth is presented in the form of creationism, or in the manner of the creation myths of the nomads and their doctrine of emergence, or in the form of Neo-Platonic emanationism positing an original divine substance that, from condensation to condensation, and segmentation to segmentation, eventually becomes the matter we know on earth.[10]

* * *

To reflect on who we are, or on what really constitutes *"one-*self", begins with the idea that our waking personality—namely our daily individuality—is pinned as it were on superimposed layers of being,[11] starting first with the fact that before we are this or that person we are prototypically human beings, then—in order of decreasing importance—male or female, then of a given race, (or racial blend), then of a given culture (including religion), and finally of a given historical epoch; and, at the tail end of this descending order of layers proceeding from the vastest to the narrowest, we are a mix of the individual heredity of our forbearers and parents, on the one hand, but also, on the other, the sum of our own uniquely individual choices; it is this amalgam of both convergent and divergent trends

9 It is not that creatures such as so-called Cro-Magnon or Neanderthal man never existed, but that the theory of evolutionism always presupposes progress and not the possibility of human devolution or the degeneracy of a species, man included; those Paleolithic skeletal remains, in other words, may simply correspond to degenerate species, not evolving ones. Moreover, they raise the question, why is it that only isolated remains are discovered, never a group?

10 See Schuon's chapter *"Atma-Maya"* in *Form and Substance in the Religions* (Bloomington, IN: World Wisdom, 2002). This emanationism is rejected by some Sufis on the grounds that it establishes an equivalence between creation and Creator, a pitfall avoided by the Judeo-Christian *creatio ex nihilo*, it would seem, that is, until one ponders the absurdity of *something* appearing out of *nothing*, a dialectical conundrum that the Buddhist doctrine of voidness (*shunya*) can skirt to a large measure. More will be said about this topic in the chapter "Individuality Is Not Individualism".

11 In Hinduism there is the doctrine of the five *koshas*, or envelopes, that Divine Being takes on in its projection into the time-space continuum of creation. See Frithjof Schuon's opening chapter "The Vedanta" in *Spiritual Perspectives and Human Facts* (Bloomington, IN: World Wisdom, 2007), and "The Mystery of the Veil" in *Esoterism as Principle and as Way* (Bedfont: Perennial Books, 1981).

that constitutes our individual personality proper.[12] In other words, the *anthropos* (the notion of man as such) is the superordinate of the individual person just as *Deos* (God) could be said to be in turn the superordinate of *anthropos*. Each one of these dimensions, according to the hierarchy just outlined (be it gender, race, culture, epoch, heredity, and family) defines our personality before it becomes the idiosyncratically unique person we happen to be. This cosmological order of heredity begs the question, of course, as to what precedes our appearance in existence as *bona fide* human beings, for such an origin is materially undetectable; it can only be guessed at through spiritual intuition or by sensing what the theophanic symbols of the human form entail, or by realizing the theomorphic majesty of man as true image of God. Simply stated, the Self reflects Itself in selves and these selves begin as archetypes that fragment first into saints and heroes, then the righteous, and eventually into more and more accidental beings, all the way out to a nihilistic point of no return, as it were.

Having outlined a descending order of individuation from greater to lesser magnitude, a counter-argument could be made that from the point of view of the individual person it is really his individuality that constitutes the most important crystallization, like the apex of a pyramid, since all the previous constituents are generic and not specific, and that is in fact a meaningful distinction because, in the end, if no individual can exist without first being a supra-individual man or woman, and of a given race, and so on, it is equally true that no human being can exist without being first and last an individual, namely someone distinct from all other individuals. Paradox of sameness and difference reflecting the interweaving of the principles of the Absolute and the Infinite.

However, higher, or deeper, even than the superordinate of *anthropos*, each person partakes of two essential dimensions of reality: existence and consciousness or, to borrow from Scholastics, *esse* and *intelligens*. In other words, to be a human being is to exist and it is to know. Whatever the form of our being and whatever the contents of our consciousness, we cannot cease to be nor cease to be aware, and in being (*esse*) we partake of all Being in the sense that we are a dimension or modality, however finite, of the one immortal Self, just as in knowing (*intelligens*) we partake potentially of the totality of God's Self-awareness. In other words, even if as individu-

---

12 In Hinduism, this notion of the individual is expanded to include different kinds of *karma*, some of which like *prarabda karma*, have not yet born fruit and which are likened to an arrow, already shot, but still flying to its target. Likewise, individuals are marked by what is termed (in Hinduism and Buddhism) as *samskaras*, or knots of volitional and desire-directed tendencies, inherited and re-inherited, that determine their clinging to the *samsara* via a particular birth and, most likely, multiple rebirths.

als we may not be aware of more than our immediate flesh and emotional existence, we are in our essence pure intelligence and pure immortality.[13] There is, in other words, no intrinsically insurmountable barrier or division in universal consciousness, just as light cannot be divided or just as cosmic substance cannot be fundamentally segmented even while being accidentally refracted into countless forms; but these forms refract, finally, what is really a kind of exploded view of an impartible divine Totality. The implications of this oneness of Self are obviously profound, not least of which is that whatever an individual does to himself he does implicitly to others and indeed to the universe; no man can cheat in a pure vacuum free of all consequence; and likewise, when he shows kindness he is sweetening the universe.

Every man, every woman, sits on a veritable ocean within themselves; but they do so unawares, and the ocean remains unavowed, and thus they live in one exiguous corner of their integral possibilities. They do so, of course, as individuals and, inasmuch as individuality remains unredeemed, they do so as cosmic accidents, which amounts to living beneath themselves—or outside themselves. This immense disparity between actual—or accidental—being and true—or necessary—being can be a source of some very real disequilibrium, for the suppression of our human totality exerts over time a limiting if not crippling effect on man's ability to be joyous and free, for joy in the end derives from wholeness as well as from the Truth, both of which have a liberating effect from the cramp of individualistic existence; a fake, artificial, half-existence is a lingering death. Joy and freedom are man's theomorphic birthright for as the ancient alchemical saying declares: "nature rejoices in nature", that is to say nature blossoms and thrives when freed from the shackles of unnatural constraints. A "theomorphic birthright", we say, and not just a "birthright", because the merely human birthright can be compromised firstly by *karma*, that is, an entanglement of causes and effects entailing perhaps the lengthy atonement of a "cosmic debt", and secondly this birthright can be compromised by the vice of horizontality accruing from the fact of entering the human state and experiencing life purely passively, without ever sensing the ver-

---

13 Saint Symeon the New Theologian captures the essence of this truth in his poem *We Awaken in Christ's Body*: "We awaken in Christ's body / As Christ awakens in our bodies, / And my poor hand is Christ , / He enters my foot, and is infinitely me. / I move my hand, and wonderfully / My hand becomes Christ, becomes all of Him / For God is indivisibly / Whole, seamless in his Godhood. / I move my foot, and at once / He appears like a flash of lightning / Do my words seem blasphemous?—Then / Open your heart to Him. . ." (*The Enlightened Heart: An Anthology of Sacred Poetry*, ed. Stephen Mitchell [New York: Harper Perennial, 1989], p. 38).

tical axis which is that of self-transcendence and of spiritual realization. Put differently, our human birthright gives us access to the human state, its divine gifts, but many if not most individuals acquire this birthright accidentally, namely as no more than another step in an ongoing process of transmigration in which they enter the human state only to exit it, all of which is an incredible waste unless they can become integral human beings and not just people. The theomorphic birthright—implied in a human birth—is what gives an individual potential access to the divine realm. If an individual is oblivious to the vertical imperative, this is due largely to a profane attitude, a mark of which is found in a mundane, if not casual or even trivial, approach in enjoying life's blessings, and this attitude destroys the possibility of what Sufis know as *barakah*, a benefic spiritual influence or an aura inherent in all good things, and actualized through the beautiful use of precious things.[14]

Now the "ocean" referred to above is not the subconscious popularized in modern psychology, which is more akin to a psychic heap of moldering impressions left by our individual possibility as well as by our collective lot as human beings. This ocean then—really a heavenly vault—is the totality of the possibility of man as *imago Dei*, or image of the Creator and, as such, it obviously cannot be encompassed by the individual ego in its passionate individualism; in fact, man as archetype and man as an individual—or to be more exact man as an individualist or selfish ego—are mutually exclusive, although there is no real "mutuality" since the fragmentary ego is really a dream fabric destined to be dissolved; it disappears like a shadow once his life's curtain closes; only the blessed are immortal: they do not die when they die.[15] This ocean is not the subconscious, we say, because it is really

14 Koran: "Lo! We have placed all that is on the earth as an ornament thereof that We may try them: which of them is best in conduct" ("The Cave", 18:7). Similarly, American Indians speak of the *wakan* influence, or the aura of the sacred, accompanying all good things, and this magical influence vanishes if a person's attitude is not mindfully respectful of a situation or of an object's sacredness.

15 But, in another sense, the individual ego does not disappear at death, but is relocated, either transfigured, if pure, or reiterated in a new karmic modality if still passionally bound to the wheel of existence of births and deaths; the whole mystical doctrine of merit is premised on this fact. What is dissolved at death, no doubt, are the earthly specifics of this ego, but not what Vedantic doctrine terms the *vasanas* or innate tendencies; these will "resurface", as it were, in another life but there will be no formal connection between the two lives, so that the reincarnated soul will not recognize anything of his new world just as it will not remember anything of its previous existence. *Vasanas* determine, among other things, affinities and aversions, as well as inclinations, impulses, needs and the like. Likewise, the trace of merit (or of demerit) continues to reverberate across the veils of reincarnation, just as the salvational impetus of Divine Mercy never ceases to resonate in the hearts of all

the supra-conscious, for in fact it is the individual being who is asleep and therefore it is he who is unconscious with respect to this reality; in other words, this reality is in fact dreaming the individual—if we may paraphrase the Taoist philosopher Chuang Tzu's dream of a butterfly—and not vice-versa. If it is objected that the term "subconscious" is merely a dialectical convenience meant to explain that man's latent possibilities are dormant by contrast to man's outward wakefulness, which is not incorrect, we will nonetheless have to specify that the modern notion of the subconscious amounts finally to a simulacrum if not a kind of clever parody of the hypostatic and invisible degrees of divine Reality because the so-called "collective subconscious" does not extend beyond the psychic plane of becoming and metamorphosis—by contrast with the deathless plane of the Spirit, that of the true Eternals.

The tautology, "true Eternals", is intended to establish a distinction with the makeshift "eternals" or the doctrine of archetypes of modern psychology that combines a mixture of psychic fragments with pieces of archetypes; that is to say, psychology, and especially psychoanalysis, has too personalistic a notion of collective urges and their so-called "archetypal" images. To take one example: the model of the "Hero", morally inspiring as it could be, ends up being miscast or trivialized[16] because the whole notion of evil—or of lethal darkness—which the hero (always solar in his function) is meant to overcome turns out not really being "evil" in itself. Lo and behold, in psychoanalysis, this "evil" corresponds to the denied "shadow" of our true but as yet unrecognized self; namely, it corresponds to allegedly repressed fears or those parts of himself the hero is not yet "mature enough" to confront and integrate. The banality of this assumption, which reduces the entire notion of evil to a psychological phantasm, undermines the notion of the hero—and ultimately of God—not least because the true hero hails from a supra-psychological realm, the sacred domain of the Spirit. Now, this is not to say that the psychoanalytic doctrine of the "shadow" is not partially correct on its level; but what has to be said, however, is that the true archetypal Hero dwells at a lofty remove from the trivial moral dilemmas dear to a bourgeois psychology titillated by grandeur, but impotent to realize it because it has no clue what it is to be a warrior or a saint, let alone a hero or martyr, for these states require the ever prompt and total readiness to sacrifice one's life, literally so if necessary. Now dying—

---

transmigrating creatures as it seeks to redeem individual souls and to restore them back to their heavenly substance.

16 Or misappropriated by the likes of a Jung, and notably and brilliantly by a Joseph Camp-bell in his *Hero with a Thousand Faces*.

spiritually if not physically—is a highly inconvenient outcome for the ego which, for obvious reasons, psychoanalysis wants to spare from any risk of permanent extinction while exalting this ego in every promiscuous way possible, but in a manner that seeks to bypass the staunch renunciation and purification that are the hallmarks of any true heroism. The saint seeks renunciation; the profane ego seeks indulgence. The saint wants to validate God; the ego wants to validate itself as god.

The "psychological subconscious", moreover, is not intelligent or lucid—two of the attributes characterizing any state involving the Spirit— but opaquely and polymorphously conscious, and functioning more like a buffer zone between soul and body. Thus the sensation-driven psycho-drama psychoanalysts are fond of analyzing is something of a tragi-comedy, suffocatingly banal when all is said and done because centered on the tribulations of man's ego, possibly magnified by grandiose references to cosmic archetypes that can feed an individual's sublimist sense of "specialness" if not his delusions of divinity. However, as stated above, this psycho-drama does not unfold for an instant on the plane of the Spirit,[17] access to which presupposes, as a pre-condition spiritual humility, or the extinction of individualism, though not of individuality proper; this humility which is the virgin bride of the Holy Spirit.

*   *   *

If one were now to formulate these considerations in a completely different manner, by reducing them to their most basic reflexes, one could say that the key to happiness is to consider, whom do we love more: God or ourselves?[18] Most people, even when professing to love God, continue in

---

17 Jung's notion of the "collective unconscious", intellectually enticing as it may be and ac-cidentally right in some of its premises, is too complex a subject to be dealt with here. But to base a doctrine of man's ontology, as Jung does, on a "common brain structure" (see Jung's "Introduction" to *The Secret of the Golden Flower*) is not only a materialistic as well as an evolutionist assumption, but also an inversion of the cosmic order of things, because the "brain structure" Jung has in mind is "determined" before it is a "determinant", that is to say it is an "effect" before it is a "cause". Moreover, the question of what determined this struc-ture in the first place eludes all psychoanalytic investigation; but somehow this question never occurs to psychologists, just as, on its plane, the "nothingness" quantum physics pos-tulates is never defined by physicists, leaving aside the fact that "nothingness" can never be pure nothingness, i.e. something that by definition cannot exist except as a dialectical foil.

18 Echoing Jesus' question to Simon: "Lovest thou me more than these [the other disci-ples]?" (John 21:15). Meister Eckhart's challenge of such a distinction is worth a comment. The great Rhenish preacher affirmed that since "there is no order and degree in the One . . . therefore, whoever loves God more than his neighbor, loves well, but not perfectly"

fact to love themselves more—wanting "to save their life", thus being in risk of losing it (Matt. 16:25)—be it simply because their own existence is so much realer to them in its existential immediacy than that of an invisible God.[19] Yet, the seed of happiness is to be found in loving God more, for in loving Him we love our essence, no less; in fact, the greatest irony for the ego bent on self-gratification is to discover that our ultimate self-interest coincides integrally with God's, just as, correlatively, to ignore God amounts to harming ourselves.

Integral spirituality requires reversing the priority held by the human pole over the Divine, or that of outwardness over that of inwardness. Expressed in Christian terms, this becomes then: to efface oneself— virgin purity of soul—so that Christ can shine, for, as Christ tells Saint Catherine of Siena, in the archetypal equation of dis-individuation: "I am He who is and thou art she who is not."[20] In universal terms, this means that man cannot meet God directly except through the sacred mold of the prophetic substance,[21] namely the mold of perfect man, because "only the son can know the Father". Death and resurrection, symbolically operated through the grace of the divine man, means: firstly recognition of God's transcendence—extinction—and then union through God's immanence—fulfillment—, respectively the *fana* (self-annihilation) and *baqa* (subsistence) of Sufism. One of the signal talents of a gifted spiritual master or even of a good director of conscience, is to continuously force the ego of an aspirant out of its "comfort zone", because complacency is the enemy of self-transcendence. In parallel to the master's keeping the disciple providentially "off-balance" is the fact that it is not uncommon for

(twenty-fifth article in the papal bull *in agro dominico*, condemning a number of Eckhart's propositions). We are exceedingly loath to criticize Eckhart, but we have to say that, in our opinion, this proposition merited criticism: the human plane, being the plane of meaningful distinctions, entails alternatives and degrees and therefore choices; no man can avoid these, not even a saint, and thus to love God (or Christ) more than ourselves or our fellow men is a natural hierarchical preference even though—to rejoin Eckhart—it ends up in a love that finally benefits both our neighbor and ourselves. Hence, it is not possible for an individual to choose to love God and neighbor equally at the outset, for to do so risks overvaluing our neighbor at the expense of God, otherwise why would Jesus have even raised the question?

19 About God's "invisibility" or hiddenness ("my face shall not be seen", Exod. 34:23), see the chapter "Satan Is Not an Atheist".

20 Quoted in Titus Burckhardt, *Siena: City of the Virgin* (Bloomington, IN: World Wisdom, 2008), p. 54.

21 Prototypically, the Logos, whether as the Word of God made flesh or in its microcosmic form as the heart-intellect.

the sincere aspirant, embarking on the spiritual path, to start out possibly being uncomfortable with the master himself and, in fact, even with God— "Oh that I had ever been born!" Yet this very discomfort can be proof both of the validity of the method and of this aspirant's sincerity, for it is part of the preliminary phase of mortifying extinction.

Transposing this equation now onto the plane of principles, we will say that what is a quandary for theology—but not for metaphysics—can be mitigated or even overcome by understanding the distinction just alluded to between "God as transcendence" and "God as immanence". For man, namely the human individual, there can be no immanence without prior transcendence: God cannot be fully approached as Self until He has been first understood as Truth and, by practical consequence, as Law. While the spiritual path entails processes occurring simultaneously—since man exists also in the timelessness of pure being—there is nonetheless a normal sequence in which purification precedes union, extinction enlightenment, death rebirth; indeed, the necessary premise for remembering—the Platonic anamnesis—entails a prior process of unknowing, of stripping the soul bare of its erroneous preconceptions. Otherwise immanence without transcendence is the devil's brew as can be seen, once again, in so much of so called New Age mysticism[22] which does not feel bound to exoteric religious dogma and prescriptions—the monotheistic doctrine of hell, for example, being usually the first doctrine to be discarded, along with the ever inconvenient notion of sin.[23] But to reject formal religion or orthodoxy and dogma, in favor of a kind of subjective spiritualism, often combined with aspirations to enhance one's personal potential, inevitably leads to a false esoterism since real esoterism cannot disavow exoterism—quite to the contrary[24]—just as the essence is not meant to disavow formal religion,

---

22 It could be objected that the term "New Age mysticism" is a contradiction in terms, but we do not think so, because "the Spirit bloweth where it listeth. . .".

23 However exoterists themselves, infected by psychologism and democratism, are now also discarding those notions—psychologism by trying to explain every "sin" and democratism by denying true inferiority.

24 In a deeper sense, however, it is really exoterism that disavows esoterism—true esoterism being always of one substance with universal orthodoxy or the "nature of things", the *fitrah* of the Sufis or the *sanatana dharma* of the Vedanta. We recall Schuon mentioning to us once that "only pure esoterism is perfectly orthodox", and indeed where else would orthodoxy derive its legitimacy save from the Spirit? Be that as it may, the role of esoterism is to pursue the implications of exoterism to their ultimate degree, but it will do so in a manner that exoterism cannot encompass or accept, at least formally. Thus if exoterism affirms the uniqueness and oneness of God, and does so with unarguable absoluteness, esoterism will carry this truth to the very depths of the doctrine of the identity between the individual

or the sap the tree. To assume otherwise, namely to bypass preliminary atonement (meaning "at-one-ment") would be, for instance, tantamount to confusing nudism with holy innocence before God;[25] common man cannot just disport himself in the shame of his fallenness, he needs to overcome himself first and does so through dignity and appropriate modesty.

*   *   *

What does it mean to say "I am not the Self" and yet "I am the Self"? These are self-cancelling affirmations. The key here is to understand that "I am *not* the Self" constitutes the indispensable basis for declaring "I am the Self"; or, the understanding that we—as individuals—cannot in any way be the Self provides the indispensable precondition for understanding the continuity of substance of universal selfhood; only the divine is fit for the Divine. Indeed, for an individual born in a still religious civilization, there are two essential character traits blazing in the firmament of his world: the reverential fear of God (principle of otherness—alterity) and the love of God (principle of identity—ipseity); they are also the human counterpart of the negative and positive polarities governing the ebb and flow of creation—the outbreath and inbreath of existence. These aspects of reverential fear and love—or respect and devotion—derive in turn from the "hard and soft" principial polarity of the Absolute-Infinite existing *in divinis*. Conversely, the Absolute-Infinite pairing, when transposed onto creation, becomes that of Heaven and manifestation, or *Atma-Maya*.[26] Hence, in front of the

self and the one Self (*aham Brahmasmi*), for its implication is that nothing then can exist outside of God; but exoterism, taking its stand on the duality between Creator and man, can only reject this affirmation categorically.

25 The grossness of nudism stems from mistaking the fleshly banality of our unregenerate self with a kind of primordial naturalness, or of assuming that an unclothed casualness is a kind of innocence. The one is a parody of the other, because the appeal of casualness, or of being "just oneself", lies partly in the laziness involved in not wanting to truly overcome oneself, to say nothing of being oblivious of what the extraordinary majesty of man as *imago Dei* entails. If we had an inkling of our eternal human archetype we would, like Adam and Eve, run to hide out of shame. And, likewise, if we encountered someone embodying this archetype, we would be fearful: "If thou hadst observed them closely thou hadst assuredly turned away from them in flight, and hadst been filled with dread of them", we read in the Koran ("The Cave", 18:18) about encountering the youths in the cave, who are the true initiates in the Spirit.

26 *Maya* is usually defined in opposition to *Atma*, being equated with illusion and ignorance, which is of course a crucial principle. But *Maya* is also the *Shakti* of *Atma*, and in that role it represents the radiation of *Atma* in creation, what Schuon termed the "Principle of Divine Reverberation" (see *Spiritual Perspectives and Human Facts*, chap. "Contours of

transcendent mystery of *Atma*, man is effaced, disciplined, and rigorous; yet, by virtue of the immanent mystery of *Atma* shining through *Maya*, man can also radiate, create, and be joyous. The two traits of fear and love are inseparable: without love, fear can become crippling or turn into the zeal of bitterness, or possibly determine an attitude of abject servility instead of being reverential respect, which is ennobling; and without fear, love can become casual temerity or presumption, or damnable familiarity.

Modern man, to generalize, neither fears God nor loves God, because to fear and to love Him is essentially to put God first, or to put Heaven before the world (*contemptus mundi*), which is as much as to say—in Scholastic terms—to put "necessary being" before "possible being". It is also to understand that the human cannot do without the Divine, while not divinizing the human just as much as not humanizing the Divine.[27] Man cannot answer the question "Who am I?" without first understanding that "I am nothing" and therefore "I stand in awe before my Maker and, by extension, before my fellow human beings", and yet that "I exist and thus I am all-embracing love" and therefore "I rush in love to my Maker and, by extension, to my fellow human beings". Who am I? I am profoundest respect and infinite love.

A host of spiritual, as well as psychological, reflexes result from these two fundamental attitudes: reverential fear, in its vital core, corresponds to a healthy sense of proportions—yea "the beginning of wisdom"—that is anchored first in an awareness of our creaturely nothingness before our Maker: "eat thy bread with quaking..." (Ezek. 12:18). And this "fear", this reverential fear, will normally be the leaven of one's faith. At the same time, this fear of God, if it is to be more than cringing abasement, requires a positive complement, that of holy devotion, or love: "He delivered me be-cause He delighted in me" (Ps. 18:19). It must be understood here that God's omnipotence entails, metaphysically, his all-mercifulness, for He could not be all-merciful were He not omnipotent. Hence, His very majesty before which man goes pale and must avert his gaze, hides His loving beauty which redeems man in ecstasy of joy.

---

the Spirit"). Ramakrishna referred to two different aspects of *Maya*, one being *vidya Maya* (awareness or *vijnana*) and the other *avidya Maya* (non-awareness or ignorance) (*The Gospel of Sri Ramakrishna*, section 16, chap. 1). There is, in other words, a *Maya* leading us to *Atma* and one leading us away.

27 Of the two fallacies, the second—namely, humanizing God—is less problematical be-cause God takes on a human face to address man, which means that He also tolerates the tendency to over-humanize Him—unless this "over-humanizing" veers into paganism or idolatry, because then He has to contend with competing "gods", as it were. Worth noting is the fact that paganism is ultimately a back-door entry to the first heresy, that of divinizing man, by mythological proxy one might say.

What can be lost sight of is that these qualities—the principles of which determine our humility and charity (or *vacare Deo* and *agape*)[28]—correspond not merely to basic dispositions of the human soul, but, as mentioned above, to the most profound of cosmic realities in that they govern macrocosmically the twin pulse of attraction and repulsion, or of day and night, heat and cold, as well as, when transposed, the masculine and the feminine poles at the heart of the universe. At their core, they are also connected to life and death, in that they correspond to the twin forces of expansion and contraction, or of abundance and sacrifice, or the summer and winter solstices.[29] And, translated microcosmically, there are a series of human traits corresponding to them, the methodical spiritual prototypes of which are summarized in all true spirituality in the mutual injunction of *oratio* et *jejunium*, namely of "prayer" and "fasting" or activity for God and poverty for God—renunciation and affirmation. Their universality is found everywhere, such as in Buddhism, in the mystery of the *Pratyeka Buddha* (solitary detachment) and the mystery of the *Bodhisattva* (radiant manifestation).[30] Or they correspond simply to inwardness and revelation, as summarized in the biblical phrase: "I sleep, but my heart waketh" (Song of Songs 5:2).

In a derived sense, but still connected to reverential fear, we would like to mention the qualities of solemnity and dignity found in most tribal and semi-nomadic people, as well as in still rural people where religiousness still has a meaning. Not least, reverential fear is the foundation for the Biblical quality of venerability.

Now, a factor that undermines the Biblical venerability of man, and that exerts a distorting influence on the whole notion of individuation in general, is the issue of demographics. In using the term "demographics", we have in mind the rampant growth of mankind's numbers leading to catastrophic overpopulation: by its nature, overpopulation is socialistic, enslaving, and ultimately debasing for the individual, because the relationship between

---

28 For *agape*, see 1 Cor. 13:1-8: "Though I speak with the tongues of men and of angels, and I have not charity, I am become as sounding brass, or a tinkling crystal. . .".

29 In describing these pairings, we are not attempting to establish any direct parallelisms between the poles because some pairings are made up of two benefic qualities, others of opposite or even conflicting qualities; but all these pairings modulate the duality of creation, whether in positive or negative mode.

30 See Frithjof Schuon, chap. "Mystery of the Bodhisattva", in *Treasures of Buddhism* (Bloomington, IN: World Wisdom, 1993) and "The Two Paradises" in *Form and Substance in the Religions*.

the quality of an individual and overcrowding is inversely proportional.[31] In other words, wherever populations multiply to exceed certain optimal ratios, the individual is subjected more and more not only to a *de facto* dictatorship of the masses, but collective standards or norms are skewed downwards following the law of quantitative pressure and inertia that has to accommodate the greatest common denominator, as opposed to what would be ideal for a guiding elite; in such a universe, the outcome to the question of "Who am I?" is increasingly at the mercy of overwhelming collective trends that trample qualitative options. Collectivism, and the vulgarizing sociology and philosophy that supports it—or the "reign of quantity", to borrow from the French metaphysician René Guénon—is the great enemy of a noble individualism which is the archetype of man. Nomadism, to take now the opposite end of the spectrum of civilization, guarantees that only the worthiest individuals survive and the severity of this natural selection affects—mostly positively—the quality of the genealogy of a race, at least in a cyclical epoch such as ours where the pole of matter predominates over the pole of the spirit. That said, the integral possibility of man is to be found in some balance between civilization proper, with its possibility of cities or great cultural bastions sheltered from the rigors of brutish and possibly demeaning survival, and nomadism proper which, at its best, is meant to have a raw revitalizing effect on civilization and on man's individual mettle, just as ice or fire purify nature.[32]

* * *

When the Hindu scriptures affirm that "the Self is the one and only transmigrant" this is a colossal ellipsis meant to emphasize that God—or the Godhead (*Atma*)—is the sole real. It is a dialectical ellipsis on the same scale as to say with the Buddhists—but reversing the equation now—that *samsara* (manifestation) is *Nirvana* (Heaven) or, in other words, that *Maya* is *Atma* or that the creation is reducible in the final analysis to God's Being since God alone is Real, or that man is divine. "Glory be to Me", cried Al-Bistami.[33]

31 We are aware of the different statistical studies, some of which come to differing conclusions about whether or not human population is leveling off or continuing to increase. Whatever their conclusions, and whether or not the earth can sustain present and future masses of individuals, it is clear that the sheer quantity of people has decisively overwhelmed their quality.

32 See Ibn Khaldun's *Muqaddimah* or philosophy of history, in which he examines the unstable but vitalizing balance between nomads and city-dwellers, as well as Arnold Toynbee's exploration of the impact of stress and ease on the survival and growth of civilizations.

33 Bayazid al-Bistami was a foremost Sufi proponent of the doctrine of extinction (*fana*),

THE MYSTERY OF INDIVIDUALITY

In metaphysics—but not in theology—it is possible to speak of everything being reducible to the Principle;[34] likewise, it is possible to speak of the Principle being reflected in manifestation. However, both formulations—because they are formulations—contain a double-edged sword effect. Thus the first one, in reducing everything to the Principle, wishes to defend the transcendent primacy of the Divine, but risks doing so at the expense of any reflected (or temporal) reality that manifestation may have, otherwise how could it even exist for an instant? Whereas, the second one, allowing for the reflection of the Principle in manifestation, recognizes the mirroring of the divine Cause in the effects and thus lays the foundation for the divine essence of all creation, but in so doing risks laying the ground at the same time for the classic error of pantheism—as well as of idolatry—in which the effects are divinized. Of the two formulations, one declaring the incomparable uniqueness of the Cause and the other the relative equivalence of the effect with the Cause, the former which defends God's uniqueness is the safer one for it avoids the risk of idolatry or of ensnarement in the cosmic illusion. Yet it is still an ellipsis, and therefore it comes at a price which in rejecting the reality of the world—or rather the *relative* reality of the world—renders the existence of the world incomprehensible because even an illusion has some degree of realness however ephemeral. Be that as it may, to say that "the Self is the one and only transmigrant" is finally an ellipsis meant to challenge logic, but in a manner of a Zen *koan* that explodes a logic that is merely profane.

Yet human logic retains its relative rights, and therefore it can be argued that it is certainly not in its capacity as the "sole Real" that the Self, or *Atma*, is a transmigrant—namely a state of being presupposing an individual soul. And were we to assume, for the sake of argument, that the sole Real could transmigrate, would It not *ipso facto* abolish the *samsara* if It did so as pure Self? The invincibility of the Self radiating as Self would burn all veils. Of course, It does abolish the *samsara* ultimately through the *mahapralaya* or the apocatastasis; however, to concede this, in other words to

---

or of "annihilation in God" (*fana fi'Llah*). The full quotation reads: "Glory be to Me; how great is my Majesty!" We have taken the liberty to capitalize "Me" (in contrast with printed versions of this quotation) since a lower case "me" would be pure heresy, in which case the statement would not have survived the centuries.

34 The term "Principle" denotes, in metaphysics, the "supreme primary cause" and is thus a synonym for God or, more exactly, the Godhead or ultimate Divine Essence. The "Principle" is often defined in contrast to "manifestation" or everything that is not this Supreme Principle. Other synonymous (but not completely identical) pairings are: the Absolute and the relative (Vedanta: *Atma* and *Maya*), the Real and the illusory, Substance and accident, Essence and form, God and the world, Cause and effect.

say that the Self eventually reabsorbs all of manifestation at a given point in time in the future, is then to concede that there is a "before" and "after", as well as a beginning and an end and a whole duration—or countless durations, in between.[35] And this then is also to concede that individuality can exist "outside" of the Self. This distinction between Self and non-self—or of a separation occurring within the Self, or of distinction within indistinction if one prefers— is captured in Krishna's declaration to Arjuna: "I am not in them [human beings]; they are in Me" (*Bhagavad Gita*, 7:12).

Not surprisingly, to assert, in its purest form, that the Self alone is real and that therefore the world and man are nothing, not even a dream finally, is a formulation that is dialectically alien to Judaism, Christianity, and Islam, which, like Vishnuism in India, are religious perspectives that emphasize the quasi-absolute duality between Creator and creation or that between God and man.[36] When seen from the human vantage point, this perspective, limited as it is by time and space (and history), is obviously legitimate for a human being; he can in fact have no other vantage point short of attaining *maha-samadhi* or ultimate extinction in Godhead. Thus, from the perspective of the three monotheistic revelations, in which the creator and legislator God is supreme, man as God's ontological "masterpiece", has a role to play, whether as *pontifex* (man as "bridge-maker" in Christianity) or vice-regent (*khalifah* in Islam). As a result, man, on pain of not being able to think at all, is entitled to formulations and definitions that take into account gradations of Reality, provided he does not exaggerate the reality of these gradations at the expense of the One Supreme Reality.

Of the three monotheisms, one might say that, dialectically at least, Christianity comes closest to jeopardizing the formal exclusivity of the Absolute, what with its doctrine of the Trinity—dividing the One into a tripartite "absolute"—in which the idea of the Principle made flesh is specified, along with the idea of Mary being the "mother of God"—another colossal ellipsis. In essence, however, these doctrinal formulations attempt to capture the realness of the Divine both in Itself and in its cosmic radiation, of which man is, archetypically, the quintessence in creation. That said, it goes without saying that the absoluteness of God is paramount in

---

35 This is summarized in the *Srimad Bhagavata Mahpurana*, 2, 9:32, 34 thus: "Before this universe was, I alone was. . . . After manifestation I continued to be, in Myself as well as in the form of the world of phenomena; and when the universe has ceased to exist I will be. . . . Just as one may say of the sensible elements that they have entered into all living beings (since these beings live by them) . . . or that they have not entered into them (since they constitute them *a priori*), so also one can say that I entered into these living beings (as such) or that I did not enter into them (since there is no reality other than I)."

36 Buddhism sidesteps this whole issue by omitting the explicit mention of God.

these monotheisms—especially in Islam, which came, one might say, as a "corrective compensation" for Christianity's human theomorphism, just as Christianity had to compensate or "humanize" Judaism's legalistic rigor by restoring the primacy of love over law. Nonetheless, and in contradistinction with the pure metaphysical reductionism of *Atma* being the sole Real, in all three monotheistic religions God's absoluteness is an absoluteness that presupposes the presence of man and therefore that of his relative reality as "reflected Self".[37] Islam, which is the last revelation, has the providential advantage of summarizing in an unsurpassable manner the twofold doctrine regarding the absolute reality of God and the relative reality of man in its twin testimonials: "There is no divinity save the Divinity" and "Muhammad is His messenger". In other words, to paraphrase, this testimony bears witness that God alone is real, and yet at the same time asserts that the *avatara* is a reflection of God on earth, because "I and my Father are one", as Christ declared.[38]

*   *   *

We have seen that the question of our root identity touches on the question of *theosis*, namely of the realization of the Divine, or to quote once again Christ's words: "Be ye therefore perfect, even as your Father which is in heaven is perfect." In Buddhist terms, to understand the Buddha ultimately means attaining Buddhahood oneself,[39] because so long as the "Eye of the Heart" remains sealed, man cannot understand anything except indirectly or through the veil of obscurity, whence the necessity of faith which is a "seeing without seeing". Thus, the mystery of individuation—which is finally that of God assuming the human state prototypically—entails the mystery of sanctity or an understanding through the heart, the immanent and deathless source of light and life in every human being. And even

---

37 The Andalusian Sufi, Ibn Arabi captures this perfectly in his *Fusus al-Hikam* ("Ring Settings of Wisdom"): "For divinity requires that [thing] over which it is divine and lordship requires the servant, otherwise they would have no meaning or existence" (1:119, cited in Michael Sells in *Mystical Languages of Unsaying*, p. 93). At the same time, Ibn Arabi rectifies or compensates for this affirmation right afterwards by specifying: "But in reality lordship is the same as identity." However, we cannot detail this logical aporia or "irresolvable dilemma" further at this point.

38 An interpretation that exoteric Islam could never countenance, of course, and one for which the Jews wanted to stone him.

39 Although, to borrow from Mahayana Buddhism, the actual realization depends on Amitabha's Grace—the grace of the *bodhisattva*—never on individual efforts alone. All man can do is to prepare the tinder; Heaven provides the spark.

though this doctrine of the "Eye of the Heart" is the key of keys for understanding what man is, modern psychology finally knows nothing of it. Yet this key is found in every tradition prior to the advent of the modern world, including so-called primitive people; without it, the human soul is condemned to wander on indefinitely through the *samsara*.[40] In Hinduism and Buddhism, this key is referred to as the Third Eye; however, because it is non-organic, its material existence is unverifiable and it takes then but one short modern step to declare it non-existent, as if non-material equaled non-real. But man cannot know God, and therefore "who he is" except through God, that is to say, except through a faculty that transcends the limitations of the rational, empirical human ego as such—leaving aside the question of grace, for the ego cannot have a true vision of any reality transcending it without the help of Heaven.[41]

To the question, then, how is one to follow in the quest of the *mysterium individuationis*, a mystery leading finally to pure Selfhood, requires entering into the wake of the Socratic adage of "knowing thyself". Now, quite obviously, few souls—very few souls indeed[42]—will have the intellective (noetic) gift of a Ramana Maharshi, who when he inquired inwardly to himself, "Who am I?", then immersed himself into a blessed self-reflective plunge that took him from unveiling to ontological unveiling, as effortlessly as a river is reclaimed by the ocean, into the very roots of selfhood

40 Thus we find in the Oglala Sioux medicine man, Black Elk's account a reference to this Eye of the Heart: "I am blind and I do not see the things of this world; but when the Light comes from on High, it illuminates my heart and I can see, because the Eye of my heart (*Chante Ishta*) sees all things. The heart is the sanctuary at the center of which is a small space where the Great Spirit (*Wakan Tanka*) lives, and this is the Eye of the Great Spirit by which He sees everything, and with which we see Him. When the heart is impure, the Great Spirit cannot be seen, and if you should die in this ignorance, your soul will not be able to return at once to the Great Spirit, but will have to be purified by wanderings across the Cosmos. To know the center of the heart where the Great Spirit dwells, you must be pure and good and live according to the way that the Great Spirit has taught us. The man who is pure in this way, contains the Universe in the Pocket of his Heart (*Chante Ognaka*)" (quoted in Frithjof Schuon, *The Eye of the Heart* [Bloomington, IN: World Wisdom, 1997], p. 9n). In the monotheistic religions, the "wanderings across the Cosmos" referred to are synthetically encompassed in the doctrines of purgatory and hell.

41 Schuon comments: "The ego as such cannot logically seek the experience of what lies beyond egoity; man is man and the Self is the Self" (*Esoterism as Principle and as Way*, p. 32). This single axiomatic statement should put an end to all kinds of fruitless speculations and experiments about self-realization or enhancing one's divine potential, which are contradictions in terms since the Self alone knows its own.

42 "At the end of many lives, the man of wisdom resorts to Me, knowing that Vasudeva [the Supreme] is all that is. Such a great soul is very difficult to find" (*Bhagavad Gita*, 7:19).

wherein his heart-identity merged with that of the Divine Self. Rephrasing the Socratic "know thyself" (*gnosi seauton*), one would like to say, combining the powers of a dispassionate introspection with devout contemplation before the mystery of Being: enter into thyself, into thy innermost self, and gaze and gaze and gaze. The rest lies in the hands of divine Grace, for only God can repossess Himself and thus cure the wound of duality since He always was One to begin with. In essence, the mystery of individuality touches upon a triple mystery: we in God, God in us, and God in Himself. Or respectively: mystery of Faith, mystery of Revelation, mystery of Holiness.

CHAPTER 3

The Iconic Figure

The greatness of My glory shall overshadow thee; lions shall fear thee; bears shall protect thee; wolves shall flee before thee, and I will remain thy companion.
(Mechthild of Magdeburg)

Every traditional human collectivity has been inspired by an emblematic human archetype, a prophetic, royal, or heroic figure—*pontifex maximus* or "greatest bridge-builder" between Heaven and earth—holding a role that is the human and yet preeminently divine face of that civilization. The sacred imprint of this prototype is projected onto society and assimilated by the masses in the measure that a collectivity can still do so post the Golden Age. It is repeated in innumerable human variants that are shades of the same iconic mold; such a figure spawns saints and saintly men and women in its wake, and, for the rest of society, serves as the moral exemplar by which a collectivity can overcome its proletarian tendencies. We shall remember here that a collectivity itself represents in sum a macrocosmic individual and therefore is meant, in its way and when properly inspired and guided, to function as a type of normative model for individuals. But, when unguided, it succumbs to the law of gravity of its passions.

This overarching iconographic figure is meant to offer a model of true man—and true woman too, quite obviously—while representing a model image of each man's individual essence. The paragon model for this figure are the great prophets, come on earth as the embodiment of the Logos, or the fully noetic human incarnation of the Spirit of God made man. For Christianity, this figurehead is the wondrous and incomparable example of Christ, understanding however that this image has lost much if not most of its former vividness and spiritual potency the more it became appropriated by a sentimental religious bias that diluted and dissolved, when not distorting, its original gnostic reality.[1] In Islam, this figure is the paragon

---

1 This bias will, over time, inevitably reflect the day to day conventions of a given social setting; this has led to a more and more sentimental image of the Savior fitted to the customs of the times. At the extreme, this image ends up bearing only the vaguest or even no resemblance at all to the archetype; for example, in the modern West, priests dress more and more like their parishioners, until all meaningful distinctions between sacred and secular are lost, and therefore lost too is the sense of the real Christic image as men hurry to update the intemporal to serve their mundane needs. In stark contrast to the Christian West, the Eastern Church has maintained the iconic figure of Christ as seen in the solemn dignity of the Orthodox patriarch priests as well as in the sacred iconography decorating the churches which, in substance, if at all, has not succumbed to individualistic modern art so far.

example of the prophet Muhammad—and the *barakah* (the perfume of the divine) or the *Ruh Muhammadiyah* (the Muhammadan spirit) permeating everything, from the dress to the architecture, in ways both concrete and subtly mysterious. Yet, here again, this image has become fanatically appropriated in modern times and thereby distorted if not mangled by extremists who are often brutally oblivious of their prophet's exceptional aristocracy of bearing and fineness of manners and magnanimity of comportment, and not least his spiritual serenity. Likewise, for Eastern civilizations, the Buddha has served as the radiant exemplar, imprinting a monastic example of serene effacement and ineffable otherworldliness, expressed among others by the breathtaking multitude of monks as well as nuns one finds in the Far-East; for instance, we are told that almost half the population of Lhasa, the capital of Tibet, was at various times peopled by monks. On the feminine side we find, in the West, the heroic figure in Judaism of the prophetess Deborah[2] and, in Christianity, the silent image of the co-redemptress Virgin Mary, "full of grace", while in the Islamic world we have that of the daughter of the prophet Muhammad, Fatima. Hinduism has the image of Sita, the wife of Rama, the seventh *avatara*[3] of the God Vishnu, she herself also being considered as an *avatara* but of the Goddess Lakshmi; and we also have the complementary feminine archetype of Radha, consort of Krishna.[4] One might also want to add that the masculine *avatara*'s iconographic majesty is also sometimes compensated by a child version of it which, in Christianity, is seen in the cult of the Child Jesus, whereas in Hinduism the prophetic figure of Krishna is often depicted in a child form, the *bala Krishna*.

We mentioned, for Hinduism, the complementary icons of Radha and Sita—Radha as the divine mistress and erotic lover, free to love outside of

---

2 Not less than seven women in fact are accounted as prophetesses in that religion, and some commentators will add the names of Rebecca, Rachel, and Lea to that number. Furthermore, one will recall that, in essential Judaism, woman is considered to be an embodiment of the *Shekhinah*, or the highest wisdom; in fact, the *Shekhinah* (as the *Ruach Ha-Kodesh*) is equivalent to the Holy Spirit in Christianity—the Spirit's interchangeability as masculine or feminine personification being part of the mystery of the essence.

3 A salvific descent and human personification of God on earth.

4 Sita is the iconographic model of the perfect, duty-bound wife, whereas Radha is the model of divine love; they represent complementary possibilities of feminine perfection. This complementarity of female icons is not as well developed in Christianity and Islam, which both exhibit an ambivalent sense of what could be hazardously termed the "free woman", but what is in fact an embodiment of love that transcends social conventions. In some ways, the complementarity can be likened to that between exoterism and esoterism, or to that between erotic love and chaste love, at least inasmuch as pure eroticism shares an analogy with esoterism in its need to break free from all earthly shackles.

all social conventions, and Sita as the model of the virtuous, humble, and devoted wife. Such a polarity exists in Christendom and Islam, albeit in an essentially suppressed mode: in Christianity, we have the figure of Mary Magdalene, the first to see Christ arisen, and archetype of the forgiven sinner, though the Dionysian genius of her love, if we may say, cannot be accounted for properly in this religion's inherently moralistic terms; and in Islam, there is the lusciously beautiful and willfully intelligent figure of Aisha, the "favorite wife of the Prophet", in whose arms he died; she too has been passed over mostly in silence in this religion.[5] Neither of these iconographic figures found much of a social archetype in either of the great civilizations of Christianity or Islam in the way that Radha did in Hinduism, a religion that harmoniously accommodates seemingly every archetypal spiritual possibility known to mankind.[6]

The stellar iconographic models that heralded sacred civilizations are further supported by the cult of saints typical of traditional cultures, saints whose names are given to children, thus weaving a web of spiritual filiation through which all men become virtual children of God; similarly, theophoric names[7] were common in the Ancient pre Judeo-Christian Middle East, and later in Islam. In stark contrast, our age is the first and therefore the only one in history to be defined in the absence of a supreme prophetic figure—and the sowing of saints following in his luminous wake like stars—and this void could likely pave the way for the advent of an anti-prophetic figure because individuals cannot exist long without the support of a figurehead; the need to worship is innate to man: remove God, and remove the saints, and the void will eventually be filled with idols, if not with demons.

In civilizations where icons and frescoes—the visual counterpart of the liturgy—are part of the divine language of revelation (Hinduism, Buddhism,

---

5 From the beginning Aisha fell into some measure of disrepute when she instigated political strife leading to a war with Ali, Muhammad's son-in-law.

6 The often over-moralistic adulation of the Virgin Mary, in some sectors of Roman Catholic Christianity, and of Fatima, in Islam, based on their virginal or "desexualized" merits, could not easily accommodate the opposite and highly erotic persons of Mary Magdalene and Aisha; and yet both of the latter are also iconic prototypes of womanhood in their own right, prototypes which therefore have to be found by definition in paradise. That said, Mary Magdalene cannot be set as a complementary pole to the Holy Virgin, whose incomparable and majestic loftiness transcends all comparisons. Moreover, a civilization cannot have two "contending" archetypes: it must choose one or the other—although, once again, Hinduism proves here to be the exception, given its amplitude.

7 Or names "bearing the god", such as Apollonius, from Apollo in Greek, or Abd al-Haqq ("Servant of the Real") in Arabic.

and Christianity in particular),[8] this iconic image is enshrined in sanctuaries and reflected by the attitude and comportment of priests, monks, and the faithful in general, whose character is molded by it. Mention must also be made of the elderly who, in these traditional societies, often realize a kind of saintly dignity, impassivity, and gravity, coupled with a sweetness reflecting the temporal proximity of their agedness to Heaven, and also due to their having finally overcome so many of life's battles and passions. In a secular civilization, however, and one that prizes physical appeal and dynamism—both idiosyncrasies being psychologically consistent with the doctrine of progressivism, which is anti contemplative by definition, contemplativity being related to the notion of repose in the divine center— old age is often something people flee from, desperate as they are for an immortality sought in a "fountain of youth" understood really as a fountain of physical vitality, and not of holy innocence; but such an emphasis can only lead to disillusion because, under normal circumstances, the process of aging is meant to correspond to a transfer of outer beauty to inner beauty, or the transfiguration of accidental beauty into eternal beauty, and not to the clinging onto a withering youth.

A word now regarding the role of iconography in a traditional civilization, given sacred art's central role in perpetuating the iconic figure. More specifically, with respect to the veneration of images, it must be said that, for all their importance, paintings and statuary can also prove to be a double-edged sword due to the constant temptation to yield to an overly humanized depiction of divine figures, to say nothing of the unfortunate deification of central historical figures that may be far from holy. To illustrate this general point, Giotto's frescoes—to take one central example—provide a whole teaching of how Heaven can touch earth in all daily aspects of life; however these frescoes constitute at the same time the outer limit in narrative realism that such images can safely employ without sealing the door to the archetype. In other words, if an image becomes too graphically literal, its transcendent or supra-formal symbolism risks becoming over-shadowed by a fleshly realism that, finally, defeats the image's original purpose since it is precisely this supra-formal essence that it is meant to exemplify, and hence to convey the presence of the supernatural. In the

---

8 But Islam compensates for this lack of human images with the living imitation of the Prophet, whose hieratic imprint is seen on the faces of all traditional men, to one degree or another; this imitation has been one of the most striking features of this religion, part of which may stem from this religion's relative youthfulness compared to others, although the essential cause is no doubt to be found in the fact that in Islam each man is his own priest, whence the scrupulous need for each individual to model himself on the prophet instead of relying on a priestly intermediary as one finds in other religions.

case of Greek and Roman statuary, their very human perfection—and ironically given their plastic ideal—ends up excluding the divine archetype owing to too slavish a duplication of the outward human form in the inert material of stone or marble;[9] one cannot, after all, infuse breath into stone to make it seem living—stone being lifeless in its substance—although, in compensation, stone, owing to its very inertness, lends itself ideally to stylization. A measure of naturalism in art (either painting or sculpture) is effective but only if compensated by a balancing measure of stylization that restores the subject matter of this art to its spiritual archetype. In other words, stylization works to the measure that art's naturalism is transfigured because outward nature cannot be duplicated literally by the artist; what he must seize via the artistic medium is a form's intellective purpose, the artistic composition serving then as the mirror of the soul of whatever object is depicted and not merely as the repetition of its physical form with no other purpose than to achieve a virtuoso kind of imitation, which finally is enslaving in that it cannot help the viewer overcome the bonds of matter.[10] When the symbolism of forms in human representations is understood, the inert rigor of stone can then lend itself to the carving of the fundamental nobility of hieratic attitude and posture. This can be seen in some of the statuary ornamenting Gothic churches where saints are aligned like impersonal stalactites, reflecting their immortal station as holy witnesses to the Divine; and likewise in some Egyptian art, where their archetypal individuality is crystallized in a sacred and still semi-abstract humanization of the eternal Principle made man.

The same limitation, or contradiction, of too literal an art applies to Renaissance and Baroque art onward; in Scholastic terms the defect of this humanistic art is to glorify accidental being to the detriment of necessary being—or the discursive over the essential, the temporal over the intemporal—not to mention the risk of idolizing purely fleshly existence, and this cult corresponds finally to the whole post-medieval shift in society's center of gravity from other-worldliness to worldliness. Sacred art, to be true to its vocation as witness of the Divine—in contrast to the pure naturalism of the Renaissance outlook, wherein fleshly man displaces God in physical realness—must include the symbolic or hieratic dimension alluded to, because man is *spiritus* and not just *corpus*. But, seen more broadly, naturalism and hieratic symbolism need not be mutually

9 "They [mankind] know only an outward part of the life of the world, and are heedless of the Hereafter" (Koran, "The Romans", 30:7).

10 Modern art, of course, has broken those bonds, mostly (but not always) in the lower direction of chaos and not of that of a higher harmony, to say the least.

exclusive, as some of the Hindu and Buddhist statuary proves; in medieval Christian art, however, they are usually very much exclusive. Indeed, medieval Christian artists favored the spiritual content or the symbolism over the form, treating the latter more as an accessory to the symbolism, the depiction of a hieratic attitude taking precedence over all other considerations. Or perhaps, if artistically gifted, the medieval artist may have depreciated the form on purpose so as not to allow a secondary or outward perfection—that of the human shape—to overshadow an essential one, that of the Spirit.[11] Or else, the literal human form could be stylistically de-formed on purpose—as in the art of icons where heads are enlarged and torsos narrowed and verticalized—to emphasize a transcendental spiritual essence; medieval statuary did much the same.[12]

That said, it should be specified that by "form" we are not referring so much to the polarity *forma* (*spiritus* or "intelligent principle") and *materia* (substance), which are the ruling poles of sacred art, but to the quality of execution. Hence, to reformulate our first statement, one could say that traditional Christian art subordinated *materia* entirely to *forma* in the sense that the plastic manifestation of truth was not to be perfected at the expense of this truth. Needless to say, this priority of the Principle (Truth) over its formal expression totally determined the mentality of traditional man as well as reflected it; man's earthly wellbeing was always premised on, if not subordinated to, his everlasting wellbeing, and his art reflected that priority.

Now these stylistic "shortcomings"—that is to say the often crude imperfections in sacred art's representation of the human form—proved too big a temptation for Renaissance artists not to "improve upon", and in fact they did so with spectacular success; but the improvement came

---

11 Interesting to note is the evolution of the crucifix in Christendom. Originally, the cross was depicted without the body of Christ. Then, when the body was introduced (apparently only in the fifth century A.D.), it was often that of a fully resurrected and robed Christ— a Christ in Majesty—and only later came the image of the agonizing Christ (See John Chrisholm Lambert, *A Dictionary of Christ and the Gospels*, passim [Edinburgh: T. & T. Clark, 1906]). Recourse to such a literal depiction and the transition from royal to suffering Christ coincides, one might say, with the sentimental decline of man's worship. In other words, it could be assumed that the Christians of the first centuries, who revered the empty cross, had a more naturally intellective faith than the passionalistic Christians of the Renaissance and Baroque periods. Or it might be said that as man's faith declines, religion resorts to more and more literal, if not sensationalistic, imagery in an attempt to revive it; unfortunately, such means also compromise the sacredness of the mystery because of the very outwardness of fleshly realism, precisely.

12 By contrast, an emphasis on divine immanence can "afford" to be more naturalistic, as seen notably in the Kangra Hindu miniatures.

at the price of a fatal exchange in which the Spirit essentially lost out to the flesh, and Western society has never recovered from this reversal of poles. Mention is made of this, of course, without reference to the risk of exaggeration found in sacred art itself, a risk that led no less than a Saint Bernard to proscribe images in Cistercian sanctuaries—a proscription that included even the illumination of manuscripts—and this at a time when religious representations still heeded the rules of sacred art. Iconoclasm, clearly, can take on many different forms, some of which are legitimate such as Islam's exclusion of images, given the passional tendencies of Semites to divinize figurines—to say nothing of this religion's providential cyclical anticipation of an "idolatrous" disaster such as the Renaissance to come, and in so doing enshrining the Biblical world all the way up to the threshold of the modern world; and some excessive such as Protestantism's ransacking of Catholic sanctuaries, though perhaps the pomp and splendor asphyxiating some of the late Middle Ages' Catholic Church does not quite absolve Protestant iconoclasm, but it certainly explains the provocation it represented.

* * *

Leaving these considerations aside now and to resume with our earlier trend of thought, every true civilization has been based on a supreme Divine Image which, when taken in its essential traits, can be basically divided into a static or contemplative prototype, that of a priest or saint, and a dynamic or action-oriented prototype, that of a king or a hero, or respectively that of a contemplative saint and that of a active warrior— these models echoing in turn the "heart and mind" polarity discussed earlier.[13] Both images are complementary reflections of the "personality" of the Creator, which synthesizes the dual functions of the Absolute that unifies and saves, on the one hand, and of the Absolute that creates and legislates, on the other and, in so doing, separates. And these images are also a symbolic reflection of God become man. In this sense, true kingship, far from being simply the repressive force of autocratic power equaling absolute corruption—a favorite democratic refrain[14]—ideally radiates out

13 Or salvation and justice. In the animal kingdom, this duality is indirectly reflected in the division between predators and non-predators. See also the chapter "The Crook and the Flail" in our book, *On Awakening and Remembering*.

14 Which is refuted by the traditional role of the king's fool, precisely, whose function was to foil a monarch's pretention to divine absoluteness; in other words, not all autocrats were blind to the risks of power; this issue, we propose, is in fact mostly a latter times problem as monarchs gradually became less spiritual.

to the very periphery and lowest rungs of the social order: the image of the true divine monarch—providential image of God on earth—serves to remind each individual of what he is in his theomorphic essence and thus provides each individual with a true and often majestic scale of perfection that offers him an inspiring chance of rising above himself and attaining to a true standard of dignity and nobility that no proletarian government can provide him with.[15] Quite to the contrary: a proletarian egalitarianism, by reducing man to a low or utilitarian common denominator, destroys man's chance at rising to his ideal stature as created in the image of God, a royal station of imperishable worth. In fact, a "proletarian egalitarianism" is a contradiction in terms since far from enhancing equality, it enhances inequality by forcing individuals to live beneath themselves or to share an artificial bond of a false or forced equality with other human beings that violates all the norms of equilibrium within the cosmos, an equilibrium that is based on the hierarchical—although also complementary—differences in human degrees of worth, quality, and giftedness. In other words, the equality of man cannot be established at the expense of an individual's capacity to surpass himself, otherwise one is establishing equality based on what is most outward in men, namely, their physical survival. Democratists will counter that what is at stake here is equality of opportunity, and, taken in the abstract, that sounds like a fair principle, but the notion of equality becomes easily overwhelmed by socialistic tendencies of quantity over quality that eventually suppresses quality. Man's equality resides, positively, in his potential sainthood, namely in his common divine essence, which he shares with all other men, and not in his human limitations; and, negatively, it resides in his equality before death which makes no distinction between potentates and paupers; but not least, it resides ultimately in his equality before God's mercy which is always accessible to any man, regardless of his station in life.

To develop some of these points, it is worth noting that true democracy, or true egalitarianism, is inversely proportional to numbers: in other words, the smaller the human community the more naturally egalitarian it is; that is why the nomadic culture is the most egalitarian there is, although much

---

15 In Buddhist terms, the monarch's central duty is to be a "noble wheel-turning monarch", namely a ruler that inherits from Heaven the role of preserving divine Law, that is to say the Wheel of *Dharma*, so that his subjects and even the earth will prosper. (See the Pali canon of the discourses of the Buddha, *Cakkavatti-Sihanada Sutta*, III, 59-63, quoted from *In the Buddha's Words*, edited by Bhikkhu Bodhi [Boston: Wisdom Publications, 2005], pp. 139-141). Such a role cannot be left to the chance fortunes of democratic election, but requires a heavenly investiture, although such a proviso is obviously a dead letter for all secular forms of government; but we must mention it nonetheless.

the same could be said *mutatis mutandis* of villages and hamlets prior to the city cultures of the late Middle Ages. For instance the autonomous lifestyle of so-called "barbaric" tribes surrounding the Roman empire, who lived in settlements that were semi-permanent, or any society whose buildings were still made of wood, fostered in all individuals a bracing self-reliance and it is this quality that lies at the heart of a natural egalitarianism in which each person had to achieve a large measure of independent fortitude, for the survival of the group depended directly on the strength of each individual member. By contrast to wooden structures, edifices in stone tend to establish, over time, a feudal hierarchy of center versus periphery, and thus of mighty versus weak, and finally of *de facto* superiors versus inferiors. Nonetheless, just as there is a divine prototype for equality—a community of saints, utopian as this may sound in our epoch—there is a complementary, and just as divine, prototype for hierarchy for there are inevitably degrees in God's majesty, and therefore degrees in paradise,[16] and thus degrees on earth.

Vertically, if the figure of the monarch is majestically premised on a paragon model for mankind, the uppermost point of which touches the Divine, it is balanced horizontally on the complementary aspect of his role of father of his people; in this role, the monarch reflects the role of God as father of the faithful and this model is reflected from the center of the kingdom all the way out, in diminishing circles, to the kingdom's periphery, through the fiefdoms and manors, each ruled by lords with their indentured peasants, each lord serving as a figure-head father for the people attached to his lands. This is a status that elected officials can never truly duplicate for a father is a father for life, and this familial structure of society corresponds therefore to a natural norm that no other political system can match. And there is no need to bring up here the question of feudal injustices, or the fact that democracy (or egalitarianism) cannot magically abolish such injustices; in fact, it can only modify the modalities of injustice without solving the problem. Hence, it would be seriously short-sighted to underestimate the devotion peasants could harbor for their estate's lord and lady, and vice-versa obviously; indeed the loss of this relationship to the advantage of populist representation—often communist in spirit—is incalculable. The communistic element is premised on denying any privileges to elite human beings, while, hypocritically, securing them for party officials or bureaucrats, and at the same time catering to a human collectivity's mass propensities that choke idealism.

---

16 "Those are they who are in truth believers. For them are degrees of honor with their Lord" (Koran, "The Spoils of War", 8:4).

In establishing possible causes for the absence of a prophetic or—by regal extension—of a kingly figure serving as the cornerstone of a social edifice, we have just seen that this modern absence is partly the result of an egalitarianism, which comes down finally to a quasi-religious devotion to averageness, an averageness that is finally as oppressive in its way as tyranny in that it can crush true excellence. By definition, moreover, such egalitarianism implicitly resents the idea of anyone's superiority and thus, by implication, resents the principle of hierarchy. And, following in this vein of logic, the inescapable conclusion is that this phobia of superiority ends up, whether inadvertently or otherwise, compromising the idea of God as ruler or king, with the consequence that God—if one even still believes in Him—is relegated to a benign background role, becoming a kind of avuncular figure that is, if not totally merciful, at least impotent; and in fact this is one of the reasons that the modern psyche of the average citizen, ruled by humanist sentimentalism, is simply unable to muster the reverence for a majestic, commanding, and awe-inducing God.[17] The disappearance of God as the "Lord of Hosts" coincides with the democratic rejection of autocracy, whence the reliance on the ballot box for resolving all issues and the recourse to the slogan "mass makes right" proffered as the blunt rebuke to the totalitarian argument "might makes right".

A corollary effect of this populist prejudice is that whatever the collectivity does or enjoys becomes the *de facto* criterion for defining what is normal for man; in other words, there is an assumption that if enough people want something, or if enough people are busy doing something, then that "something" must *ipso facto* be right—a collective form of peer pressure, if one will. But the question is rarely if ever raised whether a whole multitude can degenerate or, put differently, why it would not degenerate if left entirely to its own recourses, that is to say shorn of divine guidance? In other words, if left to itself to grope for solutions, a multitude cannot but surrender its fate to the law of averages, which always operates in a downward spiral[18] because if the majority—as opposed to an enlightened elite—becomes the arbitrator of who should lead, then compromise[19] becomes the

---

17 "God" becomes just "the man upstairs", or "the old man", and other such semi-affectionate but profoundly inappropriate monikers that are the predictable casualties of egalitarian casualness.

18 Evolutionism, of course, posits the idea of an ascentional collectivity, a fantasy that conveniently covers many sins, not least a flight from God.

19 The problem with the obsession with "compromise" is that it is reverently equated with

dictating (or bullying) mechanism of right and wrong as opposed to a real ideal which, by definition, is rarely or never to the taste of a populist majority which wants to bring everything down to a common denominator decided as much by inertia as it is by the absence—or at least irrelevance—of prophetic figures. Makeshift governance, and makeshift leadership for that matter, can never replace true prophethood or kingship, or what amounts to Heaven-bestowed anointment. At its worst, democracy turns into a kind of demonocracy—permissiveness exploiting the charter of a misguided notion of freedom to usher in ever more degenerate lifestyles.

A deeper cause for the present-day absence of a prophetic figure comes from the debasing of true elites, or simply of paragon figures, for this is one of the outcomes of the locust-like spreading of humanity, a phenomenon in which numbers are inversely proportional to quality, as has been noted earlier.[20] And more fundamentally yet, there is the question of the cyclical state of remoteness of our epoch from humanity's divine origin that influences a process of collective deterioration; this has been outlined, among others, in the Hindu theory of the four *yugas*. It should be noted that in referring to an "elite" we do not mean to be blind to the unconscionable degeneracy of aristocrats, whose monstrous pamperedness enraged normal God-fearing men thus setting the stage for bloody revolutions, especially in France, Russia, and later China; however, the evil effects of these social upheavals far exceeded the evil of the cause, and did so precisely because

---

fairness when in fact the polar ends of a compromise may be vastly unequal, particularly if one of the parties represents a true principle or is clearly more enlightened. For instance, why should believers compromise with atheists? Or why should anyone compromise with a Communist? Compromise, to be valid, requires a minimum of symmetry between the two poles of the negotiations; but dogmatic egalitarianism inevitably obscures this. An example of a legitimate compromise might be between laws balancing church and state or, secularly, between government and free enterprise.

20 Many factors have intervened to favor the rise of a proletarian human being—too many to examine in detail in a single chapter—one of them being modern medicine; but another has to do with the advent of modern warfare where, to take one spectacular example, Europe's elite young men were systematically killed during the two World Wars and even previous to that during the battles confronting rows of soldiers free to fire on each other at will; the front ranks were invariably led by the crème de la crème of men, be they the finest bred or simply the most gallant. Entire strata of gifted human beings were systematically wiped out during those wars. Another factor was the genocidal purging of the elites by the Communist Chinese and Soviet dictators. These tragedies account for the proletarian rise or the advent of what the Hindus designate as the *shudra* mentality that replaces the extinction of the *kshatriya* or warrior and princely caste. Socialism, and especially a Communist socialism, are the form of government that a proletarian "egalitarianism" engenders, and such an outcome is not just confined to non-religious societies, as can be seen with various plebeian versions of Islamism that are frankly Communist in spirit.

the cause (social injustice) was more of a trigger than a central detonator. Thus, in the end, in the case of Holy Mother Russia, the liberated serfs, as well as the Russian population at large, were very cruelly served in losing the Tsars in exchange for their new Bolshevik taskmasters, because to be ruled by a prince guarantees at least that a human being lives in a society where lordship is still a viable concept, therefore allowing him, in principle, to be—by reflection—a lord in his own home if not outside, whereas to be led by a maliciously petty and pedantic, if not sadistic, proletarian commissioner means everyone becomes a base serf, namely has to dress, eat, think, and behave as a proletarian worker, and is, of course, forbidden to be religious since the state is the only god, and devotion to it the only religion. In such a setting, the reigning "iconic" figure now becomes an insensitive foreman or bureaucrat, if not a brutal dictator. However, as mentioned above, *noblesse oblige*: the so-called elite's deviation from their God-appointed duties as role models doomed them to become the hapless accomplices in their own downfall.

Be that as it may, it is also important to understand that the term "elite" is not strictly synonymous with aristocrats; thus this term should also include the possibility of the noble farmer, whose yeoman virtue and piety made of him a bulwark of society. And not least there is the example, in a country like the United States of America, of the frontier-bred pioneer who was raised with a sturdy Biblical ethos of self-reliance under the sun and before God; the legacy of these rural virtues is now rapidly receding with the dwindling of that very frontier's heritage as it is gradually overrun with sprawling urban blight, the step-child of industrialism—a phenomenon, incidentally, that is unknown in traditional societies where the pursuit of profit is never totally divorced from religion, and where the promise of endless affluence is not the exorbitant goal it becomes in essentially secular societies.

*   *   *

As creation grows in remoteness from its celestial origin, the realities of human weaknesses assert themselves over time with indefatigable and crushing persistence; social inertia gains in force, leading to inexorable moral decay except, that is, for periodic restorations of the original ideal in which the bond with Heaven is temporarily renewed and refreshed, either through a new religion or the apparition of great saints. In the case of religion, Heaven has to adjust, as it were, to mankind's cyclical degeneracy, offering a message and a set of prescriptions not meant necessarily for an elite but accessible to a majority of human beings because, as Schuon has pointed out in several instances,[21] Heaven intends to save the multitudes and must therefore provide a message open to everyone; too stringent an ideal actually produces the opposite effect, as seen, for example, in the late medieval imposition of celibacy on the clergy as a whole, when it should have been reserved for monks alone, as it had been for twelve centuries previously. In other words, religion normally addresses man in his waywardness, be it expressed as sin (Christianity), hypocrisy (Islam), or rebellion (Judaism), and will provide a theological solution that has to take into consideration man's profane nature and not just his contemplative genius, whence the heavy emphasis on obedience and the relentless threats of damnation and lurid descriptions of the torments of hell. In that sense, the gnostic essence of a scripture like the Koran, being the book of the last great historical revelation, is veiled by a massive emphasis on man's errancy, much of this sacred book being concerned with stern exhortations, warnings, and threats, whose sobering repetition, though interjected with poetically marvelous descriptions of God's mercy, is intended to instill the sharp fear of God and of eternal punishment in the obdurate hearts of a *Kali Yuga* collectivity. In that sense, the Koran is of a markedly different tenor than scriptures such as the *Upanishads*, even though both scriptures find common ground in the celebration of God's grandeur, as well as that of creation's primordial sacredness.

This compromise in scriptures between inspiring idealism and sometimes gruesome intimidation, or between the majesty of lordship and the misery of penitence, is a factor that must be borne in mind at all times when assessing the divineness of a saintly figurehead who embodies such a message. Moreover, when Heaven clads itself in a human garment, it accepts some of the humbling necessities of earthly life, sharing the physical wretchedness and daily indignities of mortal men and women in their flesh-bound existence; as a result the messenger representing the saintly model may strike a skeptic as disappointingly human even while remaining luminously immune inwardly from outward limitations. In fact, the veil of the physical body can induce not just skeptics but the very devotees themselves to over-humanize the divine personage—the prophet or, to speak in Buddhist terms, the *bodhisattva*—but each for very different ends: devotees may over-sentimentalize this personage until he becomes "all too human"—more a product of their individual feelings and aspirations than a real "god-man", whereas skeptics, for their part, will say that since this divine personage—an angel amongst men—needs to eat and sleep he is

21 See, for example, "To Accept or to Refuse Revelation" in *From the Divine to the Human* (Bloomington, IN: World Wisdom, 1982).

but a mere mortal like all of us and therefore not deserving of any sublime status, and even less of reverence. In the end, every person sees but himself projected into another; hence to recognize a saint is to have the capacity for sanctity oneself, just as the inability to recognize a saint can be due to one's own spiritual limitation—the inevitable scarcity of saints in an overwhelmingly secular age notwithstanding.

Now if even saints cannot escape the censure of mortality as well as physical shortcomings, how much more then will the human defectiveness of every ruler not be an issue? It may seem impossible that a monarch could dare claim a divine mandate; but this is where a distinction has to be made between a human being and a cosmic function, or between an individual and an archetype, or—metaphysically—between the accident and the essence. In a traditional society, function transcends individuality just as the essence takes precedence over the accident. This relationship has become reversed in modern societies, partly due to humanism, psychologism, and democratism, all of which tend to focus on the individual at the expense of the function and, by extension, at the expense of the archetype.

In practical terms, this reversal of priorities leads to a number of assumptions about different types of government. Thus, when comparing different forms of polity, it is assumed that kingship is automatically more corrupt or tyrannical—for being autocratic—than a political system premised on an elected president or prime minister, the implication being that a democratically elected head of state would automatically be more efficiently held to account than a monarch—or that his corruptibility would be more easily disposed of. But, leaving aside the possibility of manipulating the electorate into selecting a duplicitous leader, the issue is less the risk of corruption, which exists in any society, than of preserving the nature of the function itself which, when it represents a glorious and heavenly symbol, has a role to play that transcends whatever gifts or probity—or lack thereof— its royal bearer may have, so much so, in fact, that one might be tempted to say here that the exception justifies the rule: the sagacious monarch, rare as his earthly occurrence may be, justifies the curse of enduring the accession of a string of petty or even corrupt potentates because at least the people will still have access to a sacred archetype embodied in the function itself and this, in turn, helps to determine the quality of their status as vassals, for in reality we are all vassals of God. By that token, better then to have a supreme function than a perfect president.[22]

---

22 In the case of the American democracy, we shall grant that a president of the stature of a Lincoln can make one dream of democracy's excellence. But, finally, a man of Lincoln's wisdom and mettle is not a proof as such either for democracy or against monarchy, because one exceptional individual cannot redeem the pragmatic averageness of a function become essentially mundane, if not profane, and thus devoid of spiritual inspiration.

Pure democracy, as mentioned previously, works best only among elite nomadic tribes where the possibility of tricking one's peers is almost impossible because the necessity of having to face the elements in their raw severity is a trial by fire that only the stalwart and the meritorious can measure up to. Moreover, there are obviously non-material factors that decide the choice of a true human exemplar. Thus, in a culture still linked to Heaven, namely in which heeding auguries still makes sense, one notes a prevalence of prophetic insights guiding men, not to mention the manifestation of heavenly signs anointing a chosen leader; these signs can consist of a special immunity in battle, hunting prowess, exceptional aptness of intuitive intelligence, and other tokens of supernatural favor, not least being regal bearing or prophetic charisma. Obviously, the disappearance of such reliance on Heaven is hardly a mark of progress, but points rather to a society's disinheritance by the cosmic Spirit,[23] when not its disgrace.

By contrast, humanism—or at least liberal humanism—is dedicated to civilizing man according to a social ideal that pays lip service to religion while disowning it in practice since it tries to seal off both the chasm of hell underlying cosmic manifestation and the promise of paradise overarching it, as it endeavors to insulate existence from any supernatural incursions—either because it does not understand them or because it does not believe in them. In keeping with this philosophy, it seeks to promote a comfortable and predictable existence sheltered from all "act of God"-type calamities.[24]

---

23 One could of course simply use the term "God" instead of "cosmic Spirit", but in reality there is a vital principle or intelligence operating as a delegate faculty of the Creator on earth, and thus we want to specify it since it is immanent in all creatures and in natural phenomena without being directly equatable with God as such. It is the *Aql al-Awwal* of the Sufis, or the "first Intellect" and in Hinduism the *Buddhi* or "universal Intellect". This function is also embodied by a prophet, such that every prophet is a manifestation of the heavenly *buddhi* on earth.

24 For the secularist, a tornado is not an "act of God" but a meteorological phenomenon; likewise, an earthquake is a tectonic accident; creation is considered to be purely inert matter devoid of any consciousness whatsoever, whereas for ancient man it is essentially a materialization of the divine Being and its phenomena express therefore the movements of the Spirit. That said, these viewpoints are not mutually exclusive, because it is difficult to assess whether a phenomenon such as an earthquake is just a random part of nature or truly an "act of God". We assume that devoutness of prayer can work miracles in protecting a medieval town in the Middle Ages from natural disasters, but one can also assume that to a large extent God allows nature to be, leaving it then up to man to seek divine protection or not. Hence, establishing a direct correlation between a natural disaster and punishment from Heaven is not necessarily obvious. The destruction of a town like Pompey might be a good example of the former case, namely of a people forfeiting God's grace. And we also find in

Nevertheless, it is understandable for man to aspire to a civilization free of injustice, where every effort is undertaken to promote wellbeing, peace, and universal concord, where the so-called "sanctity" of the individual and of property are guaranteed by laws. But then what? Only God can, in the end, provide this immunity, though not necessarily on this earth, which remains the realm of imperfection and decay. And when did the so-called "sanctity" of a man's life and possessions start to outweigh his moral worth, and why indeed should they, leaving aside all questions of the crucial principle of personal property and of immunity from persecution? Virtue is the true gold standard of mankind. Protecting individuals irrespective of their moral worth is a problematical feature of a secular civilization aspiring to define ethics outside of religion, which alone is their mainstay. Ideally, it is individual merit that gives to law its sacrosanct underpinnings—but an individual merit based, of course, on a divine prototype, barring which there can be no standards: "Why callest thou me good?" Remove the divine exemplar upon which any real standard depends, and law will be divorced from divine justice and become the pragmatic or opportunistic tool of the mighty and the wealthy, or the chicanery of scoundrels finding wealthy means to rewrite justice; such outcomes are unavoidable in a secular world aspiring to divine ideals outside of God. Part of the reason for this is the divorce between religion and justice, which is both a sign of the times and a cause. By contrast, in nomadism, man's wealth and possessions are more correlated to his moral worth, and justice more correlated to merit, and merit is premised on God's favor with an individual, thus validating his relationship with Heaven. Be that as it may, there has to be a quasi-sacrosanct principle defending personal property in any society, barring no better recourse, otherwise the weak and unsuspecting would be plundered to death; our considerations do not challenge this right, to the contrary.

Worth noting here is that the correlation between moral worth and wealth is the basis for the belief linking a monarch's moral worth and the fruitfulness of the crops; this belief determines then that in times of famine monarchs risked losing their mandate: the elements themselves, as it were, would stand in judgment over them. But such a relationship between ruler and cosmos entails a religious civilization guided by God. In this respect, one cannot forget that some "autocrats" were deeply religious, if not occasionally saintly sovereigns;[25] in fact, in India it is considered that

the Koran many examples where God speaks of the disasters He visits on unbelieving or idolatrous peoples, further specifying that they should be taken as warnings for believers.

25 In the West, King Louis of France and King Edward the Confessor, Alexander Nevsky, probably Emperor Constantine the Great, and Charlemagne, not forgetting King Stephen I,

saintly monarchs ruled for millennia before the advent of the *Kali Yuga*, the terminal age in which dissension and war have become predominant. Regardless of whether they were literally saintly or not, this assumption reflects on the nature of the function itself. In this respect, regicide is ultimately a crime against God: only a king has the right to supplant a king, except in certain exceptional instances in which the people act as the "voice of God"; but then one can presume they are acting, not out of sacrilegious passion, but as a rightful instrument of God's justice.[26]

As pointed out above, even if the representative of God on earth, whether a monarch or a pontiff, is corrupt, that is no grounds for cancelling the function, because bearer and function are not situated on the same level. To illustrate this by means of a religious example, one can take the traditional rite of the confessional: the priest effaced himself before the function so that in principle (or theurgically) it is Christ himself who received the penitent's confession for, in fact, it is he alone who has the power

patron saint of Hungary. In the Middle East, there is Saladin, and much earlier, we have the examples of King David and of Solomon. In the East, there is the example of the great ruler of the Maurian dynasty and propagator of Buddhism, Ashoka, or that of King Ikshvaku venerated in the *Vedas*. Moreover, a king can be an *avatara*, such as in the case of Rama who later even became an emperor. Raja Raja Chola I of the Tamil Chola dynasty in India was considered to be a descent of Vishnu: a temple copper plate inscription states: "Having noticed the marks [on his body] that Arulmozhi [the future Raja Raja Chola] was the very Vishnu the protector of the three worlds, descended on earth [Utama, the reigning king] installed him in the position of *yuvaraja* (heir apparent) and himself bore the burden of ruling the earth." And the recognition of a ruler's avataric scope could cut across religious lines, such as in the case of the Muslim emperor Akbar, who was equated (not without possible exaggeration) in the Hindu poetry and songs of the time with Rama. However we do have the striking case of the Japanese Prince Shotoku appearing in the guise of a *bodhisattva* in a dream-vision to Shinran, founder of Jodo-Shinsu Buddhism, which set Shinran on the path to enlightenment. Mention could be made, also, that one of the Bible's books is entitled "The Book of Kings", which is not insignificant. And no list of beneficent rulers would be complete without including the names of Marcus Aurelius and Pius Antoninus, who were part of "the Five Good Emperors", and who embodied the ancient stoic virtues of *pietas*, *gravitas*, and *dignitas*. Not least, a king could be baptized by a saint as in the case of Clovis, who converted to Christianity and was anointed by Saint Remigius in a small chapel in Rheims which later became the site for the cathedral in which the kings of France would be crowned.

26 In ancient China, the emperors ruled according to the "mandate of Heaven", in which they executed their function as the stewards of Heaven on earth. The man chosen to be an emperor could—in principle—originate from any stratum of society, even from the peasant. And there are several instances in which regimes oppressing the people were overthrown through popular revolutions; this can also be the cosmos' manner to oblige men, who are normally underlings, not to become overly passive, just as it prevents rulers from becoming overly assertive; such is the nature and necessity of the ebb and flow of power on earth.

to shrive him; if the priest's lack of sanctity were considered to invalidate the confession, then society would be deprived of a gate to Heaven in that it would be impossible to find enough saints to perform the office in order to meet popular demand. Now, it is crucial to specify that the trappings of the confessional, consisting in a booth and a grated opening[27] veiling the individuality of the priest, is an absolute key to the spiritual efficacy of the confession itself—which, lest one forget, is a sacrament—whence its necessary theatricality in the noblest sense of this term, or the need for a divine staging, if one will, that in hiding the officiant reveals Christ; the "impersonality" of this mysteriously sacred setting highlights the priority of the function over the officeholder. Modern face-to-face confessions, in which the priest listens to a penitent in the capacity of a friendly advisor, are trivial and worthless, if not frankly Luciferian in cases where the priest starts playing the role of a kind of psychoanalyst, because then the ego of the believer is likely to be mollified instead of mortified. It should not be difficult for anyone to understand that a face-to-face confession ruins—utterly and irrevocably—the idea of the penitent placing himself before Christ.

*   *   *

Now to extrapolate what was said about functions to a social and architectural setting, the sacred import of these functions is mirrored not just in their executors but also in the very structure of ancient towns in which the priestly office expressed by the sanctuary—whether a church, temple, or mosque—occupies a privileged station, along with its counterpart the executive office, namely a fortress or a castle. A remarkable feature of travelling in Western and Eastern Europe is the prospect of countless medieval towns in which one sees houses clustered like sheep around a sentinel church serving symbolically as a shepherd, whereas, above the town, one sees the fortress serving, in turn, as a shield and protector of the figurative shepherd and social herd.[28] All poetic and romantic notions aside—and all wretched utilitarian considerations notwithstanding—this architectural coupling is eloquently representative of the dual faculties of man's theomorphic nature, the church representing the heart and the fortress the

---

27 With a possible crucifix hanging over the grill, not to mention the kneeler, and the fact that the confession itself and the response should be whispered.

28 American rural towns, by contrast, increasingly made the courthouse their focal center, and modern cities now have massively gleaming buildings owned by enormous commercial interests towering over their skylines.

mind. In such an architectural setting, an individual can never completely forget who he is, and what his vocation should be, and what the wager of human existence entails; in fact, this kind of urban structure provides him with an educational and formative mold. Moreover, the symbolism of these main edifices—the sanctuary and the fortress—fostered the salutary awareness of never letting one's guard down because the omnipresent threat of an enemy was a concrete daily reality.[29] This explains why many towns became themselves walled fortresses (integrating castle and church within the same perimeter) with iron gates that were locked at night; this image evokes the idea of the city being patterned on the human body with its organic functions and openings, the streets being like arteries, the market place corresponding to the organs of assimilation, the heart to the church at the center, the watch towers being the eyes, and the seat of local authority being the head.[30] Hence, overcoming the threats that rendered walled fortifications obsolete was not necessarily a net gain for society since peace and civility, however desirable they are in principle, when achieved in this base world normally induce men to relax and so to lose much of the urgency to transcend themselves. Soporific mediocrity may seem harmless enough when compared to battle injuries, but its harm to the soul is incalculable; slackness and degeneracy are cousins. Not least, the feudal structure of towns inspired a vital and proud independence for its inhabitants, who were wont to resist occupation by foreigners, the latter themselves being the proud product of their own walled towns or else fiercely free men of the steppes. In mentioning this we are not either extolling warfare or refuting pacifism, but acknowledging that man in our darkened final age cannot transcend himself without the goad of struggle nor can he do so without being prepared to die for eternal values; he has to earn, so to speak, his immortality with his mortality *in mutua funera* ("in mutual self-assured destruction").

It could be argued that the development of such fortified towns centered on a church was only a phase in a continuum of history which could never become permanent, and therefore such towns, and by extension kingdoms, cannot serve as a useful model for civilization, given their temporariness

---

29 Pacifists are of course appalled by epochs riven by military conflicts, but political peace is not always a desirable good if it breeds moral stagnancy. Thus a Thucydides says of the ancient Athenians: they "regard peace as a far greater calamity than laborious activity" (*History of the Peloponnesian War*, 1:70).

30 Saint Catherine of Siena takes this analogy between a city and man even deeper by declaring that "the city [Siena] is the image of the soul, the surrounding walls being the frontier between the outward and inward life. The gates are the faculties or senses connecting the life of the soul with the outer world" (Titus Burckhardt, *Siena: City of the Virgin*, p. 53).

when situated on a grand scale. The answer is that, brief as this phase may have been when taken in the unfolding of centuries, it nonetheless corresponded to an ideal or at least to a norm—always within the harsh and often brutally demeaning context of the *Kali Yuga*—since these towns' political independence still reflected something of the archetypal spirit of freedom found among primordial nomads, albeit transposed into the hard fixity of stone.

*   *   *

If we could free ourselves for an instant from the collective hypnosis that makes almost everyone nowadays automatically assume that our present world represents a kind of enviable norm due to overwhelming numbers of people thinking the same thing, we might grasp what a true man could be in the most qualitative and timeless sense of this word.[31] But such an insight entails two major provisos: firstly, breaking free from a cocoon of relentless cultural, as well as hereditary, conditioning which, unless one is exposed to a truly normative civilization or to a paragon man, is virtually impossible to overcome; and secondly, an integral sense of the sacred or of what man's theomorphic essence consists of, for to remove the sacred is to abolish at one fell stroke all true scale of perfection. Moreover, in order to free ourselves lastingly from this cultural hypnosis it is hardly enough to inveigh with fervent moralism against "a modern culture of fornication and depravity", because the antidote espoused, alas, is most often a narrowly self-righteous notion of sin that evinces little understanding of what primordial man or the *fitrah*[32] means; and the unnaturalness of such a morality is partly why conventional religion is so easily spurned either in favor of libertarianism or of counter-cultural, New Age refittings of traditional Eastern or even of American Indian or Australian Aborigine spiritualities—to mention but a few of the more popular cults—as also in any of a new variety of improvisational Evangelistic cults animated by an ecstatic

---

31 Thoreau attempted this in secluding himself at Walden, bathing in a pond while imagining he might be bathing in the waters of the Ganges of far-off India in the epoch of the Rishis, and not in the vicinity of Massachusetts' puritan hamlets. And indeed, wilderness can be an antidote for the snare of time or the slavery of living in a set epoch; living before the mountains, valleys, streams, open fields, or forests is to live before the Creator in the timelessness of nature. Emerson too tried to stand tall under the empyrean, modeling himself on immortal principles not colored by an epoch's self-serving conventions.

32 The *fitrah* is an Arabic term for the "innate human nature" which Muslims, of course, rate in Islamic terms. But we use the term non-confessionally as the Sufis use it, meaning "primordial norm"; indeed, this is a key concept for defining man in depth.

subjectivism claiming inspiration from the Holy Spirit. Yes, indeed, "The Spirit bloweth where it listeth", but this does not mean "It bloweth just anywhere", and certainly not at our beck and call.

Now, in our modern world, what is impossible for the collectivity may be possible for an individual: in order to grasp, both through intuition and imagination, what it was to be a man in another century, in a totally different culture, such as that of the Middle Ages or, further, that of a wandering nomad prior to the advent of the great city cultures, and to be able to do so free from the warp of modern standards presupposes having a sense of the sacred as well as, in parallel, a sense of the heroic; it amounts, in other words, to having a sense for the significance of the prophetic model described above, namely of recovering and perpetuating the iconic figure.

When all is said and done, however, it is the cyclical and tragic fate of this iconic figure, who inspires a civilization to embody a divine archetype, to be ultimately either misunderstood or destroyed for, to paraphrase, no man is a prophet in his own culture: it is the destiny of a prophet to start as a stranger to his people—"the Son of man hath no where to lay his head"— before he is adopted and culturally enshrined. And yet, in the final legacy of his civilization, however many centuries later, he ends up once again as a stranger.

CHAPTER 4

Kingdoms and Nations

Roman, remember by your strength to rule
Earth's peoples—for your arts are to be these:
To pacify, to impose the rule of law,
To spare the conquered, battle down the proud.
(Virgil, *Aeneid* VI:1145-1154)

God cannot be likened to a president or a prime minister, assuredly, but He can be likened to a king or to an emperor. Given this, is a kingdom or is a nation more appropriate to the nature of man? Or, put differently, in what social setting can a human being best fulfill his integral vocation? The answer may strike everyone today as obvious, in fact the question may seem quaintly ridiculous: has not democracy, and the freedom it fosters, laid all such speculations to rest? But it should not be, especially since the vaunted notion of democratic freedom is fraught with ambiguities, foremost among them being that freedom cannot be unconditional otherwise it is self-cancelling. In other words, while the notion of freedom itself is sacred, a boundless or indiscriminate freedom benefits counter-forces that exploit its generosity against it. Moreover, freedom is often confused with permissiveness with little or no serious consideration to how permissiveness undermines the very bulwark of freedom itself, because permissiveness eventually turns to perversity, the law of inertia prevailing. The antidote to permissiveness is discernment, without which freedom veers into chaos; discernment, however, is almost always equated by free-thinkers with censure or discrimination, if not frank prejudice, all the more as all authority, which under normal circumstances would help decide such matters, has become essentially functional or opportunistic, not to mention open to endless calling into question, which means that it is not real authority.

As mentioned previously, the idea of the individual entails that of the collective individual or of society. In practical terms this means an individual is subordinate to a community of individuals and especially to a society whose collective interests should coincide with the old adage *vox populi, vox Dei* or "the voice of the people is the voice of God".[1] In that respect, the individual as an individualist cannot have interests that override those of the commonwealth, for he represents a fragment that finds its completion

---

1 We say "should", a reservation that leaves the door open for the possibility of degenerate collectivities, in which case the adage no longer holds.

83

in the common good. However, in a more fundamental sense, the One comes before the many—or Adam before men—and therefore a society is ultimately no better than its most outstanding individual, or select individuals, whose eminence obviously influences the collectivity's overall welfare, as well as its level of wisdom, the quality of its aspirations, and finally its competence.[2] A gifted individual can forge an empire, or at least set a lofty standard for everyone which allows even the humblest to benefit from by association, and this kind of inspiring excellence can never be the talent of a collectivity as such. Conversely, a collectivity can be detrimental to the gifted individual in clipping his wings, so to speak, not least religiously,[3] or may even banish him should he prove too much of a gadfly.[4]

Society as a whole always tends towards a "middle of the road" averageness or a type of stasis that it will defend, zealously if necessary, from anything threatening to upset it either from above or below; and it is basically right in doing so because this averageness corresponds to a certain equilibrium without which society could not function as it wends its way between the lash and goad of individualistic extremes. However, every equilibrium needs to be challenged from time to time so as to avoid a potentially unhealthy stagnation, which means that all social orders depend on periodic renewals to be refreshed and revivified; thus the uneasy balance between individual freedom and collective priorities has its providen-

---

2 Emerson was prompted to write in his essay "History": "There is no history, only biography"—a comment he penned upon reading the biography of the Mohawk Indian chief, Joseph Brant-Thayendanegea by William L. Stone (Robert Richardson Jr. *Emerson: The Mind of On Fire* [Berkeley: University of California Press, 1995], p. 316). The debate of whether history is made by events or by individuals does not make a whole lot of sense to us since our planet is not just driven by blind geo-cataclysmic events or social upheavals; rather there are intelligent and determined individuals who make choices. That said, there is also the question of historians who see divine design in history (from a Virgil, through Jewish and Christian historicism, to a Toynbee and a Christopher Dawson), a theory that seems supported by the advent of the great religious revelations which both create and crystallize a civilization, and do so through a prophetic figure. What makes sense is the idea that individuals appear by destiny (there is no such thing as blind fate) in the historical setting in which they become the levers for accomplishments unobtainable by nature or random circumstances alone; for, seen from above, neither nature nor circumstances are ever purely random. Now, if it is true that great individuals are born into great epochs, it is also the case that great epochs spawn great individuals.

3 Thus Schuon comments: "The average *Sunnah* [the religious and social imitation of the example of the prophet Muhammad] prevents the ordinary man from being a wild beast and from losing his soul; but it may also prevent a man of outstanding spiritual gifts from transcending forms and from realizing the Essence" (*Understanding Islam*, p. 80).

4 As seen, for example, in the fate of the Athenian aristocrat and general, Alcibiades, to whom Plato devoted two of his dialogues, and not least the fate of Dante exiled from Florence.

tial tension in choices oscillating between the safety of dependable moderation—the stability of the masses—and the necessity for periodic bursts of boundary-shattering inspiration in the person of visionary individuals. We hope to be forgiven for expounding platitudes here, but sometimes the obvious bears repeating so as to set the stage for larger traditional ideas that, for their part, are no longer well understood—ideas, it should be added, whose self-evident rightness for most of mankind's history have suddenly lost relevance today. For example, any pretense to autocratic power, which was considered not only normal in societies modeled on kingdoms but indispensable and in fact a proof of a sovereign's legitimacy if not charisma, is largely reviled in our epoch as totalitarianism or fascism owing to a culture steeped in liberal humanism, as if a truly wise autocrat—Plato's philosopher-king for instance—were not a supreme human possibility, or as if there could not be benevolent absolutism, or also, in the reverse sense, as if sovereigns never had to answer to a council of elders or even to popular forces that regulate their absolutism.

In tribal or nomadic societies, gifted individuals are the obvious leaders, and after the establishment of civilizations consisting first of wood then of stone dwellings, but still prior to the advent of the industrial age, mankind from antiquity onward was ruled almost exclusively by kingships, as well as by the reflection of kingship radiating through the network of principalities and fiefdoms ruled by lords who maintained their personal human prestige through both prowess of arms and of character.[5] This fragmentation of kingdoms, many of which existed under the aegis of the Holy Roman Empire or some other form of empire, reflected the proud self-assurance of the ruling princes and fostered a kind of regal or at least fierce independence that, in principle, empowered individuals to rise to their fullest strength from having to contend with formidable rivals. Mention should also be made that traditional rulership was in many instances decided via purely pragmatic means of competition, and not by hereditary appointment or bequeathal. Seen from God's vantage point, the importance was to secure the best ruler and this often entailed abrogating a traditional lineage, and allowing a usually violent power struggle to decide the outcome; indeed, this would be the only way to refresh sclerotic customs.[6]

---

5 Interestingly, a residue of this decentralized form of governance still existed until fairly recently. Noted Catholic historian Christopher Dawson gives us a glimpse of this: "In reality England consisted of thousands of miniature monarchies—often highly autocratic ones—ruled like the medieval State by the temporal power of the squire and the spiritual authority of the parson" (*Beyond Politics* [New York: Sheed and Ward, 1939]).

6 This point is well made by the anthropologist M.E. Combs-Schilling regarding Sunnite Muslims: "The Sunni stand in between [Shiites and Khawarij], taking the reasonable posi-

In the inexorable transition from tribal to feudal age, the feudal age still preserved many of the characteristics that defined noble nomadism: self-reliance, valor, independence, pride—spectacularly reflected in the art of heraldry—, all of which are qualities premised on man's need to surpass himself to achieve true moral excellence and heroism. These qualities also ensured that political boundaries fluctuated rather freely according to the worthiness of individuals and societies that upheld them, and did not congeal too rigidly according to strict linguistic unity or economic advantages. This perpetual instability of boundaries maintained, therefore, a more natural division since effective autonomy depended on the concreteness of the respect both earned and imposed by heroic individuals, as opposed to the semi-abstract divisions that characterize modern nations, which once declared legally sacrosanct by bureaucratic fiat end up obstructing the organic need for repositioning found in the ever-shifting reordering of alignments typifying the life of warring tribes and warring kingdoms. These ancient political shifts, when seen from high above, resemble those governing nature, such as the swinging shifts in a river's course, the rise and fall of mountains, and the eroding and reshaping of great landmasses. No doubt, it will be objected, the political configurations of nations also shifts, but it does so either much more slowly or pent-up inequalities are artificially suppressed until rent apart by catastrophic conflicts that could have been lessened had a more natural form of re-ordering prevailed from the start.

Yet, to take the contrary position for a moment, it could be reasonably argued that the modern system of political boundaries has its advantages, as found in the charter of nations guaranteeing sovereign countries immunity from persecution, and also in the benefits of global peace and economic security ensured by common national as well as international rules, all of which are a necessary premise for prosperity, along with appreciable legal guarantees of protection of property and self—none of these having ever existed on such a large global scale in previous civilizations.[7] But

---

tion that, in terms of political authority, *it all depends* [italics ours]. Sometimes a blood descendant is legitimate, sometimes not. Sometimes communal election is pivotal, sometimes not. Sometimes a monarchy is appropriate, sometimes not. Sometimes military rule is legitimate, sometimes not" (*Sacred Performance* [New York: Columbia University Press, 1989], p. 87).

7 The Magna Carta was a forerunner not only of the principle of common law but also of the Charter of Nations, if one will. As is well known, its central tenets were to limit a king's autocratic power and to set the foundations for later parliamentary rule. However, one should bear in mind that the necessity for a Magna Carta resulted from the fact that the barons who "revolted" had no other choice than to limit King John's power from the

our contention is that such stability and security actually work best—or more naturally—under the aegis of an empire which does not impose the arbitrariness of state divisions cutting across ethnic or tribal lines, and that therefore does not suppress the cultural vitality of minorities through the forced homogenization of citizens under nationalisms; these nationalistic unities can be relatively artificial and therefore do not correspond to the nature of a people at large. Moreover—when contrasting a civilization based on kingdoms with one based on nations—one will want to note that, contrary to a nation, the principle of a kingdom depends foremost on the lordly ideal of a crown or a throne, as well as on the sacredness of the altar: remove the throne and remove the altar—to echo Joseph de Maistre's famous pairing[8]—what is left to hold a people together? Or, what is left to inspire men? And what is left to protect individuals from a bloodily divisive chauvinism against which only a true king can provide the magnanimous shield? For monarchy is, by definition, neither racist nor political.[9]

And this bears pondering: without global economic prosperity, the vaunted international stability humanists promote will be quick to fracture, and if a worldwide depression should become a reality—or when it becomes so—there will be none of the redundancies found in the systems of kingdoms to absorb any massive social shocks and disruptions; if worldwide famine, epidemic disease, or economic collapse threaten, entire nations will crumble, and perhaps the world itself, given the interlocking nature of modern economies, sustained furthermore by "fiat currencies", which are another expression of the opportunistic values prevailing currently in a world not upheld by any true authority that could guarantee them.

lack of competing alternative monarchs. In other words, England, and to a certain extent other European kingdoms, were developing a too central and, frankly, "pre-nationalistic" model of authority, whereas traditionally, barons who rose up could in earlier epochs rally around an alternative monarch. Therefore, the Magna Carta was the tool to compensate for an over-centralization of power and not a repudiation of the political ethos of decentralized kingdoms competing for power, as had previously been the norm for centuries.

8 See *The Saint Petersburg Dialogues.*

9 For example, "The country of Yugoslavia was created—rather artificially, as later became obvious—on the downfall of the Austro-Hungarian and Ottoman empires after World War I. Following the brutal internal wars of the 1990s, Yugoslavia broke into seven independent countries: three majority *Eastern Orthodox*: Serbia, Macedonia, and Montenegro; two majority *Roman Catholic*: Croatia and Slovenia; and two majority *Muslim*: Bosnia and Kosovo. The 'Republika Srpska', with a chiefly Serbian (*Eastern Orthodox*) population, is composed of northern and eastern enclaves within the territory of Bosnia, and enjoys self-government" (William Stoddart, *What Does Islam Mean in Today's World?* [Bloomington, IN: World Wisdom, 2012]).

Without wanting to enter into a discourse about purely political issues—what if not chaff in the wind?—a few comments should be made here about the nature of a nation, since understanding this will shed some light on the role and destiny of an individual. First of all, one ought rather to speak of "states" and not "nations" since the original idea of a nation entails that of a group of people sharing a common language, religious culture, and ethnicity—parameters that very often do not fit conveniently into the modern reality of a state. Hence, the correct definition of a "nation" corresponds to a natural distinction, such as reference to the Iroquois Nation, and not to a political unit per se. In contrast, and by definition, a state is more or less nationalistic, and potentially if not effectively racist to some degree or another—or at least jingoist, since it is based on promoting the superiority of a narrow cultural bias which is defined *grosso modo* through the political exclusion, if not depreciation, of other cultures;[10] and such nationalistic preferentialism becomes then a *de facto* tyranny over the minority cultures that may continue to exist within the geographic boundaries of that state. To take one example, once the Armenians fell under the narrow geographic interests of post-Ottoman Turkey and the fanatic promotion of Turkish nationalism under Ataturk, along with the abolishment of the Caliphate, nothing protected them—or the Greek and Assyrian minorities—from the horrors of genocide and deportation.[11] By contrast, the loose gatherings of tribes and later of

10 Modern exceptions such as the United States of America, Australia, and Brazil are essentially "artificial" creations dictated by social and economic opportunity, and therefore do not fit into the original definition of a state. Their mandate is premised on ethnic and religious pluralism and thus corresponds, in some ways, more to a kind of ersatz empire functioning in effect as a state.

11 Another example: the Basques, who are a distinct people with their own language, were artificially divided between two nations after France and Spain's modern political boundaries gelled, and because of this division they lost a relative autonomy they had enjoyed since Roman Antiquity. Similarly, the Kurds, since the modern advent of nations, are now divided among four different countries. And the situation of tribes on the African continent was rendered disastrous by the imposition of nationalistic divisions that destroyed the viability of tribes which, when existing as one, enjoyed a certain power and autonomy, but once divided were reduced in some cases to the status of pariah minorities exposed to random slaughter. An extreme example of nationalistic racism would, of course, be the Third Reich's ambition of racial purity. Regarding this, the Third Reich is a contradiction in terms because its leaders tried to make an empire out of what was really a nation and these are mutually exclusive concepts given that a true empire is, by innate charter, universalist and therefore inherently (and benignly) tolerant of a multitude of human sub-groups; in fact, it depends on the successful existence of minorities for its own political and economic viability.

principalities that characterized centuries of mankind's history prevented the rise of monomaniacal state ideologies as seen especially in the twentieth century where in some instances a demonic ideology was grafted onto a nationalism. The natural system of checks and balances offered by free-floating tribes, and later by semi-autonomous principalities, also prevented minorities from being crushed and exterminated, and of having their cultural identity quasi-razed from the earth. Thus, Jews were never safer in history than under imperial pan-European or pan-North African empires, and never more imperiled than in nations—be they imperialistic in scope as Ferdinand and Isabella's Renaissance Spain or as Communist Russia became.[12] Not least, nations, by definition, tend to resort to political scapegoats in times of adversity; this is the dark side of nationalistic patriotism that is not well understood. Now, to bring up an opposite point of view: "Distrust all governments!" a Christian idealist might declaim, and quoting Saint Augustine: "what are kingdoms but great robberies? For what are robberies themselves but little kingdoms?"[13] Fair enough! Yet, men must be governed in some fashion.

All cultures, quite obviously, are different and therefore more or less mutually exclusive, but it fell to the modern world to erect these differences into quasi-sovereign absolutes. Proponents of nationalism will argue that modern states are but the crystallization of ancient historical trends; true, but they do not seem to perceive that the creation of states corresponds ultimately to an unnatural or opportunistic fragmentation of mankind based on essentially secular, and therefore on what can only be relatively petty, interests—notwithstanding the question of patriotism which in itself (in its romantic and even spiritual essence) corresponds to a noble instinct because rooted, precisely, in the soul of a people and not just that of a nation. In counter distinction, and to repeat, an empire can richly and effortlessly accommodate multiple cultures and is therefore not discriminatory to ethnic groupings or if it becomes so, this narrowness is the prelude to its fall.[14]

---

12 And it should surprise no one that in Bismarck's fledgling Germany, the patriotic mystique of Prussian Junkers and Christian Pietists could not accommodate Jews, considering they could never be truly "German".

13 Augustine, *City of God*, Book 19, Section 17.

14 For instance the glorious Mughal dynasty collapsed once and when the last of his dynasty, the emperor Aurangzeb, in an act of religious zealotry, tried to enforce Islam to the exclusion of the other religions that had hitherto thrived under his tolerant predecessors. Likewise, Ferdinand and Isabella's persecution of their Jewish and Muslim subjects heralded the end of the Spanish Empire. Many of these Jews, incidentally, found welcome in the imperial Ottoman lands, as well as in the English and Dutch empires, while Spain went from powerful empire to minor nation, not in one fell swoop, certainly, but irreversibly.

That said, modern empires, such as the British or even the Spanish empires, which are more economic than truly cultural, cannot be compared in substance to empires that inaugurated an entire tradition such as the Holy Roman Empire, the Roman itself, the Persian, the Mongol, the Tang Dynasty, or the Mughal, and Ottoman empires, except outwardly—or horizontally—in their hegemonic similarities, that is to say, they cannot be compared in depth or vertically because the religious splendor and cultural genius of a Ming or Ottoman empire eclipses that of any modern empire, incomparably so.[15] And it is this vertical dimension of spirit that is a key for avoiding the trap of establishing false analogies that tempt historians and sociologists to see similarities where there are none, except on the most outward material plane.

Having brought up the problem of artificial divisions, briefest mention has to be made of a false reversal of these divisions as espoused by advocates of a "one world government", who in wishing to solve injustice and to promote world peace and prosperity will end up ruining mankind. The reason is that traditions and cultures thrive on the stimulus of polar contrasts which a forced homogenization can only destroy.

*   *   *

What is easily overlooked, in modern assessments of ancient societies, is the degree to which rulers in traditional worlds, even bloodthirsty ones, had to answer either to saints, wise priests, monks, or hermits. In Western North Africa there is the tradition of maraboutism, a socio-political network anchored by saintly teachers (*murabat*), if not by living saints (*awliya*), whose tombs dot the landscape and are the destination point of pilgrimages.[16] The prevalence of such spiritual men deeply influenced the run of society in all epochs and, of this, right up to the threshold of our modern world. For instance, it is noteworthy that as recently as Tolstoy's nineteenth century Russia, the roads were still travelled by wandering mendicant monks and

---

15 Even so, it is worth noting that any latter empire with a sovereign at its head, such as the Hapsburg Empire, retains some of the sacred legitimacy that constitutes the moral foundation of kingship in general. In fact, we know that the so-called Holy Roman Hapsburg Empire was "neither holy nor Roman", but it still retained the hierarchical trappings of its ancient prototype, and this is of key importance for restraining the forces of plebian democracy, oblivious of nobility and inclined to trivialize all grandeur. It bears noting that the rise of democracy coincides with the rise to power of the merchant classes, or, in Hindu terms, of the *vaishya* merchant caste displacing the *kshatriya* warrior class.

16 Linguistically, the Arabic word for "saint" (*wali*) is connected to the derivative word *wilāya*, meaning "sovereign rule", thus coupling the notions of sanctity and sovereignty.

saintly men—many of them self-effaced beggars[17]—who were known and revered by the people. Indeed, it is difficult to convey to the modern reader what the atmosphere of those epochs could be, suffused as they were with a palpable aura of spirituality, even of miraculousness: the Divine imbued the air, so to speak, and all the social customs were laced with sacred formulas; buildings and homes were adorned with icons, possibly sacred statuettes or effigies, not forgetting sacred inscriptions, and people might wear amulets that had been consecrated or blessed at sanctuaries, or they might own talismans.[18] Many monasteries and hermitages—both in the East and in the West—were set perilously on sheer cliff walls, suspended between Heaven and earth as it were, a spectacular testimony to the faith of men and also to the meaning of human life on earth meant to unfold before the portals of Eternity. And saints mingled with the crowds; for instance, in Russia there was the *starets*, or revered elder, reputed to have miraculous powers and healing gifts; and the Jews, for their part, had their *tzadik* ("righteous one") who was also renowned as a miracle worker and whose word was readily revered as God's word; fortunate the inhabitants of lands where God's voice could still be heard! Such spiritual men can only be the fruit of a social system in which the sacred is truly operative and this fact alone surely offered a measure of consolation for whatever oppression the serfs endured; at its worst, the earthly lot of serfs in such a pious society fulfilled the function of a station in purgatory and cannot therefore be likened to the alienation in some godless urban hellhole that modern sociologists might equate it with, due to an inability to measure society's spiritual dimension or to do so in non-political or non-economic terms.[19] Indeed, a sociologist is unlikely to grasp the crucial importance of this distinction unless he

17 In traditional countries, and in contrast to the often importune panhandling we know of in the West, there used to be a whole etiquette for begging, the premise of which was unobtrusive humility and gratitude based on piety and fear of God.

18 In another context, accounts of the life of Padmasambhava (an Indian sage revered in Tantric Buddhism), provide a glimpse of a traditional world unimaginable for present-day men, one in which deities or powerful spirit entities literally competed with mortals. That said, a margin for pious exaggerations must be allowed when assessing such accounts; but the atmosphere of the supernatural penetrated daily life everywhere, and that is the main thing.

19 However, accounts of the oppression of serfs have to be balanced with the fact that noblemen's estates were, on average, peopled with tenant farmers that saw in their patrons a fatherly figure. Also, the prosperity of both lord and servant was anchored in this familial bond that no political system can replace, not forgetting the deep piety that patrons and peasants shared in common when celebrating countless religious ceremonies, including the literal sharing of communal marriages, births, and deaths. This feature is rarely given its proper due in social treatises premised mainly on considerations of wealth and poverty and on the seemingly undislodgable assumption of class warfare.

has a pious heart; but then a "pious heart" would amount to an automatic disqualification when rated by the sterile standards of "objectivity" within modern academia.

Be that as it may, a telling fact is that in today's world almost no one—in the modern West at least—knows what a real saint looks like because virtually no one knows what Heaven or the sacred is;[20] for moderns, traditional societies rank as inevitably backward, and hence all of their people and customs are deemed likewise to be so. No doubt, a central reason for this ignorance of the sacred is that there is nothing left in the West untouched by the modern world which, for its part, is essentially an anti-civilization since it is the first one in history to develop almost exclusively on an industrialist basis, the exorbitant development of which has led to the near elimination of tradition. One proof of what is an unparalleled situation is the disappearance of sacred art and sacred architecture in the West, as well as, in a minor mode, the obsoleteness of craftsmanship as a feature of daily life; whereas in a traditional civilization craftsmanship was virtually a manner of being involving most of society, handmade artifacts dictating a rhythm of life that mirrored nature's stately pace that was the very opposite of our frenetic lifestyle premised on ever more stringent productivity.[21] The disappearance of both folk and sacred art coincides, in other words, with the disappearance of the trace of Heaven on earth; and if this trace vanishes, how can one expect people to imagine concretely what the miraculous looks like unless they still harbor an intuitive sense of the sacred as it is manifested in virgin nature, the first and last bastion of God's revelation? But translating the homilies of nature into civilized or man-made forms cannot be done in an arbitrary manner; if sacred architecture knows how to transpose the pattern genius of mineral and vegetal motifs, as well as the geometry of the cosmos, into buildings and possibly statuary, it does so through holy inspiration or revelation, not through an individualistic improvisation.

---

20 As mentioned in an earlier chapter, in its priests the Eastern Orthodox Church has preserved the iconic model of Christ, whereas—as Schuon once commented to us in person—the Pope in the Western Church was modeled on the Roman emperor. The Western Roman Catholic Church, for its part, under the modernizing impetus of the Vatican II Council, has now set up a kind of "assembly line process" for canonizing saints, with a criterion of selection based on choosing candidates mostly for their social contributions to mankind, spirituality having become inseparable from welfarism.

21 Gandhi tried heroically but futilely to revive the hand-loom industry in India, but he found himself powerless to contend with the implacable efficiency of machine-made garments. Though thousands of miles away, the infernal steel mills of Lancaster did their part to destroy rural India and, by rebound, traditionalism everywhere.

It is therefore not by accident that the Middle Ages is generally seen as the "Dark Ages", and is depicted that way despite being romanticized by artists, dreamers, and poets or simply by lovers of crumbling stones. Ancient civilizations, almost invariably, are examined through the preconceptions of socio-economic and scientific parameters that rule modern thinking and not sufficiently—if at all—for the wonders that they exhibited both religiously and culturally; nor do moderns seize the collective soul of their peoples, remnants of which may still be seen in the daily atmosphere found in still traditional streets and bazaars.[22] Their sacred art, even when admired and treasured by modern collectors, is seen not as an expression of a spiritual perfection, unsurpassable and therefore fully sufficient unto itself, but either as an interesting stage in man's progress or as a dispensable, almost accidental luxury, a kind of extravagant frill subsidized by oppressive overlords. There is of course some truth to this—*errare humanum est*—but our point is that even if there were ornate excesses, these "excesses" nonetheless fitted within the parameters of an artistic style still governed by sacred criteria.[23] Consequently it is easy for a modern sensibility to miss the theurgic benefit such art may have on the multitudes, all the more as esthetics in a religious tradition are never purely decorative, let alone frivolous, but transcribe a symbolism meant to transmit the intelligent nature of the cosmos itself.

On a grandiose scale, a building such as the Taj Mahal has to be seen both as the synthesis of a sacred lotus become edifice as well as a paragon expression of an entire tradition; that is to say, its creation entailed a knowledge of Heaven on the part of its builders while presupposing a vast substructure of cultural elements dictating every aspect of the lives of the subjects of the Mughal Empire, from dress and manners, to the style of their cities, their music, their paintings, not least their language, gestures,

---

22 Islam preserved the Biblical world of Moses and Christ, as Hinduism did that of the *Puranas* and *Upanishads*; but these worlds must be experienced directly to be properly appreciated.

23 True, once ancient cultures pass an apogee point, they are bound to degenerate; but even in their gradual degeneration it would be simplistic to compare them stroke for stroke with modern equivalents. Certainly, the Egyptian, Babylonian, and Meso-American cultures were guilty of titanism, and the Prometheanism ensuing from this laid the foundation for the ever-present inclination for man to eclipse the Divine. And this outcome resulted furthermore from the excess of human realism of the Egyptian and Meso-American statuary; in fact the Meso-American culture veered eventually into the nightmarish. In contrast, the Hindu and Buddhist cultures escaped such architectonic phantasmagoria largely unscathed, whatever "gigantism" they exhibited being still restrained or still fitting a social context in which the Divine preserved its preeminence, which proves the relative legitimacy of such art in which size is meant to convey greatness.

and general comportment, of which this building was a bejeweled apo-
theosis. Seen in this manner, the Taj Mahal is no longer an extravagant
creation wrought from the tribute of "exploited and oppressed multitudes",
but a pinnacle symbol of a whole infinitely precious way of being, sparkling
and coruscating in thousands upon thousands of facets that are a reflection
of the Mughal interpretation of their dream of Heaven on earth. Indeed,
the animating genius of traditional societies derived in a majority of cases[24]
from the revelation of a divine Center crystallized on earth, which rever-
berated in endless magical reflections. In a traditional society, man is surrounded by the supernatural and the sacred. In the West, this factor held
true for civilization through the Middle Ages, but changed radically after
the Renaissance when a once sacred medieval civilization was supplanted
and then later gradually uprooted by the advent of the industrial revolu-
tion—the all-devouring machine age—along with the proletarian revolutions it ushered in that swept Europe in several decisive phases. A forerunner of what became the proletarian age started in Cromwell's England and
also with Peter the Great's Russia, then in Robespierre's France, and finally
in Lenin's Russia where the Bolsheviks ruthlessly attempted to exterminate
ancient Holy Mother Russia.

To resume our topic, in olden times sultans and maharajahs, too proud to
bow before men, would however consent to stoop before penniless hermits
or risk their throne, because even if the sultan was "the shadow of God on
earth"—as the Ottomans referred to him—the mightiest of rulers was still
but a mortal among mortals.[25] On a perhaps quaint note but nonetheless
tellingly profound, the tradition of the jester, or king's fool, is another relic
of bygone eras unknown to modern rulers; with the elimination of the
jester—notably in England following upon the beheading of Charles I—
this tradition came to an end, thus signaling by the same stroke the end of a
monarch's real power because only a true autocrat, in the very best sense of
the term, would require a fool. It was the fool's role to remind the king that
anything divine he represented, through the symbolism of his function,

24 Two singular exceptions are pagan Greece and pagan Rome, which are like forerunners
of the modern utilitarian world. However, Greece was not always pagan, and Rome had
its stoic ethos and its imperial glory modeled on the "gods"; the humanization and ration-
alization of sacred symbols did not develop unilaterally at the expense of the supernatural
even though it ended up laying the foundation first for the Renaissance and then for the
industrial age to come.

25 Whence in the Bible Ezekiel warns a potentate: "Because thine heart is lifted up, and
thou hast said, I am a God, I sit in the seat of God . . . yet thou art a man, and not God. . . .
Wilt thou yet say before him that slayeth thee, I am God? But thou shalt be a man, and no
God, in the hand of him that slayeth thee" (Ezek. 28:2, 9).

was entirely dependent on God's awesome grace, and therefore he was well minded always to beware of becoming a fool himself should he forget that,[26] a caveat now void because rendered unnecessary in a republican age by the loss of meaning of the royal function—a loss further reinforced by the symbolic irrelevance of presidents or prime ministers, who are for the most part easily replaceable functionaries. In other words, there is no need to "mock" a monarch, and far less a head of state, who is powerless. Perhaps a dictator would warrant a fool to foil him, but, precisely, a dictator is what he is from scorning humility.

What is more, rulers in traditional societies not only had to deal with saintly hermits, whose blessings mattered—a sterling example of which is the story of King Ajatshatru placing himself at the feet of the Buddha[27]— but also, strange to say, with potent curses if they deviated from the proper stewardship of their kingdoms. Curses, as well as spells and omens and the like, are all now relegated to the storehouse of superstitions belonging to a credulous people. But in a universe still not sealed off from the supernatural, a curse is, outwardly and in some respects, the obverse of a blessing; it is in fact worth pondering that a people for whom a blessing, or a curse, has become a trite relic of the past, are a pale shadow of a true humanity, because only a real person—not a mere citizen—can himself, standing before God, bestow a meaningful blessing or for that matter a curse or, more accurately defined, an imprecation such as King David's: "Let death seize upon them, and let them go down quick into hell" (Ps. 55:15).[28]

*   *   *

Now a word on context: no man, however great, can be divorced from a civilization. As stated above, traditional civilizations—all questions of their very real problems notwithstanding—were premised on the reality of the "next world"; this priority meant that mundane issues could never assume overriding importance: everything a man was in his flesh and blood, and everything he owned, could only be relative and therefore could never be-

26 Traditionally, in Morocco, the heir to the throne was subject to what is termed a "ceremony of mockery".

27 See the *Samannaphala Sutta* ("The Fruits of Contemplative Life Sutra") from the *Digha Nikaya* discourses of the Pali Canon.

28 A prototype of both a blessing and a curse can be found in this quotation from Genesis, where God speaks to Abraham: "And I will bless them that bless thee, and curse him that curseth thee" (Gen. 12:2).

come an absolute goal in itself. According to this logic, food and shelter, for instance, had to meet certain minimum subsistence standards as opposed to being quasi-absolute ends in themselves. Thus, issues considered to be "social problems" today and that modern man believes have to be solved imperatively and on a massive scale—such as food, wealth, education, health, and the like—were never viewed traditionally as intractable problems to be permanently overcome, but rather as unavoidable imperfections, the wound and scar of life on earth; such problems were cosmologically "necessary", hence irresolvable in their root, because, quite simply, earth can never be Heaven.

For instance, a problem like poverty never had the social stigma associated with it today: a measure of poverty was considered as a "normal" condition of life on earth and even had a noble archetype, that of renunciation. Now, to avoid any misunderstanding, it should be clear that poverty should not be left to fester, because misery is demeaning and, as mentioned above, in a traditional civilization constant succor for the downtrodden was an active religious duty. But succor for the poor is one thing, and the ideal of eradicating poverty from the face of the earth is another, not to mention that the issue of exorbitant progress and measureless material wellbeing create in turn exorbitant expectations which soon create exorbitant lacks. "My kingdom is not of this world", we keep mentioning and so too in the Koran we find the refrain that "the Hereafter is better for you than the present (world)" ("The Morning Hours", 93:4), meaning that earthly solace may not always be forthcoming from God and this in view of obliging the soul to remember and hence to rely on the excellence of the next world; it is a universal law that if suffering is relieved too quickly, or too completely, it can lose its salvific virtue. Put differently, in attempting to solve all of man's problems here and now there is a risk that the soul's flight-impetus for salvation will be clipped.

As a result, traditional man resigned himself to fate on a daily basis, accepting morally and out of spiritual principle the periodic swings in fortune; in fact a key part of his happiness depended precisely on his spiritual capacity for resignation to God's will. Transposing this attitude of pious fatalism—if not of holy resignation—to a whole collectivity entailed an outlook in which an individual person was not considered preeminently in terms of his "rights" but foremost in terms of his obligations and responsibilities; sacrifice took precedence over comfort, at least where such an alternative presented itself.

Humanists consider that they have invented "human rights" and, undeniably, there is certainly a logic to social justice pursued for its own sake; by this we mean that obvious abuses need to be rectified as such, wherever, however, and whenever they occur. Yet, logically, it has always been the prerogative and mandate of the great religious revelations to re-establish and preserve a measure of justice on earth and to protect the poor, the needy, the oppressed, and the dispossessed—indeed, one's salvation depended on one's charity. Therefore, social justice was never divorced from religion but always presupposed the need for gaining God's favor—injustice being equated with a loss of God's favor, precisely, or as karma allowed by God. The key coupling of holy resignation with holy trust were the twin poles that shaped the spiritual quality of an individual—resignation determining his humility, and trust inspiring his generosity. The aspect of holy resignation, when allowed to penetrate to the very marrow of an individual's soul, created in turn a social atmosphere that lessened ambition, greed, and conflict while predisposing contentment along with simple needs; meanwhile the aspect of holy trust fostered an attitude of hope and generosity and by extension of spiritual solidarity that made it easier for individuals to share the goods of Heaven's bounty. Not least, it should be noted that both of these attitudes are antithetical to progressivism.

At this point, it seems appropriate to introduce a crucial caveat: until now the term "tradition" has been discussed in a manner in which we may seem to endorse traditionalism indistinctly, or even to equate it with an ideal norm. However, this term should be restricted ideally to a civilization still based on a divine Revelation, in other words, on a civilization incorporating three central pillars that can be summarized as Truth, Beauty, Virtue. To detail these: Truth, namely a correct doctrine and a corresponding magisterium based on a supreme divine Truth; Beauty, namely the esthetics seen both in the social customs, or the etiquette of religious courtesy, and in the architecture—especially sacred architecture—not to mention the arts and crafts in general, including clothing; and lastly Virtue or a religious ethics governing correct behavior. Otherwise, the term "tradition" is compromised by the passions and inertia of the human collectivity expressing it; deteriorating customs undermine this term, not to mention superstitions or even abhorrent practices that are not any the more venerable for being ancient. For instance, too often in "traditional" societies it is women that are made to be the scapegoat for the weaknesses and passions of the men.[29]

---

29 For example, the barbaric practice of genital mutilation—wrongly termed "female circumcision"—is abusively disguised as being part of hallowed religious tradition, when it is a raw crime against nature, partly based on the fear of women's charms. In effect, women are made to pay the price for the men's lack of self-control, when it is really the weakness of the males that should be prosecuted; but since it is men who rule, they are liable to twist religion—and tradition—to their muscular advantage.

To repeat, a true civilization gives precedence to what is of immortal value to man, in contrast to what is only of temporal value, and it will therefore promote for society a healthy sense of priorities in which the Hereafter takes precedence over this world—at least *de jure*, if not *de facto*, depending on circumstances. By way of contrasting the possible conflicts modern man faces when obliged to choose between this world and the next, and as difficult as this is to express, we want to take one example illustrating the real challenge this question of priorities can present: modern medicine allows—and has no choice but to allow, given its newfound prowess—infants unfit for a normal life to live, thus weakening society. Now part of the problem for opting for saving a life without regard to social consequences stems from a loss of a sense of the reality of the next world; in other words, if one could truly believe in the concreteness of the next world (and of God's mercy), one would not be so desperate to keep infants or patients alive at all costs, thus divinizing—implicitly and unwittingly—the flesh over the Spirit. This paradox is typical of the reversal of poles governing the modern world, the reversal entailing the priority of this world over the next. In mentioning this, however, we are not advocating removing machine life support systems purely and simply, we are merely noting the social aberrations following in the wake of extreme "progress", which places decent and moral people today as never before on the two horns of a real dilemma. And indeed, modern solutions may solve the immediate problem of an infant's survival but often at the expense of a far greater problem, which is that of overpopulation in this case, as well as at the cost of the weakening of society, since nature's natural means of selection are impeded. But modern solutions rarely do more than displace ancient problems, or modify modalities, without solving the fundamental issue of the world not being Heaven.

In this light, the industrial development of our present civilization can be seen as a hypertrophy meant—in part, it would seem—to compensate for the moral deficit of man's shrinking spirituality, a spirituality understood to have been the reigning quality of the *Satya Yuga* (the "Age of Truth"), the first of the four ages of creation, namely, the one situated closest to the primordial paradise, if not overlapping with it. Hence, as spectacularly brilliant as the invention of industrialism and machines is—of man taming the forces of nature—it is inconceivable that an archetype for our modern industrial civilization will be found in Eternity; for all of its genius, it is finally not only unnatural but inherently utilitarian and hence mostly ugly, if not alienating, and therefore contrary to the spiritual nature of man; and yet it corresponds to a promethean possibility of man's genius that has to be exhausted before our cycle of creation closes.

To expand the above point: machines are developed to compensate for man's physical helplessness; but account should be taken of the fact that a human being is ideally suited to an environment in which a horse should be the fastest means of transport; to go faster than a horse, in other words, takes man outside of norms he can comfortably deal with psychologically. Thus the introduction of machines permitting men to travel at previously unimaginable velocities shattered cosmic ratios premised on the inherent physical limitations of the human body—limitations that have their normative as well as their symbolic meaning. Among other things, velocity, which is inherently dispersing, not only ends up flattening the geographic meaningfulness of the immensity of distances, as well as compromising the depth of human relationships by its shallowing impatience, but also contributes to the acceleration of time; and this acceleration, in turn, impacts the fate of a civilization by promoting a mystique of dynamism: doing (effort) gradually overwhelms being (contemplation). By contrast, ancient wisdom reminds us that "haste is of the devil". Not least, haste is also the rhythmic counterpart of the cult of change and innovation—essentially fostering infidelity towards tradition—whereas for primordial man change was the enemy of the sacred monotony of his ways, a sacred monotony that echoed the course of the stars' circling an invisible center, and of the majestic rising and setting of the great luminaries, the sun moving timelessly as a luminous shuttle between the two solsticial edges of creation's weaving.

Reversing the priority of the Hereafter over the here-below—in fact turning traditional civilization's immemorial hierarchy upside down—is the story of the modern world, starting with the Renaissance which co-incided with a shift from the geocentric perspective to the heliocentric, a transition that turned out to be deeply symbolic. To honor man's timeless needs entails, first, redressing this upside-down perspective, namely by re-storing the Divine to its rightful preeminence, otherwise one ends up mak-ing a god of the individual by default, not to mention that man liberated from God turns into a potential monster: as man continues to eat of "the Tree of Knowledge" he stands next to an abyss held in a petri dish, ready to clone himself and to discard God once for all. Yet a more insidious trap—echoing the false immanentism discussed above—is that of individualizing God, namely appropriating the Divine so that God becomes the *imago ho-mini* instead of man being the *imago Dei*. Better in that case, and in some respects, an atheist crudely denying God than a heretic believer disfiguring the whole notion of spirituality, because it may be easier to dismiss the atheist than a charismatic "spiritual" impostor.

True rulership has always entailed a reference to a divine origin, be it hereditary investiture—"king by the grace of God" or "Son of Heaven"—or merely the sacred investiture inherent in the fact that a king is modeled on the heavenly Sovereign; in other words, the function of kingship has its own sacred magic.[30] If such an assessment may strike some modern scholars as extravagant, then they should consider that the presence of a king cannot be fitted to an atheistic society, these two possibilities being mutually exclusive; it is proof, in other words, that the crown and the bishop's rod belong together. The concept of a nation, by contrast to a kingdom, is organized essentially around secular ideals within which the possibility of a purely atheistic government is not only completely possible, it is increasingly the norm, at least among "advanced" nations. This occurrence then begs the question whether it is preferable to have an ill-functioning kingdom or a well-functioning nation—that is to say with respect to its subjects' (or citizens') ultimate welfare? The contrast can be sharpened even further by asking: is a peaceful democracy preferable to a brutal kingship? One merit of such questions is to show that it can be difficult to compare epochs very dissimilar in tenor and purpose, and in a way it is unfair to compare an epoch's best features with another epoch's worst, which is really what these questions amount to. Perhaps the most reasonable conclusion would be to remember that epochs are best compared when assessing their global characteristics and, crucially, to do so with a scale of values that includes the totality of a collectivity's prospects, that it, not just its material wellbeing but its eternal becoming. That being the case, one will want to remember that in a traditional (and virtually sacred) society, man stands at the edge of Eternity, both physically and philosophically. The daily proximity of death in ancient worlds, as well as its stoic acceptance as a natural part of life, determined both the relativity of this world and the concreteness of the supernatural world which, when integrated through religion to this world, was no longer an abstraction or a grandmother's tale. In such a society, men and women's souls were imprinted with an otherworldliness that was enhanced by a daily awareness of life's precariousness, a precariousness that modern science is endeavoring to overturn with every ounce of its unbottled genius. Be that as it may, it is worth remembering that tradition, in the integral sense of the word, is not just stuffy convention or a lame obsession with outworn customs or the perpetuation of comfortable

30 Or as Schuon formulates it, referring to the role of the emperor in ancient China: "it is really the Throne that created the emperor" (*In the Face of the Absolute* [Bloomington, IN: World Wisdom, 1994], p. 115).

prejudices—though it can degenerate into all of these—but the resounding echo of Divine Revelation preserved through time in customs and crafts.

Revelation comes like a lightning bolt out of the heavens, in a cosmic flash of God-bestowed insight, the thundering reverberations of which must then be crystallized into forms and rituals so as to be preserved against the inroads of time; "By the Scripture that maketh plain, Lo! We revealed it on a blessed night . . . whereon every wise command is made clear" (Koran, "Smoke", 4:1-4). In turn, these forms need to be periodically refreshed so as not to ossify and decay. Thus, tradition, in the fullest sense, is a solemn pact with Heaven borne out by man through adamantine fidelity to the original revelation.

Perhaps the decisive difference between kingdoms and nations (or political states) comes down to deciding whether man is a delegate image of God on earth or if he is the citizen-child of secular revolutions and progressivism. "My *kingdom* is not of this world" (italics ours),[31] Christ stated, and one interpretation of this saying is to conclude that one cannot find Heaven on earth. This assumption was essentially taken for granted by all civilizations preceding the Renaissance, when the view of the universe underwent a pendulum swing from the theocentric to the anthropocentric; in this reversal, man became—owing partly to Copernicus' heliocentrism—a peripheral being flung at the cosmos' outer limits and no longer the center around which the sun rose and set; here is where the birth of relativism originates. Yet, at the same time, the great irony is that even though man was no longer the center of the Ptolemaic universe— with all the stars circling him according to the apparent movement of the galaxies—he ended up becoming *de facto* a god in that he basically ceased deferring to an invisible deity and took over full command of his terrestrial destiny; the irony of this bears emphasizing: the heliocentric perspective determined both a relativization of man, and ushered in the birth of modern existential angst, and yet at the very same time it heralded the assumption by man of godlike powers to alter the face of the universe itself. But the inconsistency is not really an inconsistency: so long as man was the symbolic center of the cosmos and was understood to be created in the image of his Lord, he was compelled to be humble precisely because of that image's holy symbolism and metaphysical import. This displacement in man's social and spiritual center of gravity produced a total realignment of priorities of unprecedented magnitude, unleashing the development of an absolutely unparalleled material progress that has, among other things,

31 We have cited these words of Christ multiple times because they are the key to a whole outlook. The ability to heed them in a meaningful way is what differentiates a traditional world from our modern world.

blinded both man's sense of cosmic and of eschatological proportions; he became both titanic and autonomous. The nub of the problem—and this is a perennial concern—is that man, when left to his own devices and passions, seeks immediate and, if possible, total gratification; indeed he logically wants to seize the whole world for his own use and enjoyment. But the choice facing each individual finally has always been between this world and the next world; thus, for a social order to be truly effective, it must establish priorities that remind man of this life's ephemerality, thus sparing him from placing his treasure in an edifice built on sand, while reminding him of the Eternal. And this means that the political structure of a society ought ideally to be articulated along those lines, starting with the supreme functions of its rulers. By that measure the essence of kingship is to reflect Godship on earth.

CHAPTER 5

Individuality Is Not Individualism

Brahma satyam, jagan mithya, jivo brahmaiva na aparah.
("*Brahman* alone is real, the world is neither real nor unreal,
and the individual soul is no different than *Brahman*.")
(Shankaracharya)

Thou wast perfect in thy ways from the day that thou wast created,
till iniquity was found in thee.
(Ezek. 28:15)

Verily We created man of the best of stature
Then We reduced him to the lowest of the low.
(Koran, "The Fig", 95:4-5)

The Lord's declaration to Moses, "I am that I am", is the supreme ontological statement the Divine can make of Itself in a language men can understand.[1] God, in making this statement to Moses, utters an essential declaration, speaking non-hypostatically,[2] namely outside of time and beyond any states, or before all determinations. This primordial declaration expresses the epitome of the Absolute's Self-awareness; and this Self-awareness constitutes the first premonition of the possibility of duality, but not of duality itself since self-awareness—at this ineffable level—is still part of the Self's ontological *prajna* or unity of wisdom. In other words, the Self would not be the Self if It were unconscious: the Self is both Being (*sat*) and Consciousness (*chit*); It both "is" and "knows".

In this sublimely sacred self-awareness, there is the objectification that "allows" God to both be and to know at the very same time, and in knowing Himself as Self the premise for the first creative impulse towards duality of self is set into motion, in the manner of a sacred echo in the fertile void of totality; these are the origins of Principle and Substance. In so doing, this

---

1 The Hindu Advaita Vedanta sage, Shri Ramana Maharshi said about this Biblical phrase that no formulation of God "is indeed so well put as the biblical statement 'I am that I am'". Although he mentioned that similar formulations can be found in Hindu scriptures, such as the famous *Aham Brahmasmi* ("I am Brahman", *Brihadaranyaka Upanishad* 1.4.10), he considered none so pithily complete.

2 "Non-hypostatically": from the Neoplatonic notion of "hypostases" or "hierarchical stations" of the Divine, e.g. Beyond-Being, Being, Creation.

impulse self-engenders images—or reflections—of the original One Self in a growing profusion of modalities that, *mutatis mutandis*, mirror and retrace the original oneness of their divine origin through radiation. Yet, very importantly, such blissfulness of being does not translate immediately into what we humans know as creation, but it does produce a series of divine hypostases that eventually end in the creative act which is repeated "everywhere" and co-eternally with God's being, and in infinite endlessness. Thus, God creates in an act of supreme noetic intelligence in which the creature-to-be is featured as an *ideos*—to borrow from Plato's doctrine of the divine "ideas"—in the Divine Mind. Creation is not, therefore, the fruit of a blind impulse struggling for the light of day, but a theophany. Once it emerges at the level of matter, however, the seed of the future creature then exists unconsciously in the embryonic darkness of the substance receiving it; but this was not its fate earlier, namely when the creature lit up archetypally in God's Mind.[3] In fact, matter itself—or more exactly the prototype for matter[4]—is luminous before it becomes congealed into the opacity and hardness as we know it, at least from the outside, since inside it is transparent energy. If we were to search for the origin of the individual in this darkened secondary substance it would be to start from the periphery and not from the cosmic center as we must.

*   *   *

The essence of the word "individuality" rests on the principle of indivisibility. Now who else can claim, in the strictest sense, the status of being undivided if not the Supreme Self? And yet, the mystery of existence is that each individual self can be "one-self" in the virtually supreme sense in that each creature is insuperably absolute: unique, non-duplicable, occurring only once in eons of history, never to be repeated again, because that is why an individual exists. Stated as such, this is a rather astonishing claim to distinctness, but the uniqueness is really due to the principial uniqueness of the Absolute projecting Itself in a fragmented manner into the relative, rather than through any individual merit; that uniqueness also happens to be the biggest stumbling block to understanding the meaning of our cosmic paternity in the Absolute, so much so that man, engrossed with his

3 Likewise, at the level of manifestation itself, souls, according to Plato, drink of Lethe and then shoot away "like stars" to their birth, either in human or in animal form (see the eschatological myth closing the *Republic*).

4 Not to be confused with the proto-matter of evolutionism, which is but a refinement of the material definition of matter.

individual uniqueness, ends up competing with the Absolute Itself: "Hath not man seen that We have created him from a drop of seed? Yet lo! He is an open opponent" (Koran, "Ya Sin", 36:77).

To illustrate this principle of individual distinctiveness, we could ask in the form of a *koan*: is each snowflake truly unique? Apparently, each possesses its own irreplicable pattern; are we to wonder then at an individual's naïvely literal sense of uniqueness? This principle of non-duplication of individual selves illustrates the inexhaustibility of the Divine Principle expressed through creation. Clearly, however, the illusion of uniqueness—making each one of us feel that he or she is an autonomous self in his or her own right—has to be an illusion. But if it is so intrinsically, it is not completely so extrinsically inasmuch as the Supreme Self can project Itself into myriads of tiny selves and thus lend them a kind of "mini-absoluteness" reflecting Its own absoluteness, just as the image of the one sun can be projected into myriads of water drops;[5] such an image is only an analogy, and therefore only a partial representation of our point, but inasmuch as each drop of water can reflect the sun, then each drop incorporates the image of the sun integrally, but without ever being the sun except by remote participation. At the same time, there is not only reflection via separation but reflection via identity, or a merging of substances between divine cause and human effect which Rumi captured very well in his immortal words: "You see yourself as the drop in the ocean, but you are also the ocean in the drop."

In cosmological terms—and to borrow from the ancient Sankhya philosophy—it is as if the individual cosmic principle or *Purusha*,[6] in incarnating Itself in cosmic substance or *Prakriti*,[7] could become

5 If we look at birds, each bluebird for example conducts itself as if it were the only bluebird in existence, as likewise does each hawk or swan: they hold themselves with a smartly proud erectness and total alertness and behave with absolute gravity of purpose as if they embodied the very archetype of the divine thunderbird itself, with all due consideration for their different levels. On this score, incidentally, human beings have in fact much to learn from them as far as dignity of posture and total vigilance of comportment is concerned; indeed, to know and to reflect the Absolute is first to be dignified and alert.

6 The Divine Self projected in human form at the pinnacle of manifestation.

7 Definitions of *Purusha* and *Prakriti* vary: for some, *Purusha* (lit. "eastern dawn") is pure Spirit whereas *Prakriti* (lit. "that which gives shapes") falls exclusively on the side of creation and mostly material creation at that, namely the distinction between supra-formal and formal manifestation. Or this polarity corresponds to the distinction between "Self" and "non-Self". For us, it is the duality between the masculine pole of the Absolute and feminine pole of the Infinite projected into Manifestation (see Schuon's *Esoterism as Principle and as Way*, chap. "The Mystery of the Veil") or, to paraphrase Guénon, the distinction between "essence" and "substance", or what in effect amounts to the distinction between "intelli-

infinitely segmented and thus apparently divided—without however having its wholeness impaired in the slightest, since its "body" belongs to a pre-formal order of being (pre-creation).[8] According to the Sankhya philosophy, *Purusha* is the creator God[9] manifested in a human form. His cosmic dismemberment—as that of Osiris in the Egyptian myth—is both symbolic and literal because, being transcendent with respect to creation proper, and also appearing first as pure consciousness, he cannot be actually divided; but there is a substance drawn from him—*Prakriti*—which, in its outermost projection becomes fragmented in the process of creative separation, as operated through the three *gunas* of *sattva*, *rajas*, and *tamas*,[10] or of creation operating through gradual degrees of differentiation ending up in a terminal point of separation from the divine Cause.

gence" and "existence". Or, if as Spirit, *Purusha* is equatable with *Atma*, then *Prakriti* would be the *Shakti* (or energetic radiation) of *Atma*, and in that sense would be equatable with *Maya*, but higher *Maya* as the created splendor of the Absolute, what in Sufism is known as *tajalli* or the glory of God expressing Himself in Manifestation.

8 According to René Guénon in *Man and his Becoming according to the Vedanta* (Ghent, NY: Sophia Perennis, 2001, pp. 46-50), commenting on the *Bhagavad Gita* (15:16), there are two *Purushas*—which echoes the formulation of Shankaracharya in his commentary on this chapter and verse—an imperishable *Purusha* and a perishable one, whereas the Supreme Self (*Atma*) declares: "Because I transcend the perishable and am even higher than the imperishable, therefore am I known in the world and in the *Veda* as 'Purushottama', the Highest Spirit." We assume these two beings are comparable, if not basically identical, to the two *Atmans* likened to two inseparable birds on the tree of life mentioned in the *Upanishads*, respectively the Supreme Self and the individual self (*Mundaka Upanishad* 3.1.1).

9 See for instance *Rig Veda*, hymn 10:90. However, technically speaking, the Sankhya being a cosmological doctrine (*darshana*) is neither metaphysical, nor theological, and thus does not elaborate on the principle of the personal creator God (*Ishvara*). But such a divine entity can nonetheless be inferred in that its definition of *Purusha* as "Supreme Spirit" entails what other sacred philosophies would consider to be "God", or the creator God; and certainly the ancient philosophical schools of Hinduism incorporate the Sankhya cosmology into their doctrine of the Divine.

10 *Prakriti*, defined here as universal manifested substance (which is the prototype of creation itself as pure potentiality, and thus pre-existent but still non-determined and therefore determining), is passive with respect to *Purusha* but active with respect to creation; it is the *natura naturans* of the *materia prima* or principle of creative fruitfulness of original substance. It consists of three cosmic modalities or *gunas*: *sattva* or the "intelligent, luminous, ascending principle", *rajas* or the "active, expanding, fiery, and passional principle", and *tamas* or the "descending, dull, inertia bound, and tenebrous principle". These *gunas* can be envisaged in a vertical sense moving from light to darkness, or from intelligence to ignorance, or from pure activeness to pure inertia (or, in moral terms, from virtue to vice), or they can be envisaged in a horizontal sense, in which case the two separative *gunas*—*rajas* and *tamas*—no longer fulfill a negative role, but merely a cosmological role respectively of polarization and of condensation, in which case *sattva* can be said to act as their underlying unity.

To specify: although the principle of *Purusha* is "non-producing" in itself, *Prakriti* can be said to be drawn from him, comparably as with Eve drawn from the body of Adam. And just as *Purusha* himself is indivisible despite his sacrifice, so too *Prakriti* remains perfectly virgin despite all of her productions because she still represents Divine Being projected as creative substance: "Thou art all fair my love, there is no spot in thee" (Song of Songs 4:7). In metaphysical terms this means that even though the relative is prefigured in the Absolute—and, *mutatis mutandis*, creation in *Prakriti*— the Absolute is not rendered conditional to any degree whatsoever by the relative's existence (or pre-existence). Strictly speaking, creation is pure *Maya* or "non-reality", but depending on the relationship with *Atma* (the Absolute) one could say that creation can have a delegate reality *of its own*, which means that it is neither completely real nor completely unreal: it is not "real" since it is not the Principle, which is the sole, eternal, unchanging Real; yet, being a reflection of the Principle in space-time manifestation (the realm of *nama-rupa* or "name and form"), it partakes or echoes— through its breathing and life—the realness of its divine Prototype, for this earthly life, although changing and mortal in its modalities, is nothing in its essence other than life itself; in other words, it is deathless in its primal indistinction, but not so in its formal distinctiveness. It is here that one needs to be careful not to confuse life with its material forms, the latter of which are in constant need of vivification to preserve them from contamination and degeneration. To illustrate this: a tree thrives so long as its sap vitalizes it, but its freshness, strength, and vitality comes from its sap; and when the sap withdraws, the tree dies. But where is the sap? Likewise, man derives his consciousness and vitality from the Spirit, which though unseen, is inherent to his body; otherwise his body returns to the earth whereas his soul is but a hue, its light being the Spirit.

*   *   *

These preliminary considerations may seem unnecessarily complex, but they are essential for grasping the root of the process of individuation. The idea of individuality, namely of the indivisibility of the eternal Self refracted as soul or differentiated Consciousness and Personality, rests on the static and silent essence of *Purusha* (the Supreme Person), while Existence—the "*being*-ness" of creatures—derives from the dynamic vitality of *Prakriti*.[11] In other words, our individuality could not exist

---

11 This sequence would seem to place "being" hierarchically beneath "consciousness", and this is so inasmuch as "being" in creation follows the intelligent projection of it, much as heat follows light. But in the Absolute Self, "consciousness" and "being" are indissolubly

were it not for its root identity with the Self both as supreme egoic (or self-intelligent) principle and as being, namely as life translated into a creature: "He it is Who did create all of you from a *single* soul" (Koran, "The Heights", 7:189, italics ours). Thus our life—or rather our existence, mortal as well as posthumous—is ontologically nothing other than the life of the Self itself—translated intellectively through *Purusha* and articulated existentially through *Prakriti*—and our consciousness is nothing other, again in its supra-individual essence, than the intelligence of the Self projected through a series of hypostatic stations ranging from the Non-manifest, to the Pre-manifest, and finally to the manifest proper which consists in our daily experience of the world we happen to live in, or the "waking state", what is termed *vaishwanara* in Vedantic philosophy.[12]

In microcosmic terms, the reflection of the Self as "Supra-Being" is represented by the Heart-Intellect—*increatus et increabile*,[13] as Meister Eckhart formulates it—or the immortal supra-individual faculty in man;[14] next, the reflection of the Self as "Being" would correspond to the higher soul in man, namely the non-corruptible or the holy archetype of our individual soul, our experience of which would be, inwardly, our objective conscience of the Divine and, outwardly, of right and wrong and of good and evil; and finally, the Self in its individualized or broken reflection as "outward being", which is our passionate or corruptible soul in need of reformation and salvation, a soul that is temporarily locked in matter even though not ultimately bound by the physical body's final corruption.[15] Thus,

---

one, as seen in the tantric *yab-yum* representation of the interlaced male and female divinities representing respectively "compassion" (*karuna*) and "wisdom" (*prajna*). To be noted, and contrary to our delineation above, the masculine principle is considered here as being dynamic (embodied as "compassion") whereas the female is static (embodied as "wisdom"); these polarizations are reversible depending on the hypostatic level involved. In other words, and to follow our previous analogy, "light" is personified here by the female principle and "heat" by the masculine.

12 But, to avert the temptation of a false pantheism, it must be emphasized that creation as such emanates from *Prakriti* and not from *Purusha*; in other words, *Purusha* is independent of *Prakriti*, but not *Prakriti* of *Purusha*.

13 "Uncreated and uncreatable".

14 "Supra-individual" but also the faculty of the supreme personhood of *Paramatma* reflected in the individual self. In other words, the Supreme Personhood is supra-personal but not impersonal.

15 In Sufism, we find the distinction between four degrees of "soul", ascending from the animal soul (*an-nafs al-haywaniyah*), next the passional soul (*an-nafs al-ammarah* or "soul which incites" to evil), then the discerning or intelligent soul (*an-nafs al-lawwamah* or "soul which blames"), and finally the intellective soul (*an-nafs al-mutma'innah* or "the soul at

in a broad sense, our individuality, in its personal or temporary distinctness from the Supreme Self as such, embraces an ontological range which at its uppermost point corresponds to the pre-manifest Self (*Purusha*)—as well as to pre-manifest Being (*Prakriti*)—and, at its outermost point, corresponds to the manifest ego (*atman*); it does not however include the non-manifest Self (*Paramatma*), even though It is mysteriously inherent in our being. To use an analogy, this triple condensation from the supra-formal to the formal resembles the transition from pure light, to heat, and finally to form. According to that analogy, then, the individual and transmigrating soul is basically an igneous entity, neither pure light nor pure form, but partaking of both light and form. There are, of course, any number of different divisions that apply to the creation of man, but, at the risk of over-simplification, we need not concern ourselves with them here.[16] Reversing and transfiguring this process of individualizing condensation is part of the spiritual way; in other words, the spiritual path corresponds to an alchemical dis-individuation in which the individual self is extinguished in the universal Self, in order to be reborn, but now of the Spirit. At the same time, it enables a gem-like crystallization of numerous individual archetypes, for, to borrow an image, there can be an infinite number of star-like images of the supernal Sun; the process of disindividuation is not meant to abolish individuality as such, as has been mentioned earlier, but to restore the true image from its individual distortions. This dual process is summarized in an alchemical saying: "The body must become spirit and the spirit body."[17]

*   *   *

It is by design that we choose to reference the Sankhya doctrine of *Purusha* and *Prakriti*—we could also have referenced the Platonic notion of the demiurge—for it enables the notion of individuality to be discussed in a

peace"). See Titus Burckhardt's *Introduction to Sufi Doctrine* (World Wisdom, 2008).

16 For example, Mahayana Buddhism recognizes some 89 levels of consciousness (*Vinnana Khanda*) and in medieval Christian Hermeticism one finds diagrams charting the ascent of the soul through literally dozens of spheres, ranging, among others, through multiple hierarchies (or hypostases) of angels equated with an equal number of cognitive faculties (*intelligentiae*), and four animic spheres corresponding to the "celestial soul", the "rational soul", the "animal soul", and the "vegetative soul", etc. For a profound discussion of these dimensions proceeding from the Principle to Manifestation, see Frithjof Schuon's chapter on "The Five Divine Presences" in *Form and Substance in the Religions*.

17 *The Glory of the World* (or *Table of Paradise*), an anonymous alchemical treatise forming part of *The Hermetic Museum*.

cosmic and thus non-religious framework; indeed we intend to present the nature and process of individuation as such and not as interpreted by religious revelation, at least not *a priori*.[18] Yet, the whole notion of individuation cannot finally be separated from the religious; thus we shall now say, borrowing from the language of religion, that in creating man God created a perfection, for man is the *imago Dei*, no less,[19] the *Adam Kadmon* of the Kabbalah or the *Insan al-Kamil* of Sufism, the *Chen Jen* of Taoism, or the *Arhat* of Buddhism. However, the specific term matters not; what matters is to understand that a perfect Creator could not create anything less than a perfect being[20]—perfectly intelligent, perfectly good, perfectly strong, and perfectly beautiful, as well as perfectly holy—on pain of not being God: in other words, He could not create a being who was anything less than co-essential with Himself for He could not[21] step outside of Himself, being the Divine pleroma or "infinite Totality"—redundancy intended. In the words of the Bible: "Who is the image of the invisible God, the firstborn of every creature: for by him were all things created. . . . And he is before all things, and by him all things consist" (Col. 1:15-19). One could discuss in indefinitely complex terms a process that, in its essence, comes down to this: first, the Self *being* aware of Itself as selfhood and, second, the Self *becoming* aware of Itself as a separate object; the distinction here between "being aware" and "becoming aware" is to avoid describing just one aspect because the Supreme Self is simultaneously a Non-Aware Awareness. Or, simply stated, the Self is aware of Itself first inwardly and then outwardly, one might say.

Now the "being aware of Itself" is, to borrow from Neoplatonism, both the awareness and the object of awareness (*noesis* and *noema*) leading to the first bipolarization, between substance and object, but still *in divinis*.

---

18 We could also have referred to the Aristotelian distinction between matter and form, or potency and perfection, or the later theological refinements of this theory under Aquinas and Duns Scotus.

19 Christianity speaks of Christ, the perfectly begotten "son of God" and even Islam, which just like Christianity is loath to praise man, recognizes not only the Prophet Muhammad's "mighty stature" (*khuluqun azim*—Koran, "The Pen", 68:4) but also man's original loftiness when first created: "Verily We created man of the most excellent stature, then We reduced him to the lowest of the low" (Koran, 95:4-5).

20 Athena springs full-armed from the head of Zeus, in a parthenogenetic process. Parthenogenesis is a term borrowed from biology to indicate the "virgin birth" or the asexual development of an embryo without the intervention of male fertilization. We use the term here in a transposed and cosmological sense.

21 To say "could not" might seem to imply some kind of limitation in God, but it is merely a dialectical manner of emphasizing that God has to be God or else He is not God.

To quote from Plotinus: "The One, perfect because It seeks nothing, has nothing, and needs nothing, overflows, as it were, and Its superabundance makes something other than Itself. This, when it has come into being, turns back upon the One and is filled, so becomes its contemplator, *Nous*. Its halt and turning towards the One constitutes being, its gaze upon the One, *Nous*. Since it halts and turns towards the One that it may see, it becomes at once *Nous* and being."[22]

The implications of this premise are manifold and profound. The mystery is that the Divine Self, in being aware of Itself, and thus in effect setting the premise for what will become creation, can segment Itself into myriads upon myriads of reflected selves that while existing as distinct from one another, in an exploded mode as it were, yet mirror the indivisibility of their origin just like the sparks from some great supernal fire reflect the whole; this is the One becoming many and yet forfeiting nothing of its Oneness just as light is not diminished or increased by its refraction. But this primordial division—initially an immanent and still blissful differentiation[23]—initiates the first relativization, but still *in divinis*, before in due course ending in external separation, with the terminal concomitants of suffering and conflict familiar to mankind. Hence the Absolute cannot duplicate Itself as pure Absolute, for quite obviously there can only be one absolute. Yet—and at the risk of repeating ourselves—something of the uniqueness of the original Principle has to be reflected in the refraction of the One in countless individualities; and this is part of what constitutes the uniqueness of each individual, not least the inability for an individual to be anyone other than himself. In other words, the uniqueness of individuality becomes—painfully on the plane of division—a solitude reflecting the soleness of the unique Absolute, a separation that can only be overcome on earth through love and compassion.

Of all creatures, only man has the power to deny the Absolute, which is the power to deny the Self and therefore, by cosmic extrapolation, to reject his own true self, because only the non-self "burns" in hell, as Jacob Boehme specified. In Hinduism, these two paths—namely the choice

---

22 Quoted in *Neoplatonism and Gnosticism* by Richard T. Wallis, Jay Bregman (Albany, NY: SUNY, 1992), p. 213. The language of "overflowing" becomes in Eckhart that of *bullitio* and *ebullitio* ("boiling"—or "bubbling"—and "boiling over"). And since we mention Gnosticism we take this opportunity to say that we are not endorsing, even implicitly, any of a number of Gnostic heresies that are misrepresentations of Neoplatonism clumsily combined with Manichean residues that confronted early Christianity. Our understanding of *gnosis* is based on the etymology of this Greek word which means "wisdom" or "knowledge of the *Nous* (the Self)", and not on the historical movement that borrowed this term.

23 From which is derived the Platonic principle of Eros animating the cosmos through duality.

between Heaven and "hell"[24]— are called the *Deva Yana*, or "path of the Gods", and the *Pitri Yana*, the "path of the ancestors"; they are associated respectively with "light" and "smoke", the gateway to the *Deva Yana* passing through the southern solsticial door of minimum light leading to maximum light (winter or midnight point) and the *Pitri Yana* passing through the northern solsticial Sun Door of peak light (summer or noon point) but marking the beginning of dwindling light.[25] The "Path of Smoke", in this scheme, includes not just Tartarus but the entire realm of transmigration. Thus, already right here on earth individual souls are actively engaged in walking either on one or the other of these paths. May it be that of the *Deva Yana*, the essence of which is to recognize the trace of the One Self in our individual self. As for the *Pitri Yana*, its riddle results from answering wrongly the question: "Who am I?" If the answer is "I am other than the Self", namely an "individualist", or if the answer is that "I love myself more than the Self", the cycle of transmigration cannot be broken. Only our archetypal individuality *in divinis* can be "saved" and thus delivered from the wheel of birth and death, for in truth it was never undelivered.

*   *   *

Before proceeding further, it is necessary to address a problematical misconception: the paragon human being described above should not be confused with any "superman" fantasy, such as the Omega Man of a Teilhard de Chardin's so-called Liberation Theology. This idea of a "pneumatic Christ" that can be attained collectively as the human race evolves is really a parody of the doctrine of *theosis*, namely the sanctification of man through the spiritual path (the *unitio deificans*), whence its appeal precisely for unhumble souls. It is the direct and promethean inversion of Christ's words, "My kingdom is not of this world", for *theosis* ("making divine")[26] is premised not on the macrocosmic transfiguration of creation as such, but on the individual soul's microcosmic transfiguration from the human to the divine—or at least, holy; which transfiguration in turn benefits, or at least

---

24 In theological terms, "hell" amounts to damnation, but this term can also be amplified to include all the non-central states in the wheel of the *samsara*, namely those covering the cycles of transmigration. For man, to reenter the *samsara* amounts to losing his central state as *imago Dei* and that is a type of hell even when not being hell proper.

25 *Bhagavad Gita*, 8:23-26.

26 The Christian basis for which are the famous words of Saint Athanasius: "God became man that man might become godlike" (*deiformes, sed non Deus*), a maxim that became the centerpiece of Eckhart's doctrine of *die Geburt* or the birth of the Son in the soul.

atones for, the inevitable degradation of the creation itself. In other words, this human perfection is to be sought entirely inwardly, not outwardly, for it corresponds—to paraphrase Schuon—to a supernaturally natural virtuality in every man, which is the capacity of returning to the primordial state. It is this very Edenic virtuality which is conferred through baptism, for instance, or through spiritual initiation such as the Hindu *diksha* or Sufi *bayah*; but, to reiterate, this restoration of man's Edenic virtuality does not contribute directly to the collective betterment of humanity, except in the measure that the world always benefits from the prayer and grace of saintly men and women.[27]

Now to digress a bit, but to cover some necessary background in order to situate individuality in a larger context: spiritualities—*orthodox* ones, that is—are premised on a rigorous detachment from the world, causing individualists see in them a disheartening negativism[28]—really a misunderstanding of the *via negativa* of mysticism—to which they oppose an "optimistic", "generous", "faith in man" euphoric philosophy premised on the mirage of mankind's endless progress. In contrast to the trivial optimism described above, one will want to recall the superhuman penances endured by mystics in ages past, not just for their own sins but also for those of the world, as they strove heroically in solitary prayer, willing to endure super-human penance and displaying a bodhisattvic altruism, while plunged in the *abyssus caritatis* or the "infinite abyss of selfless love". They did so with a compassion heedless of all self-comfort and earthly fruits, those being left entirely to the Lord, whose measures are not man's.[29] But this compassion was directed at dying for other souls—both on earth and in purgatory—and was centered on God and not on the betterment of humanity, for the

27 Heaven may have a social mission for a given saint, but a saint does not approach Heaven on that basis, which would amount to putting the cart before the horse, or namely of making of God an appendage of one's plans for saving the world. And what if God does not wish to save the world? No one considers this, and yet this is the doctrine of the Parousia, or Second Coming of Christ.

28 Hence a quote of the Persian Sufi Junayd: "He who fears God never smiles", a grim formulation no doubt, but far less so when one considers the nothingness of the individual before his Maker; it is meant to counter the smiling, smugly insolent self-comfort of the superficial man who has no fear of God or of the next world.

29 And not just in ages past. As recently as the twentieth-century, Christ tells Sister Consolata, an Italian nun and "victim soul", one might say, in that she lived a life of total mortification: "Live annihilated and enclosed in a single and continual [prayer]: 'Jesus, Mary, I love you, save souls.' Nothing else; the rest does not exist for thee" (quoted in Father Lorenzo Sales, *Jesus Appeals to the World* [New York: Alba House, 2004], p. 104). The lives of Saint Theresa of Lisieux and of Saint Bernadette of Lourdes are also examples of such a sacrificial devotion, and more recently of a Padre Pio, the Italian saint and stigmatist.

world will be the world and cannot therefore be redeemed; any true mystic understands this. Thus, it has been left to our modern age to invent an "activist compassion" set on improving if not transfiguring the world,[30] and not surprisingly given that "social spiritualists" (to give them a name) have no idea what sacred tradition is; or else they somehow manage to see the sacred in an electronic world of global connectedness.

Formulated differently, nothing in creation operates outside of the principle of the circle; therefore there can be no possibility of an absolute or a linear progress, only of a relative transformation within archetypal, therefore principially preset, parameters: each creature—and each age, and each creation—emanates out of a mysteriously invisible and ubiquitous sacred center that projects itself in different substances, reflecting the prototypical marriage of *Purusha* and *Prakriti* described earlier, namely the original proto-cosmic bonded polarization found in the heart of all forms of life. Therefore, if the circle—Plato's sphere when extended in depth—is the principle of manifestation, a circle that according to all nomadic cultures had to be preserved unbroken,[31] then nothing can escape the circle; if such is the case, on what principle then can evolutionists base their fatuously linear notion of "endless progress"? The fallacy of this thesis is that by all sensible measures this kind of progress is as unnecessary as it is impossible—when in fact the perfection of a creature lies nestling in the egg, so to speak, and its post-partum extension is only the material reverberation of its embryonic genius. Correct, evolutionists might respond, insisting that this is exactly their claim: mankind is still progressing towards that peak extension. But the problem of this theory is that not only are a species' characteristics defined *in divinis* for "all of time"—this is the whole premise of a species' uniqueness—but the theory

---

30 True, one finds examples of religious utopianisms in preceding centuries that were meant partly to be social exemplars; however, these communities were not experimental models intended to be transposed to all of society. By contrast, the Teilhardian idea of a "noosphere" (from the Greek *nous* or "mind"), namely of a supreme collective state of higher consciousness, is a kind of cosmic megalomania not least because it is an arrogation of the traditional idea of the Universal Intellect or of the Cosmic Spirit—in Sufism, Ibn Arabi's *Ruh al-Kulli*—which exists independently of man, although refracted as *intellectus* in the intellective heart of man's soul. To be logical: if mankind is progressing to a mythical "noosphere" or a realm where the *nous* ("mind") rules supreme, then the notion of Heaven becomes dispensable, and God useless, because traditionally the *nous* was the realm of the Divine, namely a realm inaccessible to collective man.

31 The lodges of nomads—American Indian tipis and Mongol yurts—are very often circular in form, sometimes with a tent pole in the center, or an opening in the roof, symbolizing the *axis mundi*, or the central and transcending axis of the Spirit.

itself is mired in materialism, no matter how sublimely defined,[32] because true creation begins at a pre-material or supernatural level, in which the embryonic process we know of is not yet operative. Following in the wake of the Platonic doctrine of emanationism, as well as heeding creation myths the world over, the genesis of a manifestation follows a series of pre-determinations in which the divine light undergoes a process of darkening and solidification as it moves from pneumatic infinity to, ultimately (in our universe), material coagulation, or from luminous essence to formal solidity. And a crucial premise to all this is that creation is foremost an act of intelligence in which God conceives of something and the very conception of it results in a creation; indeed, the very word "conception" combines the dual meanings of an idea and its genesis within a womb; in this case, the womb is the divine Mind. In the Koran, this process is described thus: "But His command, when He intendeth a thing, is only that He saith unto it: Be! and it is" ("Ya Sin", 36:82). This is the primordial—and still atemporal—"Be!" (*kun* in Arabic) in which God no sooner conceives of something than it is, propelled by the emphatic instantaneity of his flashing Mind; and then from resounding logoic echo to echo it reverberates out into the primordial substance, *Prakriti*, and finally to the outer reaches of the cosmos before returning, undergoing any number of "material"[33] and non-material metamorphoses—via transmigration, notably—in the process. However, ultimately, man is restored to God only by returning to his supreme original nature *sub specie aeternitatis*, which the Koran expresses thus: "As He brought you into being, so return ye unto Him" ("The Heights", 7:29).

Now it is true that, again following Plato[34]—and most if not all of the different creation myths of indigenous peoples the world over—that a phase of chaos preceded the ordering of our present creation as the counter-shock rupture between the spiritual and material orders; thus, in a relative sense, there is a kind of progress from chaos to order that

32 As with the theory of quantum physics, for example, which no doubt begs to be super-seded by an even more subtly elaborate notion of matter and sub-atomic particles, and so on *ad infinitum*, in a vain quest to rejoin the Spirit via sensory references; hence Shabistari: "In each atom a hundred suns are concealed. . ." (*The Secret Rose Garden of Sa'd Ud Din Mahmud Shabistari*, trans. Florence Lederer [Lahore: Ashraf, 1992], p. 39). This raises the question: what do we know today that this medieval Persian Sufi did not grasp perfectly, in its essence, both literally and symbolically, and did so centuries before our spectrographic instruments?

33 Or what in other realms of the *samsara* would correspond to the material density we know on earth.

34 See his *Timaeus*, in particular.

accompanies the entry into a new dimension of created reality—the breaching of an isthmus separating the hierarchy of orders—especially in the latter phases of a manifestation involving an increasing hardening of the original celestial substance as it moves out to the very periphery of its arc of projection. However, order cannot arise out of disorder; rather any disorder corresponds to the projection of a superior and eternally pre-existing order into a lesser—or denser—substance which undergoes a phase of chaos as it accommodates the creative influx, a chaos that must then be recomposed through the agency of time or of a succession of phases, whence the theories of interglacial ages and the paleontological doctrines of biology and geology. That said, it would be naïve to assume that the order evolving out of the protean disorder involves a process of evolutionary succession, because—paraphrasing Schuon[35]—species erupt out from the subtle state once the earthly framework is ready to receive them, much as the soul enters the womb when the embryo is ready. Therefore, to assume that species are the product of eons of trial and error, the haphazard process of natural selection, is senseless if one allows that each species has from the outset and "forever" its own unique reason—or genius.[36] "God saw everything that He had made, and, behold, it was very good", we read in Genesis (1:31).

Mention was made of the embryo's "readiness". The question of the exact moment of the ensoulment of the embryo is a passionately debated topic, but our inclination is to heed Aquinas' view that the rational soul created by God is not the result of the biological formation of a fetus because, following the Church Doctor's thinking, there is no commensurate causality between matter and psyche (*materia* and *anima*), the soul belonging to an altogether different and superior realm of reality. And just as thinking on the part of man presupposes an existing brain, so too the hominization cannot occur until a sequence of biological processes starting with semen and ovum, then blood, then organs, and so on, has

---

35 In this regard, Schuon remarks: "The coming of man is a sudden 'descent' of the Spirit into a receptacle that is perfect and definitive because it is conformable to the manifestation of the Absolute; the absoluteness of man is like that of the geometrical point, which, strictly speaking, is quantitatively unattainable starting from the circumference" (*Stations of Wisdom* [Bloomington, IN: World Wisdom, 1995], p. 89). Or this succinct Schuonian wisdom: "A 'minus' always presupposes an initial 'plus', so that a seeming evolution is no more than the quite provisional unfolding of a preexisting result; the human embryo becomes a man because that is what it already is; no 'evolution' will produce a man from an animal embryo. In the same way, the whole cosmos can spring only from an embryonic state which contains the virtuality of all its possible unfolding and simply makes manifest on the plane of contingencies an infinitely higher and transcendent prototype" (*Understanding Islam*, p. 107n).

36 Genus = genius.

developed before the actual soul can enter the womb (*On the Power of God*, q. 3, a. 9, ad 9).[37] This is also the position of Islam which considers that the first motion that the mother senses of the child in her womb is the moment of quickening when the actual human soul enters; the same, *mutatis mutandis*, surely applies to animals too. For modern theologians the complication arises when invoking present-day scientific knowledge about embryology not available in the Middle Ages, and even less so for Aristotle—whom Aquinas follows—about the epigenetic primordia of the organs that are the basis for the formation of the species. Our assumption is that Aquinas might have dealt with that by invoking the distinction which asserts, in scholastic terms, that virtuality is not actuality; in other words that even if the full future human being is present already in embryo, there is still a major transition point between a possibility and its manifestation, to say nothing of the fact that there is a discontinuity as well as continuity between Spirit, soul, and body. Jewish authorities, for their part, are cautious in adopting too peremptory an opinion on such a delicate matter, but there is some consensus among Rabbis in describing the embryo as a *safek nefesh* or a "partial or potential person" and not a *nefesh* (or "a soul" or "a person") outright, which term applies to the fetus proper. And Islam's doctrine, as mentioned, rests on the idea of ensoulment occurring well after conception. But, the matter is too complex for us to detail any further here, except to mention its relevance in our discussion of individuation. And, needless to say, none of these remarks should be construed as a pretext for dehumanizing the fetus which is obviously sacred.

It is all too easy, when seeing things from the outside, to overlook the fact that man's essence is uncreate; in other words, everything essential constituting man's being does not belong *a priori* to the order of creation itself but only *a posteriori*, which is why the Sufis say about themselves, "The Sufi is not created" (*as-Sufi lam yukhlaq*); and they also describe themselves as being a "son of the moment" (*ibn al-waqt*), meaning that time has no hold on them for they place themselves in the eternal Now, a "Now" that precedes and succeeds all creations, or in fact is independent of all yesterdays and tomorrows. And, as the Sufi mystic poet Ibn al-Farid specified, God made a pledge of mutual love between Himself and man that was given "before man's soul was clothed in the shadow of his clay".[38]

And this brings us now to the following question: is man's material form the mold of his "evolving nature", or is the psycho-physical cladding of his celestial nature (soul) a projection into *materia*? In other words,

---

37 See also *Summa Contra Gentiles*, II, Ch. 89, 11 and *Summa Theologiae*, Ia, q. 119, a. 2.

38 We are paraphrasing and quoting Reynold Nicholson's gloss of Ibn al-Farid (see Reynold Nicholson, *The Idea of Personality in Sufism* [Lahore: Ashraf, 1964], pp. 22-23).

does man follow form or does form follow man? Evolutionism answers this question by focusing on the effects of the outward on the inward; thus it assumes that an animal's mimetism (or mimicry), for example, is the result of its adaptation to its environment. While the theory of interactivity between a natural setting and the shapes and pigmentation of animal forms and appearances is grounded in biological reality, the question that evolutionists leave out is the possibility of an original symbiosis existing between an environment and its creatures before their materialization, that is to say before their actual creation, namely when they still "existed" *in divinis*. In other words, evolutionists take apparently no account—because they are unable to do so, given their strict materialist epistemology and also given their utilitarianism—of the counter-argument that creatures and their environment are all part of one and the same type of cosmic intelligence. For example, a deer's camouflage is not so much the product of an ersatz defense mechanism, but the expression of this animal's primordial (or original) oneness with his environment, in the sense that a deer is like the animal embodiment of a faculty expressing a holistic—and deeply intelligent—pre-unity with the forest which, in turn, is itself like a reflection of this animal's soul. Or, the deer is the genius of the forest, the forest being like the unconscious part and the deer the conscious dynamic principle, both being finally indissociable. If so, then this animal's "mimetism" is the effect of a much deeper cause than the utilitarian need for survival.

Transposing this logic, a human being's erect body, as well as the intelligence of his features, is a symbolic expression of man's centrality in creation that enables him both to know—and to be—the Absolute. But more broadly, a same divine principle can manifest in every natural realm; thus the solar principle finds an expression through certain animals like the lion or the stag for the four-legged creatures, the eagle or the swan for the winged, perhaps a swordfish for the fish, or a dragon-fly and a praying mantis in the insect realm, and so on. In every animal, insect, vegetable, and even mineral realm there are creatures which are like direct embodiments of the solar principle, whereas the other creatures either reflect a lesser likeness to the sun, or are more representative—to speak analogically—of the symbolism of other planets. In alchemy, the ruling prototype is gold and the other metals are like shades of solar gold; the entire alchemical process—which mirrors creation's hierarchy—outlines the process of the ascension of light back to its heavenly prototype, according to a cosmic ladder in which lead (in this example) is situated on the bottom "rung", being the "darkest" (or heaviest) of the metals, and so on.[39]

---

39 It would be tempting, again for the evolutionist, to equate his science with that of al-

* * *

If one were to find oneself in the midst of teeming multitudes at the pilgrimage in Mecca, or at the *Kumbh Mela*[40] on the shores of the Ganges where hundreds upon hundreds of thousands, sometimes millions, of pilgrims assemble, what would strike us the most, the similarity of everyone or the differences? In other words, is it the individuality of the participants or is it their impersonality? The answer actually is both, because to be given life and a personality by God means to express the One Self in a particular mode; but since the Self cannot be expressed perfectly and completely by any one person—otherwise that person would not exist apart from the Self—It must be expressed by many people, which means every individual will express It in his or her own particular way. At the same time, it is as if the Self, being inexpressible and really formless—*para-Brahma*—were to compensate for that unnameableness by allowing Itself to be named— partially—by an infinite number of creatures, so that each creature, and each individual human being, were like a syllable in naming It in a manner in which the One Self would still be readily recognizable—through our common humanity—but also in a manner revealing the endless variety of qualities stemming from the infinitude of Being.

In essence, our personality is the fusion of two principles: that of the Absolute, whence our uniqueness of being one separate person; and of the Infinite, whence our idiosyncratic distinctness in the sense of being one unrepeatable variant among countless other souls. This twofold principle accounts for a kind of double objectivation of the Principle of *Atma* become *atman*. The uniqueness (deriving from the Absolute) and the distinctness (deriving from the Infinite) may seem to be two different ways of describing the same attribute, but they are not: the uniqueness—even though every other soul repeats this uniqueness—corresponds to an individual's wholeness, namely the uniqueness of being born alone and of having to die alone. In material terms, this uniqueness accounts for an individual's physical body fashioned in the image of God: each human individual

---

chemy, positing that just as alchemy's great work is the transfiguration of lead back into gold, so too is evolutionism's great work the transfiguration of animals back into a human or even supra-human prototype; but this parallel actually occurs outside of creation, namely in transmigration, or in realms where the Self repossesses all of its individual modalities across supra-terrestrial time, and not in creation where each species is the crystallization either of an archetype, a partial archetype, or even its inversion.

40 A gathering popularized by Shankara in the eighth century, who encouraged believers not only to be purified in the Ganges, but to be purified through the company (*satsanga*) of holy men and holy teachings.

shares the same divine prototype and is therefore its absolute and separate epitome; this prototype is what determines his autonomy or the fact that he can move by his own powers, freely and independently of any other creature. Now, the paradox is that this person's singleness is replicated *ad infinitum* by numberless other individuals, each being equally "absolutely unique" or separate; this is the mystery of sameness in variety and this is why each individual is entitled to say "I" as if he or she were the sole self because he or she is a miniature version of the one Self.[41] By contrast, the principle of the Infinite determining the individual distinctness of a person (their individualization), derives from the Infinite's capacity for indefinite originality of variation which means that no one is, was, or will be quite like us—ever—a rather astonishing fact on the face of it, but proof of God's limitlessness. However—and this is a key—both an individual's uniqueness and distinctness are premised on an archetype *in divinis*, and this archetype can repeat itself, but never quite the same way. And this leads us to a question: is our individual particularity the effect of an archetype's perfection—albeit projected in an endless variety of uneven modes—or is our individual particularity due to our individualistic idiosyncrasies? Here the answer has to be that *intrinsically* our individuality corresponds to a perfection, otherwise we would not partake of any reality whatsoever; but *extrinsically* our defects can add an extra "twist" to our individual distinctness, but a twist that is accidental and non-permanent since what matters fundamentally is our potential perfection—namely, the possibility of sanctity as well as of archetypal beauty—which is the enduring basis for our claim to immortality, the substance of which is our blessedness in Heaven; and such a possibility is only for those who in fact have overcome their ego's idiosyncratic separateness, while realizing its divine singularity. The lukewarm Christ so despised have no place here.

Hence, depending on the point of emphasis, the *principium individuationis*[42] is the single most heinous of sins because of the fault of egocentrism—and, by extension, egoism—that it entails, namely of mistaking one-self for the Self—to whatever degree—and therefore, in so doing, denying the Self from shining through us, as well as arrogating prerogatives that can only belong to the Self, such as self-importance,

41 And this is also why murder is a capital crime.

42 In Vedantic terms *ahamkara*, from *aham* or "ego", meaning literally "that which makes me". Separated from the Self, the *ahamkara* impetus is governed by *rajas* (the fiery or expansive *guna*) and also by *tamas* (the dull, inertia-determining *guna*), and not by *sattva* (the luminous and ascending *guna*). Unreformed, it leads to pride, passion, pettiness, on the one hand, but, on the other, to indifference or hard-heartedness. In other words, there is a dynamic deviation and a static one.

dignity, justice, and so on, whence the emphasis in Christianity of each individual being "the worst of sinners" a notion, which despite its logical absurdity, has its point in the alchemy of spiritual poverty, for without this lowliness man cannot be saved. And yet, as we have seen, the *principium individuationis* is nothing other, in its essence, than the Self projecting Itself into manifestation (or duality), and therefore the core of individuation is holy inasmuch as it can be, as it should, a transparent vessel for the Self but obviously not inasmuch as it identifies itself apart from the Self.

Be that as it may, we have left unmentioned an essential component of an individual and that is the feature of impersonality. It may be paradoxical to consider such a feature since it may seem like the negation of all individuality, but if an individual is on the one hand a synthesis between the Absolute and the Infinite, he is on the other hand also a combination of form and substance: the form is what makes an individual recognizably unique, as mentioned above, but this form is at the same time a particularized expression of an underlying substance, namely an individual's common humanity and without this impersonal substratum, which defines all men, an individual's distinctiveness would be utterly alienating; only God can be perfect Form and perfect Totality. Hence, if an individual can manifest the Absolute, at the same time he is nothing before the Absolute, and it is this combination of reality and nothingness that comprises the totality of an individual, or rather the egolessness of a saint. The aspect of impersonality derives then from our nothingness before God, whence the need for self-effacement; but this balances the pole of affirmation or that of our realness through God. Formulated in Buddhist terms, the Buddha is *Shunyamurti*, or "manifestation of the sacred Void".

And this brings us to another important point that may be obvious to many, but not necessarily to all. If spiritual life involves overcoming our ego, the state of egolessness itself does not lead to a kind of trans-individual wonder: in achieving spiritual realization a soul does not just become invisible or nameless or an exact copy of another egoless being: it becomes fully itself in a manner that allows it to be immortally recognizable in Heaven and on earth.[43] In fact, egolessness enhances what is divinely unique about our personality, in that this identity is one bestowed on us by a spark of the Divine Itself in a manner that allows God to manifest Himself through the genius of an individual temperament and particular character traits brought to their acme of perfection thanks to sanctity, or perhaps heroism too; these traits become then like the peculiar facets of a

---

43 In Dante's *Divine Comedy*, the poet recognizes all the deceased souls as he journeys through hell, purgatory, and not least Heaven.

diamond through which the light shines in its brightest effulgence.

Finally, what we love about another person is their qualitative personality. Thus, to take an example, it is the "Lincolnness" of a Lincoln that is so appealing, namely his personal expression of the virtues of stoicism, integrity, compassion, and nobility of intelligence combined with a disarming sense of humor; the unique synthesis of those qualities is what determined Lincoln's special originality. His stoicism, moreover, is made even more appealing because of his spiritual suffering, a suffering undergone in sweetness given his humility and compassion. Without those personal touches, his stoicism would no doubt be less appealing. However, were it not for the spiritualization of Lincoln's qualities and virtues, these attributes would have no profundity. Indeed, spiritual faith is the measure of man.

*   *   *

We cannot close this chapter without referring to a key concept in Buddhism and Hinduism, namely that of *anatta* (or *anatma*), that is "no-self"—a refreshing perspective after the fever of individualism. Taken in its most literal sense, this doctrine suggests that the personality we have is nothing more than an aggregate of impressions, feelings, and thoughts that are temporarily (or accidentally) held together by our physical body in an unstable alliance for the duration of an earthly existence, no sooner than to be completely and utterly dispersed upon death and the dissolution of the flesh, with therefore no *post mortem* individual subsistence.[44] This doctrine is really a reverse variant of the doctrine of the One or sole-subsisting Self, the main difference being that instead of emphasizing the absoluteness of the Self (*Atma*), it takes the opposite point of departure by emphasizing the nothingness of individual experiences. By that token, the entire creation

---

44 The Scottish empiricist David Hume would probably have embraced this concept, he who coined the idea of the "bundle theory" to explain what, purportedly, is the same idea of individual things lacking an essence. We would not have bothered noting this were it not the need to give an illustration of what a traditional doctrine can look like when iterated by modern philosophy. Some modern Buddhists have in fact applied Hume's term to their version of "*anatta*", which is not surprising since the human mind is basically the same across different cultures. Now to be perfectly fair, we suppose many a Buddhist would no doubt argue that there is some posthumous continuation of psychic elements in the sense that even if, upon the death of the individual, these elements do indeed disaggregate, they are then partially recombined in another soul entity, albeit now with other psychic strands, themselves the fragments of previous soul entities. We presume that the Hindu doctrine of the *samskaras* and *vasanas* could be interpreted in such a manner, but all of these considerations fit under the doctrine of metempsychosis, which is too complex to detail here.

becomes a mirage, an illusion, in which ephemeral beings and creatures come and go eon upon eons, like ripples on the same oceanic substance. However, to say that the Absolute alone is Real, does not mean—as we have had occasion to mention several times—that the relative is totally unreal; by contrast with the Absolute, the relative is of course non-real in itself—or non-real ultimately—but in its reflection of the Absolute it is partially real since it is the Absolute itself radiating in refracted mode.[45]

Very well, Buddhists and Hindus will say, but these aspects are the fruit of *avidya* or ignorance and the moment the individual self, through intelligent consciousness, realizes his underlying oneness with the Self, the image vanishes, merging back into the infinite divine substance, with not the slightest trace of its former distinctness. This definition strikes us as being too synthetic in the sense that it excludes intermediary notions, not least the idea of the sanctified ego which persists in some individual fashion in paradise, otherwise there would be no intercession from the saints (Christianity) or from the Buddhas (Buddhism). In other words, one would want to specify that an individual, upon attaining spiritual realization, certainly subsists as a recognizably distinct individual, whether on earth or in Heaven, while being transparently open, as it were, to God who then radiates through the medium of that sanctified self. There is no reason for the saint to simply disappear; in fact, on the contrary, there is good reason for God to now enjoy the fruits of his grace because, to reiterate, in creating man God created a saint and that is why He created man. Put differently, it seems absurdly pointless for God to create man only to have him vanish and totally disappear in the supreme union as if he never had been. Metaphysical purists would even claim that the individual never existed at all in the first place; if so, then God would be totally without friends.[46] At the same time, the nature of love is to merge, but in a manner that distinctness combines with indistinctness; to lose either pole is to end the attraction, namely the aspect of love which is the whole basis of union.

In affirming the above, it is not a matter of discounting the reality either of *nirvikalpa samadhi* (objectless ecstasy), or the *unio indistinctionis*

---

45 Contrary to a common misperception, the Buddha himself apparently never affirmed the doctrine of *anatta*, but rather that of *shunya*, the doctrine of the sacred void underlying all of manifestation, both earthly and divine. In the "Connected Discourses" of Theravada Buddhism, the *Samyutta Nikaya* (4:400), Gautama Buddha was asked if there was no soul (*natthatta*), a doctrine traditionally considered to be equivalent to Nihilism (*Uchedavada*). His response: "Both formerly and now, I have never been a nihilist (*vinayika*), never been the one who teaches the annihilation of a being, but instead have been one who teaches about the source of suffering and its ending."

46 In Islam the term for saint is *wali'ullah* or "friend of God".

(union without distinction) of Christianity, or the *fanu'l-fana* (extinction of extinctions) of the Sufis; what we are saying is that a subject can contemplate and be merged with the Divine through ecstasy while still retaining his or her individuality, transfigured and totally luminous as it then becomes. To borrow a metaphor, it is as if a candle flame recognized its identity with the solar orb but still remained a candle flame; who is to say that this candle flame—in its igneous or luminous substance—is not the Self, and yet who is to say that this flame is not distinct? And who is to say where the distinctiveness ends or begins in this confluence of light? Or who is to say what best defines a flame: is it its form or its substance? In other words, the contemplation of God can take place both in union and in separation, both inside and outside, immanently and transcendentally—albeit there are hierarchical levels. It is as if the individual self and the Self can merge and demerge—even concurrently—in a "fusion without confusion"[47] in which the Self "breathes" the individual self in and out, just as the individual self—simultaneously and reversely—"breathes" the great Self in and out through being breathed in and out by the great Self. The Self knows and loves Itself through our self (now purified and rendered immaculate by Grace) in a ceaseless act of timeless communion in which distinction can be said to be, in essence, another mode of indistinction, just as the sacred Pythagorean numbers do not really divide unity but express its multifaceted radiance. Or, transposed, these are again modulations of the One Infinite: the non-dual dualism, *Prajna-Paramita* or Wisdom-Compassion, of the interlaced masculine and feminine deities that was mentioned earlier.

To argue now in the reverse, if the proponents of a totally literalistic mystical extinction were correct, then the subject experiencing supreme ecstasy would not survive the experience: he would die on the spot. That said, in the *unio indisctinctionis*[48] consciousness can merge between God—or, more precisely, the Godhead[49]—and the human soul owing to the immanent co-essentiality of the soul with the Divine; such a state

---

47 To echo Ananda Coomaraswamy's famous point.

48 Bernard McGinn, in his remarkable series of *The Presence of God*, comes back to a distinction between the *unio indisctinctionis* proper (as celebrated by Hadewijch and Eckhart, among others), based on absolute identity, and the more usually recognized *unio spiritus* (spoken of by a Saint Bernard of Clairvaux) in which the distinction between servant and Lord is maintained in the rapture of union. In some ways this distinction would echo the distinction Christ made between "friends" and "servants" (see John 15:15).

49 For wherever there is God there has to be the duality of the servant and the Lord; only in pure Godhead are such polarities transcended, whether through contemplative consciousness or after the *maha pralaya*, the ultimate reabsorption of creation into supreme Non-Being.

leads either to a temporary cessation of individual self-awareness or to a continuously conscious inherence of the soul's substance with its Divine Essence; but in both cases the individuality, blessedly transfigured as it now is, still exists just as a mirror filled with sunlight still keeps its mirror nature while reflecting the sun in its most dazzling of brilliance.

And these thoughts bring us once more to an important point: when mystics speak of annihilating the ego, or the complete extinction of the ego, one will want to bear in mind that the ego to be ridden of cannot be the ego as such, but only the passional or fallen ego. In reality, one might say there are three egos: 1.the individualistic or passional ego, fallen and thus in need of redemption; 2. the primordial ego of Adam before the Fall, that of perfect man as manifested on earth through prophets and sages; finally 3. there is, if one may say, the Divine Ego, or the Self. The individualistic ego must enter into the mold of the prophetic ego in order to be able to rejoin the Divine Ego. Thus, to quote Saint Iraneus, God became man so that man might become God, and God becomes man through the prophet or the sage. This doctrine was at the heart of Meister Eckhart's teachings, and indeed he further elaborates it by stating, with his usual boldness: "If you want to know God, you should not just be like the Son, rather you should be the Son himself."[50]

To avoid any unfortunate ambiguity in the point being made here, the following may be said: the passional ego corresponds to a deviation or an inversion of primordial man; that is why it is in need of conversion, of a turning around, which will feel, to the profane ego, like a turning upside down when in fact it is a turning upright. To grasp the implications of conversion, one could say that the ego as such has two dimensions, one static, the other dynamic. But in the fallen ego, the static dimension freezes and thus leads to a hardening of the heart. And the dynamic dimension— the prototype of which is either vital faith and love when oriented to the inward, or right action when oriented to the outward—becomes (again in the fallen ego) agitation, restlessness, and dispersion, and an inability to find repose. Thus, on the one hand, what is hard or congealed in man must be melted and, on the other hand, what is scattered must be gathered and re-centered. Individualism corresponds to the outward ego and individuation to the converted or to the archetypal and inward ego. Fallen, or outward man, and especially worldly man, is soft where he should be hard and hard where he should be soft. When conversion is completed—by the unction of the grace of Heaven and not by individual will—man becomes both

---

50 Quoted from Bernard McGinn, *The Harvest of Mysticism in Medieval Germany* (New York: Herder & Herder, 2005), p. 148.

gentle and strong at the same time, thanks to the bracing elixir of the now converted heart, whose wishes are at once strengthening and appeasing: "I sleep but my heart waketh", we read in the Song of Songs.

* * *

Each person represents an individual possibility partly reflected in their life, or cycle of moments and phases from cradle to grave. Now if one could look at an individual outside of time, his human possibility would be seen as a type of instantaneous circle in which the sequence of phases from youth to old age would appear in a kind of synthetic totality. But to be a creature means to live in time, and thus to live out each aspect in a succession of distinct modes since it is not possible for a soul locked in a flesh and blood body to live several phases at once on the formal or material plane. However, man's center of consciousness is situated, as it were, at the center of the circle of his possibility—a center where the human intellect and the Divine Intellect meet, and indeed are one. For an individual, access to his immortal center is theoretically possible at any given moment in that his center is ageless because it is timeless and therefore also perfect because joining with the Divine. Therefore, no one is compelled in principle to be just a youth or just an old person; there is always access to the freedom of the ageless center, which also coincides with our moral conscience, since living up to oneself really means to live up to our deathless essence which stands as a witness over our self-expense, if one may so term it,[51] namely the manner in which we spend our vital capital—to echo the Gospel parable of the sower.[52] But to transpose this idea to its macrocosmic conclusion, we are presented in Zen with the image of the master having the disciple dab a point with the paint brush, representing his individual possibility, then of painting a circle around this; by so doing, the master indicates that the point can radiate out to include the whole universe for, in essence, we are not just an individual dot, but, through the perfection of our circle, a compassionate part of the whole circle of creation. Thus, in being truly one-self, we merge into the boundless mystery of One Self, because our life or being is also Being itself and our consciousness is Consciousness in itself.

51 See the Koran, "*Qaf*", 50:21 and the famous metaphor of the "driver" and the "witness" which, we assume, stand microcosmically for the passional will (or the desire nature) and the faculty of consciousness (or the intellect).

52 See Luke 8:4-8.

CHAPTER 6

Beyond Good and Evil

Why callest thou me good? There is none good but one, that is, God.
(Matt. 19:17)

Wherefore, my brethren, ye also are become dead to the law by the body of Christ.
(Rom. 7:4)

Man, seen from outside, is born at the fulcrum point between good and evil, or between adoration and revolt. No other creature has this momentous leverage—or supreme privilege—of choosing virtue, namely immortality, or its opposite, oblivion; this is one signal proof of man's divineness of substance because only a creature of god-like dimension can reject God—or the Good—, free-will being, in essence, a divine prerogative. Now, the choice of rejecting God is also the freedom of rejecting freedom, for freedom and God cannot be dissociated.[1]

In everyday practical terms, freedom—or free-will—consists in man's ability to choose between one good over another good or, morally, to choose between right and wrong, or between good and evil, and it is this choice that represents a dilemma which some spiritual thinkers believe should be transcended because, for them, showing any preference always presupposes partiality, namely a self-interested ego. In other words, according to this perspective true spiritual detachment is impossible so long as we betray some favoritism in our choices, because a preference reveals and perpetuates egoic being. But to speak of individuation is to speak of choice, and to speak of choice is—vertically—to speak of good and evil.

The domain of earth is a symbol not just of our fleshly world but also of all of the innumerable samsaric worlds found outside of Heaven (the *Brahma Loka*) dotting cosmic manifestation; therefore, our earthly existence recapitulates, symbolically, all of existence in the *samsara*. And these non-heavenly worlds are ruled by vertical opposites because the good reflected in them cannot be unalloyed; it mingles with corruption and is therefore precarious, not least for the reason that these worlds themselves are not enduring as are the heavenly realms. As a result, creatures situated outside of the immortal Elysian Fields, have to expiate their otherness from God through suffering and loss, and even damnation which is the ultimate

---

1 Freedom is the reflection of the pole of the Infinite in manifestation.

ransom of duality or the ultimate pulverization of every false otherness that stands up against God. It may be argued that even the Elysian Fields themselves are finally reabsorbed into Godhead, which is true, but their outwardness with respect to the Divine Essence is not the outwardness of our earth—or of realms similar to our earth.[2]

Beneath—or outside—the celestial sphere, we enter into the realm of opposites, a cosmic sector ruled by the contending poles of light and darkness, being and non-being, life and death, happiness and suffering. Thus, to say that one wishes to transcend "good and evil" really means that one wishes to transcend negative oppositions, but not that one intends to transcend the Good as such, because the Sovereign Good (the *Summum Bonum*) cannot have any real opposite since it coincides with Reality and hence with Totality; thus there is nothing, within the metacosmic realm, that is situated "outside" of It. Furthermore, there is no symmetry between good and evil, not least because evil is only a perversion of the good and thus does not have a substance of its own: its reality is that of a shadow albeit a shadow's effects can be ravaging; but, it should be noted that evil's destructive power derives completely, and *a contrario*, from the force of good subverted and not of itself. Now if the principial Good cannot be opposed, the manifested good can be opposed on the cosmic plane, although never in a fundamental manner—save by man—since the other "oppositions" belong simply to the order of imperfection, decay, or disease and therefore not to evil proper.[3]

Even so, can one still ask whether it is possible to transcend good and evil on this cosmic plane, the good being here an opposable good—or a relative good—in the sense of being a good that can stand in contrast not just with evil, obviously, but in fact with another good? The answer to this question requires a subtler explanation. Put differently, this is the same as asking: does every individual good reflect the Sovereign Good? Or does it reflect It perfectly? The answer is "yes and no", or "yes" but perhaps only partially. This is where a distinction can be made between what in Christian theology is known as the "morally good" (the *bonum honestum*) and the

2 Metaphysically speaking, the heavenly realms are not perpetually enduring, but compared to the non-heavenly realms, in which separation predominates over unity, one could say that unity and not separation determines everything in them, whence their perfume of eternity. Moreover, in the heavenly realms, we assume that polarities are complementary, the antithetical polarities being found only outside of them.

3 It is possible, in other words, for man to oppose truth and virtue on earth, and hence for him to oppose God either directly or by implication, something that no other creature can do.

"Sovereign Good" (the *Summum Bonum*).[4] Pseudo-esoterists are prompt to pride themselves in what they think is their capacity to stand above the "morally good", or above what they dismiss as "exoteric" morality, when in fact they themselves are not even above flattery. But to imagine that one can be above exoteric morality is really to misunderstand the nature of morality as such, because even though a distinction can be made in some fundamental respects between exoteric—or social—morality and essential or universal morality, no human being can legitimately place himself outside of the notion of morality as such. If one is to be "the morally good", then it can only be in the name of a higher or fuller morality.

Profane man for his part, especially if he has a "good character" and is "nice" or good-natured or even kind and thoughtful, has no sense that he needs to atone for anything. Of course, a criminal may have the same conviction, but we are not speaking here of gross immorality or of a psychopathic monster, but of a person who would be considered to be "good" by any socially acceptable standard, namely of someone who does have a conscience; and that is precisely why this person's complacency is so problematical. Now, all things being equal, to have a "good character" is obviously not nothing: it can be the fruit of "good *karma*" and therefore may not be devoid of original merit—or, more accurately, of merit accumulated in a "previous existence"; but it corresponds more to a fund of goodness passively acquired at the moment of birth and hence to a fund that can be easily squandered away since ease of being can lead to carelessness or to a false assumption that all is fine. For example, getting along well with people and being a decent person may dull spiritual vigilance, and this is a critical lapse, not to mention that it may lead to a kind of unconscious presumption about one's individual merits; in fact, being popular may be quite a misleading yardstick regarding our intrinsic merit; conversely, some of the most strictly moral of individuals may not be easy to get along with, precisely because of their high ethical standard, and a "not nice" trait such as gruffness may even be a mark of virtuous seriousness, or of a personality not fond of tolerating fools. But, in the end, being loved by God and not just by men should be every man's paramount concern.

Now, this example of a good but non-religious person leads us to a classic disclaimer: atheist freethinkers believe that "one can be good without God". In other words, for such people morality does not require a divine basis to be fully moral, or so they assume, but without pausing to consider the shallowness of such a definition of goodness, for if the essence

---

4 A third category is that of the *bonum utile*, or what is of practical use, namely a utilitarian good; but this is not relevant to our topic because it is a purely pragmatic and thus a non-moral question.

of goodness is holiness ("wholeness"),[5] then one cannot separate goodness from God; only the saint would be truly good, not in himself obviously but because he is united to the source of the sole good which is God. By removing the Absolute from their equation, relativist humanists then leave goodness to be "graded on a curve", so to speak, a human curve naturally, that is to say one presupposing a widening degree of ignorance or blindness, if not increasing arbitrariness, and certainly one that rejects the ideal of an absolute moral perfection. Moreover, when a sliding scale standard is used, brokered through ever-shifting compromises and the convenient rationalizations of the averageness dogging multitudes, then it becomes difficult to differentiate true goodness from social expediency. In such circumstances, the notion of the good ceases to be a truly superior standard; instead, it becomes adulterated into something that does not inconvenience the majority of people, at which point the whole idea of goodness itself becomes a relative affair, a utilitarian goal centered on psychological happiness and no longer on the divine epitome of absolute goodness.

Profane humanists may counter that because man cannot know God, man is then just as arbitrary in establishing what or who God is, in which case "divine edicts" are really nothing more than abusive human interpretations about what is or is not Divine.[6] But this opinion is wrong on several counts: firstly, it denies the possibility of Revelation, namely of God speaking to man; secondly, it denies the objectivity of the heart-intellect, as well as of its extension which is the moral faculty of the conscience of right and wrong; thirdly, it denies the infallible instinct for the Absolute which is inherent in man, otherwise he would be nothing more than a rational animal—an instinct, incidentally, that can only originate in God Himself since God is its self-referent object; and fourthly, as previously mentioned, and not least, it denies the possibility of an absolute good, the *Summum Bonum* of the Platonists, the notion of *Dharma* of Eastern philosophies, or that of the Tao.

Be that as it may, even abusive interpretations of religion presuppose a supreme divine Entity; in other words, there is always enough of the truly divine in morality interpreted—or misinterpreted—by men so long as the Divine remains the standard of reference, however indirect or human-

---

5 "Hale" and "health" also share the same root as "holy".

6 In a twist on this fact, the "profane believer"—preposterous as this term may seem—will rashly assert that he needs no temple to worship God in. What he overlooks is that he cannot address God before he has had a sack and ash cloth conversion; to think otherwise is insolence. However, post such a conversion, he would be entitled to heed Christ's injunction to worship God neither on Mount Gerizim nor in the Temple, but "in spirit and in truth" (John 4:24).

ized or even distorted. The fact of the matter is this: either there is God, in which case to refer to Him means that He can guide us despite our abuse of things in his Holy Name, or there is no God, but then there would be no goodness worthy of the name either. Hence, better in the end to have imperfect religion than no religion, and that is often the only choice available in an imperfect human society; the point is, however imperfect or awkward religious morality may be when in the hands of men, it still refers to God as opposed to an ersatz morality defined by atheists which is inherently meaningless because it is based finally on nothing except the opinions and conveniences of erring humans.[7] Furthermore, even if atheists believe morality can be defined by man, they are still forced to borrow, wittingly or unwittingly, from a heritage of religious morality in order to put this morality into practice; one cannot, after all, reinvent the wheel: religion = morality. Finally and not least, even a standard that is subject to corruption or degeneration still remains a standard and that is why people are able to recognize its corruption in the first place; in short, corruption can only occur if there is something that is not corrupt at the origin.[8] The very notion of morality, in fact, is proof of man's divine origin.

*   *   *

Man is fundamentally good, or so it is affirmed by many philosophers and even by many Christians for whom the idea of Christic redemption is not effective if it is not stated as a doctrine of all-encompassing love—a love excluding no one, absolutely no one. But what does this assumption do to the doctrine of hell? If love must exclude no one, then the doctrine of hell promulgated in all the religious revelations becomes a mere rhetorical gimmick and not a cosmological necessity; in fact, it would be a titanic lie, and diabolically malicious at that. Be that as it may, the idea of God's "goodness" defined in such humanistic terms, if accepted literally, eliminates the idea of the God of Judgment, and all the more so if man is inveterately

---

7 Such is the type of morality a Camus wanted to promote, albeit tinged with dread despair—of course! What else can anyone expect of a "godless moralism", for ultimately this is a contradiction in terms? However, it is worth noting that Camus' despair was unconsciously spiritual in that his "absurdism" concealed a longing for salvation that he could never justify rationally. We point this out to be equitable, as well as to note the paradoxes a nonetheless intelligent soul faces in the wasteland of modernism.

8 Of course, the main example here is that of religion: the possibility for religion to become corrupt or degenerate does not disprove the principle of religion, which is based on a suprahuman notion of the good fitted to man's weakness and ignorance. Neither does disease disprove health.

good. However, if evil exists, then too there has to be an extreme possibility of evil, and hence a cosmological necessity for hell; otherwise evil would triumph, or else there is no evil. And to understand the cosmological necessity of hell means that one must understand the full consequences of what man's freedom and intelligence entail.

Yet, oddly enough, the affirmation that "man is fundamentally good" is not altogether wrong, provided it is situated correctly. What should be said is not that this or that individual man as such is good but that man "created in the image of God" is good; in other words, by virtue of man's theomorphic essence all individual men have access, in principle, to a divine kernel of absolute goodness in their innermost essence. But, quite obviously, this cannot mean that all individuals will benefit from it because with this divine kernel comes the gift of freedom and that freedom, precisely, includes the possibility of rejecting God and by extension the Good—otherwise it would not be freedom. Therefore, a given individual can forfeit his divine essence, leaving aside the fact that some individuals are inherently evil, and are therefore unredeemable; but to understand the implications of this latter affirmation requires situating the individual in the larger context of the *samsara*, namely that of transmigration.

As alluded to above, to believe the contrary, namely that man is inherently good, is by implication to question Divine Justice on the one hand, as well as to debase the whole notion of goodness on the other, and therefore to underestimate the nature of evil itself. Not least, it is also a clever-sounding manner to peddle our own human goodness cheaply—in the hopes of easy mercy for our faults—and therefore to shirk the deeper implications of our human vocation as creatures of God. Indeed if God is merciful He is also rigorous; this means that the very quality of His mercy is highlighted by the rigor of His justice, and not the contrary as is so often assumed, namely that proof of His mercy is the mildness of His justice; to assert this is to reverse a cosmic equation. In practical terms, to assume that none of our human failings are serious enough to warrant eternal hell is *ipso facto* to make light of profanity or to minimize the notion of sacrilege, to say nothing of sin itself. Moreover, to suppose that even the most heinous human being still possesses some kind of goodness in his core—and is therefore deserving of our love—is to blur the distinction between good and evil itself, because the reason evil is "evil" is because it not only disavows the Good, but seeks in fact to exterminate the Good, absolutely and utterly; that is why it is evil and that is why it is unredeemable. And here believers can be as culpable as secular humanists, for they can carry the notion of "goodness" to absurd extremes, for instance in the manner in which they may apply the exhortation "love thine enemy"; yes, indeed, but not blindly. These words of Christ are meant firstly to neutralize passional enmity, namely to break the cycle of karmic vendettas, and secondly to affirm a general principle of goodwill towards all men in virtue of their inherent theomorphism—in principle at least, because to extend goodwill to an overtly evil person risks our facilitating his evilness, thus making us complicit in this evil to some degree. In other words, what Christ wants to promote is a profound predisposition to forgive our fellow man in virtue of his potential if not effective goodness, and not the idea of literally forgiving someone who does not wish to be forgiven or who does not repent. We regret having to belabor the point, but the sentimental notion of the innate goodness of mankind is so deeply ingrained in humanist education that various arguments have to be brought to bear to situate some of the pitfalls of this issue.[9]

Free will is the measure of man's intelligence just as, in turn, his intelligence is the reason for his free will: there would, in other words, be no free will without intelligence, and vice-versa. However, in the last analysis, man's goodness does not belong to him: "Why callest thou me good", Christ asks. Goodness is really situated outside man inasmuch as man is defined as a separate creature from God.[10] In fact, without God man is nothing but ignorance, weakness, faithlessness, error, treachery, passion, and blindness. "God alone is good", Christ affirms. How then could individual man ever situate himself "beyond good and evil", he who is not even good?

*　*　*

To return to the question of religious morality applied to a civilization, it is worth pointing out that a body of laws and morals is not meant to lay down the foundations for an ideal society, but to establish a pragmatic norm that is ideal for a collectivity—though not necessarily for its most gifted individuals—while still reflecting the trace on earth of a celestial ideal that obviously can never be duplicated literally given the imperfection of all things earthly. As such, a moral code is intended above all to forestall myriads of evils, rather than to promote myriads of goods. As with any compromise,

---

9 Remove law and order and it will become quickly obvious how "good" mankind really is. In other words, the only reason many human beings are "good" is because of the very threat of justice and nothing else.

10 Hence Meister Eckhart: "The fount and living artery of universal good, essential truth, and perfect consolation is God, God only, and everything not God has in itself a natural bitterness, discomfort, and unhappiness, and does not make for good, which is of God and is the same as God, but lessens, dims, and hides the sweetness, joy, and comfort that God gives" (*The Works of Meister Eckhart*, ed. Franz Pfeiffer [Kila, MT: Kessinger Publishing, 1992], p. 311).

the interests of the more qualitative human individuals can be sacrificed for the good of the collectivity, that is to say, sinners and saints have to abide by the same rules when living together even though the rules are meant for the sinners. When criticizing such a moral code—in the name of what far-fetched utopian alternative, one might ask?—modern man forgets or dismisses the evils that such a code is meant to forestall. And because traditional moral strictures may curb or crush a particular good or liberty or pleasure—such as dancing—that may be perfectly licit in itself, modern man throws out the whole apparatus of religious morality as being repressive, without grasping that the relative human benefit gained comes at an immense cost, whereas for a traditional morality the same human benefit lost comes at an immense gain.[11]

What these considerations come down to is that the perfect solution or the perfect world that humanism aspires towards does not exist and cannot exist on earth, and this for cosmological reasons, because society can never be a paradise; it can only—in the best of circumstances—be an imperfect reflection of it. To take a few examples, the prohibition of meat in Hinduism, or of wine in Islam, or of making graven images of the Divinity in both Judaism and Islam, none of these prohibitions singles out an object that is necessarily a cause for sin in another religious tradition; this is where it is appropriate to speak of an "exoteric" or opportune morality as opposed to essential morality as such. The different restrictions of the religious traditions mentioned have to be seen not in isolation but in terms of a total cultural and even ethnic context; thus, if a Semite has a propensity towards idolatry, edicts prohibiting images have a purpose, but one that need not be transposed automatically to other cultures whose people may have a vastly different mentality and for whom the presence of images may, on the contrary, be vitally necessary to anchor and nourish popular faith—their absence leading just as surely to irreligion, as the presence of images can lead to idolatry in another society. But iconoclasm, corresponding as it does to a necessity in the spiritual economy of a society, has been a feature of all of the great civilizations; the question then becomes one of accentuation or of degree, so that in Christianity one finds a profusion of icons in the Russian and Greek orthodox churches, but an austere elimination of them

---

11 An example is the case of children born out of wedlock, formerly a cause for shame, today virtually the norm but at the cost of the degradation of the whole society, because only a fool would not concur that children benefit from being raised in a religiously and socially homogeneous environment of a two-parent household. Now, with the "benefit" of social and moral freedom allowed adults with nary a hint of stigma, they are free to have children outside of wedlock in a "structure" so loose that it has turned into a continuous social experiment.

in Protestantism—partly the result, it must be noted, of the pagan excesses of Renaissance Catholicism which offers us a fleshly, even quasi-orgiastic spectacle of their abuse. One of the most incredible "changes of heart" occurring at the center of a revealed religion is the case of the Renaissance Catholic Church's adoption of an iconography celebrating the thickly sensual and earthly chocking-out of the heavenly. This spectacle of a once religious art turned profane almost overnight, and de facto idolatrous through over-humanization, is precisely the risk the Semitic prohibition of images sought to preempt. The "idolatrous" dimension here is the future "religion of man" this fleshly and spiritually opaque art laid the foundation for.

To resume our earlier thread, the question of a social morality compelled to choose between the lesser of two evils—as opposed to opting for the truly ideal—can present issues of near inextricable complexity. Thus, to take one particularly difficult example, the status of "woman" in Islam: there is an apparent paradox in that woman in this religion is originally elevated to a sacred or quasi-divine status, the very loftiness of which suggests a zealous veiling in a society where men can behave as beasts. But this praiseworthy notion of protecting beauty becomes distorted, in the hands of the vulgar, through an often harsh moralism where woman ends up being punished for the passion of men who cannot—or do not want—to control themselves; the price she has paid for that is reflected in the sometimes brutal customs that humble if not humiliate her publically, forcing her to wear sometimes barbarically lugubrious accoutrements designed to foil male lust. Thus woman does indeed have a lofty status in Islam,[12] but this status corresponds in practice more to a principle or a paradisal dream than to a living reality; this is partly due to the nature of the *Kali Yuga*, but not entirely so for, by striking contrast, woman's public status among the desert nomads is vastly superior to her urban status.[13] In its essence, the loftiness of the idea of veiling—and the excellence of the original impetus must be emphasized—associates woman not only with the gardens of heaven on earth, reflection of the celestial *jannat* of gushing fountains,

---

12 At least ideally, because she is also considered to be a dangerous temptress and the cause of civil strife; indeed, the term *fitna* in Arabic means—not without astuteness—both "civil strife" and "woman".

13 Among social examples, Hinduism traditionally extended women, on average, great dignity, notwithstanding the dreadful custom of the dowry, whose modern variants can ruin the parents of a daughter and in fact can wreck a girl's status for life despite this custom's original symbolism of associating woman and preciousness. However, reconciling idealism and realism in the *Kali Yuga* becomes increasingly difficult to achieve as the cycle declines: true idealism becomes more and more impracticable in the exploding population of *shudras* and pariahs that characterizes our world, where all demand rights equal to a maharaja's.

"beneath which rivers flow", but also with the wine of love, not to mention with the ineffable beauty of the Divine Essence, the *Dhat*. Yet, the fact that other religious traditions recognize in their own manner the notion of the *Shekhinah*, or the sacred feminine,[14] and do not resort to such an alienating extremism of defenses, proves that in Islam the practical application of a once noble impetus stems from the crude lack of self-domination of men in general. Yet, one would like to think that true manhood rests in self-domination and not in brutal oppression.

In a sense, woman is really too esoteric a possibility, as presented in Islam *de principio*, to ever hope to be understood properly by the masses *de facto*, who then mistreat her out of a tortured combination of reverence, fear, and passion.[15] That said, it is crucial not to extend the decadence of a noble principle, as illustrated by the masses of latter-day Islam, to earlier epochs of that civilization where the splendor of safeguarding that principle finds a unique mode of expression displayed not just in the people's mode of dress, but also in an unparalleled architecture celebrating the walled sacredness of the inward—"the kingdom of Heaven is within you"; here the genius of Islamic art as seen in recessed courtyards, hidden gardens, and abodes, and not least in the genius of customs keeping the essence veiled, carrying a perfume of paradise on earth. And, needless to say, a culture that recognizes the mystery of beauty's sacredness has to be intrinsically noble.

Beauty and nobility notwithstanding, and to further explore the paradoxes resulting from the clash of sacred idealism and the unavoidable barbarity of human nature, the irony—which is not lost on profane free-thinkers—is that religion can become anti-religious, so to speak, due to its own excessive moralism. In other words, a religious moralism that becomes obsessively fixed on the idea of "man as sin" can overplay its hand to the point of forgetting that man is God's noblest creation; and therefore, in punishing man to an unnatural extent creates a backlash where nature eventually avenges itself from excesses it cannot absorb short of dying.[16] It is here that the providence of Islam comes to correct the sometimes over-zealous ef-

14 The *Shekhinah*, of course, refers to the Divine Essence as such, which is neither masculine nor feminine; but traditionally, the essence is often depicted as feminine and it is the cosmic prerogative of woman to embody that owing to her mystery of inwardness.

15 No wonder God prohibited wine to Muslims; we suppose He could not prohibit women also, but presumably not for lack of wanting to!

16 *"Chassez le naturel"*, the French say, *"il revient au galop"*, or "chasing away what is natural ensures it will come back apace" (literally "at a gallop"); this is akin to over-bending a tree or a huge bow which at some point either breaks or snaps back violently.

forts of both Judaism and Christianity to penalize man's sinfulness, for Islam restores a balance between this world and the next; it does so through its sacramentalization of the natural pleasures of the flesh, which are legitimate so long as they are not abused and especially if they are consecrated. Thus, taking the broadest possible view of mankind, not only do we find correctives within a single religion itself,[17] but also between religions—for instance the crusades—and therefore between different historical epochs and cultures, showing us that history is a series of tendencies and counter-balancing movements, although in the end these cannot reverse humanity's implacable cyclical drift away from Heaven. However, even if the tide of mankind's descent cannot be definitively stayed, the cosmic and historical counter-balancings are meant to restore and to preserve a primordial equilibrium that is each time expressed anew, and dazzlingly so for awhile, through the genius of each new traditional civilization, thus helping to slow down or offset the general cyclical decline of humanity at large. To take an example of this kind of counter-balancing, part of the providence of Buddhism was to restore a spiritual equality of humanity that Hinduism, through the excesses of an over-stratified caste system, risked destroying, just as, in turn, part of the providence of Hinduism was originally to erect a caste system meant to protect the spiritual essence of the best of men from intermingling with the rising proliferation of baser men over time, thus sheltering society from degeneration. But even a Heaven-revealed solution cannot avoid the warping and ultimate deformation that comes from this clash between the ideal and the vulgar; in the end, such cosmic interventions can only be compromises, recalling the Buddhist doctrine of the *upaya*, or "heavenly stratagem", designed to save the largest number of souls with an often blunt morality but at the expense of promoting a spiritual ideal or perfection unattainable by the masses. A proper understanding of this dilemma is crucial for situating religious "excesses" in a realistic context or for understanding the necessary limitations of moral systems applied, not to an elite, but to the common man who is unfaithful to his divine vocation and prey to cravings, passions, and vices uncontrollable save for religion's strictures.

Having said this, we are loath to say anything about religions that may undermine their prestige and doctrinal credibility; religions' enemies abound in the *Kali Yuga* and we do not want to give these any more reasons either to gloat in their profane freedom or to criticize an institution that is divine in its origin, coming as it does initially straight from Heaven. How-

17 For instance Christ asking Saint Francis in a vision to repair his Church which is in ruins ("Francis repair my falling house"); or Krishna appearing to the warrior king Arjuna on the battlefield to restore justice.

ever, if it is only natural for the faithful to revere religion devotedly in all of its aspects, beliefs, and precepts, it is also necessary to point out that religion is purely Divine only at its origin and in its ultimate goal, which amounts to saying that it is completely sacred only in its intemporal substance. But, in the human span stretching between divine origin and divine end, religion cannot be absolutely sacred in all of its forms because, outwardly, it is the product of the encounter between God and man, or between Perfection and imperfection. Furthermore, this encounter is not with man as such in his sacred and majestic Adamic prototype, but with man as he happens to be socially, culturally, and temporally in the cyclical crumbling of time. It is this "religion"—or what amounts actually to the imperfect human dimension of religion[18]—that pseudo-esoterists, incidentally, imagine transcending: these "esoterists", equipped with a certain horizontal intelligence or culture—but lacking a true vertical intelligence—notice the stiff limitations of a given religion, be it that of its dogmas or eschatological symbolism, but at the same time they are unable to translate the real meaning of these dogmas and symbolism, and are therefore unaware of the extraordinary realness and wondrous profundity of the sacred they are dismissing. Now, even assuming that someone might be competent enough to recognize the limitation of form (by contrast to the essence), he should then not forget that every man carries within himself, generically by virtue of his collective humanity, the stigma of the Fall; therefore no one should lose sight of the fact that fallen man as such is not entitled to transcend—let alone dispense with—the rites or liturgy or sacred symbols in themselves, but only their humanized excesses. Hence, to take one example, if, for a Christian exoterist, the image of the passion of Christ stimulates his piety in direct measure to the graphic depiction of the Savior's agony, we would say that it is not morally incumbent on an intelligent believer to revere the sensationalization that the gore and agony of the Crucifixion can lend itself to; however, it is incumbent on him to humbly respect, if not be shaken to the very core of his soul by, the dolorous greatness of the sacrifice of Jesus' last moments on earth; indeed, the essence of Christian compassion redeeming the cosmos is to be found in this image.

The question of revering the spirit of religious forms, but not necessarily their over-humanized literalness, requires further explanation because the

---

18 We recall Schuon saying something somewhere about exoterism being a kind of betrayal of religion, and that only esoterism is true to the original message of the revelation, because only esoterism understands the integral nature of man and therefore of God who created him. Similarly, the German romantic poet and playwright Schiller could state daringly but also nobly: "Which religion do I profess? None of those you mention to me. And why none? Because of Religion" (*Mein Glaube* ["My Credo"]).

truth is found somewhere between the twin excesses of an iconoclasm blind in its fury and a devotionalism that can be just as blind in its quasi-idolatry; it is therefore crucial not to rashly reject one in the name of the other. On the one hand, man—especially collective man—needs some concrete and palpable religious symbols to grasp, otherwise he is left shoreless before the immensity of the divine Void. At the same time, when Heaven provides him with forms—in principle sacred—this can incite a tendency towards a type of massive literalism as well as a type of idolatrous pantheism which truly contemplative and intelligent men will recoil from—"Sufism is all courteousness", it is said, which reminds us of Dante's *cuor gentil* or "the gentle and noble heart"; this is the essence of spirituality. The difficulty, where applicable, arises partly from the limitation of earthly forms to properly receive a divine imprint in that the fathomlessness and ineffability of the Divine cannot be accommodated without some awkwardness by the earthly mold, whence the necessity for and the genius of sacred symbolism. However, this collision between a perfect Spirit and an imperfect earthly mold is seen in the possible clumsiness of the artistic form, be it a statue, a painting, or even scripture itself, to say nothing of the faithful's own human ability to express the Spirit; but the incompatibility between form and essence can be more than overcome by the intelligence of the symbolism depicted. That is also why, among other things, saints or spiritual masters can be underestimated because their human body and even their personality can partially mask their spirituality, giving unperceptive people the impression that they are merely human, or "just like us"; but a saint should not have to walk on water to be revered. That said, a saint, even a *bodhisattva* or an *avatara*, can suffer from illness, irritation, sadness, or any number of human traits or ailments;[19] but none of these affect his essential selflessness, or the God-consciousness, which rules his entire life, day after tireless day. That is to say, a saint, who is a man who has died to the ego and therefore to the world, lives in a state of permanent awareness of God—all his reflexes take God into account everywhere—while at the same time having to endure the humbling vicissitudes and mortifications inherent to the flesh and to physical outwardness in general, namely of having to exist on earth with a corruptible body and surrounded by objects all fated to decay. Thus, there is a certain unavoidable contradiction between the saint's luminously selfless inward state and his outward state, and it is this outward state that he shares with other men, but without being determined by it in his character—or morally—except in the most external of senses,

---

19 "And they say: What aileth this messenger [of God] that he eateth food and walketh in the markets?" And: "We [God] never sent before thee any messengers but lo! They verily ate food and walked in the markets" (Koran, "The Criterion", 25:7, 20).

such as having misgivings, discouragement, being upset, and the like. In the Koran, God often speaks to Muhammad saying "do not be discouraged" or "do not be aggrieved". In fact, in the Koran the prophet Hud, anticipating this problem, asks a skeptical people: "Marvel ye that there should come unto you a Reminder from your Lord by means of a man among you, that he may warn you?" ("The Heights", 7:69).[20] And, in the *Bhagavad Gita*, God in the form of Krishna enjoins Arjuna to be of a firm disposition and not swayed by either gain or loss, which is another form of enjoining man not to be swayed by "good and evil".

Needless to say, man as such cannot transcend man; however, he can—*Dei gratia*—transcend the fallenness or imperfection or outwardness of man, so as to be freed "from the law of sin and death" (Rom. 8:2); or he can transcend ignorance, passion, vices, in other words every limitation inherited by post-Edenic man. And he transcends vice through virtue because virtue corresponds to essential man just as vice corresponds to accidental man, for it is in virtue that man resembles God most, whence this Sufi supplication: "I seek pardon for all in me that is not God."

*   *   *

Though man cannot transcend the duality of "good and evil"—because, as mentioned, to transcend the Good is senseless—there are however several possible meanings to this statement which can make it more intelligible. If it means that the duality of fortune and adversity are to be transcended, that both gain and loss, health and sickness, joy and sadness are to be treated with serene dispassion, then there is a profound point to it because these dueling polarities implicate the ego's wellbeing; according to this logic, to be overly affected by changes of circumstances is proof that the ego has not yet been overcome, because the Self—as well as the spiritual aspirant inasmuch as he can identify with the Self—remains essentially unruffled in its innermost substance by all such shifts in fortune; in other words, the believer's happiness—or his faith—should not depend on outward circumstances but on his relationship with the Divine; and that is why it is said the Sufi is "not created" (*lam yukhlaq*). By that token, the supreme saint is the man who is no longer just this being, but who is identified with Being itself in its immovable fullness; no filling or emptying touches him: "This is full, that is full; though this fullness comes from that fullness all that remains is fullness itself".[21]

---

20 The same argument is also made in chapter 50, "*Qaf*".

21 From the *shanti mantras* in the *Upanishads* (see *Brihadaranyaka Upanishad* and *Isha-*

Yet, regarding detachment, it would be pure pretention to claim that a human being could be entirely indifferent to extremes of adversity, unless he were made of stone or in a state of permanent *samadhi*; to be a human being is to have feelings and sensations, and thus it is not "feelings and sensations" which must be transcended but allowing them to overrule our intelligence, or to disrupt our serenity and trust, namely the qualities betokening the sincerity of our faith in God. Rather, what one should say is that the true sage's "love of the Divine" remains unaffected by changes in fortune, and not that he cannot suffer like another human being does. Fluctuations of circumstance are transcended through detachment or equanimity because wisdom—as well as faith—teach us that through all the tribulations of existence, God is still God and therefore remains ever-merciful; in other words, the Sovereign Good, like the sun, remains undiminishedly good and radiating whatever our earthly fate may be. Likewise, microcosmically, the access through our heart to the Sovereign Good remains totally open at all times because our heart's core and the Sovereign Good are one and the same and thus cannot be blocked by any earthly trials—trials, incidentally, which can originate also from a super-abundance of wellbeing or riches, and not necessarily from suffering or indigence, whence the admonition in the *Bhagavad Gita* (12:18) to treat pleasure and pain alike.[22] And this is in fact another possible meaning for the affirmation of "transcending good and evil".

Another possible meaning is that the plane on which good and evil collide is finally a relative plane since on the level of the *Summum Bonum*, all negative dualities vanish because the Sovereign Good, being Totality, has no opposite; nothing can exist outside of It. Hence, the "good" manifesting on the secondary plane is really a relative good, even though it partakes of the Good as such. Earthly joys and pleasures fit into this category and are therefore of the kind that can be renounced. But in concrete terms, the evil that can beset them—be it through mere deprivation or be it through corruption—and especially the notion of sin occurring from the abuse of these pleasures, this risk of evil (or sin) can become irrelevant for someone

---

vasya Upanishad). The term "fullness" is synonymous with the Absolute.

22 In this same chapter 12 of the *Bhagavad Gita* (verse 17), mention is made of man "re-nouncing good and evil"; this seems to be the common translation, but it is one open to misunderstanding. Our assumption is that reference here is not being made to absolute "good and evil", but to what is "beneficent" and what is "harmful", or as one English trans-lation offers: "who renounces both *auspicious* and *inauspicious* things" [italics ours]. The "beneficent" or the "auspicious" is not quite the same thing as the pure Good; this is a cru-cial nuance that goes to the heart of this chapter's thesis, for the relative good can indeed be renounced, but not Good itself, as we keep on remarking.

who has realized such a luminous depth of purity that temptation is no longer even a possibility.[23] Such is the nature of the pneumatic mystic, whose soul ascends naturally to Heaven and cannot fall since for it the law of gravity operates in reverse mode: in other words, Heaven's attraction, for this soul, overwhelms the pull of gravity.

However, even non-pneumatics can in principle, presumably through purification, attain to this level of "sattvic attraction", as a Hindu might say. And indeed this is the deeper meaning of this passage from the Epistle to the Galatians: "If ye be led of the Spirit, ye are not under the law" (5:18), and which Saint Augustine formulates thus: "Love God and do what thou wilt";[24] in other words the pure cannot act impurely no matter what he does.[25] It should be specified, nonetheless, that if those "led by the Spirit" will not do certain things that morality finds reprehensible, it does not mean that they will necessarily heed every moralistic injunction; the medieval French mystic Marguerite Porete, for instance, makes this very clear, saying that pure love is restrained by nothing.[26] We have already pointed out that if social morality can be disregarded then it can only be in the name of a supreme morality—in the sense of the Vedantic declaration *Tat tvam asi*, "thou art That" namely the "blessed Self" (*Chandogya Upanishad* 6.8.7)— and not out of libertine impunity, let alone a licentiousness claiming a divine freedom as spurious as it is self-serving—the classic excuse of false mystics who claim they are above the law and therefore that everything they do is blessed and who further assert that even religion itself must be transcended to reach the Divine, when in reality it is their narcissism that convinces them of their goodness and therefore induces them to presume that everything they desire and do cannot but likewise be good.

---

23 The English mystic, Lilian Stavely, describes a "higher part" in the "intelligence of the soul": "Separated from worldly things by an impalpable veil, it rests above all such things in serene calm, and strangest of all, has no comprehension whatever of sin and evil: when we enter this part of the soul and live with it sin and evil become not only non-existent, but unthinkable, unimaginable: we are totally removed from any such order of existence" (*A Christian Woman's Secret* [Bloomington, IN: World Wisdom, 2009], p. 89). What she is alluding to, finally, is a degree of *samadhi*.

24 *Ama Deum et fac quod vis* or *dilige, et quod vis fac* ("Seventh Treatise from the Epistles of Saint John").

25 And here we rejoin Krishna's injunction in the *Bhagavad Gita*: "Be, O Arjuna, free from the triad of the *gunas*, free from pairs, free from acquisition and preservation, ever remaining in the *sattva* (goodness), and self-possessed." (2:45). Krishna specifies to be "free from the triad of the *gunas*", but not from the *guna* of *sattva*, and this corroborates our thesis.

26 *The Mirror of Simple Souls*.

To amplify the above considerations, one can also consider "beyond good and evil" in the specific manner of some saints, for example Saint Teresa of Avila, who said: "Not for the Heaven Thou hast promised me am I moved to love Thee, and not for the dread threat of hell am I compelled to cease from offending Thee."[27] The basis for this statement—which echoes that of some Sufis who want to refuse Paradise for the sake of God alone[28]— is that, to paraphrase what was said earlier, when Heaven speaks to man It is obliged to address an all too average mentality which is inherently passionate, more or less mercenary, and perhaps cowardly, a mentality that is easily cajoled, flattered, or intimidated and that will not be motivated to seek salvation except both through the attraction of great rewards and the fear of dire threats. The crudeness of that mentality, as well as its childishness, is something that appalls noble mystics—such as a Marguerite Porete or a Saint Teresa of Avila—who are moved by the pure love of God and not by the prospect of personal gain or loss. Thus, inasmuch as this sense of gain and loss can be a spur to a baser self-interest, nobler aspirants will disdain those lures and scare tactics as impediments to true mystical union. Hence, the deeper meaning of going "beyond good and evil" could be synonymous with the idea of looking "beyond Paradise and hell" in the sense of "beyond reward and punishment", notwithstanding the unfortunate implication that anyone might dare scorn Paradise. In truth, however, it is not Paradise as such they are rejecting—despite certain appearances—but, first, the enticement of some bribery intended to reward a soul "for being good" and, secondly, the greedy sensualist's vision of a Paradise overflowing with food, merriment, and luxury, and all manner of delightful carnal pleasures that, precisely, we are told to renounce on earth. There is indeed something singularly unappealing in the image of men being unable to be virtuous except on condition of receiving an honorarium in the Hereafter, as well as in the image of a God "forced" to lure souls with the bait of pleasure, souls who would otherwise remain indifferent to His message and envoys.[29] At the same time, realism forces us to concede that it would be extravagant or

---

27 "Sonnet to the Crucified Christ". And the Spanish mystic goes on to say: "And though there were no Heaven, I would love Thee still, and though there were no hell, yet I would fear Thee."

28 On this topic, see for instance, Frithjof Schuon, "The Two Paradises", in *Form and Substance in the Religions*.

29 The Koran, in particular among all sacred scriptures, talks tirelessly about marvelous rewards or of threats of a ghastly fate if God goes unheeded. But such divine dialectics— all questions of its symbolism notwithstanding— finally sheds light on the nature of man much more than on the nature of spirituality. In other words, this scripture addresses man of the *Kali Yuga*, not of the *Satya Yuga*.

BEYOND GOOD AND EVIL

unrealistic to ask the average man or woman to give up the world just for the sake of God, a "God" that for a sensualist can only be an abstract entity. Pascal's wager comes to mind here, which he crafted for libertines or any person loath to give up earthly comforts for an invisible God; indeed, how does theology appeal to a worldly mentality that believes "a bird in the hand is worth two in the bush"?

On the other hand, if such a pragmatic motive has its place spiritually, then it should also be understood that some men and women are naturally attracted to God for the sake of the Divine as such; for these, then, the expression "beyond good and evil" carries some real meaning; their heroism lies in the wager of risking everything for God alone.

* * *

More profoundly, however, there is a degree of union that transcends not only the world, but Paradise as well, or at least the idea of Paradise as a realm where a soul can taste of God while still in a state of separateness, namely of loving God in a subject-object duality and which, therefore, is not the ultimate degree of union. As alluded to earlier, mention has to be made of two different levels of selfhood, the one of sanctified realization or the *unio mystica* and the other of the *unio indistinctionis*, a degree of union in which the difference between the human subject and the Divine object is erased; these heavenly degrees could be said to reflect respectively, in man, the difference between salvation (or blessedness) and realization. The first type of union involves a distinct subject, the sanctified soul, enjoying union with a distinct object, God, whereas in the second type of union, the very notion of union is ultimately shed since the knowing and loving subject is reabsorbed totally in God's being which—as Eckhart emphasized—is characterized by the absence of all distinctions—absolute Selfhood or Godhead (Eckhart's *Gottheit*). Now, by definition, such a degree is unattainable by the individual ego's own initiative and therefore it is not a degree of union that can be aspired to by design; it simply happens by supreme ontological beingness (ipseity or selfhood) in which the knowing and affective subject is formlessly reabsorbed into his root ontological identity in the Self beyond time and space; moreover, this union is operated entirely from the Self "choosing" to absorb this subject, in actual fulfillment of a oneness that had never been sundered in the first place. Likewise, there is Paradise as ordinarily conceived and then there is the Paradise of the Essence, without there being a clear dividing line between the two because the Self is as such wholly One, and is therefore the One blissfully aware of Itself through all the human gradations of mystical consciousness. And in being aware of Itself as One, the Self *ipso facto* abolishes all otherness.

To open a brief parenthesis here, we must not forget in all that is said about man situating himself beyond good and evil, that it is really only God who can be said to be beyond such polarities, and not man, who as such is pure outwardness and therefore bound to polarities. Thus a Sufi such as Ibn al-Farid can make God say: "These are in Paradise and I care not; and these are in hell and I care not."[30] A surprising statement, on the face of it,[31] which however not mean that God is indifferent, as human language would suggest; we surmise rather that his unity remains undisturbed by any duality, either blissful or painful.[32] Thus there is a dimension in God which so totally transcends duality that any creation—or rather manifestation, since the reference is to Heaven and hell—ceases to exist as outwardness, while still existing inwardly but then understood to be so immanently bound to Godhead that its very separateness is actually an element of the fullness of the Supreme Self; in other words, totality is not totality if it does not encompass the possibility of separation. At least, such an interpretation can apply with regard to "those who are in Paradise", where immanence prevails over transcendence; but it is far less clear how this applies to "those who are in hell" because, precisely, the dimension of hell is premised on separateness not as qualitative distinctness but as alienation. However, it is truer to assert that God's oneness allows for no gaps than to say that God's infinity allows for gaps; thus, in a certain sense, God's infinity may seem to conflict with God's absoluteness (or oneness) since it entails duality; but all duality, whether blessed or conflictual, exists within—never outside—an underlying unity, and it is this unity that remains forever total, unriven, undisturbed, no matter what the existential experience of individual creatures may be. Now, in empirical terms, the painful dimension of duality as separation is clearly a paradox—and a bitter one for the creature in the pangs of suffering—but it is similar to the mystery of death occurring within the substance of life. Thus, to paraphrase Ibn al-Farid's quotation, this could perhaps be said: "These are living, and I care not; those are dying, and I care not" for, as is stated

---

30 *Ta'iyyatu'l-Kubra*, v. 746, quoted in Reynold Nicholson, *The Idea of Personality in Islam*, p. 31.

31 Because being attributed to the personal God when what is involved here, we assume, is the supra-personal Godhead who alone is "entitled" to make such an affirmation.

32 In this sense, and according to Bernard McGinn, Eckhart "insists that God is above being and goodness" (see *Harvest of Mysticism*, p. 97). McGinn mentions that Eckhart criticizes the onto-theology of Aquinas, because God as *puritas essendi*—which Eckhart identifies with *intelligere* (or the act of intelligence)—is beyond both being and anything knowable that can be ascribed to Him.

in the *Bhagavad Gita*, life and death are one and the same for *Atma*: "the wise grieve neither for the living nor for the dead . . . the unreal hath no being" (2:11, 2:16). Duality, in other words, is a by-product of unity and therefore can never be a truly independent reality as such, no matter how great the agony of a given creature trapped in duality; in fact, the pain is really the part's agonizing tribute to a unity denied. In that sense, man can take his stand, intellectually and spiritually, either in the substance or in the accident, his faith actualizing the permanently underlying divine mercy without being able to abolish separation outwardly; but even then, when mercy is actualized, the outward that was a shackle becomes a lever according to the principle of grace that "my yoke is easy, and my burden is light" (Matt. 11:30). For the believer, the whole cosmos conspires in his salvation.

However, to return to Ibn al-Farid's poem, we might also paraphrase the second assertion ("and these are in hell and I care not") as follows: "As to my bounteous mercy, I remain unperturbed while ceaselessly saving the worlds and beings." In other words, from an essential perspective, it is permissible to say that God is detached even from his own infinite Mercy; and in a certain ecstatic sense it might be said furthermore that God's self-ecstasy overwhelms the awareness of a duality, adding that the very fullness of that self-ecstasy is precisely what provides mercy's irresistible force because by nature it radiates heedless of any obstacles, repossessing all separateness continuously and forever.

* * *

In closing, mention was made of two levels of selfhood, but in actuality it would not be improper to recall the doctrine of the "triple ego" or three levels of subjectivity mentioned earlier in the book: one is the outward ego, that of imperfect man in need of conversion and purification—the fallen ego if one will. Then we have the ego of perfect man, of the prophet or *avatara*, the model as well as the mold for the reformation of the fallen ego: "no man cometh unto the Father, but by me" (John 14:6). Finally there is the Divine Ego, or the one Self. Now, these three selves are all found in each individual ego, whether potentially in common man, or virtually in the faithful, if not actually in the saints. The immanence of the Divine Ego in the individual ego can be likened to that of water with respect to the drop, or of fire to the spark: it is not that the individual ego can encompass God but that the Divine Intellect within its innermost heart is of one substance with the Divine itself. This Divine Self, or essence, is beyond all dualities, but since the individual cannot be identified with It as an individual, the individual cannot transcend duality so long as he remains an individual;

or, put differently, he cannot transcend duality, let alone good and evil; or he cannot do so and yet remain an individual.[33]

If concentration on the Unmanifested (*avyakta* or "incomprehensible to the senses") is a self-cancelling proposition for the individual or fragmentary ego, it is nonetheless a conceptual possibility—as well as an ontological possibility—and therefore also a human possibility in the sense that the world in all of its aspects can be contemplated as void (*shunya* in Buddhism) since all of its manifestations are ever-changing, impermanent, and therefore, like mist, melt before the sole Real. In that sense, the world as well as one's ego and its myriad play of impressions, thoughts, and desires, and all dueling dualities can be seen as a suffocating sheath that the spirit in us longs to slough off. But setting such a goal, as the *Bhagavad Gita* warns, is difficult and dangerous for the individual ego because there is a risk of trying to reach the Absolute through bypassing man—or rather of doing so bypassing everything divine in man, starting with the virtues;[34] without self-noughting, the ego can instead become fatally inflated and mistake its-self for the Self. The more usual path back to the Self proceeds through the conscious choice of the True over the false, the Real over the illusory, the Good over the bad and then, having properly recognized this duality in its fullest implications and consequences, to concentrate wholeheartedly and at every level on the True and on the Sacred; indeed, when the Good is properly discerned, It will naturally and *ipso facto* attract the totality of the individual aspirant, just as evil, when properly identified, will *ipso facto* repel the soul; this is why there can be no integral spiritual path without prior discernment, that is to say: without an acute awareness of good and evil, precisely. The rest lies in the hands of God.

---

33 Schuon addresses this problem: "The conclusion of all these considerations is the following: in order to be able to conceive of transcending egoity, it is first of all necessary to thank God for having given it to us; before seeking to 'transcend' or to 'objectify' mental faculties and with them sensations, thoughts, and emotions, it is necessary to know how to make a good use of these faculties. One can only go beyond the mental and psychic faculties in the measure that one has realized of them a sufficient perfection; to attempt to go beyond them *a priori*, on the basis of an initial program and without further ado, can have the most harmful of effects and amounts in principle to a suicide; luckily, were it not for the incredible tenacity of human nature, things could be much worse" ("Reflections Concerning a Letter", undated).

34 "The difficulty of those whose thoughts are set on the Unmanifested is greater, for the goal of the Unmanifested is hard to reach by the embodied being" (*Bhagavad Gita*, 12:5).

CHAPTER 7

Satan Is Not an Atheist

The fool hath said in his heart, there is no God.
(Ps. 14:1)

Thou believest that there is one God; thou doest well:
the devils also believe, and tremble.
(James 2:19)

And remember when thy Lord brought forth from the Children of Adam, from
their reins, their seed, and made them testify of themselves, (saying): Am I not
your Lord? They said: Yea, verily. We testify. (That was) lest ye should say at the
Day of Resurrection: Lo! Of this we were unaware.
(Koran, "The Heights", 7:172)

Let us for an instant imagine a godless world. Or, rather, let us imagine a
world in which man would be the sole god. And, to the point, let us then
raise this question: can man be a sovereign of his universe without God? In
other words, what is man without God? The truth is that a godless world
could not long be sustained, for without at least some reference to the Divine, all values would turn to dust or become a matter of pragmatic, if not
tyrannical, self-interest; and a self-interest heedless of anything but personal needs would lead to the cutthroat disintegration of society. A godless
society is something utterly inhuman because the Divine is the ultimate
bulwark of Reality and hence the mainstay of all values. The essence of hu-
manness is man's capacity for godliness; remove the Divine and everything
unravels. Such a bulwark is fictitious, the atheist will aver, but if so then it
is not a bulwark; or there can be no bulwark. In that case, if one knows how
to ponder things in depth, then there could be no Reality either.

Strange to say it takes a measure of intelligence to deny God; that is,
were it not for our God-given intelligence we would not know how to deny
Him. That is, the very faculty that allows us to understand things is also
the faculty that can lead us into cerebral foolishness, in the sense that human intelligence, when not directed to a noble goal, can become the very
instrument of man's undoing. Now, in denying God, it does not occur to an
atheist where this notion of "God" originates, or rather that such a notion
could never arise in the absence of a God—namely, he does not grasp that,
first of all, what does not exist is unthinkable. Nor does he grasp the full
implications the gift of intelligence itself entails, a gift that would be inex-
plicably gratuitous save for the Supreme Object it is fashioned for, because

149

it is always the object that explains the instrument, and not vice-versa. The gift of intelligence, moreover, presupposes the capacity of consciousness, a capacity that by definition has to preexist matter because matter cannot engender something non-material like consciousness, to say nothing of supreme attributes of consciousness such as wisdom and virtue. In fact, atheism comes down philosophically to a form of materialism, of belief namely in the supremacy of matter, however refined the science.

There is no more mediocre person wandering the broad face of the earth than an atheist, for his perspective of the universe is bounded by the four corners of his ego-myopia; in an act of presumption, however unintentional, the atheist assumes, existentially, that his little self is the measure of this universe. And the lukewarm too partake of this inglorious station; that is why Christ spewed them out of his mouth for, like atheists, these complacent creatures, while hedging their bets, profit richly from being human beings but have no wish to fulfill the vocation a human birth presupposes, which is to know the Divine. "But", the atheist provocatively asks, "why should we believe in a God no one sees?" Or, "Were God so obvious—or so great—how could anyone then not notice Him?" All questions of a prodigious dearth of imagination aside, the answer is that the lot of man on earth requires faith, inasmuch as he is estranged from his divine origin. Conversely, everyone has to believe in something, otherwise they could not arise in the morning; if belief in God is rejected, what instantly replaces this credo is belief in oneself, for man cannot live without faith in something. Fair and well, the atheist may rejoin, this is precisely a formula for credulousness if not superstition; and indeed it can be, but this objection sidesteps the main issue which is that the Greater is what determines the lesser, and not the other way round as his secular logic posits. In a word, the mediocrity of the atheist resides in this: at heart or by default, he really believes only in himself, or in what his immediate existential situation dictates, and there is something unwholesome, even contemptible in such a limitation, as if the atheist wanted to hoard the priceless gift of life and the miracle of intelligence all to himself. But the unavowed premise of such a reflex is that he—profane man—becomes the epitome of creation, at least in the absence of any other contenders. And in that miserliness of soul he calls to mind Christ's parable of the servant entrusted with one talent, whom the master said would be "cast into outer darkness" after his having had "taken away even that which he hath". Transposed to our analogy, the symbolism of the talent becomes that of the miracle of our birth in a central state, which is a gift loaned to us for our spiritual fructification while on earth.[1]

---

1 Matt. 25:14-30. In essence, this parable echoes that of the sower and the good seed (Luke 8:5-15), with all due allowance to the difference in metaphors, because the seed in the second

"Cast into outer darkness", Christ declared. Why such harsh a sanction if this servant did no more than faithfully safekeep his master's talent, not spending it, though not investing it either? The problem is that an atheist, far from being "the epitome of creation", is the epitome of indifference to Heaven and of dullness of soul, no matter how humanly charismatic he may otherwise be; there is a deadness in his heart, however buried beneath a professed love of humanity. Is it his fault? An invisible God gives us everything while leaving us stranded in major risk of doubt as to his very existence—"I girded thee, though thou hast not known me" (Is. 45:5). Again, is it really the atheist's fault? To offer one clue, and this cannot be minimized: doubt in a Creator derives finally either from taking oneself implicitly for a god, by over-estimating oneself in some degree and measure;[2] or else it can derive from having absolutely no imagination about what the incomparable grandeur of the human state entails, and in that case the lack of imagination—or the intensity of the doubt—coincides with some degree of unuprootable self-contentment, consciously or otherwise, which leads us in fact to the same cosmic dead-end. From an ontological standpoint, however, there can be no excuse, for if indeed man is created in the image of God, he carries then this imprint eternally in his substance, that is to say he carries it before his entry into and after his exit from the human state; therefore he can only ignore it through some active denial of his conscience; his paltry excuses to the contrary will not hold up tomorrow at the Day of Reckoning where he will sharply remember what he was so conveniently wont to forget today. But, in the last analysis, man is judged by his own divine essence; that is to say, his immortal substance, will stand in judgment over him. "And every soul cometh along [on Judgment Day] with a driver and a witness" (Koran, "Qaf", 50:21).[3]

There is a paradox in the fact that God can, in principle, save a vicious sinner whereas He can do nothing with easygoing human indifference because He can do nothing with an insipid soul that has no lift, namely that does not want to transcend itself, or that does not shudder at a celestial

---

parable is the word of God; however, both the talent and the seed are a gift from God and call for a proper investment, which entails having faith.

2 "And those who do not seek for a meeting with Us [God] say . . . Why do we not see our Lord? Assuredly they think too highly of themselves and are scornful with a great pride" (Koran, "The Crierion", 25:21).

3 The "driver" is understood to be the individual will and the "witness" man's divine intellect, a faculty which, individualized, becomes man's conscience. Schuon formulates this aspect as follows: "For the final judgment is none other than an aspect of the possibility represented by a particular man. By definition, a possibility wants to be what it is, its nature is its will to be" (*From the Divine to the Human* [Bloomington, IN: World Wisdom, 1982], p. 52).

token; one can tame fire or melt ice, but do nothing with sludge. God can convert a Paul of Tarsus persecuting Christians and transmute him into a paragon of a man, but what of a comfortable atheist, smug in his knowledge, incurably blind to creation's theophanic majesty? No epiphany can touch the soul of he who, imbued with himself, be it only out of lazy inertia, is incapable of being truly good—or, for that matter, even of being bad; or of he who can detect no greatness in his fellow man, thereby forcing everyone else by implication to be as banal as he himself is content to be. Incidentally, the essence of chumminess is the trivial and finally false camaraderie founded in avoiding our human greatness *sub specie aeternitatis*. True friendship, the one surviving all earthly trials, can only be founded on the awareness—and love—of the divine in one's neighbor, and this requires a measure of solemn respect and an exquisite dignity of manners.

By contrast with the denseness of the atheist and the impotence of the agnostic, the principle of evil, in raising itself against the Divine, ends up praising God *a contrario*, whence, of course, its utter heinousness. However its very militancy is a form of recognizing God's grandeur, and this suggests the possibility of a *coincidentia oppositorum*—a "unity of opposites"[4]—even though this does nothing to cancel the opposition on the plane of such oppositions, nor needless to say to lessen the evilness of the opposition; this must be made very clear. If opposing the Divine is a form of proof of God it is in the manner of a reverse proof, that of the most radical opposition possible, no doubt, but thereby a spectacular proof in its own right, for were there not the Sovereign Good, there would be no evil either.

The conflict between these two poles—their appearance of irresolvable dualism—has often led man to deal with them in an alogical or quasi-Manichaean way[5] in an attempt to account for radical opposites while trying to avoid logical contradiction; or else in trying to preserve the idea of the good in its earthly modality. Reconciling such antinomies can lead to theological inconsistencies which irreverent and clever freethinkers take full

---

4 The Bible expresses this via the ellipsis of suggesting that God created evil: "I form the light, and create darkness: I make peace, and create evil: I the Lord do all these things" (Is. 45:7). Or, the Koran: "I seek refuge in the Lord of the Daybreak, from the evil of that which He created" ("The Daybreak", 113:1-2), and other passages, such as God's seeming tolerance of Satan (see for instance Koran, "The Heights", 7:11-18). Also worth mentioning is that the Lord's Prayer implies something analogous in the plea: "And lead us not into temptation", in other words, why would He (the Lord) ever want to "*lead* us into temptation"?

5 Strict logicians may object to our use of the term "alogical", asking what the difference is between "alogic" and "illogic". The difference is that between an inaccurate but still valid description of something real and an erroneous description of the same thing—hence bearing in mind that the inaccuracy may be a factor of the difficulty of conveying in human terms the complexity of the reality described, and not something involving an error of appreciation.

advantage of to disprove both religion and God; they mock the blind faith of believers who believe in the unseen, as if the testimony of a blind man about a fire should be discounted simply because he could not see it. Yet, this is precisely what happens with atheists when discounting the credibility of faith: their position is that the burden of proof for demonstrating the existence of God should rest squarely with believers for believing in such an Entity and not with themselves for denying It. What they conveniently forget, however, is that the nature of the proof entails a twofold hurdle: firstly, surmounting the division between the natural and supernatural (or between the visible and the invisible) and, secondly, surmounting the obtuseness of the viewing subject. In other words, why should the small-minded atheist, pinned in a narrow material universe which he swears by, and locked in his subjectivity which he also swears by, have the exclusive prerogative of dictating what the full breadth of the provable should be? Why should a man trapped in a hole be allowed to pronounce judgment on the metacosm? This is a case of blindness prescribing what vision should be. Indeed, by what right does the person who knows less—or whose imagination cannot overleap certain boundaries—set the parameters of Reality that can never be full-fathomed by man? It is as if someone who had been raised exclusively in a winter landscape would deny the possibility of flowers blooming or of leaves springing from dry branches. How does one prove spring in winter? All things being equal, fairness demands at least that the person who believes in the greater should be the one to enjoy the benefit of doubt, not vice-versa.[6]

This brings us to a reverse problem that in some ways mirrors the myopia of the skeptic, namely of a religious purism that, sublimely intent in preserving the Divine from any earthly stain, ends up robbing this same Divine of all human concreteness. The dilemma for religion, when confronted with the opaqueness of profane man—or of having to combine the ineffable with the corruptible, or the Absolute with the relative—is that it feels obliged to resort to an artificial idealism, one that while securing the sovereignty of the sacred also ends up making Heaven all but incomprehensible or unreal, and, what is worse, of doing so accidentally in favor of disbelievers. It is this kind of dilemma that has led to the genesis of various sects—such as the Cathars, and at least some of the Gnostics before them—to isolate the Divine from any relationship with matter and, in so doing, of widening the divide between Heaven and earth until it becomes unbridgeable. True, the heresy was less in these aforementioned sects' idealism than in the radical exclusivity of their position leading to a

---

6 The allegory of Plato's cave comes to mind here.

reverse absurdity from the one described above, namely to state that the Divine—in the form of Christ, in this instance—could never be incarnated in flesh. We find the same kind of acrobatic disclaimers in Buddhism where doctrines proclaiming that the Buddha never assumed a real human form, only an illusion of a form. Such ideas, when taken to their logical extremes, unfortunately end up ensuring that man can never approach God on a human basis or even know Him—unless extreme and permanent abasement before God, in which human ignorance is praised, be considered to be the only adequate mode of knowledge for a human being. The truth is that religion, of necessity, has to be a balancing act between the rights of Heaven and the "rights" of man—rights man receives by virtue of his divine essence, needless to say. Now, by understanding how inextricably interwoven some of these issues are, and how any dogmatic formulation can trigger a possible counter-reaction, allows us to see how intelligent men can be induced to judge religion over-hastily, for religion is a miracle of light and wisdom and yet, at the same time, a bulky compromise between Heaven and man. The aspect of miracle gives religion its incomparability, the compromise its comparability; and it is often difficult for human beings lacking in contemplativity, or in metaphysical insight—not to mention in faith—to sort these out properly.

In a normal society,[7] that is a society based on a central spiritual revelation and sustained by a living sense of the sacred, the Divine suffuses the atmosphere everywhere, and all the architecture, arts, and crafts remind one of Heaven; in such a setting, atheism cannot take root; it is a conviction that only a madman would dare sustain. By contrast, one of the consequences of the break of modern civilization from religious tradition is the disavowal of the Absolute, which is religion's central doctrinal premise, and consequently the proliferation of relativism; and this relativism corresponds terminally—in the absence of the Absolute—to a deterioration if not to a dismantling of original wholeness; and it is then that the notion of God is either rejected or so misunderstood to the point of becoming virtually useless. As a social or collective phenomenon, this deterioration and ultimate collapse occurs only at the end of a cosmic cycle. By the term

---

7 The question might be asked, what is a "normal" society? A normal society is one that is theocentric and not anthropocentric; or one could say it is "uranocentric"—from the Greek *ouranos*, meaning "heaven". In using the term "uranocentric" we seek to broaden the connotation of the term "theocentric" which, although intrinsically sufficient, might for many readers conjure up images of an abusive theocracy, something the term "uranocentric" does not. Rather, the latter term conveys the whole dimension of sacred architecture, the arts and crafts, and traditional dress and customs; in short, it is a complement to the term "theocentric" which, for its part, covers more the doctrinal dimension.

"end" we mean that secularization cannot occur as a collective phenomenon until the final stage of such a cycle. However, atheism for its part, along with philosophical doubt and skepticism, develops the moment the gap between Heaven and earth becomes effective; thus we read in the *Vedas*—the oldest extant literature known to mankind—"There is no Indra. Who hath beheld him? Whom shall they honor?"[8] Whence the obscure—and heroic—merit of the believer's faith; for man by himself, that is to say in his individualism, is a *de facto* atheist until converted.

*   *   *

When attempting to assess the right balance between Heaven and earth, or the manner in which the spiritual must be integrated with the temporal, one will want to bear in mind that the Divine is the only valid cornerstone of any true scale of values;[9] consequently, one is entitled to assert that nothing has value unless it is connected in some fashion to God, and by the term "God" we mean the most supreme qualitative instance—or Intelligence—imaginable and this has to be the Absolute or else we end up in pure nihilism. Unpalatable as this may be to free-thinkers and secularists, no culture can prosper that is not rooted in a sacred cult,[10] and no cult can be termed sacred if it is not religious in essence. This axiom, of course, works in reverse in the sense that an anti-culture can thrive up to a point by vampirizing a defunct religious tradition, which is exactly the fate of the modern world, for society cannot function without a body of morals, and in its turn morality depends on religion. Whether man understands this or not, or whether he likes it or not, man is forever *homo religiosus* and the day this is no longer so is the day the world ends. Indeed, all of man's cultural heritage, namely his customs and ceremonies surrounding every stage of birth, marriage, and death, derives from religion and it is therefore religion that gives value to his life, because religion—and spirituality, when religion is taken in depth—is the only manner of recognizing the Divine. Thus all attempts to define society by excluding customs that derive from religion would end up dismantling society's very foundation, because no society

---

8 *Rig Veda*, VIII.89. Or: "Before whose majesty and mighty manhood the two worlds trembled: he, O men, is Indra. Of whom, the terrible, they ask, 'Where is he?' Of him, indeed, they also say, 'He is not'".

9 Of course, in removing God from the equation, the atheist denies then the immortality of the soul, a convenient omission that releases him from any eschatological finality when assessing his earthly decisions and actions.

10 Indeed, the very etymology of the word "culture" presupposes a "cult".

can be erected on opportunistic motives. Likewise, all efforts to fashion totally new customs in the complete absence of religion—or to divorce new customs from any kind of a religious basis—can only amount to nothing, or worse, an alien wilderness. The most secular or man-made of customs, if they are to have any meaning at all—and no matter how profane the celebration—can only be derived, however obscurely, from some religious prototype, because birth, marriage, and death ceremonies are ultimately meaningless without the seal of Eternity. Put differently, a relative value is no value at all; without the ray of Heaven, light is a mere glare.

With this background in mind, we can now return to the question of belief in God. A bit of a sly question to ask is: can a villain be a believer? Or rather: is a person truly a villain if he is a believer? Or, reversely, is an atheist *ipso facto* a villain? The answer to all these questions is that a villain is someone who is evil, whether or not he is a believer; and if he is a believer, his villainy is all the more unpardonable.[11] As to the possible villainy of the atheist, the question is that he may not be evil per se, he may even lead a life that is ostensibly virtuous; but his irreparable sin is to throw away his chance at salvation and thus to bypass the vocation of being born a human being, for in forfeiting such an august vocation he does permanent harm not only to himself but, by implication, he injures his fellow men;[12] indeed, and as mentioned above, how can we love our fellow men well if we love not God, for to love another person well is finally to love what is divine in him—or to love him because of his potential divineness—and, in so doing, we help redeem him by addressing his true nature. The atheist's atheism may be due to an infirmity of the will—an inveterate indifference to Heaven, for example—or it may be an active choice, a rebellion against God as in those who are militant atheists, believing that religion is the root of all evil. Either way this person is a spiritual cripple but not necessarily evil per se. Perhaps the dilemma of asking whether an atheist is evil can be answered thus: while an atheist may not be evil, it is—all things being equal—an evil to be an atheist; there is a world of nuance in this *distinguo* which, in the last analysis, only God can solve. However, an atheist's willful rejection—or his hard-hearted ignorance—of redemption amounts to removing himself from the ray of divine mercy, whatever his posthumous

11 Eckhart captured the irony of this type of contradiction in one of his famous aphorisms: "The more they blaspheme the more they praise Him", meaning that all things prove God in their way, which however is of no benefit to the blasphemer, unless he repent.

12 It could in fact be said that every man and woman should be a saint, or strive at least to be one for the sake of others, because in allowing ourselves to be morally imperfect we allow ourselves to disrespect our fellow men, which is a form of harm; no one can be morally imperfect in a vacuum.

outcome. Nonetheless, when speculating about such matters, one must be circumspect about individual cases, for it is possible that the substance of a soul may never be revealed on earth, not until the trumpets of Judgment Day resound and the lids of the graves are removed and souls hasten to their Maker—and not forgetting that "the first shall be last" (Matt. 20:16); in other words, an ostentatious believer may amount to less in the Lord's eyes than a bereaved atheist, depending on circumstances.[13]

In an impulse of misplaced envy, some people—agnostics especially— admire an atheist for "having the courage of his convictions"[14] and for "facing the universe alone in a supposedly heroic stand of self-reliance", bravely going against the grain of fearful sheep-like parishioners, while deriding believers for cowardice and for cringing before a father-figure God meant to allay their childish fears. What is one to conclude from such a misplaced admiration? That man is some kind of superhuman god who can stand up to earthquakes, floods, and, not least, to death? Or, that religious fear equals childishness and stupidity, or in other words that such a fear is never objective or never based on a lucid sense of proportions that has the humility to understand what man's insuperable limitations are, of a humility mindful of the fact that man can be crushed like an ant? Moreover, fearlessness by itself proves nothing since it can be born either from courage or from blindness, either from intelligence or from stupidity, to say nothing of the fact that a healthy fearfulness is finally a measure of wisdom when dealing with what is objectively majestic or what is objectively terrifying.[15]

To further sharpen the contrast between atheism and faith, we shall raise another question: can an atheist be virtuous and a believer a sinner? Again, yes—or "yes to some extent"—because a believer may be, for example, a bad citizen and an atheist a good one. However, in the grand eschatological scheme of things, the virtuousness of the atheist is by definition inherently superficial, just as the sinfulness of the believer is inherently

---

13 This is ultimately a complex question, not with respect to the absurdity of atheism, but of the nuances in individual cases. In fact, it is certainly possible for God to forgive some atheists, given that there may well be extenuating factors explaining a given person's atheism; some people are accidentally atheistical from having been abused in their youth by spiritual hypocrites, for example, or from being the numbed witness of a ghastly genocide; these could be termed accidental atheists, victims of the *samsara*'s vicissitudes if one will, while understanding that nothing happens by chance. But logically, atheism as such is unforgivable.

14 To wit, Coleridge affirms: "Not one man in ten thousand has goodness of heart or strength of mind to be an atheist", which he then repeats for emphasis (Letter to Thomas Allsop, 1820). However, Coleridge himself was apparently not an atheist.

15 "The fear of the Lord is the beginning of wisdom" (Ps. 111:10; Prov. 9:10).

accidental, at least with regard to their final ends, and therefore, in both cases, neither trait corresponds finally to their owner's true substance once stripped of their earthly shell. And as mentioned earlier, there are also accidental atheists—just as there are superficial believers—in the sense that some people can be provisory atheists, so to speak, perhaps precisely out of disgust for religious abuse or stupidity; or their anti-religious bias may be a kind of intelligent defiance begging to be contradicted by true spiritual wisdom, not by dogmatic moralism. Also, strange to say, it is possible for example to love Christianity while hating Christians—a humanly unsustainable attitude, of course, because no one can exclude themselves from the human race by loving a credo and not at least some of those who espouse it; but the point still holds given the idiotic or even reprehensible behavior of some believers, all the more unacceptable in that they profess to be believers, precisely, or namely the very people that should set an example of godliness.[16] Also, some people are stale believers; in other words, they are believers out of convenience or convention and not by conviction. In fairness, one will have to note that there are also evil believers, logically absurd as this may seem, otherwise there would be no hypocrisy, or Pharisees.[17] But leaving such fine points aside, the main argument is simply this: no matter how genuinely virtuous an atheist may appear to be, his rejection of God is no light matter: how could his merit finally measure up to that of a true believer, because the merit of a believer has a supernatural component that adds incomparable luster to his destiny, a quasi-miraculous essence in fact. Hence, to assume that an atheist can be literally just as good as a believer, as some people aver, is to ignore what goodness is, and it is to ignore that the essence of goodness is premised on the supernatural. Conversely, it also amounts to overrating the human, and doing so of course at the expense of the Divine.

Furthermore, as we touched upon above, one cannot overlook that, strictly speaking, every man is a *de facto* atheist even if he is a *de jure* believer, at least until he has been sanctified: "but we are all as an unclean thing, and all our righteousnesses are as filthy rags" (Is. 64:6). Not least, we must beware lest, out of misplaced charity, our tolerance of an atheist hints at a tolerance with our own corruptible self, for many of our attitudes end up being sympathetically self-referent, that is to say until spiritual conver-

16 The Thirty Years War is one good example of such unchristian behavior, although sectarian violence is to be seen everywhere across the ages and, we assume, is tolerated by God since despite its crudeness, it prevents man from taking spiritual matters lightly.

17 Some of the Mahayana Sutras mention wicked monks destined for hell, and Jesus for his part said: "Not everyone that saith unto me Lord, Lord, shall enter into the kingdom of heaven" (Matt. 7:21).

sion (a turning away from ourselves) has become effective. The saint's ego, by contrast, is blessedly theocentric: he sees the universe and man—and himself—only in reference to God, which means that he sees man in God and God in man.

*   *   *

God is an objective Reality and therefore the notion of God is an objective concept—in fact the realest there is. This may sound like the most basic of truisms; it is however pregnant with implications that are easily overlooked but that go to the heart of the atheist problem. To reformulate: as man stands before Reality, he faces essentially two possibilities: there is, on the one hand, God as such, and then, on the other, man's belief in God; these two are not the same thing. Or: we have God and religion, and these two things likewise are not equivalent. It is of course inevitable that God be associated with religion—nothing could be more logical—but the *distinguo* is that in religion God is not necessarily God as such. The very same could also be said, in turn, of religion: there is religion premised on the relationship between "man as such" or archetypal man—the *imago Dei*, direct and still incorrupt—and God, and this is the *religio perennis* or the *fitrah*, or the *sanatana dharma*, namely the primordial religion underlying all religions; and then there is religion premised on "fallen man", or "collective man" post the golden age, and these are the various exoterisms combined to some extent with semi-confessional esoterisms. Some will object that such distinctions are only too obvious but impracticable since the "God as such" referred to is inherently unknowable, or that the religion premised on "man as such" is a Platonic abstraction that, in practical terms, is meaningless when divorced from men. But that is not our point: what we are saying rejoins a more intermediary position, one namely that recognizes that God has spoken in each of the great revelations and that therefore His being is fully present—as pure Divinity—in each of their religions' sacraments, and at the same time our position rejoins a viewpoint acknowledging that in religion God inevitably takes on a veil—disguising or lessening Himself as it were—thus enabling man to be able to deal with Him indirectly or by sacred substitute. Hence both affirmations are true: on the one hand, "religion *is* God" and, on the other, "religion is *not* God",[18] and this is the paradox. If both truths are combined, then one could say that religion is, on the one hand, divine *in its essence* and, on the other, sacred *in its form*,

---

18 Or, if that is too ill-sounding: "religion is divine", but not all in religion is divine since it involves concessions to fallen man.

but that religion is not necessarily divine as such—except by darkened reflection—in its formal literalness, otherwise there would be no veil; indeed, one of this veil's functions is precisely to cover the Divine, and, in principle, providentially so.[19] But, in taking on a human face, God risks appearing merely human and that is where secular humanists scavenge for their arguments to dismiss religion as an anthropomorphic fallacy, and the believers, alas, often assist them by their own fervent ineptitude in dealing in too sentimentally human a manner with God and his saints.[20]

To say that God, or the Divine, is an objective Reality is to say that It—the Reality—exists before and after any of man's conceptions of It, as well as before and after religion. Eckhart, ever audacious, formulates it thus: "before creatures were, God was not 'God'". This is to say—for the purposes of this argument—that if God is a reality at least equal to the reality of a majestic mountain standing before us, then the description of this mountain by men—not to mention its possible negation—cannot logically be realer than this mountain. And yet, the reality of God, for most men, is based on the description of this Reality—or its negation—and not on the immediate reality of the Divine Object itself. The challenge then is to be able to grasp the Reality in itself, at least conceptually, so that our personal ssessment of it is determined not by other people's, or even other cultures' measures, but by the Reality Itself. However, this amounts to conceding that man can only grasp the Divine by ceasing to be man—man as outwardness—since the lot of man banished from the Garden of Eden is to have to know the Truth only from afar and indirectly; to know the Divine Object directly, man has to somehow jump over his own shadow, which is to say that barring supernatural assistance, man is fated to know God only through a veil or abstractly. However, this divide can be surmounted conceptually through metaphysics, certainly, but also to some extent through theology because man can transcend himself intellectually. Otherwise, or existentially, man must begin to know God through abasement. Thus Moses, speaking to God in the desert of the Sinai, asks: "Show me Thy Self that

19 The Buddha is said to have remarked that he was neither a man, nor a god, which is an important *distinguo*. In Scholastic dialectics, a *distinguo* is the art of making a subtle distinction between two aspects of a truth, neither of which can stand alone. In the Buddha's statement, there is a *cedo* and a *nego*, i.e. he concedes (the concession or *cedo*) that he is more than human but at the same time denies (the refutation or *nego*) that he is a god. The *distinguo* is the contrast between the two affirmations. The same *distinguo* applies to our definition of religion just made above. The rest is a word to the wise.

20 For example, some of the Renaissance paintings show the birth of Jesus with so chubbily realistic a depiction of a baby that, contrary to icons, there is not the slightest hint left of the majestic theophany of the event.

I may gaze upon Thee. He [God] said: thou wilt not see Me, but gaze upon the mountain! If it stand still in its place, then thou wilt see Me. And when his Lord revealed His glory to the mountain He sent it crashing down. And Moses fell down senseless. And when he woke he said: Glory unto Thee! I turn unto Thee repentant, and I am the first of true believers" (Koran, "The Heights", 7:143).

While it is certainly true that God can only be fully known by man in the heart, namely in a *unio mystica* finding its fulfillment in man's deepest subjective core,[21] this does not mean that Reality is reducible to an individualistic solipsism in which the whole universe is but a state of personal consciousness projected out onto a grandiose scale. That would be a kind of megalomania, a massive distortion of *Advaita Vedanta*'s formulation that the Self alone is Real; it would be a distortion because such a solipsism involves reversing the poles Substance and accident, namely of allowing the accident to believe it is the Substance, or of having the nature of the Substance being defined by the nature of the accident, or the Real by the unreal; this is like handing the asylum over to the inmates. And yet this is exactly what has been happening across the centuries, especially since the Christian Middle Ages, where man in his outwardness—or in the profane fact of his earthly existence—has become the measure of the universe, instead of being the measure of the universe in virtue of the *Spiritus* he embodies, for it is this *Spiritus* that is really the measure of the universe.

*   *   *

The above comments serve to highlight a crucial distinction found in creation, namely the relationship of continuity and that of discontinuity with the Principle, or First Cause. Creation starts as theophany and as such is an expression of the Creator's Wisdom, Beauty, Goodness, as well as Power,[22] and this is the aspect of continuity; yet, at the same time, being other than the Creator, creation is separation, limitation, and ultimately opposition, and this is the aspect of discontinuity. Discontinuity, however, does not occur at the outset since the opening phases of the creational meta-phenom-

---

21 The *visio Dei*—knowing God in the mind—is an indispensable preliminary to full mystical union and therefore it should not be lightly discarded as is done by pseudo-Zen practitioners and others in what amounts to a suicide of our God-given intelligence: one does not slay rationalism by destroying *ratio*.

22 Or, following Plato, of the True, the Good, and the Beautiful, a triad echoing the Vedantic trinity *Sat-Chit-Ananda*, in which case "Power", mentioned above in the text, is assimilable to the element "Goodness" in Plato's delineation and thus to the Vedantic element *Sat* or "Being". In other words, God's being equals both Goodness and Power.

enon are part of an inherently static plenitude of celestial radiance[23] that only "later", from emanation to emanation, or reverberation to reverberation, eventually descend, through increasing remotion, to denser, more congealed possibilities, of which our material world is like a terminal point in the outward cosmogonic projection.

Situated in this context, the demonic principle now sits, on the one hand, at the point of total opaque density and massive hardness and, on the other hand, at the point of total disaggregation or dispersion. There are in other words two points of cosmic inflexion, one for creation as form and one for creation as rhythm (or motion): the initial form is pure perfection and glory and the initial rhythm is pure joy or adoration; however, in the outermost phases, form eventually becomes separation (discontinuity) and no longer revelation (continuity), while rhythm becomes revolt and no longer adoration. In tracing this arc of projection from the non-manifested (*asat*) to the manifested (*sat*),[24] one will recognize two opposing motions at work in creation, and by extension in history: while creation as a whole tends downwards,[25] and mankind with it, towards a cosmic abyss, there is simultaneously a parallel ascent (the *deva yana* or "path of the gods") compensating the descent (the *pitri yana* or "path of the ancestors"), otherwise there would be a free fall. Microcosmically, this twofold axis or movement is retraced in the inspiration and expiration phases of all creatures. The ascent referred to, however, becomes harder for mankind to maintain over time since it cannot overcome the ultimate downward spiral of the world itself as each cycle of manifestation tends towards its foreordained end. We are speaking of course of a given creation, of a given world, since creation as such is perennial or co-eternal.[26]

In Hindu terms, our reference point is the doctrine found in the *Puranas* in which a cycle of creation is subdivided into four *yugas*; the

23 The reference to a "static" plenitude means that the dynamic pole is still self-contained or beholden to the simultaneity of God's majesty in blissful shaktic devotion as of "yet" unaware of its dramatic potential for "otherness" from the Principle.

24 In Vedantic terminology: from the non-existent to the existent—the "non-existent" being really the supra-existent.

25 Or, according to another symbolism, it tends outward, namely in the form first of an expansion that turns eventually into dispersal, or an expanding fullness that turns into a fragmentariness as the hold of the divine Center onto the periphery weakens; in this symbolism the analogy is that of proximity versus distance, or of the contending centripetal versus centrifugal tendencies ruling the cosmos.

26 In given traditions, however—such as Christianity—creation has a set beginning and ending which is empirically, symbolically, and spiritually correct and therefore *de facto* absolute in the experience of the beings existing within it.

mahayuga (or unit of four ages) itself is part of an immense *manvantara*, but the actual number of cycles and ratios of duration are not what concern us here. What is relevant to our discussion is first the idea of a progressive degeneration and secondly what this process entails. According to this ancient doctrine, creation is exteriorized through the dynamic relationship between the three *gunas*, or cosmic tendencies: *sattva* or the luminous ascending tendency, *rajas* or the fiery expansive tendency, and *tamas* the darkening and descending tendency. In the *Satya Yuga*, or Golden Age (the "Age of Truth"), *sattva*—or wisdom and spirituality—is the sole operating *guna*, the other two remaining latent in *Prakriti* or the primordial substance, whereas in the three following *yugas* all three of the *gunas* are exteriorized in a hierarchical ordering. Thus, in the *Treta Yuga*, or second age, the hierarchy is that of 1. *sattva* (light), 2. *rajas* (passion), 3. *tamas* (ignorance and depravity). In the third age, or *Dwapara Yuga*, *sattva* is replaced by 1. *rajas* as the ruling *guna*, followed by 2. *tamas* and then 3. *sattva*—moving from first to last hierarchically. Finally in the fourth age, or *Kali Yuga*, 1. *tamas* displaces *rajas* as the predominant *guna*, followed by 2. *rajas*, with 3. *sattva* again hierarchically last—or, actually, the most inward—as in the preceding age. According to this ordering, the last age is an inverted mirror reflection of the second age, whereas the first age transcends the other three and, as such, is essentially atemporal and therefore *a priori* immune from the degeneration of the following *yugas*. In the fourth age, moreover, given that creation is reduced to its most material of modes, man as a result lives captive of his body and mind, alienated from his more spiritual bodies, not least his "body of bliss" or, as Hindus teach, *anandamaya-kosha* (heavenly body), and also his "body of intelligence" or *vijnanamaya-kosha* (body of discernment and wisdom). Also, in the latter ages, *sattva*, or sanctity, is not absent, but gradually withdraws from the world, becoming more hidden, in keeping with the "repudiation" of *sattva*, which nonetheless continues to act, however invisibly. The cosmic series of transitions described retraces, in essence, the stages from pure spirituality to a loss of spirituality.[27]

The modern confusion—where relevant—comes from projecting onto the outward or material plane a perfection that the outward plane cannot encompass because it is the plane of imperfection or of separation, limitation, and finally degeneration; therefore creation's original perfection cannot be regained from the outside, no matter how much the utopianism of progress is dressed up as spirituality or explained as the workings of a divine Providence. Indeed, such an assumption, fed in part by the dazzling

---

27 Another traditional way of describing this succession of cosmic ages is through the ratio of virtue to vice which shifts, in the first age, from consisting of three quarters virtue and one quarter vice to three quarters vice and one quarter virtue in the last age.

albeit relative advances of molecular science and quantum physics, is in its own fashion a parody of the Christian millennialist doctrine of "Rapture" foretold, in which the living blessed will be reunited with "them which are asleep" in Christ (Thess. 4:15-17); however, and crucial to note, this "Rapture" occurs post the destruction and purification of the world.[28] Paradise outside of God does not exist and never will: "The kingdom of Heaven is within you."[29] And here again, the evil whisperer is at work, dumbfounding man with the prospects of a kind of physical immortality, or of special mental powers, visionary insights, and extraordinary earthly achievements which, for all their spectacular promise, are in the end non-spiritual and therefore cannot escape the defunctness gripping all material things; they will collapse finally like an air-filled balloon and mother earth in its primordial timelessness will have the last word; grassy plains and forest-canopied valleys will extend again to the edges of heaven in silent wind-rippled majesty, oblivious of the civilizations that had briefly intruded into their impassive immensity.

*   *   *

Now for *de casu diaboli* proper. A central question: does the devil exist? And this question is not quite the same as asking "what is evil"? Seen from the perspective of Neoplatonism, evil does not exist per se as a conscious entity opposing God, but only in the way that darkness exists as the absence of light. And although the idea of evil as a conscious entity, namely Satan, has been more fully developed in Christianity and in Islam than other religions (with the exception of Zoroastrianism), no less an authority in the Christian sphere than Saint Athanasius echoes the Neoplatonist perspective: "God alone exists, evil is non-being."[30] Set against this perspective is the dramatic personification of the devil in both Christianity and Islam, compared to the near total absence of an equivalent figure in

28 The scientific advances are "relative", not in themselves of course, but in their effect on society which is regressing existentially or morally in reverse parallel to material progress. Compared to crude barbarianism, modern man may justifiably feel "advanced", but the problem is that not all so-called barbarians were "barbaric", far from it. One of the less visible aspects of modernism is its patronizing attitude towards earlier cultures; yet that is of course the very definition of philosophical progressivism.

29 Or, "My kingdom is not of this world."

30 *On the Incarnation of the Word*, chap. 1. Athanasius, it will be recalled, is the author of the quintessential formulation of *theosis*: "God became man that man might become God."

Hinduism and Buddhism,[31] as well as in Taoism. Such a disparity between Western and Eastern perspectives about such a seemingly central issue, and therefore one that we might expect to be universally recognized, may be related to the fact that the non-monotheistic religions place much less emphasis on the individual; and yet, the voluntaristic perspective, stressing personal merit and demerit, is found equally in all religions, whence in all cases their highly developed doctrine of hell. Thus the ideas of evil and of the devil do not overlap perfectly, because as just noted it is possible to have a detailed eschatology of hell, without an equal emphasis on the notion of the devil.[32] And here we must distinguish between the relevance of a figure such as Satan in monotheism and his quasi non-existence in other religions—because to say he is less relevant in a number of religious traditions does not imply his non-existence; we shall return to this point.

In the Biblical allegory of the Garden of Eden, there is the tree of the knowledge of good and evil from which man is enjoined not to eat lest he die. One interpretation of this tree's symbolism is that in eating of its fruit man will awaken to the awareness of duality as *separation*—not that of duality as such—and from this separative awareness fatally ensues estrangement from God, and "in sorrow thou shalt bring forth children" (Gen. 3:16). Here then is the beginning of suffering, the scourge of mortality, and by extension the possibility of evil which in essence is the possibility for man to turn against God and therefore against the Good; and to turn against the Good is *ipso facto* to conjure suffering. Prior to this awareness of duality—of duality as separation—man lived immersed in a beatific sense of unity, or at least of a complementarity that prospered on blessed unity. And this situation (or hypostasis) explains that it is possible

---

31 Hinduism, through the *Vedas*, has a notion of the *asuras*, who are like deviated gods which the gods themselves must battle, but there is no central personification of evil. In Buddhism, mention is made of Mara, but he is hardly a central figure in this religion's soteriology and eschatology. Buddhist cosmology is extremely complex, recognizing dozens upon dozens of realms set along a vertical axis, at the bottom of which is the realm of Naraka which corresponds to the monotheistic notion of hell. But neither Buddhism nor Hinduism detail an ongoing battle between men and devils, or between God and Satan, or at least one which believers need to take account of in their daily existence, as is the case in the Christian and Islamic universes. And there is of course the cosmological perspective of Manichaeism, which however has not survived the permanence of the central revelations.

32 These eschatologies do not correspond exactly to the monotheistic ones in that "hell" in Hinduism and Buddhism is not permanent but a realm that souls journey across in their karmic expiation of sin (or rather in their expiation of ignorance, or willfulness, since the notion of "sin" is not part of the dialectics of these religions). Incidentally, a metaphysical argument can be made for hell—in the monotheistic teachings—being "everlasting" but not "eternal", and this would coincide with the teachings of the Eastern doctrines.

to have unity in diversity, because the creation existed before the Fall; in other words, it is important to emphasize that the very fact of the creation does not immediately entail that of the Fall for the motive force of creation is initially intelligence, love, and joy, not separation, opposition, and banishment. Hence, the real problem in duality is not duality as diversity, but duality as division—or outwardness—where man's sense of personal identity (individualism) is now defined as operating outside of God (or separately from Him) and not within Him. Once the individual sees himself as independent from God, the ramifications of this can lead ultimately to revolt—a promethean ambition being as it were the ultimate exercise and bitter fruit of the gift of freedom mishandled. No doubt, "existence" means etymologically to "stand outside", but existence does not in and of itself equal opposition; for existence to become opposition entails an active, conscious choice on the part of an intelligent being, the fact of existence itself being something altogether neutral.

The temptation for man in the primordial paradise to explore duality was overwhelming, for curiosity, like an insane itch once aroused, cannot be suppressed; but Edenic innocence may have endured unclouded for a timeless period before the impetus for cosmic outwardness emerged, because the age closest to the divine Center is infused with this Center's timelessness.[33] That this separative impetus was a latent dimension inherent in creation means that it could not not assert itself over time given that creation cannot be the Creator. Now, why would an omniscient and loving God bestow on man the capacity to harm or even to destroy himself, one might ask? Part of the answer can be found in resigning oneself to the ontological necessity of All-Possibility, because by nature the principle of All-Possibility—originating in the pole Infinity—must exhaust Itself and this includes, as Schuon has pointed out on a number of occasions, the "possibility of the impossible". Moreover, since man has the capacity to know through division and analysis—discernment (or *viveka* in Hinduism) being the crown jewel of that capacity—it is inevitable that, over the unraveling of time, man will carry this kind of intelligence to its final degree of cosmic disassociation, if for nothing else than that it can be done.

It is of capital importance to grasp what the active role of man as willful intelligent consciousness is in enabling this principle of separation,

33 If the question is raised how a modern-day human being can "know" these things, the answer is: through the timeless faculties of intelligent speculation and metaphysical intuition. Cosmic and meta-cosmic realities cannot be grasped empirically but they are in principle accessible to metaphysical and mystical intuition. And, of course, there is the legacy of the sages, not forgetting that the "spirit bloweth where it listeth". Also, the beginning is mirrored in the end, because they are adjacent points on the same circle of time.

because nature in herself—*Prakriti*—is totally neutral or innocent and therefore virgin, so it cannot on its own engender separation and even less evil. Evil, to become effective, entails intelligent consciousness or rather the possibility for this intelligent (and loving) consciousness, once projected into manifestation, to become perverted; in other words, evil is not just an elemental, blind cosmic phenomenon, nor just a neutral Neoplatonic "absence of light". To grasp this, however, we need to define what is meant by the term evil: thus, to say that natural catastrophes, or famine, or disease, are evil is no doubt an overstatement unless one were to conclude that a people struck by such calamities had, somehow, forfeited the grace of Heaven, as we find many examples of in the monotheistic scriptures where God says that He visits upon renegade nations dread afflictions. But these calamities are not so much an expression of evil as they are a cosmic consequence that can be unleashed in response to man's perversity of will. Hence to say that nature has an evil side would be to reverse the entire equation because, in truth and traditionally, it is not man who is the innocent victim of cruel nature (the humanist version) but rather nature that becomes the echo of his waywardness—much as, microcosmically, an individual's abuses to his health will be reflected in his physical body. All the same, one should be wary of supposing that every calamity inflicted upon a nation occurs as a result of such a harsh calculus, because nature "prunes and cleanses"; this is an ordinary part of its homeostasis, so to speak, such that some of what are termed "acts of God"—earthquakes, floods, hurricanes, and the like—are just the fate of creatures on earth: landmasses collide, volcanoes erupt, mountains crumble in landslides, and great rivers overflood their banks. Furthermore, the law of the jungle—cruel as it seems from the outside, namely when divorced from a total cosmic context eluding our profane awareness—is a reflection of the law of Unity preserving itself through, and despite of, the warring competition of creatures; thus the law of the jungle conceals a ceaseless redemptive process operating as part of the unity of creation when maintaining itself outside of paradise, a process taking on a brutal aspect in the outermost fringes of creation where the separation between forms and creatures is quasi-bsolute.

But to return to the question of evil implicating man's consciousness—his intelligent consciousness—and not occurring wantonly, emphasis has always been placed in sacred scripture on the measure of freedom man has for deciding his fate, and more especially on the fact that Heaven's wrath can be stayed by even one pious soul, thus sparing a whole town from God's punishment. Freethinkers, proud of their social maturity, really chafe at the notion of a punitive divine wrath; but this wrath, a necessary dimension of divine Justice, can be likened to the blight visiting a neglected crop—for Heaven stands ever ready to bestow blessings: "We would have opened for them blessings from heaven and earth, but they disbelieved, and so We seized them on account of what they did" (Koran, "The Heights", 7:96). Such a scriptural statement suggests that man holds the outcome of creation's fate to a fairly large extent in his own hands, and this indeed is the doctrine of the Fall in the wake of which nature—originally celestial— darkens and acquires its sinister power to erase entire civilizations.

In another sense, man partakes of existence and therefore resembles nature herself, laboring and groaning in its processes; but such a situation only accounts for nature as *materia prima* and not of nature as the *shakti* of the Spirit, as one would say in Hinduism, or in her goddess-like role as tantric consort of the Spirit, for in that role she is beautiful, fruitful, and maternal, and only turns harsh and brutal when the Spirit withdraws from her; and the Spirit withdraws in proportion to man's evilness, precisely, because evil here is the pursuit of a false independence from God or of a false otherness that ends up separating the soul from the Spirit while erecting itself as a sterile god in its own right; and this cosmic impetus—which is a conscious choice, otherwise there could be no chastisement (or rectification)—conspires to widen the rift between Heaven and earth until an extreme point of unsustainable opposition is reached. Macrocosm (nature) and microcosm (man) work as one: the outward, which is cosmically passive, reflects the inward which is cosmically active.

*　*　*

Regarding now the objective independence of evil and by extension of the possibility of Satan and of demons, let it be said that while it is true that evil has no independent reality of its own—for to exist it depends on the Good, just as disease depends on health, or death on life—this does not mean that evil could not be "impersonated" by a psychic entity. Now to speak of such an entity entails some measure of autonomous existence, for just as there are angels—which are "intelligences" or divine faculties—it is perfectly conceivable that there would be demons, namely evil sentient beings rather than impersonal cosmic forces, for the cosmos is consciousness and not merely existence, and to speak of consciousness is to speak of personification—namely the mystery of individuality.[34] Creation myths, whether among nomadic peoples or in the sacred scriptures, refer to the fact that

---

34 However, we assume that neither angels nor demons have "free will", namely the possibility of going against their nature; this is a faculty awarded only to man owing to his *imago Dei* status. In which case, the principle of individuality coincides with the faculty of free will, or namely that of a total intelligence.

good and evil exist near simultaneously[35] at the outset of creation, indeed on the periphery of the fabled Garden of Eden. And, in these myths, the angels appear—before the creation of man—as divine faculties[36] that have a degree of "personification". By contrast, evil, in its form as a demon, is an "intelligency"—if such a term applies[37]—that has become perverted and indeed the very word "demon" is derived from the *daimon agathos*, or a "good spirit", just as the *asuras* in the *Vedas* were originally gods before falling; Lucifer himself is said to have been an angel.[38] From this, we may conclude that God's awareness of the good—which is the original impetus for the creation of the good—also entails the awareness of this good's limits

35 The qualification, "*near* simultaneously", is intended to take into account the distinction of creation *in divinis* and the creation *ex divinis*, for before difference—or otherness—becomes imperfection, there is perfection. In Christian terms, the Son in his heavenly glory, or the first creation, is incorrupt and incorruptible; he is distinct from God but not apart from Him; he is, to echo Saint Bonaventure, the product of God's self-diffusive goodness—radiating goodness being the entire substance and result of the creative act in its initial phase, something that we want to keep on emphasizing.

36 Likewise, in ancient Egypt, Amun is considered as "father of the gods", who are, as it were, his delegate faculties.

37 When addressing these realities in human terms, it is virtually impossible to avoid the pitfalls either of a clumsy anthropomorphism or a cerebral abstractionism; hence, wending a middle path between the two is the only alternative. Or else, one has to resort to Taoist-like dialectics, referring to notions such as "balance" and "imbalance" or "harmony" and "disharmony", but the risks of being misunderstood are then maximal because Westerners, unlike Easterners, do not normally associate virtue with harmony, nor do they grasp the "moral implications" of disharmony, some of whose connotations incorporate "esthetics". This notwithstanding, harmony is the essence of beauty and beauty is holiness.

38 To the objection that an angel cannot fall, we can refer to the Koranic teaching that Iblis (or Satan) was made out of fire and not light; hence, a "fallen angel" may not be of the same substance as an angel proper, just as light has a dimension of luminosity and one of fire. In this sense, then, demons could be said to be psychic materializations of the heat component of light, and thus they would never have been angels in the pure sense of the term, but igneous beings, originally good no doubt albeit susceptible to corruption. Though Iblis in the Koran—as well as in Christian scriptures—is cast out and reviled, this aspect of "fallen angel" continues to haunt some exegeses; one of the strangest theories we have encountered is that of Al-Hallaj who supposes that Satan (Iblis) does not bow down before Adam out of heroic fidelity to God, for to bow before Adam, a creature made of clay, would be idolatry and disloyalty. If Al-Hallaj's supposition is correct, how then does he explain Satan's disobedience of God's command? According to Al-Hallaj, this command is apparently a "test" that God uses to try Satan's loyalty; but then, if God's primordial command is a test, who would ever obey any of God's commands? It is mystifying that such a theory comes from a Sufi who so extols the human soul's absolute identity with God, because if man and God are indeed one, then in submitting to Adam, Satan would actually be submitting to God no less and would therefore not be compromising his fidelity to God.

and this awareness is instantaneously projected to the outermost reaches of the cosmic void which, mirror-like, reflects the divine light, but no longer directly or in its plenitude. Hence God declares, in Isaiah: "I form the light, and create darkness: I make peace, and create evil: I the Lord do all these things." (45:7). What we want to say is that in being aware of Himself as supreme object, God is at once aware of this object's sacred reflection in creation but cannot not be aware also at the very self-same instant that this object is not exactly Himself, and therefore He is aware of its potential imperfection. This awareness both of perfection and of imperfection could be one interpretation of God declaring: "I make peace" (the awareness of His perfection in His reflection, or creation) "and create evil" (the awareness of the imperfection or, rather, incompleteness of his reflection).

Now evil springs somewhere from this breach in duality, a breach which is not merely existential, but cognitive as well. And this self-cognition, which then becomes also a self-willing—in its capacity as demiurgic principle of otherness—is bound at some point to explore and exploit its fullest possibility as a rival otherness to God; in other words, the *principium individuationis* contains the capacity to be other than God and consequently to turn against God, whence the possibility of evil. Nonetheless, since nothing can be absolutely separate from God this demiurgic otherness, even in its extreme mode as evil, cannot sunder its bond with God, whence its ultimate doom. If we were to borrow an illustration from the field of medicine, we could liken the nature of evil to that of a malignant neoplasm (cancer) in which the body essentially turns on itself; like evil, the malignant disease is not self-engendered ("I create evil", God declares), but depends for its existence on perverting the body's normal metabolism in order to vampirize healthy cells. Thus a person who is ill is under a dual process, that of normal life and that of the disease which operates, however accidentally, as a secondary but nonetheless fully identifiable separate entity with its own unique constellation of symptoms.

The above illustration raises the question once again whether evil can be defined as existing objectively outside of man or of originating purely within the soul of man, as many thinkers have posited? As we have seen, the potentiality for revolt against the Good exists in man, of course; but to reduce evil—and by extension, the notion of the devil—to a purely subjective possibility in human beings, namely one that has no objective or independent existence in its own right, is the most treacherous of solipsisms because, firstly, it is to attribute a god-like importance to man's role in the cosmos to confront God, which no individual has the power to embody by himself, or even collectively; secondly, it ends up trivializing the nature of evil, which then becomes defined essentially in sociological or psychological terms, for to eliminate the devil, as an objective entity, is to eliminate God by implication—leaving man then as sole "devil-less" god—because the devil derives his existence from his direct opposition to God, and therefore does not depend on man, because his existence—just as that of the angels—in fact precedes that of man. The devil is the force, the consciously malevolent entity, opposing the radiation of the Divine in the cosmos, and he opposes it not as potentiality but as a fully conscious cosmic actuality, whereas in man evil is *a priori* only potentiality. There is thus a clear difference between fallen man and the *princeps huis mundi* ("evil prince of this world").

At the same time, while it is crucial not to underrate the significance of evil as a quasi-independent cosmic phenomenon, it is important to grasp that if the "prince of this world" is allowed independence in creation, he is not independent in the Manichean sense of an absolute entity opposing the Good while subsisting on its own powers.

Correlatively, if it is true that the notion of the devil is not absolutely necessary for the religious life, as evinced by some major Eastern traditions where this concept is quasi-inexistent, this does not mean that this notion is irrelevant or unreal. To borrow again from the language of medicine, evil can reside in man like a dormant virus awaiting the right trigger of circumstances to erupt in virulent toxicity. The question then becomes: is this virus a totally foreign agent or is it an integral part of an individual? In zoological terms, the virus is a foreign agent which depends on the suscep-tibility of the individual host (the human body) to become active. Carrying this analogy over to the spiritual plane, the virus (or the evil influence) is essentially powerless to infect the host (the soul) unless the host develops a weakness allowing it then to propagate itself. And this image brings us to the following fundamental point: the core of man, his essence, belongs entirely to God and is therefore immune as such to evil; hence, evil cannot enter a soul unless welcomed and this indicates that evil, as a conscious entity, exists normally *outside* the soul and hence has no power solely of its own to penetrate the soul.[39] Understanding this mutual independency is a key to situating the difference in planes involved, because it is too im-precise to speak of evil in the abstract, as a mere theoretical point of ref-erence having no concrete existence or, on the contrary, to assume that it roams at will through the universe free to persecute and oppress man unprovoked, or also that man might be powerless to resist it. In short, evil exists on an external plane and is therefore not an intimate part of man as such, although it is an intimate part of evil people, namely individuals who

---

39 "Lo! My (faithful) bondmen—over them thou (Satan) hast no power, and thy Lord suf-ficeth as (their) guardian" (Koran, "The Children of Israel", 17:65).

identify with it or even embody it. With respect to creation itself, the vi-rus—or the potential for disease—exists as the shadow side of life, whence the ellipsis of attributing the creation of evil to God. In other words, when monotheistic scriptures say that God "created evil" this is exactly as if one were to say that in creating life He created disease and death too, as we already have had occasion to mention.[40] He does so, of course, not directly but only by way of inevitable implication since created life cannot be im-mortal and, it must be added, the occurrence of the death of the creature is by way of homage to God's glorious deathlessness which annihilates and transfigures all that is not Him, for He is the sole Real.

*   *   *

In the wake of these considerations, we feel compelled to mention a mod-ern psychological theory, in that it evinces a particularly insidious twisting of the notion of evil. According to this theory, which we hinted at above, the "devil" is but a bugbear figure born from the moralistic suppression of natural primal urges that shock a conventional bourgeois sensibility shack-led by religiosity. In other words, religion—or rather puritanical "bour-geois religion"—in order to defend certain social conventions, whelps a monster—namely the figure of the devil—to scare and repress the natural instincts of the faithful into a narrow obedientialism; intimidated by no-tions of sin, the devotees develop complexes, if not traumas, that cripple their wellbeing. And likewise—still according to this profane theory—hell is a fantasy manufactured to terrorize these impressionable faithful into adhering to what amounts to a repressive moral code upon which society is erected; this is the social part of the theory.

On a personal or subjective level, the psychological facet of this theory asserts that the believer, in an effort to repress natural urges—especially sexual ones—ends up creating, with the assistance of moral guilt, a demon effigy figure that is in fact nothing other than the deformation of his own tortured or rejected desires vengefully come back to haunt his imagina-tion, courtesy perhaps of a touch of hysteria. Now, we are not challenging the psychoanalytical mechanism, because any kind of excessive strain can have a warping effect on a person's psyche and, indeed, painful complexes can turn into *de facto* demons; however, to attribute as much power as psychoanalysis does to such neuroses for inventing a totally fictitious re-

---

40 Needless to say, though, evil cannot be equated literally with disease or death, because what makes something evil is, once again, its conscious intention to destroy the Good; hence we are dealing here with a wholly different degree of magnitude than mere disease or suffering.

ality as the notion of the devil—let alone that of God—defies credibility and inverts the cosmic order of things: there is simply no parallel between the banality of the complex and the order of magnitude of the reality depicted, for how does one explain God and the devil as being hatched from a mere complex? And for psychoanalysis to extrapolate its understanding of neuroses to the field of religion is a transgression of the epistemological limits of what should in fact be a strictly medical science, and not a credo disguised as a science.[41] And, to take now the other side of the equation, if "repression" were reversed, would that rid society of the so-called "devil" (or demons) as "open-minded", tolerant, free-thinkers imagine? On the contrary, it would unleash other demons, perhaps worse. The denial of the existence of evil as an objective entity—to say nothing of the existence of God—is to assume that religion has no supernatural basis. Moreover, what is lost sight of in this assumption that repression leads to neurosis is, firstly, that every human being has to overcome himself otherwise he will become a devil, and, secondly, that archetypally the process of repression is related to the principle of conversion as fermentation. Indeed, one of the most cogent images for the principle of "self-domination" or for the *noble* "repression" of baser instincts is the alchemist's athanor, or oven (symbol of the prayer cell), in which the precious elixir (our vital but still unconverted substance) is hermetically sealed, upon which it is then heated (the fire of concentrated prayer directed by the vow of commitment to God) so as to convert it from mortal bitterness to immortal sweetness.

In criticizing the above theory, fairness obliges us to note a converse fallacy, unfortunately found among some believers, which is to suppose that the devil could not exist did he not have a parcel of love and truth in him, however infinitesimal, as if the "degree of smallness" of this love could lessen the absurdity of the affirmation.[42] What can be reiterated is that evil is a deformation of the Good and that therefore it cannot exist without the Good just as a shadow cannot exist without light; but one cannot assert

41 The problem with psychoanalysis is less with the medical and psychological understanding of the processes of the body and mind, namely with the science of psychosomatics, than with the temptation to extrapolate that knowledge to the social, philosophical, and especially religious spheres. This too has been the major problem of modern science in general—the encroachment into the non-scientific by a perspective that reduces everything to material causes. Intrinsically, there should be no conflict between religion and science, but *de facto* it is unavoidable because a religion has been made out of science; indeed, for modern man science equals truth.

42 The emphasis on the "minimalism" is usually stated by manner of hedging one's bet, a totally unnecessary dialectical precaution when one is clear-minded about an issue.

that there is the tiniest speck of goodness enabling it to exist, *quod absit*.[43] In other words, it is not a question of ratios, let alone of percentages— statistics have damaged modern man's intelligence, forcing him to assess things too much in terms of quantities instead of principles[44]—but of frank inversion, otherwise a formulation of this kind presupposes some kind of equivalence or identity of substance, however minuscule, between evil and the good and this is a cosmic impossibility. Moreover, to believe in such a theory can sow the seeds for the devil's relative exoneration, and therefore by extension that of man's sinfulness. To be perfectly clear: not even the fact of having once been an "angel of light" mitigates the absoluteness and totality of the devil's evilness; his evilness is entirely premised on his op-position, absolute and unrelenting and horrible, to the Good, and that is why Satan is not an atheist.[45]

Moving to another perspective: one element that surprises many a Westerner approaching Buddhism—a religion ostensibly of infinite com-passion and peace—is the existence of wrathful "deities".[46] The same phe-nomenon is found in Hinduism, notably in the figure of Kali as well as in Shiva in his guise as destroyer, and in the figure of the *Kalki Avatara* or "Destroyer of Foulness", who is to appear at the end of time. They embody the terrible side of the Divinity or God's aspect as judge and avenger, exam-ples of which abound in the monotheistic scriptures—an aspect by which creation is purified and restored to unity. Now, we bring this feature up to

43 To take a graphic illustration of this point, can we assume that the decay of a fruit, or of any physical body for that matter, entails some substratum of wholeness? In a certain sense "yes" because decay can only supervene where there is a previous wholeness to undo; but "no" in the decisive sense that decay presupposes the absolute loss of the dynamic princi-ple of health previously animating this body. Thus any "goodness" (or the presence of the animating principle) in the decay would actually interfere with the process of decay which can only be fulfilled in the total absence of this "goodness". The analogy between the fruit's decay and evil is, however, not complete since evil, as we have seen, is more than the prin-ciple of decay.

44 Or as Taoism formulates it: "The sum of the parts is not the whole". For instance, there comes a point where a large enough group of trees is no longer a collection of trees but a forest.

45 "No one of mankind can conquer you this day, for I [Satan] am your protector. But when the armies came in sight of one another, he took flight, saying: Lo! I am guiltless of you. Lo! I see that which ye see not. *Lo! I fear God.* And God is severe in punishment" (Koran, "The Spoils of War", 8:48, italics ours).

46 Strict, doctrinaire Buddhists will no doubt object to the term "deities", maintaining that there are no "gods" in Buddhism, and therefore no human personifications of the Divine. However, the Buddhist equivalent of the notion of deities found in other religions is covered by the notion of *bodhisattvas*, as well as that of spirits and ghosts.

contrast it with the role of evil, because one of the functions of the wrathful deities is precisely that of guardians whose function it is to ward off evil and one can deduce from their very fierceness what the severity of their duty is, as well as the nature of the adversary they are assigned to guard against; therefore, they are also proof of the devil, if one may say, because there would otherwise be no need for them to assume such a fierce role. When considering God's goodness, it is important to understand the role of His goodness with respect to Eternity, and also what it is with respect to time or creation, for here one will have to consider also the rigorous dimension of God's mercy, for if God is to properly redeem He may need first to "punish" or purify.

∗   ∗   ∗

In closing, mention was made earlier of the fact that most people are *de facto* atheists even if professing *de jure* belief in God, and this question brings us to the mystery of faith and to what theologians refer to as being the "obscure merit of faith", without which no man or woman is truly a believer. This gift, divine in its essence, can only be bestowed by God because its intellective—and emotional—spark is really drawn from His own being. Indeed, just as man cannot create life, he cannot create faith: both are gifts of God, implicit in our very existence as human beings; they are, in fact, the obscure trace of divinity within us. Where then, one might ask, does this "obscure merit" intervene? It comes from man's willingness to believe, purely and simply, for "blessed are they that have not seen, and yet have believed" (John 20:29). All man can really do, with the faith instilled in him by his Maker, is to remove the obstacles to this faith and to throw himself at the feet of God's mercy—to throw himself mind, heart, body, and soul; this at least is the perspective found in the Jesus Prayer of Hesychasm as in that of Amidism, the perspective in Buddhism entrusting all care and help and strength to the manifestation of Amida Buddha, absolute unconditional faith in him being the miraculous antidote to the corruptibility of doubt. All the rest of the spiritual work lies in the hands of Heaven.

CHAPTER 8

Capital Punishment

Thou shalt not kill.
(Matt. 5:21)

Few issues do more than capital punishment to reveal the true mettle of a person's character. And no other issue draws a deeper divide between a traditional society and the modern world.

Only God, as the giver of life, has the right to take life away: everyone no doubt would concur. Beyond this, however, agreement crumbles. This exclusive and divine prerogative being conceded, does this entail that man is wholly forbidden to act as a delegate executioner of divine justice under exceptional circumstances? Or, put differently, does it not entail that God could exercise His absolute right to end a human life via a human instrument? If not, then what other instrument could God employ, judicially speaking? Indeed, how else could God intervene in human affairs, short of a supernatural abrogation of natural law—a bolt from Heaven type of interference—except through man as an instrument over man?[1]

Now, the entire premise for the principle of divine delegation in carrying out an execution—or any other judicial verdict—presupposes that the "minister of God" (Rom. 13:4) is no longer acting purely in his limited capacity as an individual, precisely. However, remove God from the equation and man as executioner is virtually a murderer since he is then acting on his own fallible initiative to slay another human being, and who would dare cast the first stone here?[2]

---

1 Thus God tells Muhammad in the Koran that He is the doer: "Ye slew them not, but God slew them. And thou (Muhammad) threwest not when thou didst throw, but God threw" (8:17). Krishna tells Arjuna much the same at the battle of Kurukshetra in the *Bhagavad Gita*; Arjuna's task is to perform his duty (*dharma*) regardless of the fruits, even if this means slaying his own kith and kin; and what is this *dharma* if not God in human guise performing necessary deeds by sacred delegation?

2 In the fourth century Saint Ambrose, as archbishop of Milan, apparently invoked this argument with respect to capital punishment; we suppose he affirmed this while not removing God from the equation, in which case, one would like to know what role man could play as God's delegate on earth? Fundamentally, it is really not the Church's role to intervene in mundane affairs, let alone to set up secular court; with respect to the condemned, its role should be confined to offering him the last rites, for the Church's duty is to provide care for a soul's posthumous journey. On the other hand, it should be noted that if justice is the affair of the state, it is so only so long as it is still justice, because an argument can be made for injustices becoming the province of the church should the state fail in its duty.

In justification for the elimination of capital punishment, it is all too facile to quote the injunction of Christ condemning man's killing of man: "Thou shalt not kill" (Matt. 5:21). For this injunction begs the question: do Christ's words apply to the principle of justice as such or only to crime? Obviously an intelligent sense of context is required to assess these words, otherwise were one to make an absolute of them, what becomes then of another one of Christ's masterful injunctions: "judge not lest ye be judged" (Matt. 7:1)? No reasonable person would logically interpret this statement in favor of eliminating judges and courts. Thus, if man has the right to exercise judgment—his innate faculty of discernment and sense of justice warrant this—then as day follows night he also has the right to enforce a verdict; in other words the same knowledge that enables man to arrive at a sentence enables its execution. But here the fear of man's arbitrariness is often invoked to refute one man's right to execute another man; however even if human beings are all too often arbitrary, this should not cloud the essential fact that man as such is endowed with intelligence, which means he is endowed with the capacity for objectivity, and which in turn ensures both discernment and impartiality; therefore man can—in principle if not in fact—overcome arbitrariness and be completely just. Indeed, man would not be man without these essential attributes: discernment, whence fairness, namely qualities that go to the heart of the law. As a matter of fact, it is in virtue of these very attributes that every human being is held accountable for his own actions and thus, reciprocally, it means that every human being can be the object of a judicial sentence; the logic allowing man to judge himself is the same logic allowing man to be judged by man. And this bears emphasis: man, in being just, is no longer just being man, but is acting in the name of a higher principle, in the name of justice itself, in fact in the Name of God[3] who alone is truly just.[4]

For those who counter that justice is purely man–made, we respond that the principle of justice as such transcends human interpretation; it

---

3 Every witness in an American courtroom swears on the Bible that he is telling the truth.

4 It is worth pointing out here that Christ's words "thou shalt not kill" are obviously meant as an injunction against murder (this statement could also have been formulated thus: "thou shalt not *murder*") and therefore cannot apply to the death penalty by any stretch of logic, because a legal (or just) execution cannot be equated with raw murder. To believe these two acts are comparable is to conflate justice and crime: to execute a killer is not killing; not to see the incomparable difference between the two is either stupidity or it is bad will. Moreover, there is a passage in the Gospels which makes it clear that Christ approves the ultimate sanction available to the Jewish Law as enforced by the state: "He that curseth father or mother, let him die the death" (Matt. 15:4, Mark 7:10). And the principle for the riddance of "human deadwood" can be supported by the sermon on the "true vine": "If a man abide not in me, he is cast forth as a branch, and is withered; and men gather them, and cast them into the fire, and they are burned" (John 15:6).

is based on a divine ordering inherent in a cosmic equilibrium that rectifies itself ceaselessly as well as periodically: any deviation in nature, if
tolerated initially, is eventually corrected—as rigorously as necessary—so
as to restore proper balance because Reality equals balance. This principle,
transposed to man, means that social justice is based on the necessity of
preserving a human equilibrium, especially one meant to mirror divine order on earth: society equals equilibrium; anything compromising this has
either to be corrected, removed, or destroyed. But the principle of social
equilibrium applies, of course, only to a legitimate society because a tyrannical society, or one under the control of criminals, precludes the whole
idea of justice. And, an equilibrium based on repression is not an equilibrium; a true equilibrium allows a natural homeostasis between a society's
different parts under the guidance of an enlightened authority.

While a number of points discussed here may seem all too self-
evident to traditionally-minded readers, for many modern readers penal
issues have been so thoroughly re-assessed that ancient principles are no
longer accepted and in fact are usually contested if not rejected, many in
the name of progress and for what is assumed to be a more humane way
of dealing with transgressions. Yet, the fundamental stakes of existence—
essential right and wrong, life and death, salvation and damnation—do not
change across the centuries even if social circumstances do, and despite
as confusing an epoch as ours where once sacrosanct assumptions are
being systematically questioned everywhere. These fundamental stakes
transcend customs, however society may want to interpret them; they are
like the warp in the social fabric and to modify them unduly, if not to repeal
them, is to allow the whole fabric of society to unravel. For example, by
removing the plausibility of "damnation" from the equation, society's sense
of right and wrong is inevitably blunted, flattened, or made banal; in such
a setting, crime inevitably loses some of its monstrosity, for its heinousness
is dampened by a social utilitarianism that inexorably supplants age-old
principles once anchored in religious revelation. In that case, man's vision
of the universe shrinks to fit what are predominantly material parameters
of life on earth, parameters dictated primarily by ease and discomfort,
or pain and pleasure, none of which engage his immortal soul. And yet,
only man's inveterate shortsightedness, when unchecked, can divorce our
earthly welfare from our posthumous welfare: Eternity's measures, like
the fixed stars at night, do not move relative to our earthly situation, no
matter how much society may change. And it is these timeless measures
that matter in the end, for man is not merely the product of an epoch, but
above all a creature fashioned by and made for eternity;[5] in fact, if man's

5 "Jesus Christ the same yesterday, and to day, and for ever" (Heb. 13:8).

accidental situation, namely that of being a child of his times, is placed on the scales along with his timeless essence, what weight would the former hold?

Here we want to end this section with a digression that illustrates some practical problems stemming from modernist reevaluations. In Pope John-Paul II's *"Evangelium Vitae"* regarding the inviolability of human life, and hence the inapplicability of capital punishment, we read: "We must recognize that in the Old Testament this sense of the value of life, though already quite marked, *does not yet reach the refinement found in the Sermon on the Mount"* (italics ours). What are we to make of such a statement? That Moses and all of the Old Testament prophets were morally inferior to some degree in comparison to Christ and his apostles? Or perhaps that the Ten Commandments, which are the moral bedrock of Western civilization, are merely tentative? This encyclical contains a whole social program which, in advocating the idea of religious progress (where then would Islam fit in such a sequence since it comes after Christianity?), ends up relativizing the entire premise of religious authority, for if this authority does not rest finally on its timeless sense of the Absolute, then it rests on nothing. The truth is that Christ's Sermon on the Mount does not represent an improvement— God forfend!—but instead the need to restore the primacy of the spirit to an application of the Mosaic Law that had become too vindictively legalistic, as well as pharisaical, in the hands of men. Thus, it is not the abolition of the law of the prophets, but its fulfillment, that Christ came to ensure, as he himself declared (Matt. 5:18). Moreover, comparing—by implication—the Old Testament God of "wrath and vengeance" with the New Testament God of "love and peace" is not only simplistic, but it is to misunderstand the nature of the Absolute, for both the Ten Commandments and the Sermon on the Mount, different as they are in their respective purviews, are not merely exhortations to mankind, but direct expressions of God's very own nature and, as such, unsurpassable perfections: it is the same God who spoke to Moses that spoke through Christ and thus shared his nature with both prophets. Yes, there are different divine revelations, but the monotheistic religions are meant to complete each other in a circular form and not in an ascentional one, let alone in a dispensationalist manner with a whiff of Hegelianism thrown in to suit the thesis of progressivism.

*   *   *

Justice cannot be properly defined without a proper definition of what constitutes the nature of man. There is an assumption, in humanist jurisprudence, that an individual has an absolute right to life—unconditionally so and guaranteed, no matter the circumstances, something he can never forfeit. Granted, this right has a core basis in religious ethics. However, to say it is absolutely unconditional requires some nuance; it would be more correct to say—at the risk of being accused of relativism—that it is "conditionally unconditional" or, to echo Schuon, "relatively absolute". The right to life is "unconditional" in the sense that only God can give life and therefore only God can take it away. "Thou shalt not kill," Christ reminds his disciples in confirmation of the Ten Commandments, adding "and whosoever shall kill shall be in danger of the judgment" (Matt. 5:21). Yet, this right to life is also bound to be conditional, be it merely when it collides with the rights of another human being; in other words, there have to be instances in which it can be forfeited, because nothing on earth is ever absolutely absolute, if one may say without redundancy, even though a rigid morality may insist that some things are so.[6] In fact, the circumstances making this right to life less than absolute have to do with the very absoluteness of the crime of murder itself, precisely; this is a cosmic equation. To deny another human being his or her quasi-absolute right to life diminishes by the very same token our own absolute claim to life, otherwise the equation between right and justice no longer works: there has to be a sanction literally commensurate with the gravity of the crime; dilute this sanction to any degree, and the gravity of the crime itself is, by implication, automatically lessened. Indeed, murder forgiven is life debased; but opponents of the death penalty have inverted this equation, as we shall see.

Now, if the essence of Christian morality is in fact premised on the "turning of the other cheek", it should be specified that this is an attitude meant only as a governing reflex—a rule of thumb as it were—with regard to our relationship with the world in the largest sense, a rule premised on the fundamental notion that "my kingdom is not of this world". It is not meant, therefore, as a literal way of life but rather to discourage our seeking "perfect" (or too strict) a reparation for injustices; put differently, it is meant to deliver man from entrapment in a vicious circle of endless retribution. It is meant, moreover, to remind man that to seek to obtain perfect reparation on earth is a metaphysical impossibility, for the same

6 For instance, divorce is condemned by the Catholic Church, but other religious traditions allow for it. If divorce is intrinsically evil, then the Catholic tradition would be the only true religion; or marriage would always be better than divorce, no matter how dreadful or dangerous the union might be for the partners; but such an idealism simply does not correspond to the reality of human existence. Ideals are sometimes better protected through partial concessions to the vagaries of human nature than by absolutistic proscriptions that are beyond the strength of most men to adhere to, leaving them otherwise no alternative but to transgress; and history offers us abundant examples of these, starting with the issue of divorce, not to mention that of infidelity. That said, to idealize the sacred nature of marriage is, in itself, admirable and something very much worth defending.

reason no mortal is deserving of complete exoneration given the fallibility of human nature as a whole; in the *Kali Yuga*, man is guilty by mere dint of having been born, at least until Heaven sanctifies him. Hence, "turning the other cheek" can only be taken so far before it leads to absurd dilemmas. To take one example: people are entitled to their property under the law and hence if robbed are allowed—under God—to seek proper restitution of their rightful belongings. Indeed, if "turning the other cheek" became writ into law, wolves would quickly despoil sheep: thieves and scoundrels and murderers would plunder with impunity.

Thus, when assessing a biblical or religious injunction of any kind, a distinction needs to be made—with all the risks this entails of contradiction and possibly hypocrisy—between, on the one hand, a morality applied to the world—"render unto Caesar"—that perforce takes account of different practical circumstances, and, on the other, a morality applied to Heaven. Such a distinction exists because there is an opposition between Heaven and this world, or between "my kingdom (that) is not of this world" and the "law of Caesar"; that is why there is a pope and not just an emperor, and that is why there is a division between religious and secular powers.[7] Such a distinction corresponds furthermore to the inevitable difference between realism and idealism; however, they need not be at complete variance since absolute idealism—namely, spiritual idealism—is meant to enlighten and guide earthly realism. Now, even if earthly realism may seem to conflict with celestial idealism, and even sometimes has to supplant it in the brutal arena of the world, this does not mean that it cannot be perfectly principled at its level; severe as earthly realism may have to be, it serves man on earth while in fact protecting the viability of celestial idealism, otherwise, this idealism would be defenseless; for example peacemakers need the protection of warriors.[8] Needless to say, a principled realism has, by definition, to be guided by qualities such as intelligence, fairness, and magnanimity, wherever and as much as these noble qualities are practicable, and not by implacable, legalistic righteousness which is vengeful or oppressive by definition. Such a predisposition to forbearance is always mindful, in this case, of the injunction to "turn the other cheek" and it is this graciousness that immunizes justice from being tyrannical. However, if the judge is too lenient with a criminal, he harms the peace and wellbeing of the collectivity

7 See Frithjof Schuon, *Christianity/Islam* (Bloomington, IN: World Wisdom, 2008), pp. 80-81 where some of these paradoxes are explored.

8 Pacifist purists will object to this by assuming that if everyone espoused pacifism there would be no need for soldiers; but it is in the nature of dreamers not to be realistic: earth will forever be prey to predators.

who then must live in fear of unduly pardoned transgressors in their midst; as the Chinese sage Mencius stated: "One cannot forgive a bad man without harming a good man."[9]

In raising the above considerations, we realize that we still have not addressed the popular argument against capital punishment, which maintains that man cannot under any circumstances usurp the rights of God, who alone, as giver of life, can take a life. While this argument has its validity, it only proves that an unlawful assumption of divine powers is reprehensible, not that the assumption of such powers is wrong in itself, otherwise no man could stand in judgment over another man and there would be no right to authority. "Whoever sheds the blood of man, *by* man shall his blood be shed, for God made man in His own image" (Gen. 9:6; italics ours); note here the empowering meaning of the Biblical preposition *by*. Even Christ, in his direst hour, recognized the transcendent or impersonal nature of a judge's function when he told Pilate: "Thou couldest have no power at all against me, except it were given thee from above" (John 19:11). What is more, Christ exonerated Pontius Pilate from any wrongdoing in the execution of his function.[10] Not to recognize man's power of delegation granted him by God is, finally, not to understand either man or God.

*   *   *

It cannot be our intention to revisit all the arguments raised against the death penalty, only those that we think deserve fuller mention. But firstly, this debate has to be set against the backdrop of the fading concreteness of the Hereafter in a non-traditional world or, put differently, the increasing abstractness of the Kingdom of Heaven and, conversely, of the encroaching and obnubilating realness for modern man of the here-below. Indeed, "this base world" has taken ever greater precedence over the "next world", a result of the growing secularization of modern society—a secularization whose most insidious effect may not be atheism per se but the appropriation of religion by humanism, an outcome in which the human—or, to be more exact, the perishable human—has become the measure of the Divine, thus inverting the true relationship of things. It is in this context that

---

9 We quote from memory.

10 This may be a fine point, since Christ is quoted as saying merely: "he that delivered me unto thee hath the greater sin", but constraints of space prevent us from developing our argument further here, although the general context of our chapter addresses these nuances; however, Pilate is granted judicial legitimacy principially if not *de facto* in Christ's statement about the origin of his delegate power. The reader desirous of learning more about this question can be profitably referred to Schuon's chapter "An Enigma of the Gospel" in *The Transfiguration of Man* (Bloomington, IN: World Wisdom, 1995).

arguments against the death penalty have to be situated, for they gain in popularity diametrically with man's loss of the sense of God's majesty and, by extension, with the loss of man's reverential fear.[11]

Expressed differently, the rejection of capital punishment is unwittingly based on everyday man's unawareness of the afterlife, namely an unawareness that the next world is infinitely more important and existentially realer than man's everyday flesh and blood existence. Due to a mostly subconscious reflex, men are by nature inclined to view this world here below as concretely real and therefore as being *de facto* absolute; and it is this tendency that a sacred society is meant to compensate for while inspiring a sense of the concreteness of the next world. Otherwise, as we have read somewhere in Taoism: "When this world here below is taken for the real, then the Real becomes unreal." The process takes place so surreptitiously—although blatantly for those who still have eyes to see— that most people do not realize how they have come to make of life on earth such a practical absolute that the true Absolute becomes unreal for all practical purposes.[12] Therefore, by that token, if our earthly life is the one meaningful life, then to execute a convicted criminal entails a catastrophic finality, for in depriving him of life one is depriving him of existence pure and simple. Such a profane scruple cannot, however, be uppermost in the minds of truly spiritual people who know in the marrow of their bones that life on earth is but an antechamber for life eternal, or—in the Eastern perspective—who know that life on earth is but a stage in man's journey across the *samsara*. Consequently, for a traditionalist mind an execution does not entail the finality it has for the humanist of lukewarmish faith, let alone for the avowed secularist who "knows" there is no afterlife.

Likewise, the loss of the intuitive sense of the sacred Real inevitably gives rise to the fundamental trend of modern man to overrate the body with respect to the soul, or to overrate the physical with respect to the

---

11 We see this in the triteness of language, as seen notably in the ugliness of the fashion of t-shirts bearing trivial or chaotic logos, designs, and images of all kinds—the letterings especially being one of the casualties of literacy appropriated by plebian or pariah souls. Traditional clothing, and not least that of more primitive peoples, had symbol-designs reflecting the intelligent patterns of the universe, meant to be intuitively understood by man's heart-intellect. Translated into graphic designs, the universe's cosmic intelligence is expressed in the collective genius of folk wisdom, which understood the genius of the universe's divine language and allowed man to integrate the sacred patterns and rhythms of the cosmos into his daily mode of being. By contrast, and notwithstanding a few innocent or non-descript exceptions, the t-shirt is the emblem of modern man's devotion to the casual, the accidental, or worse; certainly, there is not a trace left of man's former understanding of the cosmos.

12 A signal example of this is the attitude people in modern society have regarding aging and death: aging is resisted and denied, and death is concealed.

spiritual, while forgetting that the soul itself cannot be put to death; in other words, if the soul is the real person—as opposed to his physical body—then an execution can only mark a change of costume and stage for the soul and not a terminal elimination. Thus, if one truly believes in the soul then man's whole scale of values will shift from the material to the spiritual, and in that case virtue and character—not the unrealistic survival of the physical body at all costs—becomes the decisive element in assessing an individual's welfare, indeed that of a civilization.

This being so, then to execute another human being cannot amount to committing as irreparable an act as humanists claim. Put differently, if the "next world" is realer than this one—indeed if it is the "efficient cause" of everything real in this world—then the decision to execute another human being is certainly not irreparable with respect to Eternity, aside from the fact that God will not leave an injustice unredressed. However, it is precisely the practical concreteness of Eternity, and all the existential consequences this notion entails, that is most lacking in a non-traditional society. In simplest terms, the issue comes down to what is realer, the body or the soul?[13]

Moreover, people whose humanitarian charity is revulsed by the allegedly barbaric act of executing a murderer, tend not just to overrate life on earth but also to overrate the subjective (the over-reliance on psychological motives, for instance) to the detriment of the objective (the factualness of the deed); thus, psychologism focuses more on the motives and intentions of a person's behavior rather than the enormity of the crime, this "enormity" being traditionally the measure of a criminal's individual heinousness. Now, indubitably, intention has a crucial role to play in assessing the criminality of a transgression, because that is finally the whole point of an appropriate penalty and penance; and since we are human beings and not beasts, intention is what defines us. But there is a risk of exaggerating intention if murky speculations about a person's reasons for doing what he does dilutes or eclipses the heinousness of a deliberate deed—the element of a crime's cold-blooded deliberateness being the key.[14] The assumption that even the most horrible of deeds might have some redemptive rational explanation that would lessen its horror

---

13 In the *Bhagavad Gita*, we read of Krishna's exhortation to Arjuna for his compunction about slaying: "For the soul there is neither birth nor death at any time. . . . He is unborn, eternal, ever-existing, and primeval. He is not slain when the body is slain" (2:20).

14 This is the basis of the *mens rea* ("malice aforethought") clause in the assessment of the *actus reus* ("unlawful killing of a human being") in jurisprudence, or the connection between the "fault element" and the "physical element". In other words, intention is what determines fault, not the mere physical act of the crime.

leads us into an inextricable tangle of considerations that can end up paralyzing justice, or handicapping the appropriateness of the verdict. Not least, to posit that a murderer acts purely on explainable—and hence, one assumes, on reformable—psychological motives, or that his crime was due to purely external reasons—making him therefore the helpless victim of circumstances—overlooks the fact that his deed more likely stems from motives born from his inveterate substance, namely deriving from his personal karmic tendency.[15]

People of weak or no religious faith forget that actions of men blotted out from the "Book of Life" are rooted in a perversity of will that is karmically immune to reformation because it subscends (to coin a useful neologism mirroring "transcends") all horizontal—or social—causality. For example, two children may be mistreated by the same parents, but one becomes a murderer and the other a saint; where then, in each case, is the causality for their subsequent behavior? Yet modern psychologists, instead of inferring about a person's character from his deeds—or instead of inferring about a person's will from his actions—seek to explain a person's actions by psychoanalytical concerns that blame (be it only by implication) parents, educators, social background, traumas, on so on, in a tricky game of fishing for rational explanations that end up *de facto* disculpating an individual for their every shortcoming. Extrapolate this logic, and the entire human race will be released of guilt, in which case the blame lands on God's doorstep. How so? Because the very fact of supposing that there could be a rational explanation for a monstrous crime means that the diabolic nature of crime itself is misunderstood; therefore, by extension, its gravity—namely its diabolical nature—is minimized by implication, leaving no one else to blame save God Himself. In the eyes of a modern psychologist there are no truly, ineradicably evil people, only wretched victims—never mind the real victims, especially the murdered—in desperate need of our help and,

---

15 Nietzsche claimed that in the "pre-moral" era of mankind, actions were judged by their consequences, after which motives became, for all of religious history, the preeminent criterion; but that assumption is partially false, not just because there never was a "pre-moral" humanity, but because it was assumed that the nature of a crime normally reflected a punishable intention; that is why it was a crime, precisely. However it is really the loss of religion that enables psychological motives to assume a preeminence that threatens to eclipse the objective worth of deeds. Indeed, in sturdier times, a man's word was his bond: keeping it or breaking it was all that mattered, not the "why" or "wherefore". Nowadays, however, when an individual breaks his word every excuse is likely to be invoked. Again, this is not to say that intention is irrelevant, but rather that, all things being equal, deeds prove intention. Conversely and axiomatically, when the value of deeds is minimized then weak or devious intentions pullulate. As for the exceptions that confirm the rule, these are the province of a wise judge, not that of the lawmakers.

at that, victims who are living in an unfair society in need of reformation, forgetting that no society can ever be perfect. In fact, if anything, the really evil people might instead be those who stand in judgment over criminals for not understanding them—as if the irrational, let alone the diabolic, lent itself to reason.[16] Not least, a particularly specious objection proposes that the state, by exacting a death for a death, is stooping to the murderer's level of barbarity or even lower, for it has the choice of not "killing"[17] and therefore, in choosing execution, becomes an accomplice in a never-ending cycle of violence in which hate begets hate, and violence violence; this logic comes down to equating fair-minded and disinterested justice with murder, truly a perverse conflation since, to repeat a point made earlier, the state's motives—in principle dispassionate—bear no resemblance with those of a murderer.[18]

In a nutshell, what the humanist psychologist cannot imagine is that someone would perpetrate on his own volition a ghastly act that is entirely contrary to human nature; ergo, someone other—or something else—than the murderer must be to blame. But the absurdity of such a conclusion, in this game of circular logic, is that at some point blame must somewhere come home to roost, and this "somewhere", in the end, has to be oneself—namely the individual as a fully morally endowed human being—otherwise nothing will ever get solved in this heaping or dodging of excuses. The reason why man is man and not a subhuman creature is because he has noble freedom and therefore noble responsibility: man's divine intelligence, or his consciousness of absolute right and wrong, makes it so.

Psychologism, all told, is an outlook born finally from the disease of relativity undermining modern civilization, a perspective that places people onto the unstable ground of ever-shifting reference points which allows man to modify or even to improvise, namely to rewrite rules to fit his behavior *post facto*; thus rules and principles are now molded to man, not man to rules and principles as is the case in traditional religious morality. However, in truth, to be a man—to be a human being—presupposes certain elementary bases for behavior, barring which a person is no longer fully human and therefore is potentially at risk of forfeiting any special consideration or rights. And these rights, under normal circumstances at

16 Of course, the term "diabolic" is a meaningless if not "inflammatory" term in humanistic psychology; but what director of conscience worth his salt could overlook it?

17 "Killing" being the term used by opponents to capital punishment.

18 It has to be understood here that the state would have absolutely zero interest in the murderer were it not for his crime; in other words, the state has—to say the least—nothing against the murderer *a priori*.

least, have to be earned, for rights unconditionally guaranteed, that is to say without due consideration to responsibilities, are ripe for the spoiling if not abuse.[19] We see this same law applying in the case of social respect: no one would expect to deserve the consideration of his peers without earning it.

* * *

Perplexing as this may be to point out, it is possible to simultaneously overrate human life and to underrate it, because on the one hand human life is sacred since it comes from God and yet at the same time it is relative;[20] like all earthly creatures—and things—life is substitutable or expendable. Therefore, if on the one hand there is something absolute about a human life so that killing another man becomes a crime against both humanity[21] and against Heaven, at the very same time there is something relative in a human death in the sense that natural disasters, wars, or infant mortality— to mention but a few instances—teach us that fate makes life relative, while being eminently replaceable, as seen by the sheer number of people being born. How to do justice to these two dimensions without prejudicing either pole of this scale is the crux of the matter; in other words: how does one value human life without idolatry and how does one relativize human life without dehumanization? Such is the wager of a wise discernment that knows how to allot man his rightful due without robbing either nature or karma—or Heaven—of its prerogatives.

19 We see this over and over in the case of the Free Speech Amendment in the American Constitution, which we have termed, in our previous book, as being the devil's favorite. Judges in the United States Supreme Court essentially handle this amendment as a license to forfeit all discernment regarding permissible versus offensive speech. Thus, out of an exorbitant concern for protecting unconditional rights, an amendment originally intended to protect man's dignity of freedom has now become a shield for filth and abomination. The judges' personal repugnance of what they are protecting does not absolve their intellectual impotence, or complicity for that matter.

20 The debate on abortion faces much of the same dilemma. We shall not weigh in on it except to remark that many of the opponents of capital punishment have little or no qualms about supporting abortion or assisted suicide, to the degree that one might legitimately wonder whether they do not have things precisely backward. Be that as it may, such an alternativism shows the dilemmas that face men when adopting too rigid a position about earthly issues, because these can never involve more than relative absolutes, although "absolutes" nonetheless, whence the controversy.

21 Thus in the Koran: "whosoever killeth a human being . . . it shall be as if he had killed all mankind, and whoso saveth the life of one, it shall be as if he had saved the life of all mankind" ("The Table Spread", 5:32).

With respect to this question of overrating or underrating human life, opponents of the death penalty hold a dual but contradictory position: on the one hand, they aver that an execution is an absolute evil and yet, on the other hand, they assert that capital punishment is not a deterrent to crime. Which is it? If it is not a deterrent, then it cannot be as absolute a sanction as alleged; or else it is absolute and therefore a deterrent to some degree or other; and, indeed, the shadow of the gallows is enough to give most men the shivers—but only on condition it be made obvious through public reminders, and not concealed behind hermetic doors and antiseptic procedures. The argument that the threat of execution offers no deterrence to would-be murderers stems, once again, from a loss of the sense of the Absolute, but perhaps in this instance in a less obvious manner: in other words, if the example of an execution is no deterrent then the reverse assumption implied here—which few people detect—is that good examples would then, for their part and equally so, not be edifying. It is a question here of setting examples—good examples and dread examples; why select just one end of the equation to buttress an argument but not the other? Why, in other words, assert that a negative example cannot inculcate a healthy fear in would-be criminals exactly as a positive example can inculcate principles in virtuous men? These are twin arguments: if human beings are by definition impressionable creatures, then they must be so both positively and negatively, for these are the two sides of the same coin. These arguments notwithstanding, the main problem with the argument of the non-deterrence of capital punishment comes down to this: there can be, by definition, no statistics measuring the number of would-be sociopaths who opt not to kill out of a healthy fear for their lives from having been deterred in their murderous proclivities; they remain hidden, their urges repressed; common sense should tell us this. Yet, sociologists will counter, what about those human monsters who really are obdurately immune to such deterrence? Is that not proof of the ineffectualness of such a law? But such reasoning is to misframe the problem because one could argue that these murderers are the very ones who most deserve capital punishment, precisely because they are unreformable monsters. However, even if capital punishment is not a deterrent for a diabolical maniac—indeed, nothing is!—it surely is a deterrent for lukewarm criminals. Last, but not least, an execution provides an absolute deterrence against recidivism, while also sparing society the extraordinary costs and onerous obligation of supporting a worthless soul, for the burden of preserving an evil person is unfairly borne by the law-abiding who toil in virtue, and this is a double injustice.[22]

---

22 The first injustice is the crime itself; the second is to inflict some of its consequences onto the innocent.

It has been well said that nothing concentrates the mind more than the prospect of one's own death. Indeed, for the condemned the sight of the executioner may be enough to reduce his life to a decisive instant in which he has the chance—morally speaking—of leaping over his own shadow from sheer fright of the posthumous consequences. The impending definitiveness of his sentence could condense a whole lifetime of indifference to God into a lightning reflex of contrition in which he beseeches heavenly pardon: that one instant of keenest regret could compensate for the heinousness of the crime, although a price must still be paid both in this world and in the next; but his once sure damnation may be converted to salvation.[23] And this moment, too, namely the moment of the sentence's execution, should be that of God's victory—and justice—displayed in public.[24] Beyond this, however, there are considerations that secularists, twice stuck as they are behind the curtain of earthly life, simply do not ponder, a central one being that a murderer must expiate on earth the life he took with his own life in order to be spared the possible fate of a terrible rebirth.[25]

The so-called "humane" alternative of life imprisonment is not only not humane—rather an avowal of judicial impotence as well as of moral fecklessness—but it does nothing moreover to help a condemned man draw closer to his Maker; quite on the contrary, it can worsen his bitterness. If one could place all murderers in a monastery, perhaps there would be an argument for commutation of the death penalty, but that is hardly a realistic solution.

Surprising as it may be for some, it must be added that even if capital punishment were not a deterrent—which is an absurdity—deterrence is actually not its primary purpose: its purpose is to offer society a sentence

23 Crucial to note is that a few moments of sincere contrition can erase a lifetime of bad karma and guarantee an auspicious rebirth. In the *Bhagavad Gita*, emphasis is placed on the last thoughts a dying person has, for the intensity of this moment can have a decisive influence on the conditions of a human being's rebirth.

24 Remembering also that justice coincides intrinsically with mercy.

25 Swami Prabhupada, in his commentary on the *Bhagavad Gita*, mentions: "In *Manu-samhita* [The Laws of Manu], the lawbook for mankind, it is supported that a murderer should be condemned to death so that in his next life he will not have to suffer for the great sin he has committed. Therefore, the king's punishment of hanging a murderer is actually beneficial" (*The Bhagavad-Gita As It Is*, 2nd ed. [Los Angeles: The Bhaktivedanta Book Trust, 1983], p. 88). Secularists are "twice stuck" behind the curtain of earthly life: firstly because they share in the fleshly fate of all of mankind and, secondly, because they compound this fate in making an absolute out of earthly life; for believers, on the other hand, this curtain is semi-transparent, for their faith aerates as it were their earthly coagulation, allowing the supernatural to shine through.

on parity with the gravity of the ultimate crime man is capable of; for in offering this parity the whole edifice of justice gains in authority, prestige, and efficient respect, while assigning the crime the gravity it deserves. A healthy respect for justice is not only indispensable for the orderly mainstay of society, but also a mercy and a protection for honorable men and women, whether the wicked care or not.

Moreover, the "primary purpose" for capital punishment alluded to above is only "primary" with respect to civil order, for, in following Saint Thomas Aquinas—who distinguishes no less than *three* orders of reality which are transgressed by a criminal's crime[26]—there is also a transgression of the divine order, and this dimension is completely, and conveniently, left out in the modern debate on the issue. Thus, not only does a criminal harm his own soul and harm that of his fellow man, or society by extension, but more importantly in breaching the eternal law he offends God. As a result, Aquinas considers that the penal sentence must take into account a triple transgression requiring therefore a triple punishment: in that respect, and based on the gravity of the crime, the criminal's potential goodness becomes an irrelevant consideration as far as the social order is concerned, for there are crimes that put a man beyond the pale of earthly reformation. According to traditional justice, a criminal must expiate his crime—make *amende honorable*—while hoping for mercy for his sins, but, depending on the severity of the crime, this mercy may only be in God's power to bestow, which means that the criminal's life—or soul, if he is executed— is henceforth in God's hands, not man's. Loss of belief in God, of course, diminishes or even cancels this principle—not objectively, of course, since this principle is in fact at the very core of the whole notion of justice itself, because a godless justice is a pastiche.

*   *   *

Deterrence plays a vital role in governing society, for the stringency of deterrence is meant to compensate for the weaknesses and vices inherent in human nature, serving as a kind of public form of willpower that can help base individuals do what is not in their power to will on their own. Therefore, if condign punishment is diluted in favor of criminals out of overly humane concerns, the power of deterrence loses its edge.

In fact, we feel obliged now to bring some social context to the whole problem of deterrence, some of which we touched upon earlier. Modern

---

26 Firstly, the personal order, or that of the criminal's soul (microcosmic plane); secondly, the social order or that of the collective soul as it were (social plane); and thirdly, the universal or divine order (macrocosmic plane).

penologists, in allegedly civilized countries, have gone to extraordinary lengths to "sanitize" executions, to make them as humane as possible, and to hide them from public view; in so doing, however, they have robbed much of the spiritual meaning from justice, that is to say, they have undermined the notion of what is termed "poetic justice". Inherent in the idea of poetic justice is the fact that a criminal is meted out a form of punishment corresponding as closely as possible to the nature of his crime so that in the sentence there will be a key element both of legal logic as well as of existential concreteness; thus a sentence should not just be delivered but carried out in a manner as to serve as a graphic example; in a word, the sentence should both be just and serve as the matching existential antidote to the crime's poison.

Modern man—to single him out once again—is intellectually brilliant, but he is so basically in a two-dimensional manner: raised on a diet of rationalism, legalisms, statistics, and pelted with "facts", or overwhelmed by quantitative data instead of being governed by qualitative symbols, he is inured to the three-dimensional nature of Reality, or to what may be termed the cosmic soul of things. Inevitably, this has also affected his approach to justice, which he has tried to make as "scientific" and "humane" as possible, as we have said. By contrast, traditional modes of punishment meted out sentences meant to mirror as much as possible the nature and not just the fact or degree of the crime, because traditional man still lived in a world not sterilized by science. Hence for the modern mind, punishments such as flogging, hanging, facing a firing squad, stoning, or be it only the humiliation of being pilloried on the public square, belong on a shame list of gruesome practices unbefitting a civilized society.[27] And yet, these graphic forms of punishment reflect—in the fairest of cases at least[28]—a

27 For instance, the barbarity seen in executions in empires such as China, examples of which were on display even in the twentieth century, tend, in the mind of historians, to overshadow the larger issue of the barbarity of crime itself. No barbarity of punishment can compare to the barbarity of crime itself, a principle that should be the foundation of criminology; all the rest are secondary considerations, though "secondary" does not mean irrelevant because a sentence should obviously be fitted to the nature of the crime. That being said, sadistic practices are not justice but crimes in their own right.

28 "In the fairest of cases", we say, for one must be ever mindful of gross abuses or of justice at any price: *Fiat justitia ruat caelum*, "Let justice be served though the heavens fall." Time and space permitting, it would be worth explaining how justice has to navigate between two shoals, that of over-reacting and that of under-reacting, but we can only mention this: for the risk of not administering a sentence sufficient in strength to counter man's worst propensities, there is the reverse risk—"Piso's Justice", for example (a sentence that is legally correct but morally wrong)—namely of trivializing the clout of a sentence like capital punishment by applying it to the pettiest of crimes, such as condemning pickpockets to death as was once the case in England.

keen understanding of the spiritual dimension of a sentence, the goal of which was not just to punish but also to purge the individual as well as the society at large, because a public display of justice acted like a catharsis as well as the cauterization of a wound on the body social.[29] And this is the deeper point missed by doting humanists: man needs to be saved from himself. In other words, man, in the wake of the fall, is a potential beast, if not a demon; unless he is a contemplative, he is incapable of overcoming himself without outside help, and part of this help is provided him precisely by the threat of grim sanctions. However the threat alone is not enough to deter him if this threat is never actually exercised, just as the threat of war would become meaningless without an occasional skirmish if not an open conflict.

To accept this argument is to recognize that man is not necessarily good—only God is good!—and this is the stumbling block of profane idealists and humanist reformers of all stripes. The idea that man is inherently good is basically a modern notion forming part and parcel of the doctrine of progressivism; in other words, progressivism would lose much if not all of its intellectual appeal if the doctrine of the Fall were restored, for these two perspectives are antinomic. The doctrine of the Fall, for its part, presupposes that man is inherently and perversely capable of turning against God and, thereby, of establishing himself as a god in his own right, whether *de facto* or *de jure*, namely whether simply by default or by avowed conviction. To accept the doctrine of the Fall, therefore, is to understand that man's potential for deviation must be nipped in the bud in order to preempt the far-reaching consequences entailed by godlessness, revolt, and desecration, as well as the risk of possible damnation for himself, and into which he can drag others, if not all of society; to guard against such an extreme outcome no preventive judicial measure can be too severe—provided, as always, justice itself is not compromised. That said, even the risk of a miscarriage in justice should never outweigh the correctness of the principle; this is a critical point that benevolent humanists choke on. It is readily argued that since an innocent can be victim of capital punishment, the only way to eliminate the risk of injustice is to eliminate the sentence itself; quite obviously, such reasoning can be paralyzing because one cannot let perfection (or, rather, perfectionism) stand in the way of duty. Once

29 For example, the deeper symbolism of nailing a convict onto a cross was to return the condemned person to the sacred intersection of Heaven and earth; cold comfort for the condemned, perhaps, but a fitting framework for the transmigration of his soul which, through death, is thereby returned to the center where either it is reborn or possibly delivered. And, owing to the symbolism of this form of execution, the rupture between Heaven and earth that the crime constituted for society is thus symbolically repaired.

again, "My kingdom is not of this world"; translated, this means perfect justice is a human impossibility.[30]

There was a time when insolence on a ship earned a stiffneck a quick twelve lashes, but now only a reprimand if that much; and yet insolence, especially towards authority, is the seed of Luciferian revolt. But who understands this today? Or what is twelve lashes to teach a potential insurrectionist proper respect of true authority? Or, correlatively, of what worth is an authority if it is powerless to chastise damnable insolence? The difference in the choice of sanctions may alter the course of a destiny, possibly settling the fate for the transgressor between Heaven or hell, for these are always the ultimate terminal points in the pivotal choices we make: what a man does today on earth sows the seeds of his posthumous becoming.[31] Such a choice of fates is seen in the example of the two thieves on the Cross, one of whom rails Christ while the other asks the Savior to remember him in his Father's kingdom (Luke 23:39-43).

In fact, regarding the question of a condign sentence, we can measure the immensity of the divide between the traditional world of Christ and our modern epoch by the second thief's acknowledgment of the justness of his punishment: "for we receive the due reward of our deeds". In other words, there was an understanding in a still religious society that certain crimes triggered a like punishment. In a traditional world, the debate and deliberation centered on the ignominy of the crime and not on the purported ignominy of the form of the sentence. In mentioning all of this, however, we are not proposing to resurrect old forms of punishment such as crucifixion, because everything has its time and place; we only intend to comment on the wisdom of traditional societies which the moderns are in no position to scorn. In that respect, one form of traditional punishment that elicits horror among humanists is the Islamic law requiring that thieves have their hand cut off; this is as graphic an example of "poetic justice" as can be imagined. However, this law's justification does no more than echo the Gospel: "Wherefore if thy hand or foot offend thee, cut them off" (Matt. 18:8); the objections that this is purely a metaphorical injunction, miss the point. The sensible question to raise here is not whether the sentence is gruesome but whether its implementation spares society from epidemic thievery and swindling, for the entire prophylaxis here rests on

---

30 Interesting to note is that a majority of miscarriages in justice involve people who have already some kind of criminal record. That being the case, their loud protests of innocence ring hollow, because crime, any crime, brands one a criminal, namely someone who places himself at perilous variance with Heaven.

31 "Whatsoever thou shalt bind on earth shall be bound in heaven, and whatsoever thou shalt loose on earth shall be loosed in heaven" (Matt. 16:19).

the vital principle of "an ounce of prevention. . .". That is to say, the crime of theft, if not nipped in the bud, is of such momentous social implications that the survival of civilization depends ultimately on controlling the destructive proclivity to lawlessness in its very roots; theft unpunished is the unraveling thread. What is more, the actual need of having to resort to a "harsh" sentence diminishes in direct proportion to men's willingness to implement the appropriate sentence whenever necessary; thus instead of lamenting about the harshness of a sentence, while allowing crime to fester and grow, one should lament the powerlessness of a hamstrung justice and especially the evilness of man's unreformed heart. But "man is good", we hear the hue and cry! Alas, evil never had such an ally as a so-called humanist.

*   *   *

In conclusion, it should be added, and in fact it cannot be too strongly emphasized, that the death penalty is a double-edged sword: while it is the ultimate sanction in the hierarchy of penal severity, guaranteeing real authority to the entire edifice of justice, the risk of misuse obviously creates at the same time the risk of the most despotic of abuses; to use it, for instance, to coerce a confession,[32] is a perversion of its necessary role as an instrument of intimidation. Since its effect is absolute, it requires, to be just, absolute proof before its application.

Ideally the death penalty would be merely a prerogative that "the sword of justice" holds in reserve, rarely or never to be employed, and that should always be the intent so as to preserve its value for only the most egregious of crimes;[33] at the same time, a judiciary worthy of its name should never forsake that "ultimate recourse" so as to preserve the fullness of its God-bestowed eminence and clout. And, it must be reiterated, the notion of justice is indissolubly linked with the idea of mercy, contradictory as

---

32 The ease with which a false confession can be extracted is only surpassed by the reverence awarded a confession. It is commonly believed, that no one would confess to a crime they did not commit; however, annals of justice are filled with spurious confessions, many of which were extorted thanks to the threat of capital punishment itself which, in the hands of a skilled and fearsome interrogator, is the ultimate instrument of persuasion—the truth be damned.

33 Under the *Pax Mongolica* of Khubilay Khan—a fierce Mongol, no less!—who ruled over the greatest number of subjects the earth had ever seen, the death penalty was disfavored so that during his rule the number of executions dropped to rates lower than those in the modern United States (Amy Chua, *Days of Empire* [New York: Doubleday, 2007], p. 120). Disfavored, however, is not the same as eliminated.

this may seem at first, especially for those espousing the idea of justice's "vindictiveness"; yet, it should be understood that the idea of "revenge" is consistent with the necessity of avenging a wrong, for not avenging a wrong amounts then to endorsing a wrong by implication, an outcome that would be the ultimate injury to the victim and to society, leaving aside that the cosmos cannot leave an injustice unrectified.

Hence, if God is merciful He cannot be unjust; and to be just—in the case of God—is to be merciful whatever the outward implementation of that mercy may have to be. To repair a broken equilibrium is a mercy for the whole. The primary purpose of justice, earthly as well as heavenly, is first to maintain equilibrium, and secondly to restore it once it has been disrupted. And there can be no real mercy without proper and complete reparation. The individual is created in the image of God: this is what saves him or damns him. God knows best, yes, assuredly, but man also has an obligation to represent God on earth, an obligation that he cannot shirk without irreparable damage to himself and to society.

CHAPTER 9

On Authority

Thou thoughtest that I was altogether such an one as thyself:
but I will reprove thee, and set them in order before thine eyes.
(Ps. 50: 21)

An authority that is merely human is no authority at all. No man can set himself up as a standard unless he defer to an instance greater than himself, otherwise why would his opinions compel assent? The individual by himself is inherently nothing if not another individual among innumerable other individuals. Hence, an individual's claim to authority must rest on a principle that transcends his individuality and rejoins a universal prototype in which all individuals can recognize themselves and realize their common identity. All human authority is based on the delegation and exercise of a power that cannot belong to an individual as such, although an individual can identify himself with this power and even embody it, both symbolically as well as literally, through the scrupulous execution of his office's duty. But this power's compelling credibility—akin to what is termed the "power of jurisdiction"—has to rest on the idea of an overlord that transcends all lords. In the same manner, man's individual perfection rests on a model that transcends him because man in himself—or by himself—can never be perfect, although his imperfection does not prevent him, in theory, of having access to certitude, and therefore of knowing and partaking impersonally in the perfection of absolute authority. But certitude presupposes perfect objectivity—indeed, man is not really man except for his objectivity—and this capacity for objectivity is to be found in the heart-intellect, or what constitutes the supra-personal core of each individual, the delegate divinity within every man. Not least, without objectivity there can be no fairness, and in turn authority without fairness forfeits all rights.

Authority presupposes, at root, a supreme Divine Instance which by definition is totally wise and absolutely powerful. Remove the Divine and authority becomes the plaything of imperfect men, the object of endless debating and speculation, and risks being subverted either by the absolutism of the masses or by that of a tyrant. On the political plane, Plato has detailed the series of transitions of types of authority, moving from theocracy, to aristocracy, then to timocracy, oligarchy,[1] democracy, and finally

---

1 Theocracy, of course, being the rule by a priestly class, timocracy rule governed by the principles of honor and military glory, oligarchy the rule by a powerful clique.

tyranny—this axis describing the declining transition of authority going from a truly enlightened rulership, then being appropriated by the noble classes, then by heroes, and later passing through the popular will, before ending in the hands of a tyrant, or of a despotic regime.

Mention was made of certitude because at the heart of the notion of authority lies the idea of Truth, and hence to speak of "truth" is to speak of "certitude", namely of the fact of an objective truth that exists above and beyond the bazaar of human opinions. Furthermore, to speak of "truth"— or of a supreme object—is to imply a subject fit for grasping this truth, this subject being man who has an intelligence capable of understanding it perfectly, in principle if not in fact. This brings us to the following equation: authority equals certitude and certitude equals truth; if truth is absent, there can be no certitude, and therefore no authority. There are, of course, degrees of certitude, not to mention the possibility of false certitudes, but in the latter case the term "certitude" becomes inappropriate, and one should rather speak of a "conviction", however misguided it may be.

Certitude is the impact of Truth in man's subjective substance, or certitude is the subjective experience of Truth;[2] but to refer to a "subjective experience of the Truth" does not mean that this subjective impact equals arbitrariness since Truth is not just an idea but also an existential reality that can be experienced and expressed by an individual, and this is the meaning of certitude. But once again, this experience—or this state—is entirely premised on the objective reality of the Truth, and not on man's conjectural interpretation of it. Put otherwise, Truth exists as such whether or not any single person can measure up to such an august standard, because it lies at the heart of Reality in the form of an objectively intelligible phenomenon and not as a mere subjective phenomenon born from an energy field of blind swirling forces, of which human thinking would be a kind of noumenal variant—a hypothesis which modern science is inclined to believe, as it endeavors to trace all human thinking to brain waves, which themselves would be but the product of biochemistry.[3] The Truth, in other words, is supra-material and precedes both man and therefore the thinking of it; indeed, this is why man can think in the first place.

2 We capitalize the word "Truth" when this term is synonymous with notion of the supreme Divine Principle, not otherwise, namely when it refers to "truth" simply in the abstract. That said, consistency may not always be achievable.

3 The relationship between thought and biochemistry exists, of course, but modern science is tempted to invert the relationship since brain patterns can be manipulated, whence the plethora of theories arguing that men are but the product of their genes and physiological processes; but this correlation proves only a relationship and not a hierarchy: consciousness precedes matter—just as selfhood precedes being—and here we rejoin the debate between vitalism and materialism.

Not least, the idea of Truth also implies that of "discernment", the foundation of which lies in man's inherent capacity to distinguish the Real from the unreal and, consequently, to discern, to assess, and thus to judge. In its profoundest meaning and to borrow from the Vedanta, this discernment is that between *Atma* (the Real) and *Maya* (the unreal, or the less real), and not just between true and false because there are relative degrees of truth just as there are relative degrees of falseness depending on the subject's vantage point; man's ability to assess such distinctions is the foundation of his potential authority.

*   *   *

In a utilitarian world, there is a temptation to reduce the idea of authority to purely pragmatic or scientific disciplines, and therefore to deny it—at least partially—to thinkers, educators, the clergy, or to anyone specializing in matters involving philosophy, doctrine, and principles, namely in all domains that cannot be verified by physical laws. Moreover, formerly noble certitudes, such as articles of faith about man's divine origin, have become subject to systematic revisionism as well as to what is termed "deconstruction", or to what really is the insanity of a hyper-critical mind which, unleavened by the wisdom of contemplation, is left to spin on its own cerebral skepticism, whose stepsister is cynicism. Part of the problem here results from the degeneration in modern times of the meaning of knowledge, and therefore of the notion of Truth itself—a notion declared obsolete, if ever it existed, in an age ruled by relativism. The irony is that such degeneration would mockingly occur in the wake of a doctrine of endless progress. Indeed, progressivism, this central article of faith for the humanists, while extolling the assumption of mankind's ever-increasing knowledge, actually ends up undermining the whole premise of knowledge itself since the guiding principle of progress presupposes a parallel principle of relentless obsolescence in which all previously acquired knowledge is either held in suspicion, reinterpreted, or debunked. Unperceived, but underlying this dismantling of tradition, in what amounts to a suicidal trend, is a headlong flight from a sacred center—or a sacred origin, the premise of all traditional civilizations—in favor of a fictitious supreme omega point, a quest that, barring heavenly intervention, is bound instead to lead mankind into oblivion because unreachable—the fate of all chimeras madly pursued. It is not that science has not discovered "extraordinary" new things, but that the prestige of scientific examination has been extrapolated to the whole culture of civilization, so that it is assumed everything man once knew, treasured, or acted upon is now open to complete "scientific" re-evaluation, in the name of the promise of some kind of future superknowledge, spurred by a scientific "man knows best" confidence, aspiring to a virtual omniscience, but inexistent by definition because man as such cannot overcome man; that is, he can only transcend himself spiritually, not materially. And once ancient knowledge has been discredited—never mind its formerly hallowed divine premise—man has no alternative than to be a guinea pig in his own blind, or semi-blind experiment.[4] What progressivism lacks in settled wisdom it compensates in speculative presumption: the philosophy of progress holds that mankind, having transcended its simian origins, is now engaged on a stunning journey of evolution, rising from primeval slime to sidereal greatness. But to justify its bold objective, this doctrine has to dismiss all the "legends" of a primordial Eden as fantasy, and the ancient notion of the Spirit has to be reduced to an electro-magnetic field theory that can be graphed and charted, which is as much as to say that it becomes despiritualized. In a materialistic world, one therefore that is inevitably secular, the Spirit is an outcast.[5]

*   *   *

Authority derives from the Truth, we have said, but in its social application it can derive from several founts: tradition, sacred or official investiture, electoral success, competence, merit, or, not least, knowledge itself which in fact is the basis for all types of human competence. And, of course, it

---

4 For instance, in "cracking the genetic code" science may think it can control a distant outcome, though one that it cannot possibly foresee; it is on a slippery slope to nowhere, a human twilight zone in which ethical scruples will be trampled as ever-more short-sighted utilitarian needs turn into imperative juggernauts. Here is the point: it is inconceivable that once man obtains a firmer grasp of the genetic code, that he will not forthwith feel compelled to manipulate it, whether profitably for the benefit of mankind, or so he wishfully thinks, or abusively, if tyrants get their hands on it. Here is where the dictum, "a little knowledge is a dangerous thing" might apply as the epitaph for the modern world.

5 To discount primordial or Edenic man's existence simply because there are no material traces of this era on earth—intemporal in its origin, the "once upon a time" meaning "outside of time", because eternal—is a very convenient way to reject any theory that would refute what in fact is a modern ideology jerry-rigged on material speculations. Very well, but modern scientists might in turn accuse traditionalists of resorting likewise to unprovable "facts" in order to buttress their own spiritual or metaphysical preconceptions; the answer is that traditionalists at least leave the door wide open for a divine interpretation of creation that materialists have in effect closed, at least *de facto*. Metaphysics, by definition, has no agenda since its domain is pure Truth apprehended through the heart-intellect and not just the mind alone, whereas scientism has no use for the heart-intellect and thus no use for a non-material truth hailing from what is assumed to be an inexistent Spirit. But, in fact, the Spirit's supra-existence, materially undetectable, does not equal non-existence, quite the contrary.

can also derive from divine inspiration or even, in the case of prophetic knowledge, from direct personal revelation—exceedingly rare as this last possibility is.

This is all well and good, democratists will caution, but for authority to be effective it must be recognized by the people or it becomes irrelevant in practice. Normally, such popular validation—ideally the *sensus fidelium*[6] and not just profane populism—could once be thoroughly relied upon as generation upon generation of people were all raised with an inherited and thus an instinctual as well as historical understanding of true authority. In other words, traditional man, being still normal spiritually speaking, had an innate sense of whether a leader represented divine authority or not;[7] and in turn this popular assessment compelled a leader, in principle, to remain true to his office—at least in appearance—or risk scandal, if not destitution or even death. But, after several centuries of humanistic up-heavals, Western man no longer is born either with an inherent sense of absolute Truth or of what a model human being should resemble, relativ-ism having blown such venerable notions to pieces. Humanist apologists will fervently aver, however that this is exactly where democracy stakes its validity—as against a stale theocracy, or against the tainted "self-serving" notion of inherited authority of the monarchists—because the "vital and regenerative" ideal of democracy, these secular apologists maintain, is pre-mised on the idea that cream will rise to the top, and also that the people will always know what is right better than any single individual ever can. Lost in this utopian premise, however, is that the whole idea of democracy is actually premised not on knowledge but on a vast substratum of collec-tive ignorance, otherwise there would be no need for democracy in the first place. In other words: since no one person can have certitude or perfection, then, supposedly, this intellectual void can only be partially overcome by the combined "wisdom" of many people who can together—groping and fumbling minds dialoguing—arrive at some patchwork of the best pos-sible solution, or the least imperfect of several choices, a pious wish if there ever was one because this method presupposes ignorance from the outset. Man now lives in a world where the phrase "in my opinion" decides ev-erything if this conceit can gather enough critical mass. This means that

6 The "sense of the faithful" or the knowledge Christian believers have of the Church's doc-trine. But we use the term in a universal sense to make a distinction between the authority of believers versus the semi-authority of non-believers, attributing importance to the fact of faith as being a prerequisite for competent knowledge.

7 This point presupposes a still living sense of the principle of the "iconic figure" detailed in our earlier chapter bearing this title.

pluralist democracy[8] is logically based—paradoxically and contrary to virtually everyone's assumption of it—on an implicit indictment of the very notion of man as *imago Dei* and thus of man as a competent authority in his own right. Indeed, to speak of man—metaphysically—is to speak of knowledge and therefore it is to speak implicitly of a sage. But the principle of democracy presupposes the opposite for, to reiterate, it starts from the assumption of man's radical ignorance—and without even considering how ignorance could miraculously lead to knowledge—and therefore its notion of man is not only far from flattering, it is actually self-defeating, were anyone to ponder this assumption's implications. In practical terms, this means that the only "authority" that can spring from such a speculative and error-prone ferment is, at best, a partial authority resting on a partial knowledge; for its part, any notion of certitude and hence of true authority is excluded from the outset because certitude, by definition, can never be experimental. Such a premise is of course the opposite of the traditional premise of God-given authority.[9]

Thus, if reference is made to collective man then it can only be implicitly to man as ignorance—knowledge being inversely proportional to the masses—in which case democracy can only provide a solution as the lesser of several evils, an expedient, but not an ideal solution in itself, except in the cases of tribal government mentioned earlier. However, in a densely collectivist setting, the truly good—or the truly wise—is unlikely to prevail via a democratic process, except possibly in a time of extreme crisis, because, first of all, the rise of truly good men would entail the repudiation of mankind's secularism in general, and such an outcome, in an industrial society that is growing progressively more profane, is something that would never be allowed.[10] Finally, one cannot forget that a democracy always errs, by definition, on the side of permissiveness and not on that of discernment; it errs on the side of over-tolerance and inclusion and thus is predisposed to nourish the worm that rots the apple; in other words, democracy coddles its own worst enemy in that it allows all forms of free-thinking and potential anarchy to pullulate, and these are bound in the end to undermine the very freedom which was their seed bed.

8 We have in mind populist democracy and not patrician democracy, because representational government is a key principle that is not synonymous with pure, quantitative democracy.

9 However, as stated earlier, science is making a preemptive claim at the certitude missing in modern thought.

10 There is also the reverse problem, namely that of religion being appropriated by an inherently secularist ideology dressed up as religion. Marxist or collectivist versions of Islam are one example of this, as is a Christian socialism that is evolutionist and progressivist in its basic aims.

Short of re-establishing a true theocracy or at least a monarchy pro-tecting a true Church—both total impossibilities, it would seem, in the present cycle of the *Kali Yuga*—one might still hope for an enlightened autocrat, part of whose wisdom would be to have a consultative govern-ment.[11] The principle of an enlightened autocrat rests on the idea of a po-litical leader who would be a sage, a kind of philosopher-king, as Plato proposed; leaving aside whether or not this solution is realistic, allowance should be made for the fact that such a human being can still exist, and cer-tainly existed in earlier societies. If such a person does exist, he could gov-ern better than any squabbling assembly could, since he would not have to stoop at every turn to mediocre compromises in which everyone is either repaying favors or trying to wrest a piece of power for themselves—due consideration being made however for partial knowledge, despite the fact that partial knowledge always equals partial ignorance.[12] To deny mankind any chance at having such a leader—in the name of proletarian pseudo-ideals—is to deprive mankind of the benefit of true authority, someone who could be a model leader and whose judgments society could set its compass by; someone, in other words, who could truly adjudicate after sift-ing through the merits of a representative debate and impose his decision, and if possible invoking God as guarantor while expressing the willingness to be for evermore cursed should his intent be less than honest.

*   *   *

In a traditional civilization, authority is vested in a human being whose function is to represent—if not manifest—the sacred center, or the sacred origin, the point in other words where God once entered manifestation in the form of perfect man, namely in prophetic form as an *avatara*. As such, the duty of a leader, whether the head of a church, a kingdom, or a house-hold (the *pater familias*), is to offer a human model of God the Father or of the Creator on earth. In cosmological terms, such an authority reflects

---

11 This is the basis of the Islamic *shurra* (or *majlis as-shurra*) a form of government modeled on the Bedouin idea of a council of elders or of prominent men, as well as on the ability for any tribal member (or citizen) to have personal access to this council via audiences. This model exists in all semi-agrarian tribal peoples.

12 The magic word in democracy is the idea of "compromise", never mind how unequal the merits of the two sides. The dogmatic assumption of the sacredness of compromise preempts both full discernment and true principle, because no one, in a relativist culture, would dare lay claim to certitude; therefore, no matter how right one side may be objec-tively, in a purely democratic cult of compromise, it has to trim its sails to the consensus of the ignorant or of political opportunists happy to demagogue the mystique of consensus.

the *primum mobile* or the Motionless Mover, namely the invisible but omniscient agency animating all creatures. And what the human individual occupying such an office cannot reflect, through the possible shortcomings of his personality, is normally made up for by the august symbolism of the function itself—furthermore supported by the ceremonial trappings—for this enables any chosen individual to impersonate it sufficiently, in the best sense of the term, so that the wisdom and power of that role can then be projected into society. In this respect, the structure or form of authority is vastly more important than the possible imperfection or even corruption of the holders of office, for so long as this structure exists, society functions in a manner allowing common man to benefit from its directive principle. Destroy the function, and society loses its bearings, sooner or later—and this is what has happened historically through a series of proletarian revolts typical of an epoch in which, metaphysically speaking, the accident eclipses the substance, or the shadow the Principle.

That said, it is undeniable that the momentous significance of sacred office lends itself to the reverse possibility, that of the gravest abuse; but it would be an irreparable mistake to confuse the two—namely to confuse office and holder—or to say that no man, owing to inevitable human imperfection, can be fit for a supreme office vesting him with legitimate autocratic power. Although we have broached this topic throughout this book, it bears repeating that this is to reason backwards: indeed, it is in fact precisely this human fallibility that is the basis for establishing a strong office in the first place so that the quality of the office can compensate for any lack of competence in its holder; otherwise, one would have to make the argument that since all men are fallible, then no man should have absolute power, and therefore an office reflecting such supremacy of power should be abolished. The real argument of populist zealots resembles this: since no man is exceptional—translation: since they do not want to transcend themselves—all men should be answerable to the people—translation: they should be answerable to imperfect men like themselves—and therefore all office is subject in the end to being defined by committees of like-minded citizens—translation: no office can be based on God's authority. Now, to make our position perfectly clear, we are not disavowing a system of checks and balances between sacrosanct office and popular will, because stagnation or corruption of privilege are relentless perils. Nor are we denying the necessity of competition as a prerequisite for holding office; a society's health requires an element of periodic and revitalizing challenges, and this was in fact one of the justifications for warfare in traditional societies,[13]

---

13 Capitalism follows, in its mode, the same principles (see the Austrian economist Schumpeter's theory of "creative destruction"), but it needs the oversight of strong authority to balance its hegemonic tendencies, which otherwise culminate in crushing monopolies. The

harsh as this law was, but in the end no harsher than the evils ensuing from an artificial insulation from such martial challenges, not forgetting that the moral injunction for the knights—or the *kshatriya* class—to protect the weak and the infirm has been unconscionably overlooked by modern historians for whom feudal systems have no archetype in the cosmic order, but are only antiquated phases in man's ascent from barbarism.

The traditionalist argument for kingship is that a people without a king is a people without a head,[14] just as—symbolically speaking—a people without a pontiff is a people without a heart. The story of Joan of Arc is particularly illustrative in this respect, for her homage and obeisance to her sovereign king, the weak and apparently unworthy Charles VII, finally resulted in a restoration of proper kingship—very much in spite of the man—without which France would have fallen and not become by Providence a bastion of Catholicism.[15] More broadly, to eliminate the principle of monarchy in the murky name of pluralism not only undermines the indispensable principle of a God-given authority, it also destroys man existentially by stripping away from society pageantry, grandeur, ceremonial, as well as eliminating man's sense for heavenly archetypes without which mankind is left to its own very fallible resources in a world made grayer, duller, and commoner from the absence of royalty's solar brilliance.

cosmic model for "creative destruction" is Shiva Nataraja's dance in which he is simultaneously destroying and recreating the universe.

14 Traditional people in fact so revered this principle of authority that even if they despised the ruler they venerated the function. A tragic example of this can be found in the chronicles of an eighteenth century landowner in the High Atlas Mountains, whose father was a holy man; he recorded the caliph's destruction of his father's religious lodge and entire community. He begins his book lamenting that God chose such a flawed political institution to rule the world, but never questions that the caliph is the rightful Prince of the Faithful, even while living the life of a hunted refugee (*La rihla du marabout de tasaft: Sidi Mohammed ben el Haj Brahi, ez-Zerhouni*, trans. Colonel Justinard [Paris: Geuthner, 1940]). Such a split between revolt and loyalty would be unimaginable for a modern revolutionary but, precisely, principle is no longer sacrosanct in a modern world. By contrast, reverence for principle is, for traditional man, anchored in his faith in God, and indeed both az-Zarhounis—father and son—while living desperately in craggy caves never faltered in their faith that God would rescue them even though they had lost everything on earth. "And the Hereafter is better for thee than the here-below", we read in the Koran ("The Morning Hours", 93:4), a refrain that is interwoven in the daily consciousness of every traditional man; it is the spiritual motive for enduring earthly trials without revolt and even with a holy serenity, for "all's well that ends well", as folk wisdom reminds us; and God is ever-mindful of His own.

15 This last statement is not an indictment either of the Anglican Church that was to come or of Protestantism because, paradoxically, Heaven can favor "both sides" in a conflict which may have the virtue of enhancing complimentary—albeit antagonistic—aspects of truth and tradition. But this is a rather complex question that we cannot elaborate on here.

We alluded to the notion of *pontifex*, and the deviation therefrom—as seen in the Christian doctrine of the Fall—and this notion of course finds parallels in other traditions, for example in Islam where man is defined vertically as *khalifat-ul-'ardh* (caliph or representative of God on earth) and horizontally as *nas*, meaning "man"—etymologically, a term connoting "forgetfulness". Collective man is, of course, fallen and therefore forgetful; but not all men partake to the same degree of this fallenness; thus we have mentioned that the possibility for knowledge—plenary if not infallible knowledge—always exists in principle if not in fact. And this is the profounder meaning of the Christian rites of baptism and confirmation, and of spiritual initiation in Sufism and Hinduism, which correspond to a spiritual insemination of a divine quality infused into the recipient, which then has the virtue of conjuring in the recipient his own latent excellence, because man's actualization of timeless knowledge coincides with God's conscious projection of Himself through man into the world. In the last analysis, this capacity for full knowledge cannot of course be claimed by an individual as such because knowledge, in its perfection and depth, can only belong to God or, in the cosmos, to the Holy Spirit (the *'aql kulli* in Sufism). All traditions recognize the idea of a universal spirit, or Logos, which is also defined as the universal intellect or the reflection of God's omniscience projected cosmically, so that no corner of creation is devoid of divine consciousness, at once lightning-like, infinitely gracious, and all-encompassing. Accordingly, and as delegate of God on earth, the role of man is to avail himself of the help of the Holy Spirit "that bloweth where it listeth", and that will certainly come to the assistance of a sincere office holder, whether a priest or a prince—this is "the grace of function"—provided their office be respected and their duty executed correctly according to the canons laid by sacred tradition, which are revealed originally by Heaven. The "grace of function" is, however, a dead letter in plebiscitary considerations.

Such essential or divine authority is conferred, or received, through a variety of means; it can be bestowed through anointment, apostolic succession,[16] or either by birth inheritance or blood (also via the spiritual

16 Though the term "apostolic succession" is Christian, equivalents of this transmission of authority exist in other traditions. In Buddhism, we have the *acariya-parampara*, transmission from respected elder teachers—comparable to the Jain *sthaviravali*—despite the Buddha's own apparently emphatic rejection of the idea of succession: "Be ye lamps unto yourselves" (*Mahaparinibbana Suttanta*, II.24-26). However, by the fifth century A.D. we find a luminary of the eminence of a Buddhaghosa appointing teachers to succeed him. In Tibetan and Zen Buddhism there is the lineage of *dharma* transmission from an unbroken line of spiritual teachers and disciples, illustrating the manner in which the Buddha always showed both sides of a possibility. And in Hinduism there is the *guru-shishya* (master-disciple) succession.

kinship of blood brothers), a trial by fire, or by a decision from a council of elders such as the Anglo-Saxon witenagemot. In addition, it can be bestowed through initiation (*silsilah* in Sufism), royal or spiritual appointment, and also directly from Heaven, for instance in the case of the Vedic *Agnihotra*, or rite of fire, where the officiating priest (*agnihotri*) can be chosen directly by God.[17] In each case, the electing instance should not—in principle[18]—include a greater pluralism than a council could conveniently encompass, because popular election is a fickle and unreliable measure that, by itself, usually means very little unless it confirms a choice that destiny has already established, such as selecting a victorious general; in fact, as we have seen, republicanism, *grosso modo*, is strictly a make-shift mechanism that men resort to in the absence of any effective authority, at least in situations involving a large human collectivity.[19]

Which brings us to this point: authority can be absent at both ends of the human spectrum, either because there is no need for it, the human collectivity being of such outstanding quality and intelligence that it is self-governing—and this is the case with the first Buddhist *sanghas*, the Desert Fathers, and in some ways also with noble tribes, such as the Plains Indians of North America—or else authority is absent, or relatively absent, when there is a generalized degeneration of society, which nonetheless still does not prevent some form of authority from functioning, in which case authority is diluted over administrative bodies of various kinds; but it cannot be termed pure authority, namely one rightfully containing a measure of certitude and thus of infallibility. And, of course, a third possibility of "non-authority" would be a false authority, namely a person or body of officials usurping the seat of true authority,[20] not forgetting the possibility of

---

17 Another example of such an appointment is the selection in Tibetan Buddhism of successor llamas, who are "discovered" by the signs attending the birth or infancy of a male child. But now this millenary tradition risks being referred in the future to democratic vote. No one, it seems, has the fortitude to be "out of fashion" anymore, unless from below, of course.

18 "In principle", we propose, because there are exceptions in which the "will of Heaven" may be expressed through a more universal suffrage; such a case would be that in Buddhism of the early *sanghas* or communities of monks who congregated under the leadership of a monk elected by the members, although he did not have the authority of an abbot.

19 In a social or spiritual elite, a form of "republicanism" makes sense because of the elevated quality of the average level of the members.

20 Such is the extraordinary case of the modern Catholic Church and the post-Vatican II popes who, by any traditional standard, are non-popes. The issue for the Catholic faithful is very simple: either they choose to consider the pre-Vatican II popes as true and legitimate, the last of which denounced modernism—Pius X in particular, as well as Pius XII—or one chooses the post-Vatican II popes as being true; but under no logical circumstances can

brute tyranny—although tyranny can also assume more subtle forms such as can be found in the elected tyranny of the masses whose opinions and tastes (or, rather, gross lack of them) dictate the tenor of a society through their elected representatives and do so to the detriment of elite men and women.

*   *   *

We have seen that authority can be transmitted either vertically, through divine appointment, or horizontally through tradition, or through a combination of the two. In the more particular case of a medieval trial by fire, this selection can be interpreted as a divine type of appointment in the sense that when a hero emerges victorious from wagering his life, an assumption can be made of his having earned Heaven's favor, especially if his triumph is accompanied by certain signs or omens. However, the reliability of a trial by fire selection presupposes a formal and spiritual framework, because recourse to the augury of signs implies an effective relationship with Heaven, and not extravagant wishful thinking. The fact that reliance on these signs has completely vanished in modern cultures does not mean that men have finally matured and become rational, only that Heaven has withdrawn, or that the permeability between the supernatural and the earthly, which characterized traditional civilizations, has congealed.[21] Likewise, that no secular leader is anointed—or even considered fit for an anointment ceremony—is another proof of the banality of a modern office, which is no more than that of a glorified functionary, if that much.

Perhaps the greatest irony of humanism is that it is finally dehumanizing because in "liberating" man from religion—or, what amounts to the same, in humanizing religion—it ends up divorcing man from all that defines his spiritual purpose on earth. We have the spectacle of reason trying

one accept both sets of popes as being equally true, because a Pius X and a Pius XII stood at the opposite doctrinal ends of a John XXIII and a Paul VI; to embrace both is therefore either ignorance, stupidity, or deception. Pius X and Pius XII both denounced modernism in unambiguous terms and tried to prevent the very views the Second Vatican Council's popes embraced.

21 People, unaccustomed to living in a traditional civilization, have little or no idea of the type of relationship with Heaven that permeates such a world. There is a subtle intelligence and magical language of signs and hints from the *barakah* (the divine presence) informing and guiding believers at every step. To provide an example, there are pious men in Morocco who sense a special fragrance waft into the air at the set time of prayers. And we have personally experienced the meeting of hearts that can occur in the medina, even across a crowded street, bustling with mechanized traffic and blaring horns, where *salikun* (travelers on the Sufi path) recognize each other instantly even in the absence of any insignia.

to operate intelligently while severed from the enlightening influx of the heart-intellect, the immanent source of all intelligence and understanding;[22] in such a scenario, reason can still operate, but it is like the fulgurations of a stricken star living off a dying reserve of energy with no true capacity for self-renewal despite its still dazzling aura. In fact, reason, unmoored from the stabilizing and deepening assistance of the Intellect, can wax prolific in an effort to solve everything by itself, when all it is doing is making the simple complex, thus obscuring the one thing that matters for man. Consequently, secular authority will dress itself up in omnivorous pedantic erudition or nitpicking expertise, but this is a thin disguise for a lack of true wisdom. The authority of a king is that his "yea" or "nay" has the force of a divine decree, of a mighty and venerable fiat, and what he does not explain in reams of words[23] can be validated both by the prestige of his function and, often, by the stature of his own personality. It is hard for men today to imagine what the charisma of a true king can be, but when Clovis I of the Franks, to take one example, was anointed king, the people beheld more than a man, they beheld a regal being appointed by Heaven to rule them; and the sacerdotal anointing was a ceremony instituted to convey that fact both to the ruler and his subjects. Again, the model for this ruler and the essence of his authority is derived from the prophetic envoy of Heaven on earth: "*Alleluia*. You have set on his head, O Lord, a crown of precious stones. *Alleluia*" (Tridentine Mass).

*   *   *

Authority, once again, is based on Truth and hence on certitude. And this equation leads us to consider the doctrine of infallibility. To illustrate this point, reference can be made to the well-known but problematical doctrine of papal infallibility. This doctrine, irrespective of its role in the Catholic Church, is premised on the fact that it is possible for an authority—under the right set of conditions!—to appeal to divine infallibility when promul-

---

22 Likewise, in Eastern metaphysics, the *manas* (mind) derives its light and knowledge from the *buddhi* (the heart-intellect). In the famous image of the charioteer and horses in the *Bhagavad Gita*, the *buddhi* is the charioteer, *manas* the reins, and the five horses the five senses, whereas the chariot is the body.

23 A "word to the wise" is a lost art. Legislative findings today are stuffed into gargantuan tomes that no human being could possibly read, let alone assimilate properly; it is as if men tried to exhaust an ocean of ink to explain what they rightly fear they do not understand, or as if quantity could make up for the loss of quality, or as if details could compensate for the lack of a master principle. Indeed, if "a word to the wise" no longer applies, then perhaps it is because there are no more wise to be found.

gating an opinion or decree. The lateness of this dogma's adoption—as regards the Church[24]—is due no doubt to the necessity of re-affirming the waning scope of an authority, originally granted from Heaven, to an increasingly skeptical audience; the sacred magisterium's authority was essentially unquestioned in earlier times, despite some dramatic schisms.[25] However, the insidiousness of the twin doctrines of relativism and democratism is never more apparent than in the slow corruption of the standard of certitude wherein spiritual authority—or the principle of an implicit *ex cathedra* authority[26]—has been steadily eroded until this imprimatur had to be made more explicit to counter the inroads made by rationalist skepticism.

If the notion of infallibility strikes modern man as preposterous this is not surprising given his total reliance on reason in the absence of the notion of the heart-intellect; reason, in contrast to the heart-intellect, is entirely dependent on trial and error speculation or on arguments honed by counter-arguments; in such a setting, "authority" can only be agreed upon through collective consensus. But to exclude the principial possibility of infallibility amounts to denying two central truths: 1. that man can be guided by God in some things, directly and inerrably so, and 2. that man's essence is rooted in the Absolute and he therefore has the capacity, potentially at least, to understand if not embody the prerogatives of the Absolute itself, whence the possibility for man to achieve perfection of understanding in certain specific instances. In other words, to deny infallibility as such amounts, by default, to erecting the relative as an absolute, and this is finally a contradiction in terms; in that case, it becomes virtually impossible to make binding laws, for *lex dubia lex nulla*: a law about which one is uncertain is inherently useless, because subject to endless reinterpretation and therefore never final; whence the usefulness of religion or, to be more exact, of Revelation setting down "once and for all" what men must and must not think and do.[27]

24 It was apparently promulgated in 1870.

25 But one must distinguish between challenges to a specific person, or body of authorities representing the magisterium, and challenges to the very concept of a magisterium itself; this is a later development.

26 *Ex cathedra*, which means "(speaking) from the chair (seat of authority)". Islam, more prudently, recognizes a *mufti*'s power to issue a *fatwa* (an opinion on Islamic law), but the content of this edict is binding only to the degree that the scholar issuing it merits respect. The component of "infallibility" (or of "relative infallibility"), in other words, depends entirely on the personal prestige of the cleric.

27 True, too detailed a law can rob judges of their discretionary wisdom while facilitating technical exceptions, but this is a vast topic. What religion offers are broad principial rules,

Here we must pause to consider that Revelation has always come to mankind through a human spokesman, albeit a prophet. This being the case, it should be understood that, on the one hand, if few things are more unjust than being subject to a false authority or to an individual—or a group of individuals—usurping divine right to dominate and exploit others, there can be, on the other hand, legitimate figures capable of supreme authority, something which plebeian democratism, precisely, rejects out of principle. In other words, if there can be impostors robed in ecclesiastical majesty[28]—and everyone is usually very prompt to notice this—there can also be genuine men of authority possessing supernatural virtue and wisdom, although this possibility is basically not recognized nowadays. In fairness, it should be understood that the one does not go without the other: the possibility of incompetence proves in its way the possibility of competence, just as foolishness proves wisdom. Indeed, there is no reason that authority cannot be invested in a flesh and blood human being who resembles other human beings in all outward respects, of course, but who is unlike them with respect to that special quality of loftiness of judgment. To quote from the Psalms: "Thou thoughtest that I was altogether such an one as thyself: but I will reprove thee, and set them in order before thine eyes" (50:21). And likewise, in Hinduism, it is a major offense to mistake the spiritual master (or guru) for a human being "like any other". Put differently, egalitarianism does not prevent an exceptional human being from *being* exceptional, but it does prevent him from being *seen* as exceptional in the sense of being gifted with attributes setting him above other human beings, and that is a loss for the multitudes since such a being cannot accede to a position of permanent authority.[29] Instead, people believe that organizing many fallible beings into a committee overcomes the impos-

---

such as in the Decalogue, and this is what we have in mind—the rest is "a word to the wise". The Decalogue was meant to apply until the end of time. That said, clearly each of the great religious revelations underwent centuries of elaboration through mystics, scholars, theologians, and metaphysical sages, but these elaborations were essentially part of a revelation's organic development, the fruition of the promise encapsulated in its seeds. It is in no way comparable to the revisionism that struck the twentieth century Roman Catholic Church, leading it to adapt to the modernism that it should have been combating with every fiber of its Christian soul.

28 The monstrousness of this incongruity is addressed in the Koran: "Lo! We offered the trust unto the heavens and the earth and the hills, but they shrank from bearing it and were afraid of it. And man assumed it. Lo! He hath proved a tyrant and a fool" (33:72).

29 In Shakespeare's immortal words, Caesar is made to say: "But I am constant as the northern star / Of whose true-fixed and resting quality / There is no fellow in the firmament" (*Julius Caesar*, III, i, 60).

sible possibility of a true sage which they do not believe in; both attitudes—namely accepting the notion of collective wisdom while rejecting that of individual wisdom—are equally an error because they share the same root: skepticism in the idea of the Absolute.

*　*　*

A crown does not a king make, no doubt, yet no man can be a king without one; the function is the pivot of authority: it should not be removed with impunity lest society become unhinged. This crown, emblem of a king's divine right to rule—and mirror symbol of God's crown—is the key to understanding the nature of authority, whence Charles I's famous words before his martyr's execution: "A sovereign and a subject are clean different things." Of course, the legitimacy of such authority has to be premised on justice for, as Plato said, "nothing resembles God more than the just man" (*Theaetetus*).[30]

The principle of authority implies by extension the possibility of an elite, although it should be specified that the whole notion of an elite itself pertains mainly to the unique cyclical conditions prevailing in the *Kali Yuga* and especially to its latter portion, or to what René Guénon termed the "reign of quantity"; in other words, the notion of an elite becomes especially precious in an era when quantity overwhelms quality, and therefore when quality—in the form of an elite—becomes the sole and indispensable resort for saving the values of a civilization. Unfortunately, the term "elite" now reeks of class privilege as well as of exploitation; however, this should not prevent us from recognizing what the concept means in itself, the fullest meaning being that of *noblesse oblige*.[31] Now what the idea of democracy cannot encompass—leaving aside its generally sound principle of assigning term limits to elected officials—is the possibility of promoting and safeguarding an elite; in fact, the notion of plebiscitary consultation is contrary to the whole idea of deference to an elite in that the populist assumption only takes into consideration the risk of abuse and tyranny, believing that the very notion of an "elite" can only lead to the rise of a parasite social class dedicated to inherited power, enrichment, and prestige at the expense of the masses—which assumption, incidentally, is perfectly reasonable once the Church loses its spiritual clout[32]—when in fact a society cannot really

30 Quoted from the 4th Dialogue of Joseph de Maistre's *St. Petersburg Dialogues* (Montreal: McGill-Queen's University Press, 1993), p. 127, note 32.

31 Or, to paraphrase, "for the noble-born magnanimity is a duty".

32 For an elite to be an elite, it has to be anchored in spirituality. The stamp of godlikeness is the only aristocracy.

exist successfully without an elite, in whatever field as a matter of fact. Why only the association of elite and abuse is retained in the modern mind, and almost never the idea of elite and excellence—as would be normal[33]—is partly due to the increasing degeneracy of mankind wherein the power being vested into one person—or one privileged group—is quickly corrupted and misused due to the passions of the office holder, who is tempted to translate his personal desires into a rule of law, instead of grasping what his sacrosanct obligation is to the people and, above all, to God.

In assessing these matters, it is also worth pondering the following: there is an intangible element, call it "divine grace", "charismatic genius", "super-eminent virtue", or "noble intelligence" in a superior human being that clean transcends petty politicking; this intangible essence can be defined as a spiritual quality which, if given a chance of being converted into social institutions, can permeate and radiate into an entire culture and determine the course of history. Leaving aside for now the obvious case of the great *avataras* who founded religions and whose prophetic personality determined entire civilizations, such a charismatic essence occurring in leaders can be found, for example, in a man of a Charles Martel's stamp who became the seminal genius for the entire Carolingian dynasty and served as an inspired model for the development of feudalism and the brilliant period of chivalry this notion (or polity) ushered, the noble archetype of which fashioned generations of men and women for several centuries. His victory at the Battle of Tours, where he repelled the Saracen invasion of Northern Europe, thus securing the providential hold of Christendom over the West, could never have taken place had he to defer to committees and lawyers and the conventions ruling international organizations.[34] It is this regal figure's sterling individual prowess and magnanimity, as well as his humility,[35] that guaranteed his imperishable merit; and the same intangible spirit of heroic genius coursed the veins of his grandson Charlemagne, whose reign was like the fulfillment of his grandfather's mettle. The spirit of an age, indeed the spirit of a whole culture, yea of a tradition, finds its abiding impetus in a great man and the gifted companions, heirs,

33 In some branches, however, the idea of an elite is still understood because of its indispensability. In the army, the marines are a good example of this, because second-rate soldiers jeopardize lives if not the mission.

34 Comparing epochs, such as the Middle Ages to modern internationalism, is not entirely fair, for different times require different measures; yet epochs finally reflect the cosmic state of mankind and this is what we intend to contrast.

35 He declined all the honorific titles others wanted to bestow on him, including that of kingship.

and emulators following in his wake, who also may be depositaries of his charisma; although this transmission applies especially to the patrilineal descendants, it does not do so exclusively since the archetypal genius of such figures can also flash forth discontinuously, skipping generations, if not centuries.[36] The importance of such elite originators cannot be over-rated; therefore, one can only deplore the loss of institutions enabling their ascension—or at least their radiation—, institutions that under normal circumstances should combine the qualities of the sacred and the civic for, once again, a purely civic institution has no enduring clout.[37] This generational transmission of a great man's charisma, to say nothing of the spiritual decorum and *barakah* bestowed by a central prophetic figure which is then imitated and maintained from generation to generation, is difficult if not impossible to preserve in a regime based purely on the people's will expressed through elections.

Taking now the example of the great *avataras*, if one inquires in depth about the manner in which the art and customs of Far Eastern civilizations developed under Buddhism, or where the animating spark of genius infusing their iconography and customs and doctrine was born, one will see that they are to be ascribed to the supernatural merit of the human yet divine figure that a Gautama Buddha had accumulated through extreme asceticism and total spiritual sincerity. We say "supernatural merit", because human merit alone cannot account for such a prodigy, although the human component in the Buddha's enlightenment also entails a measure of heroicalness of will, implacable self-mastery combined with supreme contemplative serenity, the keenest spiritual intuition as well as an utter self-sacrifice that are almost incomprehensible to fathom for non-spiritual men; its charismatic reverberations, enshrined in the spirituality of saints and then reflected in the masses like light on water, can last for centuries upon centuries, dimming and then refulgurating time and again. Although the Buddha had no flesh and blood descendants, he had a spiritual posterity, a "bloodline" of the spirit if one will, just as Christ did, propagated mainly (but not exclusively) through apostolic succession.[38] The case of the

---

36 For example, in the realm of spirituality, it may be that a Meister Eckhart was an echo of the Johannine spirit, namely of Saint John the apostle's gnostic wisdom.

37 Thus, even in such a devoutly democratic nation as that of the United States of America, the oath of the presidency is not rendered effective until the newly elected president has taken a solemn pledge over the Bible.

38 Not "exclusively" since there were Christian women saints, some of whom were "magistra" or teachers, and some of whom could even be considered as co-redemptresses with Christ, notably a Marguerite Porete, Angelina Foligno, a Hadewijch, and Mechthild of Magdeburg. Bernard McGinn, in his *The Flowering of Mysticism* (New York: Herder, 1998,

prophet of Islam is quite different in that it rejoins the patrilineal model alluded to above, for he had a flesh and blood progeny, a genetic feature that led, notably, to the tradition of sharifism in the kingdom of Morocco which, in turn, led to dynasties affiliated to Muhammad's grandsons, or to a unique royalty in this kingdom that although spiritual in its essence was secured and transmitted through bloodlines, hence bypassing and in fact trumping all considerations of popular suffrage.[39]

*   *   *

The great casualties of the trend of "progress" (or progressivism) are not only the notions of Truth, Authority, and Tradition, but also the notion of a sacred norm; this loss of the sense of a sacred norm explains the immense change in things and customs that the average person today typically considers to be "normal", but that are normal merely for being subscribed to passively by the majority. The desensitization of the soul of modern man, assaulted by the abnormal on a daily and relentless basis, has skewed the perception of what Reality is, to the point that no one really knows anymore what the term "normal" should connote, when in fact it is a term that, far from mirroring ever-shifting customs dictated by inertia and popularity, derives from a word founded on the notion of the True, the Beautiful, and the Good. Indeed, the terms "knowledge", "norm", and "nobility" are cognate terms that have become dissociated over time. Thus a noble person is really a person who knows, just as to know—truly to know—is to be noble, and therefore to be normal.[40]

In his Edenic state, man possessed authority inwardly and therefore did not need to be governed or directed by anyone outside himself; one could say that, geometrically speaking, his consciousness was ruled by the

---

p. 199), terms these women the "Four Female Evangelists" of thirteenth century mysticism. He also mentions the case of Margaret the Cripple, whom Christ singles out for atoning for the world much as he did (p. 197). Relevant to this chapter's theme on authority, McGinn specifies: "In order to authenticate their teaching about the path to God each of these women [the Four Female Evangelists] had to 'invent' a form of divine authorization of literally evangelical weight, that is they had to claim that their message came directly from God in a manner analogous to that of the Bible itself" (p. 142).

39 Several of these Moroccan dynasties impacted the West directly through the Hispano-Moorish empires they spawned. Indeed, the reverberations of such a paragon bloodline are near measureless and, finally, can only be properly assessed through spiritual understanding; their impact transcends sociology.

40 The Indo-European root of the word "norm" is connected to the idea of "knowledge", from which term the word "noble" is also derived: the root term *no-* becomes *gno-* in certain languages—e.g. *gnosis*—or remains *no-*, such as in the word "noble" or "nobility".

215

principle of the circle—in counter distinction with the principle of the triangle which is that of the hierarchy governing man later; figuratively speaking, immanence prevailed over transcendence because each man was a prophet unto himself, that is to say each man knew God in his heart. With the fall from grace, however, and later with the stratification of social castes ensuing from the gradual declining trend of the great cycles, man could no longer be self-directed, whence the need for the establishment of figures of hierarchical authority. In turn, authority as such implies obedience, a virtue which is first owed one's parents; however, obedience cannot be readily summoned where authority is hobbled by egalitarianism or where authority is mostly just formal, let alone unmerited. And yet, deference to authority is the beginning of self-transcendence, for as an old saying expresses it, he who does not know how to obey does not know how to rule. In obeying a true authority figure, man learns to overcome himself, this in fact being the indispensable qualification for exercising authority itself. Moreover, an authentic authority figure is a reflection of each individual's divine heart-intellect mirrored outwardly; in this sense, insofar as it is a model, it can spark in an individual the awakening of his own divine essence. Hence in assenting to a legitimate outward authority, an individual is actually assenting to his own higher nature, and this, by extension, is a manner of submitting to God via sacred human delegation; this in fact is the foundation for the absoluteness of divine authority. Thus, in submitting, man is awakened to his own immanent seat of conscience which, in itself, possesses all certitude; however, his divine kernel remains inaccessible to him without this prior obedience and submitting; and it is exactly these qualities that egalitarianism eliminates, since it spawns an entitlement mentality in which no one is humble enough to bow his head, but expects to stand shoulder to shoulder with everyone else, no matter their superiority. When equality is not balanced by hierarchy, it is forgotten that, outwardly, the general state of mankind on earth is really that of servanthood with respect to the Lord. At the same time, inwardly, man learns through this servanthood—the essence of which is worship—to imitate the Lord and thus becomes fit, *Dei gratia*, to represent the Lord's authority in public. In passing, one will note that honorific terms of address such as "your worship" or "your lordship", reserved for a person in authority, have now faded from use, becoming yet another casualty of egalitarianism.

Even the greatest of kings "will clothe themselves with trembling" before God's supreme authority,[41] indeed especially the "greatest of kings",

---

[41] "Then all the princes of the sea will come down from their thrones, lay away their robes, and put off their broidered garments: they shall clothe themselves with trembling; they shall sit upon the ground, and shall tremble at every moment, and be astonished at thee" (Ezek. 26:16).

since humility should be the signal mark of their greatness, although this humility should never interfere with their sense of legitimate majesty; false humility, is not humility. In a sense, the humility of a king is to reflect God's lordly pride; he does this by effacing himself before God so as to stand up before man, and in so doing provides average man with a chance to meet God concretely here on earth. Likewise, for man to be overcome by the grandeur of true authority is to become open to God, just as contempt for true authority amounts finally to contempt for God, because God normally makes Himself visible on earth only by delegation.

That said, mention has to be made of the aspect of invisible authority, namely of the possibility for man to efface himself before God in the secret of his oratory or out in nature, or far from heavy-handed human authority. At the risk of contradicting everything developed in this chapter, it is important to highlight the danger of worshipping human authority too slavishly and thereby for man to forfeit recourse to his own immanent conscience, fully divine in its essence, as well as the danger of depending overly on external authority figures for decisions that he alone should make.[42] This immanent conscience that every individual possesses is morally infallible, since it is the trace of the Spirit in man's soul, and yet no one should presume to project his inner infallibility onto things in the world around himself, for man's individual conscience is given to him by God *a priori* for himself and not for the world. This immanent infallibility is the seed of pure luminous objectivity resting in each man and woman's subjective depths, and which becomes then the guide for their own moral decisions, and hence is also the inescapable witness to whom they must answer to should they turn away from what is right. It is for this reason that no man can pretext ignorance on the day of judgment because to do so would be as much as to claim "I am not a man"; our conscience is the essence of what makes us human and it is therefore the essence for our authority over ourselves.

The Desert Fathers, in leaving civilization, followed the principle that God was sole authority and thus outside of this authority there were no significant other principles. To quote from Saint Anthony: "therefore whatever you see your soul to desire according to God, do that thing, and you shall keep your heart safe." Of course, such exclusive deference to immanent authority presupposes a singular profundity of soul which, in the case of the Desert Fathers, as of all true hermits, was guaranteed by their asceticism: solitude, fasting, labor, and prayer leading to the complete pu-

---

42 In essence, this is the ideal that American democracy sought nobly to promote, an ideal in which each man and woman would be fully self-accountable to themselves and not become the slaves of a tyrannical government.

rification of the heart. This same ideal of deference to the inward was later echoed by the Quietists, and is also elaborated in the key Christian doctrine of "soul competency".

Not least, an individual's capacity to recognize and hence to accept the authority in another man is, in the last analysis, a form of authority itself. In other words, the granting of authority by one man to another man is really a manner of exercising authority oneself; what we mean is that the consent to be ruled by another is itself a form of authority in that a measure of power is willingly awarded—albeit via obedience—to the person to whom rightful obedience is due. Thus what in principle starts as a hierarchical relationship ends up being a circle: in such a relationship ruler and ruled, or guide and follower, ultimately depend intimately on each other, for no man can live completely independently or be superior in all respects to everyone else; and no man can rule without the consent of the ruled, a consent which in the end can only be earned. In that manner, true authority has no power if not granted it by true obedience.

Authority derives from Truth, we have said, and certitude is the substance of competence. Now there can be no certitude without perfect objectivity and perfect objectivity presupposes utter humility. In turn, poverty before God means simplicity of soul; and, likewise, simplicity entails transparence of soul cleansed of individualistic arbitrariness; only then can God's light shine unobstructed and only then can it guide, infallibly so.

CHAPTER 10

The Primacy of Character

But let your communication be, Yea, yea; Nay, nay.
(Matt. 5:37)

The bedrock of character depends finally on a few simple things, foremost of which are truthfulness, compassion, courage, loyalty, and patience—gemlike virtues that hold the universe together. And it depends also on intelligence inasmuch as it can defined as a virtue and not just a mental faculty. But since man is complex, these "few simple things" are often exceedingly difficult to realize.

Character depends also on a polarity of virtues, a balance of positive and negative attributes, or energies if one will. In a traditional society, to say of a man, "He is beloved by his people and feared by his enemies" summarizes this polarity of virtues, for this man's lovableness derives from the "soft" qualities and his worthiness derives from the "hard" qualities. Now, to speak of a "negative attribute" may sound like a contradiction in terms, but in our world of contrasting light and darkness no positive virtue can stand on its own: generosity presupposes justice—just as justice presupposes generosity—because to give without discernment is to squander, even to harm, just as, on the "negative side" of the ledger, to punish without appropriate leniency is tyranny. Likewise—with respect to oneself—enjoyment requires sobriety, and feasting requires fasting. Now, sobriety can be ranked as a "negative" virtue, but it is just as beneficially necessary as the positive virtue of gratitude is in this same act of enjoyment; thus enjoyment without sobriety prevents gratitude just as gratitude leads to a sober sense of measure that prevents enjoyment from turning into harmful surfeit. Positive and negative qualities cannot be dissociated in the soul or defined apart from each other, just as warmth and cold are in the physical universe, indeed they are counterparts of each other. Similarly, for gentleness not to be weakness requires strength, while on the intellectual plane, contemplation, a "soft" quality, requires discernment, a "sharp" one. And the contrasts of forcefulness and peacefulness are like the characterial counterparts of the existential polarities of motion and stillness, which in the realm of behavior become activity and rest. Without such complementary alternations each character trait can turn from virtue to defect, just as, on the physical plane, activity without rest becomes agitation and rest without activity sloth.

In essence, to speak of character is to speak of virtue; therefore, one is entitled to say that to have character is synonymous with being good, just as to be truly good requires character. Now, it should be specified here that the quality of being "nice" is too often confused with being "good", when in fact to be "nice" is in no wise the same as to be good: everyone wants to be "nice"—and all too often everyone is quick to embrace people that are nice—but it is not well understood that niceness and goodness may in fact be mutually exclusive; which is to say that to be nice has value only if the niceness emanates from true goodness, for hypocrites and evil-minded people can be "nice" too, and in fact have every interest in being so in order to mask their true designs. Hence, character is more than mere "goodness" as popularly understood, that is, when this quality is reduced to niceness. But it is "goodness" when defined as the *Summum Bonum*, or the Sovereign Good which is really another term for Godliness, and a goodness, obviously, that knows how to make use when necessary of the rod, because on earth mercy has to include the possibility of rigor.

In linking character with goodness, one might be tempted in consequence to equate character simply with saintliness. Consequently, it is necessary to add that character is not just synonymous with virtue, or even saintliness, which is the essence of all virtue, but that character is also great-souledness—namely magnanimity (in Hinduism, *mahatma*)[1]—and in fact forcefulness too, because saintliness can be found in a lowly, exceedingly humble, and self-abasing format, and that is not enough to summarize noble greatness of character. Yes, "the meek shall inherit the earth", but in that case to interpret "meekness" merely as "kindness" or as soft-spoken humility[2] would be rather superficial, especially if erecting this definition as the paramount mainstay of virtue; should we then expect lions to become sheep, or Knights Templars to become nurses? In reality, this Christic homily refers, in essence, to the egolessness that does not rise up against Nature; it is akin to the Taoist "non-acting acting" (*wei wu wei*), the image of which is water that seeks the lowest ground and therefore inherits all the world, but without forfeiting any of its floodlike mightiness. Indeed, true meekness is not incompatible with bravery, far from it, just as humility is not incompatible with heroic faith, quite to the contrary. To assume

---

1 The Sanskrit word *mahatma* is composed of the prefix *maha-*, meaning "great", and *Atma* or "God", which rejoins the association just outlined between Goodness and Godliness.

2 Few if any of Christ's teachings have been more misunderstood by passionate people than this one—Nietzsche believed it created a religion of spinelessness; perhaps he forgot about the countless Christian martyrs, such as Saint Perpetua who, after being scourged in the arena, then wounded by wild beasts, helped her executioner's trembling hand by guiding his sword properly to her neck.

the opposite would be to say that strength is arrogance, when in fact true strength knows when to be self-effacing; only the foolhardy are totally fearless. The mystery is that noble fierceness and gentleness[3] go hand and hand, because no forceful quality can reach its fullness without the symbiotic presence of its opposite. To borrow some analogies, the destructive power of the hurricane arises from the gentleness of air, just as the strength of a mountain arises from its absolute stillness, and the brilliance of light from its transparency.

Notwithstanding its popular association with the idea of submissiveness, meekness is really a poverty of spirit—or lowliness—governed in essence by a pure receptivity to the Divine, a receptivity or openness which of course is extended also to the whole universe. And just like *chi* (the invisible energy-force of life)—or like ether—meekness can turn to mightiness on the slightest of promptings, taking on whatever form that circumstances require, from benign serenity to blazing love to invincible courage or, if need be, holy wrath; its lightning spontaneity comes—"negatively"—from the absence of interfering self-interest and—"positively"—from its compassion; its physiological basis can be seen in an attitude combining total relaxation with perfect alertness.[4] The virtue of meekness can be likened to the spotlessness of a mirror: this impeccability of "emptiness" allows the mirror to reflect perfectly what is reflected in it, whether soft candlelight or the blinding glory of the sun. Such is the soul of the "meek" man.

If the essence of character is kindly virtue and noble strength, then the essence of both virtue and nobility is, intellectively, the quality of objectivity—the profound objectivity in which a devotee offers his own substance in igneous oblation to his own luminous intelligence, as it were, in a process daily renewed of self-immolating utterness of denial, sometimes drawing his every breath, moment by moment, through the fire of renunciation

---

3 One of the meanings of the original Greek word *praos*, or "meekness", is that of "gentleness", which recalls Dante's *cuor gentil* or the gentle heart. And the great Saladin's instructions to his son end with these words: "'If I have become great it is because I have won men's hearts by kindness and gentleness'" (quoted in Stanley Lane-Poole, *Saladin: And the Fall of the Kingdom of Jerusalem* [New York: Cooper Square Press, 2002], p. 368). "Gentleness was the dominant note of his character. . . . The respect he inspired sprang from love, which 'casteth out fear'" (Ibid). We suspect, however, that Saladin could also be formidably fierce.

4 This is the key principle of *tai chi*. With respect now to another Eastern martial art, Morihei Ueshiba, the founder of Aikido, explains this in the following manner: "At that moment I was enlightened: the source of *budo* is God's love—the spirit of loving protection for all beings. . . . *Budo* is not the felling of an opponent by force. . . . True *budo* is to accept the spirit of the universe . . . to protect and cultivate all beings in nature" (Ueshiba & Kisshomaru, *Aikido* [Tokyo: Hozansha Publications, 1985]). One of his opponents said that fighting him was like fighting a phantom; that he could not strike him even once.

of all egoic impulses; then it is as if the consciousness of the profoundly virtuous man was a pure luminous awareness-intelligence that instantly converts all personal impulses into infinite truth and goodness. And yet, at the same time, objectivity has a cooling, refreshing virtue for, as we find in the *Bhagavad Gita*, "there is no lustral water like unto Knowledge" (4:38). By contrast, the intimate poison marring perfection of character is secret self-adoration, namely to prefer oneself over others, either practically or affectively, or by secretly allowing ourselves excuses and dispensations we are not so prompt to grant others, especially if they disappoint us.

*   *   *

Deiformity or deformity? Man can be either an image of God or a caricature of his divine archetype, as well as anything in between. The importance of the imitation of Christ—or of modeling oneself on God as human theophany—requires an exceptionally lucid understanding of what such an imitation consists of, because one wants to rise up to imitate the Divine and not to pull the Divine down to resemble us; too often the idea of man being made in the image of God results in God being made in the image of man, and this is where only the prophets, and saints, along with sacred tradition embodied by the pious and the wise, can provide a divine role model.

At birth, the frame of our destiny is like an overturned hourglass measuring out our predestined portion of days and hours; we are born upside down, in a certain sense, and must learn how to stand again. Our life is both a ransom and a harvest, the ransom of a karmic debt that must be paid out and a harvest of opportunities. In death, as every man knows, we will be irreversibly disarticulated and stripped of everything, save one thing: our character, which is our soul. Character is all we can carry with us across the great divide, for character is what we are—the individual self is the sole transmigrant, to paraphrase the Vedanta—and it is therefore our character that will set the tone for what our posthumous fate will be. Indeed, our individual modalities are donned and discarded in a parade of costumes, but "we", in our primordial essentiality as disincarnate soul, endure forever, although not necessarily as the "we" of our psycho-social daily habits and experiences.

That being said, it is delicate to establish a moral equation between our current merits and demerits and a soul's posthumous fate, because there is an element of both *maya* and divine freedom that can intermingle with our karma; in other words, our destiny is affected by interferences from the principle of All-Possibility, on the one hand, and by celestial Grace, on the other—the latter shining through man in spite of man, instilling breath into his being and beckoning him ever to rise. Without this element of divine Grace, our karma would surely be unbearable: our limitations and shortcomings would compress, crush, and suffocate us.

As mentioned above, the essence of character could be defined as "nobility", and indeed even as "kingship", or what Eckhart in his Strasburg sermons termed the theme of "the nobleman", namely someone who has attained divine "sonship" through the birth of the Word in the soul.[5] Once again, this nobleness could also be defined as holiness. However, inasmuch as nobleness and holiness can be contrasted, then nobleness might correspond more specifically to the way of heroism and sacrifice, holiness to the way of contemplative virtue and of becoming god-like— but "god-like" with all due regard for the outward incommensurability between man and the Divine. The idea of human nobleness defined as heroism is of course a vast notion which can include the idealism and prowess of the chivalric knight, the sacrificial devotion of a mother, the rugged integrity of the frontiersman forged in nature's proving ground, and countless others. Indeed, a single virtue such as heroism can serve as the moral basis for a whole cultural tradition, whether that of Samurai Japan, the Plains Indians, the Icelandic sagas, or of the *chansons de geste*. Likewise, on the contemplative side now, a virtue such as compassion can provide the inspiration for a whole religion such as in Buddhism, just as the virtue of sacrifice did for Christianity. Now, clearly nobleness cannot be defined purely as an active complement to contemplativeness, for it includes both a static as well as a dynamic pole: on the one hand nobleness is to position oneself to dwell in the sacred center and to disdain the world's pettiness and illusoriness; hence it is to follow a way of detachment; on the other hand, it is to act in the world in a manner that is generous with others while being forceful with error or injustice. The aspect of "sonship" referred to by Eckhart is the human aspect God dons, and thus, for man, it is to seek to live in a divine way, both inwardly and outwardly guided by the archetype of the Son. By comparison, merely natural virtue has no supernatural merit and therefore is likely to fade with age unlike heavenly virtue which deepens with every trial.

The two ideals, that of holiness and that of courage, can of course be fused in one person, that of the warrior-saint or the prophet. What characterizes both a heroic and a saintly life is the permanence of a lofty principle or of an over-arching noble sentiment,[6] consecrated to Heaven, a profound disposition of soul that reduces time—or the dulling monotony

---

5 See Bernard McGinn, *The Harvest of Mysticism*, p. 100.

6 "A man is made great by concentration of motive" (Emerson).

and relentless picking and pecking of hours and days—into a single instant projected continuously and luminously over thousands of moments.[7] This is the kind of love or loyalty enduring impassively like a bright star over the chattering humdrum of events; or it is an unshakeable faith that can face what mystics call a *resignatio ad infernum*[8] in which the soul is prepared to brave even hell or utmost suffering for the sake of the Beloved, believing itself completely unworthy, not even deserving of redemption. We mention this attitude not necessarily for its exemplariness or logic, but because of its courage and also because consciousness of God's perfection can induce—however paradoxically—a sense of agonizing despair in the soul about its own shortcomings and the lowliness it shares with humanity at large, whence the assumption of its total unworthiness of even being saved. The element of paradox in this essentially heroic attitude comes from the fact that—contrary to what a strict moralist may think—the despair is induced actually by a profound degree of faith and not from any lack of it; in short, it is a noble despair prepared to brave any fate fearlessly for the sake of God. Obviously, the choice of suicide is not an option because in that case despair overwhelms faith—although there may be certain rare circumstances where Heaven allows for extenuating circumstances, a very extreme example being that of Judas, and God knows best.[9] Only the truly sincere know what torment the sense of our shortcomings can unleash in the soul of he or she who longs utterly for God. Yet, at the same time, this type of passionate mysticism can verge on individualism because faith in God's mercy should normally help lessen the sting of scruples, which is another way of saying that faith without a measure of serenity is not completely faith, or it is faith clouded by some strain of individualistic

---

7 In exceptional cases such a virtue can even be exhibited by animals, as shown notably by the story of the Japanese Akita dog, Hachiko, who waited faithfully for his master at the Tokyo train station for nine long years, after the latter's unexpected death at work that had prevented him from returning home one evening. This dog lived outdoors off the handouts from benevolent strangers until his death.

8 See the Biblical basis for this attitude in Rom. 9:1-3 and Exod. 32:32.

9 We have heard of Russian officers, during the time of the Czar, who would kill themselves after hearing a particularly beautiful song, life seeming to them unendurable after such a peak of beauty. Conversely, in Japan, there is the tradition of ritual suicide, namely of submitting to self-delivered death while contemplating, if possible, an exquisite scene of nature (a flowering tree, a waterfall, or an *ikebana* bouquet) serving, through the acme of the contrast between beauty and imminent death, as a gateway to Paradise. Such ritual suicide has to be understood as a means of putting an end to an unbearable shame incurred, precisely, by the most heightened of selfless idealisms; it is in other words a pinnacle of honor that determines the extremism of the solution. Such an idealism can be the catalyst for instant sanctity.

passion. Be that as it may, part of the alchemy leading to God-realization may entail a phase of the "dark night of the soul", which can be a dread ordeal testing a soul's resolve down to its very marrow.

We have defined character as the capacity to confront the inexorable and relentless corrosion of moments that undermine baser man. For the hero these moments are victoriously transfigured into one glorious aim renewed daily; he takes pleasure in vanquishing the importunities of temptations: instant after instant he resolutely refuses to succumb to idleness or self-indulgence; he of all men knows how to turn lead into gold, or hours into litanies. Thus, in the great-souled man or woman, the heavenly triumphs over the earthly, the ideal over the trivial, love over lust, the Real over the unreal; this is the basis of supernatural virtue and of its priceless merit.

The first prerequisite for such a lofty vocation is self-domination, so as to meet the setting sun every evening in honor and not in shame, and to give a sparkling account of our day to the stars that we may join them in golden vigilance. At the same time, character is Truth; in other words, there can be no real character without Truth, for great character is to have great sincerity, which is truthfulness, not just fierceness of resolve. Reversing this equation, one can add that no one can be "sincerely in error" about moral matters because fundamental error—not mere ignorance—entails some degree of willful self-delusion, namely a degree of insincerity with our conscience. Sincerity, thus, presupposes the Truth and therefore is fundamentally premised on a sense of Reality. Consequently, to be truly sincere is to be real, which is another way of saying that Reality "exists" before we exist.

Furthermore, the following deserves mention: it is popularly assumed that to have a strong character is to have strong convictions; left out is that the objective content of our conviction matters too, and not just its intensity or vehemence, otherwise vehemence is but an expression of our passion. Or, a despotic person may seem to have a strong character, but actually his despotism masks a fundamental weakness, because despotism is not strength. Thus, ultimately, it is the quality of the conviction that leads to real strength of character. In other words, it is truth of sentiment—or, to be exact, the truth in the sentiment—that determines the depth of sentiment; the rest is histrionics, or mere subjectivity. This relationship is perhaps made clearer by reversing the equation: strength of sincerity is the reaction inspired by the reality of the object, by the objective impact it has on one's mind and soul; hence, depth of love is sparked by the direct awareness of the beauty beheld, just as loyalty comes from a clear sense of the quality of the principle, the ideal, or the person one has pledged an oath to. And, of course, keenness of perception of the divine Object determines the intensity of one's faith. Thus in the last analysis it is always the reality of the Object that determines the reality of the subject, or the quality of the Object that determines the sincerity of our feelings; in that sense, there is no true martyrdom without the prior and preeminent truth of the ideal: to die for an error is an accident; to die for God is to be reborn.

Finally, one could also say that character is love, because selfishness and strength of character are mutually incompatible, just as, conversely, generosity of soul and strength are inseparable. It is through character that we pass from seeming into being, and in being we rejoin not the imitation of life, but Life itself—the Life which is finally that of God's own immortality.

*   *   *

In defining character, reference has been made to terms one finds both in spirituality and psychology, and which may therefore convey, depending on the reader's background, either too personalistic a notion of man or too morality-centered a frame of reference; they might also conjure too conventional—or "civilized"—notions of right and wrong, or of "good and bad", and this finally could be misleading no matter how valid such definitions of nobleness and holiness may be in themselves. Therefore, we now would like to describe the meaning of individuality—and its expression as character—in more elemental terms, that is to say in terms free from the possible biases stemming from standard notions of psychology and confessional religion. These elemental points of reference will bring us back to the pneumatology—or the reflection of the Spirit in man—which has been our guiding principle from the beginning.

Existence, outside of the heavenly spheres, is governed by contending complementary poles whose very intensity of difference is also the factor determining the resolution of their opposition, since all of nature is finally circular. The most basic of these polarities, in cosmic terms, is the alternation between day (light) and night (darkness) and that between heat (expansion) and cold (contraction), along with their spatial projections as south and north. These are outward or cosmic manifestations of the positive and negative principles—or *yang* and *yin*—ruling manifestation and, in their ultimate ground, they retrace the tension between life and death (*eros* and *thanatos*), love and war, as well as between self and non-self—which are retraced, moreover, in the inspiration and expiration of creatures.[10] And, circumscribing these polarities is the duality of heaven and

---

10 These polarities are obviously not identical; we mention them only by way of illustrating the principle of duality ruling creation.

earth. With regard to "heaven" it should be made clear that it is a question here of a horizontal set of polarities, so that the pole "heaven" is really the projection of the active principle of the sky (*yang*) as contrasted with the passive principle of the earth (*yin*), in which case they function as co-equal, even though from the vertical or intrinsic point of view the pole "heaven" is hierarchically superior to that of earth given its principial symbolism; in this case one would have to speak of "Heaven" capitalized. But we are not speaking here of Principle and manifestation, of God and creation, only of manifestation which includes creation as well as the celestial realms.

Now, this polarity, when squared, gives rise to the four cardinal points and thus to any of various quaternaries, such as the four seasons, the four ages of man, the four sides of a square, the four humors of antique medicine, and so on and so forth. In principle, the initial duality and the subsequent quaternary can be subdivided quasi-indefinitely; however, beyond the cardinal numbers counting up to ten or twelve, all subsequent numbers are really minor variants—or multiples—of these cardinal numbers projected out *ad infinitum*. And the division into polarities itself is the result of the original One projecting Itself into space and time, its unity being refracted into diversity, or moving from singleness to totality, a process that equals multiplicity; in other words, if the original unity could not be divided there would be no manifestation.

To speak of existence is to speak of space, and space in turn entails a right and a left—as well as a front and a back, and also an up and a down. These dualities, rooted in the Absolute-Infinite pairing, reflect the creaturely polarity of masculine and feminine.[11] Do these polarities vanish with the absence of a subject beholding them? Yes and no—"yes" in that space is directionless in its etheric prototype, but "no" once it enters into its pre-material form, that is to say once space becomes definable in some formal manner. To elaborate: the Tibetan Book of the Dead, to cite but one traditional source, comments on the bilocation or pluri-location of sentient beings in the supra-formal realms, and quantum physics has some perception of phenomena occurring in multi-resonance levels—described as the theory of what is termed "non-local correlation"—in which past and present and future become inherently meaningless distinctions.[12]

---

11 For example, Blackfoot tepees, a circular symbol of the universe, are divided into two equal halves, one representing the masculine pole, the other the feminine.

12 It is perhaps in this fashion that special signs can precede the birth of an *avatara*, such as an aura heralding their advent, in that material existence is subordinate to spiritual existence, which lies outside of time. As a result, what appears *synthetically* (or "all at once") on the plane of spirit is projected *sequentially* in earthly existence, or what is referred to in Buddhism as being within the realm of *nama-rupa*, "name and form". The singleness

This insight lifts a corner of the veil hiding the primordial synthesis from which phenomena emerge and return, some occurring closer to the Center and others closer to the periphery, so that the closer to the Center the less differentiated (or polarized) they become and, correlatively, the farther from the Center the more differentiated (or polarized). And this brings us to the notion of the static Center (or Plato's *primum mobile*, the Motionless Mover) because motion presupposes an immobile axis around which phenomena and beings can turn, otherwise motion would amount to instant disintegration. Similarly, form presupposes a supra-formal (or formless) center, otherwise nothing could coalesce; for parts can only cohere—intimately—through the absence of a part and in this we subtly rejoin the Buddhist doctrine of the void (*shunya*).

It would, however, be completely wrong to assume that reintegration into the divine Center corresponds to pure indifferentiation or to an abolition of qualitative differences, just as, in a different sense, it would be incorrect to assume that spiritual self-abasement, or self-effacement, equals loss of self. The indifferentiation or the voidness referred to is the elimination of difference as *accident* or of individuality as *fragment*, and not of "difference" as an archetypal quality which, on the contrary, gains in greatness, beauty, or majesty as it is reabsorbed into the Divine, for then the distinct quality—or the sanctified self embodying this quality— manifests the Absolute directly and no longer the fragmenting of this same Absolute, as is the case with individualism. Indeed, as we have had occasion to mention several times, the spiritual path involves a twofold process of extinction and of manifestation—extinction before God (as transcendence) and manifestation of God (as immanence). For man, though, the manifesting is premised on the prior extinction inasmuch as this process has to occur sequentially in time; yet, this dual process can occur simultaneously upon receiving a grace for, by contrast with man's spiritual journey across life, the divine grace operates simultaneously both to extinguish and to radiate and, in fact, it comes as an earthly harbinger of the posthumous theurgical process of sanctification in which the blessed are both extinguished in God and awake in God.

These dual aspects—whose alchemy echoes the stations of night and day, or nothingness and fullness—are to be found in the dual qualities present in the perfect sage: that of total or "virginal" effacement before the Lord in which the soul finds itself, on the one hand, in a state of pure

---

of instantaneity of spirit things cannot fit into our earthly *nama-rupa* at once and forever without shattering it; it therefore has to unfold in stages and to take on formal limitations, whence this or that body type, this or that personality type, and so on and so forth.

receptivity, unblemished by individualistic preoccupations,[13] and, on the other, in a state of total and electrifying presentness of pure being,[14] because in the soul emptied of self and of the world, God pours in like a mighty waterfall, ceaselessly and luminously, yea thunderously. Likewise, in preparation for this state of virginity of spirit, the aspirant undertakes a twofold spiritual process, firstly of renunciation and self-extinction (in Sufism *fana*) and secondly of making-present the Divine (in Sufism *istihdar*): the aspirant must remove everything in his soul that obstructs the presence of the One, but at the same time he must manifest God according to his personal gifts, through a forcefully active radiation of positive qualities that may be expressed, among other things, through a burning faith, invincible strength of conviction, all-loving generosity, and a total and intense belief—or awareness—of God's mercy that pulverizes petty doubts. In a word, the aspirant gives himself to God, firstly in a process of apparent initial loss, and in so doing he then gives God to the world through his act of prayer and worship. And, once again, we find in this the polarity of negative and positive virtues.

*   *   *

Man, as microcosm, is the epitome of the greater universe—the macrocosm—and thus all the laws governing the universe from the humblest blade of grass to grandiose mega-galaxies find their echo in man; the same law directing the countless stars dotting space also governs the atoms within our bodies. Likewise, the primordial constituents of man's character, when still untouched by any cultural or psychological bias, are ordered according to the polarity of "Consciousness and Being" or mind and heart. This polarity, in turn, is also expressed through a rhythmic alternation of the static and dynamic principles of knowledge and action; or one could say the pole wisdom-love finds its expression in sanctifying action. And, as mentioned earlier, when entering solid space and time, the original duality or the relationship of *Purusha* (Spirit) manifesting through *Prakriti* (primordial substance) is further subdivided into a cosmic quaternary.[15]

13 This is the meaning of Muhammad being described as "the unlettered prophet", his illiteracy being equatable with Mary's virginity which Christ inherited, one might say.

14 Being is the opposite of nothingness, therefore *to be* is to defeat the pull of nothingness that threatens to engulf us. On earth, this battle must be renewed at every instant and that is why having character is important; character finally is all that stands between us and oblivion.

15 See our chapter "Individuality Is Not Individualism" for more on this initial cosmogonic unfolding.

In this substance's most basic manifestation (*Prakriti*) we are dealing with the Four Primordial Qualities expressed as the duality of "heat and cold" complemented by the duality of "dry and humid", or two pairs of polar conditions,[16] which then give rise to the Four Elements—two "masculine" and two "feminine"—namely of "fire and air", on the one hand, and "water and earth", on the other. Ether could be added as a fifth element, but its invisibility—or androgyny—prevents us from describing it materially[17] except to say that without the voidness of this fifth element the others could not coexist because they could neither combine with nor compensate each other, but would be self-cancelling, were they even able to emerge in the first place; their existence presupposes ether's supra-formal or subtle existence. In essence, ether is analogous to *Purusha* whereas the Four Primordial Qualities (heat, cold, dryness, and humidity) are analogous to *Prakriti* in her role of *natura naturans*.[18] By this token, the Four Elements themselves could then be seen as either the "offspring" of *Purusha* and *Prakriti*, or as the four aspects of *Prakriti* though in her role now of *natura naturata*. Yet, from another perspective, if the Four Primordial Qualities determine matter they themselves are determined, in turn, by the Four Cardinal Directions, and these four axial poles derive from the Spirit (*Purusha*) reflected in space and therefore are not part of *Prakriti* proper.[19]

16 We are still dealing with a principle of duality, but duality operating now as a quaternary. However, no matter the degree of multiplicity, everything in the cosmos is reducible each time to an underlying duality which, itself, is in turn the reflection of the principle of Unity projected into creation; that is to say Unity cannot manifest in creation except as duality, otherwise there would be no creation. It is important to note that this duality is a unity before it is a duality. Thus, intrinsically, nothing exists outside of the One (or, there is nothing but the One) no matter the diversity of modalities.

17 Ether—not to be confused with the chemical gas "ether"—could be defined as being a "non-material material" (or a pre-material) element that, according to Aristotle, was changeless except for its capacity for motion. According to the ancients it was a substance subtler than material light situated as a transition sphere between the material and the supra-material realms. Unlike the other four elements, ether transcends material causality while being vitally present in all four of the elements. It is a testament to the cosmological perspicacity of the ancients that they could account for its existence—through logical inference if not visionary inspiration—while modern physics cannot either prove or disprove it, although some modern theories, such as the notion of "dark energy" (sometimes called "quintessence"), share an affinity with this theory.

18 Terms, alchemical in their essence, coined in the Middle Ages to describe nature considered in her twin roles as active (*natura naturans* or "nature creating") and passive or inert (*natura naturata* or "nature created"), that is, determinative and determined.

19 Although they could be defined as the reflection of *Purusha* in *Prakriti*. These distinctions, complex as they may seem, are important to make because the interrelation between *Purusha* and *Prakriti* is that of a *yin-yang* interlacing, neither pole being totally void of the other.

The Four Qualities of heat, cold, dryness, and humidity are active—*Prakriti* in her dynamic aspect of *natura naturans*—with respect to the Four Elements of fire, air, water, and earth; the latter are therefore passive—*Prakriti* as *natura naturata*—being the four aspects of primordial substance, or the first *materializations* of the Spirit within the primordial substance. Yet, within each level itself (first in the Four Qualities then in the Four Elements) there is a reflection of the original Spirit-Substance duality—or of the masculine-feminine polarity—such that fire and air (the Elements) together form a masculine, dynamic, or "spirit pole" within the passive substance of the Four Elements, just as cold and humidity (the Qualities now, in distinction to the Elements) together form a feminine, passive, or "substance pole" within the supra-formal realm of the Four Elemental Qualities, which are active. And the active-passive polarity itself, which is woven in all of creation, is a reflection of the original polarity of the poles of the Absolute and the Infinite ruling manifestation. Now this duality is refracted first—within creation—in the polarity *Purusha* and *Prakriti*, then in the polarity of the Four Cardinal Directions, which taken together form an active pole with respect to the Four Primordial Qualities; but these Qualities, in turn, as we have seen, are active with respect to the Four Elements. Thus, after the principial Absolute-Infinite polarization there is the cosmic *Purusha-Prakriti* polarization and from this polarization we obtain the hierarchy first of the Four Cardinal Directions, then of the Four Qualities deriving from the Directions, and finally the Four Elements born from the Qualities.

However within each cosmic level, irrespective of its being active or passive, there is an internal polarization—again reflecting *mutatis mutandis* the archetypal division Absolute-Infinite—so that the determinative level of the Four Cardinal Directions is itself divided into an active pairing (or diurnal hemisphere) of East-South corresponding to waxing light (or day) and a passive pairing (or nocturnal hemisphere) of West-North or waning light (or night). Likewise, within the Primordial Qualities now, heat-dryness together operate as an active pole and humidity-coldness as a passive pole; and these polar pairings are reflected once again in the Four Elements themselves, fire-air forming the dynamic pair and water-earth the static pair. Now, important to note, the sequence of cosmic pairings, starting with the Absolute-Infinite, followed by *Purusha* and *Prakriti*, obey a series of reversing polarities that are inherently tantric in the relationship of attraction and repulsion they form between themselves, because the rhythm of creation depends on this mutuality of joining and separating, the dynamism of which produces the procession of the spheres. Each level of pairings follows a vertical hierarchy of levels, or a hypostatic ordering, in which each superior level fulfills a masculine or active role with respect to the subordinate level right beneath it; but this polarity is then reversed, going from passive to active, as the next level becomes in turn active with respect to the one subordinate to it, and so on down the whole onto-cosmological ladder of existence. And within each level there is a foreshadowing of the next level because even though the levels are distinct they operate also as multiples of each other according to the Spirit's radiation, the polarities directing a kind of cosmic dance, both simultaneous and at the same time successive—unity always serving as the invisible substratum of the outward bipolarization, otherwise any separation, were it to become absolute, would result in instant volatilization.

*   *   *

Projecting now these polarities into man's character, and leaving aside how these primeval poles—which manifest also as energies—are considered in different traditions,[20] we can say that the nature of primordial man—or ideal man as supreme image of the Creator—includes some combination of these Four Qualities of nature which, as we have seen, derive from the Four Cardinal Directions. To grasp existentially what the concrete meaning of these analogies can be, we must first picture man standing on earth beneath the sky, facing the luminous and warm quadrant of the south with his back to the "darkness" of the cold north, while to his left the sun rises in invincible might in the Eastern quadrant before setting in eventide beauty in the Western quadrant, and then, at nightfall, to behold the starry constellations rising in the East in one great circle overarching his earthly position before once again setting in the West. Thus man is situated in a center bounded by a circular horizon (East, South, West, North) which is itself bisected by a stellar circle (rising, zenith, setting, nadir); this twofold geometry gives us the universal image of the cross, namely that of a horizontal axis bisected by a vertical one.

The horizontal circle has four cardinal points, whereas the vertical circle has four inflection points—rising, zenith, setting, and nadir—each of which marks a decisive turning point in the sun's journey across the

20 For an explanation of the Four Qualities and the Four Elements, see Titus Burckhardt, *Alchemy: Science of the Cosmos, Science of the Soul* (Louisville, KY: Fons Vitae, 1997). And for an insight into the symbolism of the four directions as lived by the Plains Indians, see Frithjof Schuon, *The Feathered Sun*, chap. "A Metaphysic of Virgin Nature" (Bloomington, IN: World Wisdom, 1990). Also, for another perspective of the cosmic orchestration see Schuon's chapter "The Onto-Cosmological Chain" in *Survey of Metaphysics and Esoterism* (Bloomington, IN: World Wisdom, 2003), as well as his chapter "The Hypostatic Numbers" in *Esoterism as Principle and as Way*.

sky—as seen by man, of course. From this perspective, heaven and earth have two intersecting points: the Eastern edge of the horizon (the rising point or ascendant) and the Western point (the descendant).[21] In essence, the Cardinal Points spell out the sun's sacred grammar as it transcribes Reality in an outward mode for man, who himself is the microcosmic sun. Through his understanding of the symbolism of light's journey through manifestation, man—as priest and as king—serves as *pontifex* or bridge-maker between Heaven and earth. Hence man, as microcosmic sun, mirrors the physical sun which is itself, at the level of nature, a symbol of the Divine Principle. Now, each station of the sun as it journeys across the sky determines a Cardinal Direction that, in turn, expresses symbolically an attribute of the supernal (or hidden) sun's prophetic and imperial essence; this is the basis for the great luminary's worship in primeval traditions, such as in the solsticial temple of Stonehenge and others.

Being a synthesis of the macrocosm, primordial man—*paramahamsa* in Hinduism [22]—has a temperament that incorporates the essence of the Four Elements transposed into a human mode. Now, it should be specified that in referring both to the Four Qualities (heat, cold, dry, humid) or to the Four Elements (fire, air, water, and earth) we are definitely not thinking of their material equivalents in the physical body,[23] but to the fact that

---

21 For those interested in zodiacal symbolism, the apparent journey of the sun across the heavens can be further subdivided into twelve stations which correspond to the twelve signs of the zodiac as well as to the four seasons; the number "twelve" is obtained by multiplying the four vertical inflection points by three modalities (the cosmic triplicity governing the four elements). The four quadrants of the sky (East, South, West, North) correspond analogically to the four elements whereas the three dynamic modalities are the three operative modalities of these elements. Thus each of the four elements (fire, air, water, earth) has a cardinal, a fixed, and a mutable modality which recall respectively the *gunas* of the Sankhya school of philosophy in Hinduism, namely *rajas* (the expansive or fiery), *tamas* (the solidifying), and *sattva* (the luminous modality): creation, crystallization, dissolution (or transfiguration). In this symbolism, the three *gunas* reflect the horizontal action of the Spirit (*Purusha*) on primordial substance (*Prakriti*), in which case the *guna* of *tamas* does not have the negative connotation it has as darkness and ignorance, which applies when considering the *gunas* in their vertical role.

22 In the *Paramahamsa Upanishad*, this creature is described as having the four quarters for garment. The term *paramahamsa* can be translated as "supreme swan", the swan being the sacred bird attributed to Brahma; in the *Vedas* and the *Puranas*, it is a symbol of the human soul.

23 Such as we find in the Buddhist text, the *Samanna-Phala Sutta* (verse 55): "A human being is built up of the four elements. When he dies the earthly in him returns and relapses to the earth, the fluid to the water, the heat to the fire, the windy to the air," and so on and so forth. But, useful as this description may be, it is merely a material one, omitting the symbolic meaning of these elements; and it is the latter meaning that for us is absolutely crucial.

before they are either fire or water, they are a spiritual essence,[24] reducible to the primordial polarity of pure activity (masculine) and of pure passivity (feminine). Therefore, and needless to say, to appeal to the imagery of the Four Elements in order to describe the basis for man's primordial "character" is not just a poetic fancy.

As mentioned, the Four Qualities of heat, cold, dryness, and humidity, when allocated spatially, correspond respectively to the East, North, South, and West axes.[25] And each one of the Cardinal Directions has a spiritual quality that corresponds to an attribute of pure Being. There are obviously a number of different manners in which the Four Directions can be described, but we can say that the "cold" North corresponds via cosmic analogy to the character trait of incorruptibility and absolute purity, the complement to which is the "warm" South's generosity and life-giving love; and likewise, to the "dry" East there is a quality of pure dynamism or indomitable forcefulness—or of heroic invincibility—the complement to which is the "moist" West's peacefulness and repose or contemplative passivity, as well as a quality of forgivingness, nature as it were atoning with rain to compensate for excess of fire. These complementarities give us a cardinal cross or two axes which are respectively that of Purity-Generosity (North-South) and Strength-Peacefulness (East-West), the Four Qualities forming the essential traits of primordial man. Or, Incorruptibility-Love and Forcefulness-Gentleness. Or again, Detachment-Fervor and Action-Rest (or effort and play). And, underlying both pairings principially, we have the fundamental polarity of Rigor and Mercy, operative in manifestation, and, more essentially yet, of Truth and Love, deriving from beyond manifestation.

If one were to ask what a *paramahamsa* or primordial sage is like, one might say that he possesses the cardinal qualities of adamantine incorruptibility (North), generous compassion (South), fierceness of resolve (East), and sweetness of soul (West). Translated into the cardinal axes of the primordial man's soul, the North encompasses the "negative" qualities of a rigorous *contemptus mundi* or a rejection of the world: detachment, impassivity, renunciation, asceticism, and complete purity of being that

---

24 In the *Bhagavad Gita*, Krishna tells Arjuna: "Earth, water, fire, air, ether, mind, and understanding, and self-sense [*ahamkara* = individuation]—this is the eightfold division of my nature" (7:4).

25 The Four Elements themselves are the "offspring" of the Cardinal Directions (or modalities), so that the element "fire" is the resultant of the combination of the modalities of "heat" (East) and "dryness" (South); "water" is the combination of "humidity" (West) and "coldness" (North); "air" that of "humidity" (West) and "heat" (East); and finally, "earth" that of "dryness" (South) and "coldness" (North).

nothing can tempt or taint. Whereas the South, compensating as it were for the North's austerity, encompasses the "positive" qualities of welcoming love: it is all bountifulness, joy, fervor, faith, and radiant kindness. In their turn, East and West also correspond to a negative-positive polarity; first, the luminous East is the pole of victorious affirmativeness, all-conquering action, and intrepid decisiveness, the opposite of all hesitation and petty calculation, namely the quality of instant and total presentness, whereas the West, in beauteous compensation, represents the quality of peacefulness, yielding, and gratitude, or the quality of Being graciously reposing in its self-sufficient completeness.[26]

* * *

We have dwelt on the proto-cosmic qualities of the Four Directions, or their magical energies, but they could also be equated with the four seasons, the four times of day, or the four ages of man (as mentioned earlier) each of which, in their mode, retrace the same qualities. Thus, spring or childhood or innocence, as well as the morning, correspond to the East; summer or youth and early maturity, as well as noontide fullness of light, correspond to the South; autumn or ripeness of age (the time of the harvest), as well as the afternoon and early twilight correspond to the West; and finally, winter or old age and wisdom along with dignity, as well as the midnight point of the sun, correspond to the North. Indeed, nothing in creation can be properly situated outside of this cosmic quaternary.

If the primordial sage recapitulates in his very being all of these qualities of age, the seasons, and the times of day it is because his being embodies what is termed in Sufism the *fitrah* or the primordial norm, or because it reflects in Hinduism the *sanatana dharma*, the eternal law;[27] thus, by virtue of the analogy between creation and man, this sage is a living manifestation of the spirit of nature herself, embodying the Four Elements in his character, these Four Elements in turn constituting the primal modalities

---

26 We are particularly indebted to Frithjof Schuon's *Stations of Wisdom* for these insights.

27 The terms of *fitrah* and *sanatana dharma* have been appropriated by adherents of Islam and Hinduism through a kind of "religious nationalism"; but we use these in their original or essential meaning, one that transcends confessional biases. For example, for us it is the qualities of "eternity" and "invariability" and "infinity", among others, that matter in the notion of the *sanatana dharma*, and not the religious doctrine that expresses these through its maze of ritual rules, sacred as they otherwise are. The *sanatana dharma* and the *fitrah* are not based on religion; it is religion that is based on them, and it has no monopoly on these terms, to say the least.

of *Purusha*'s supreme personality reflected in *Prakriti*.[28] In this respect, the sage behaves and reacts not just through feelings, emotions, and sense impressions that move other men, but either with a kind of existential and impersonal instantaneousness or, on the contrary, with a kind of impersonal immovability found only in nature. Thus, he can react like lightning, with the fierce "fervor" of fire as it were, or remain impervious and unmoved, like the rock of ages, a veritable mountain; or again, he can have the subtleness of air or the humble suppleness of water as circumstances dictate, his suppleness of attitude being also the sign of his holy spontaneity free from the hooks of petty self-interest, emotional prejudice, or dogmatic preconceptions. These analogies could be developed in many ways, but perhaps these few observations will suffice to describe the character and nature of primordial man in his existential mode of being, a character that owes nothing finally to culture, society, or conventions.

Transposing these reflections to average man, one would like to say that while it is difficult for him to imitate nature directly—the qualities of the Four Elements incorporated into the sage's nature being a result of his holiness and not the means—he can take inspiration from knowing that all of nature reposes mysteriously in the kernel of his being. "And the Lord God formed man of the dust of the ground", we read in Genesis (2:7); the same teaching is found in the *Vedas*, and in the Koran. The analogies between man and the macrocosm or man and nature are too numerous to be mentioned exhaustively in this context. Suffice it to mention that there is a traditional analogy between the four humors and the Four Elements, blood corresponding to air, phlegm to water, black bile to earth, and yellow bile to fire. In Jewish religious commentaries, for example the *Avot de-Rabbi Natan* (chap. 21), man's body is compared to nature—when standing to a mountain, when lying down to a plain—and its individual parts to the forests, the wind, plants, and so on; we find the same parallelisms in Hinduism (in the philosophy of *Kriya Yoga*), some of which sound rather fantastic unless one understands that the formal modality described is subordinate to the elemental principle which can manifest in different modes. In that sense, moving upwardly from creation back to non-Being or *Atma*, fire is but the formal modality (or application) of the principle of heat, and heat itself but the existential mode of light, and light in turn is but the manifestation of divine consciousness and love.

Now, if the modalities of the Four Elements derive from the polarizations outlined above, their differences should not mask the unity of substance underlying them, which determines their being transformable

---

28 It is also important to understand that cosmic energies derive from *Paramatma* (the Supreme Self) who is Being and Consciousness, or Love and Wisdom, as mentioned earlier.

into their complements or opposites. Thus fire is reabsorbed into air, air is condensed into water, water into earth, which, once dried, is transformed into fire, and so the cycle resumes. Thus manifestation, when analyzed in its modalities, is nothing if not a division of original Unity beginning in the Spirit or—to be more exact—beginning in the reflection of the cosmic Spirit. *Mutatis mutandis*, all creatures and plants are in a certain sense nothing but different modalities of the sun, so that all earthly nourishment has a solar substance for origin. In discussing such matters, one can be as synthetic or analytical as one likes; consequently some balance has to be found between analytical description and synthesis—if not refreshing silence. The point is that it is important for man, when assessing these cosmic qualities, to free himself from the material grip of these symbols in order to recover their principial essence. Thus the four modalities of heat, cold, humidity, and dryness correspond in essence to the four cosmic principles of expansion, contraction, solution, and crystallization, and these principles lend themselves to an endless variety of applications, whether in nature or in man's soul.

Likewise, the sun and the moon as all the luminaries—or at least their cosmic principles—are echoed in the depths of man's heart. Thus when we say that "it is impossible for him [average man] to imitate nature directly" we mean that it would make no sense for an individual to try and imitate "fire" or "air", leaving aside the imaginative fantasies such an emulation might induce. But what can be said is that in imitating or in really imple-menting the virtues belonging to the four sacred directions, and doing so according to their essential meaning—as opposed to a more conventional-ly religious meaning—an individual can in principle return to the primor-dial norm. Thus, the virtue of detachment finds its most rigorous support in the cold North that teaches us how to freeze the soul's concupiscence; the notion of "coldness" or of assimilating the sacred power of the North can set the foundation for a moral incorruptibility that goes well beyond the merely human notion of morality. Likewise for the cardinal pole of the luminous East: to understand the medicinal power of the East means to understand the victory of light over darkness and thus to place oneself on an axis where the soul can understand and realize the noble fierceness of fire; his soul becomes open to that possibility, or to the qualities of alert-ness, bravery, and decisiveness, if not of spiritual invincibility. The same process of analogy can be transposed to the other cardinal directions and to the Four Elements which are their offspring.

Finally, it should be noted that each of the Four Elements possesses integral purity equally and totally in that each one can purify nature or the body: fire through burning, water through its lustral essence, air by cleans-ing and refreshing, and earth which reabsorbs and transfigures all corruption.[29] This is the virginal gift of *Prakriti*. Our descriptions may prove too quaintly literal for the taste of everyone, but the reader will understand that such a perspective of the Four Elements is merely a way of rendering them more concretely intelligible, otherwise their qualitative essence eludes proper description.

* * *

This outline, in which we have attempted to draw parallels between the nature of the sage and the cosmos, would not be complete without adding two more directions which, in contrast to the horizontal plane of the Four Cardinal Directions, are vertical. Again, taking as a reference man standing on earth beneath the heavens, one can draw a vertical line, the two ends of which have a zenith and a nadir, corresponding to the dimensions Height and Depth.[30] Transposed to man as microcosm, these points relate to his mind and to his heart, for if the mind is to fulfill its role of pure objectivity it needs to rise, as it were, high above things, to clean transcend the subjective in order to achieve its perfection of impersonal clarity. Likewise, it is through the depth of the heart that radical union with nature, and by extension, with the Creator, is to be found. One might say, furthermore, that these directions operate as spatial coordinates for the twin perfections of luminous objectivity and of ecstatic subjectivity: Truth and Love, or pure knowledge and pure being, or spiritual discernment and spiritual union. Transposed to character, these points can be translated as dispassionate intelligence, on the one hand, and as total depth of sincerity, on the other. Metaphysically, they rejoin the principles of transcendence and immanence, or noble loftiness of spirit and all-embracing compassion of spirit. Man, as the Creator's supreme creation and therefore mirror of nature, is utter emptiness before God since he has nothing of his own, and yet he can have a glorious station as befits his nature of envoy of God within creation. In the face of God's supreme transcendence man is nothing; yet by virtue of God's immanence in him, man is also a priest and a king.

* * *

We would now like to say a few words about virtue and morality. A virtue such as humility is understood in Taoism,[31] for instance, in a non-mor-

29 This is why references to earth as mere "dirt" are so regrettable.

30 The Plains Indians attribute these two directions respectively to the sky and to the earth, as symbolized by the eagle and the buffalo.

31 Taoism, by contrast to Confucianism, is essentially an esoterism.

alistic fashion that owes more to virgin nature than to a personalistic or willful attitude; a Taoist allows himself to be tutored in self-effacement by the purity and simplicity of a brook or by the "selflessness" of white clouds drifting across the sky instead of the definitions encountered in popular religion, which are likely to explain humility "emotionally" or volitively, namely by defining humility in terms of mortification, if not shame and guilt. Likewise a virtue like charity, for Taoism, is to shine like the sun or to bloom like a flower, whereas in popular religion, again, this virtue becomes practically meaningless when separated from its social implementation of helping the poor, caring for the sick, and exercising kindness to all men of goodwill. In other words, the risk of defining humility and charity in social terms—that is to say with respect to other human beings—is to risk reducing the essence of virtue to action or to attitudes premised primarily on man's outward behavior instead of on his inward nature; when in fact the essence of virtue corresponds to a return to divine Being reflected in virgin nature, whether this is realized in the middle of towns or in a solitary cave. God is holiness, therefore man is virtue.

However, it hardly needs saying that the person practicing true humility or charity both in a confessional religion (such as Christianity, Islam, or Hinduism) and in a non-confessional one (such as Taoism) can radiate with the very same benevolence, which points to the common divineness of all virtues, because humility and charity—simplicity and love—are qualities common to nature (*Prakriti*) herself, wherever man may be and whatever he does in the name of God. And wherever he is, and however he is, he is first part of nature herself before being part of civilization. There emanates a perfume of holiness in virtue that is detectable in all religions no matter how the modes differ across religious civilizations. Likewise, true poverty of spirit achieved in religion through the humility of deep piety leads to a transparency of soul that is bound to end up mirroring the qualities of the four elements themselves, since nature and being are one in their essence. The sanctified soul attains to a limpidity of spirit in which the glow of faith combines the qualities of fearlessness and gentleness. Divineness is universal.

When referring to a "non-moralistic" virtue it is also worth specifying that in all these reflections it could never be a question of minimizing the necessity of morality in the slightest—quite the opposite—but of understanding that there is in the *paramahamsa*, or "primordial man", a supreme "moralness" or ethical grandeur that transcends all questions of social and religious opportunism and, finally, that transcends even the definition of morality itself, since the notion of morality is premised basically on the idea of transgression which no longer applies at a primordial, let alone at a heavenly, level. In fact, contrary to many a zealous religious bias, the notion of "virtue" itself is actually a much larger term than anything the notion of morality encompasses, although it goes without saying that true virtue can never be immoral. Virtue equals divineness as such, quite independently from this or that field of human application. This gives us the following equation: morality depends on virtue, but virtue does not depend on morality in that virtue carries its own justification; being self-existent, it subsists before and after morality. It should therefore be clear that virtue cannot be reduced to the merit of avoiding sin or of overcoming defects, for it partakes, in its essence, of Godhead and eternity; in fact, from virtue's perspective, sin is irrelevant. Yet, for average man, the practice of virtue has to begin in morality proper; there is no question for him of "bypassing morality" in the lofty name of divine virtue; such primordial virtue is unattainable for the non-sanctified. At the same time, the awareness that there is such a thing as primordial virtue has the benefit of helping man to look beyond a purely social framework for his understanding and practice of morality, for being is more important than doing; indeed being is the basis for doing. Pure being is holiness.

* * *

An outline on character could have incorporated many things we can only mention in passing, such as the classical temperaments (sanguine, choleric, melancholic, and phlegmatic), each of which have an archetype, or the five castes in their universal sense (not merely in their social application as seen in Hinduism), that is to say: the contemplative and intellectually refined *brahmana* or priest; the heroic and imperious *kshatriya* or warrior; the peaceful, patient, and honest *vaishya* or merchant, farmer, or artist; and the rough but obedient *shudra* or laborer—the fifth caste (or really "out-caste") being the *pariah* although, by definition, this person is lacking in all character, precisely, since his psychic makeup is composed of heterogeneous elements of the four superior castes, which prevents him from having a homogeneous soul. Regarding the caste system, and given its importance in determining social character, it may be worth dwelling on this topic briefly. It is important to emphasize that the intrinsic nature of each caste[32] does not necessarily match individuals who are born in specific

---

32 The cosmic basis for the caste system is defined in the hymn to *Purusha* (the "Purusha Sukta") in the *Rigveda*: "From *Purusha*'s face (or the mouth) came the *brahmanas*. From His two arms came the *kshatriyas*. From His two thighs came the *vaishyas*. From His two feet came the *shudras*." These analogies are not fanciful, but are based on the idea that the social body is like a macrocosmic body, just as the individual body is a microcosm of the social body. The hierarchy of states exists archetypally before the differentiation into bodies: thus the idea of the "arms" is really a symbol of action, just as the "thighs" are a symbol of stability, and so on and so forth—the dynamic principle of "action" or the static principle

social castes; so, for instance, not all pariahs in the social sense are human pariahs in the literal sense, just as not all *brahmanas* are brahmanic or naturally contemplative, for this is where the nature of character enters, as a vertical axis penetrates (and transcends) a horizontal axis. That said, we cannot forget the individual who is "beyond caste", the *ativarnashrami*: he represents the possibility of the Spirit embodying itself in man and dwelling among men much as ether permeates the universe above and beyond the Four Elements that are derived from it; this human being can originate by social birth from any of the four castes, perhaps even from a *pariah*, and illustrates in his transparent fashion the principle of the "boundless Center" or of "the wind (spirit) that bloweth where it listeth" (John 3:8), of which there must always be some human witness. The Hindu saint Swami Ramdas, for instance, first took on the orange robe of the *sannyasin* (that of a wandering hermit who has renounced society), but then later on donned the indistinct white cloth worn by almost anyone, signifying that he had moved even beyond the non-status status of a mendicant monk. Ramana Maharshi, for his part, was an *ativarnashrami* as well as a *paramahamsa*, and here it is worth noting that these two beings are not necessarily identical: the *paramahamsa* (primordial man) includes the possibility of the *ativarnashrami*—he who is beyond caste—while embodying the totality of the priestly *brahmana* and warrior *kshatriya* possibilities; whereas the *ativarnashrami* may be a far humbler human possibility. Were such a human "airing-out" of society not possible, each creaturely determination would collapse under the crush of its exclusivity, which is to say that no matter how intense a social determination is, there is always an opening within its domain to the pure Spirit, or *Purusha*, because the universe is one before it is many.[33]

These considerations raise an important question: since the caste system is based on *dharma* or "universal law", do *dharma* and character coincide and, derivatively, do caste and character coincide? *Dharma* is Truth, or ultimate Reality: "Verily that which is *Dharma* is Truth", we read in the *Brihadaranyaka Upanishad* (1.14.14); likewise, character is truth but expressed in different modes according to the different human types. In a homogeneous social order, there is normally a correspondence between

of "stability" pre-existing all formal determinations. Likewise, the origin of the *brahmanas*, said to emanate from the face (or mouth) of *Purusha,* is an indication of their potential for knowledge and wisdom, of which the human head (or mouth = speech) is a symbol. Hence the imagery in these equations is meant to be interpreted principially, not literally.

33 It is well known in Hinduism that there were pariah saints; Gandhi, for example, mentioned there were "many many pariah saints" (*Letters to Americans*), perhaps an exaggeration but proof at least of such a possibility.

the dispassionate or objective nature of a *brahmana* and his caste, just as there is a correspondence between the commanding and martial nature of a *kshatriya* and his caste in the sense that, respectively, the *brahmana* is centered temperamentally on the unifying and appeasing principle of the One or of the Truth transcending dualities, whereas the *kshatriya*, girding his sword on his thigh, is governed temperamentally by the idea of the competing dualities—him against others, noble versus ignoble, as well as right versus wrong. To illustrate this: where the *brahmana* sees the one white light permeating all colors, the *kshatriya* sees the richness of mutually exclusive colors and will defend the glory of each. Also, the merciful nature of a *brahmana* can be contrasted with the *kshatriya*'s rigorous sense of justice and his need to compete and to defeat. Each has a role—or *dharma*—to fulfill in order to preserve and revitalize the universe or, by extension, society. Strength of character, then, for the *brahmana* will depend on a *static* quality, namely the degree of his impassivity and patience, whereas strength of character for the *kshatriya* will be measured by *dynamic* and seemingly opposite criteria: vehemence or fierceness in upholding the truth and justice, and his impatience with error, injustice, or mediocrity; where the *brahmana* displays unruffled equanimity, the *kshatriya* may display joyous enthusiasm or explosive wrath; and yet both qualities, opposite as they may appear, require equal strength in their perfection. That said, it is also true that these qualities need not be mutually exclusive in that a *brahmana* can display wrath just as a *kshatriya* can display equanimity, the first perhaps through acuteness of discernment and the second through regal magnanimity, which is to say that they will display them in a manner that accords with the basic temperament of their caste. Thus each caste reflects an aspect of the intemporal *dharma* projected, via the caste holder, into his respective social stratum. However, to repeat, the *paramahamsa* combines the qualities of all the superior castes either synthetically or sequentially depending on circumstances.

That notwithstanding, and having detailed a number of elements that explain character, it should be emphasized once again that strength of character is not just *intensity* of conviction but *rightness* of conviction. And it should be said too that strong character cannot be divorced from good character; and also, that good character is ultimately based on the divine attributes of Truth, Strength, and Beauty, which is to say that good character includes a measure of wisdom, of forcefulness, and of virtue; these qualities correspond respectively to the faculties of Intelligence, Will, and Love that summarize man's intrinsic nature.

In the final analysis, strength of character is fundamentally premised on a sense of the Absolute, the notion of which gives value to everything man believes in, loves, and undertakes. Therefore, the loss of the sense of the Absolute cannot but undermine the whole notion of character: remove the sense of the Absolute and man's vows crumble, his principles waver, his commitments falter, and his soul follows the fate of a shadow. Restore the Absolute, and man becomes radiant *rex sacrorum*, or "king of sacred things". And: "in thy majesty ride prosperously because of truth and meekness and righteousness" (Ps. 45:4).

CHAPTER 11

The Forbidden Door

Fostered by sacrifice, the gods will grant the enjoyments thou desirest.
He who enjoys these gifts without giving to them in return verily is a thief.
(*Bhagavad Gita*, 3:12)

There is a curtain before the Ark of the Covenant, a veil before the Holy Place in the Temple of Jerusalem. One finds, in medieval churches, a rood screen and, in Eastern Orthodox churches, an iconostasis set between the nave and the sanctuary.[1] These veils or screens are placed between the Divine and man—"And it was not vouchsafed to any mortal that God should speak to him unless it be . . . from behind a veil" (Koran, "Counsel", 42:51)—for who can behold the countenance of the Lord and live? The awesome holiness of God requires shrouding—"Lo, I come unto thee in a thick cloud" (Exod. 19:9)[2]—lest mortal man, glimpsing the Supreme, be felled on the spot. Various legends allude to this reality in different ways, for instance the telling of the arrival of the White Buffalo Maiden among the Sioux Indians: two men behold her but one of them, who has impure thoughts, is struck dead. And there is the legend of the hunter Actaeon who was turned into a stag when he chanced on the virgin goddess Artemis as she bathed in her unclad beauty. The legend recounts how he was then assaulted and killed by his own hounds, which symbolize the animal passions that can rend the soul.[3]

---

1 In the Eastern Orthodox Church, which protects the holy mysteries better than the Roman Catholic does, only the priest is allowed to enter through that screen, through what are aptly called the "Royal Doors" in the center of the iconostasis. However, it is traditional for the priest to bring a newborn child into the Holy of Holies and to carry it around the altar, which makes sense if one understands that the soul of an infant is still not tainted by the world. Students of history will observe that these screens are later additions; but this does not detract from their meaning, all the more as the rood screen could be considered to be no less than a reversion to the veil of the Ark of the Covenant.

2 In Islam, reference is made both to the Night of Revelation (*Laylatul Qadr*) and to the Night of Ascension (*Laylatul Mi'raj*)—the encounter between man and the Divine occurring in the blessedness of darkness.

3 In the Odyssey, Ulysses meets the enchantress Circe, who turns all men into beasts; but, falling in love with the wandering hero, spares Ulysses a similar fate. In esoteric terms, Ulysses is in fact immune to the spell of Circe's magic because, as central man, he dominates his soul. And this is also why Circe cannot but fall in love with him, just as the soul, when it is all that it ought to be, cannot elude the riveting attraction of the Spirit. Concerning the

The paradox of these veils is that the Divine, even though it is essentially infinite mercy, goodness, and beneficence, requires shrouding lest its mercy slay—if such an ellipsis be permitted. Now, it is clearly not beneficence as beneficence that is lethal, but the contrast between light and darkness that can have a shattering effect, all the more so when darkness is inveterate and repulsive of light. On another level, the manifestation of the Center—or of the One—can have an annihilating effect on the peripheral or on the many, whence the necessity for transitional hypostases, without which the appearance of the Divine on earth would signal instant and pulverizing reabsorption into the singleness of its inviolable Selfhood. In other words, without these veils, manifestation could never pass from principial potentiality to the actual manifested state. Thus, in Islam it is said that the countenance of God is veiled by seventy thousand curtains of light and darkness, without which everything His gaze fell on would be incinerated.

The brilliance and majesty of the Divine Principle is such that even its perfect creation, man—or man as the *avatara*, that is, in his form of *atmas-varupa* ("created in the image of God")—cannot be beheld directly by the angels. Thus even the cherubim are said to avert their gaze before Christ,[4] which they do partly out of fear and partly out of respect, these being really the two faces of the same attitude. Conversely, Moses, after entering in communion with the Lord, has to veil the radiance of his own face before addressing the Hebrews.[5]

The lifting of the veil—echoing that of the Egyptian goddess Isis—can only be operated after taking the marriage or the initiatic vow, both of which provide the spiritual basis or moral qualification to receive the nakedness of the Spirit; this is granted either in the form of knowledge of the Divine, in the initiatic vow, or that of the maidenly splendor of woman

tale of Actaeon above, there is another interpretation that links him to the cult of the sacred stag, whose dismemberment hearkens back to the sacrifice of a Purusha or of an Osiris. There is no direct need to reconcile the divergence in meanings given that our basic point about the fearsome (*terribilità*) aspect of the Divine still holds.

4 By way of example, a reference to this can be found in *Romanos Melodes Hymnes*, an early medieval collection of hymns for the laity gathered around the turn of the fifth and sixth centuries. The cherubim's discretion is, by cosmic analogy, a recognition of their lower order of reality. This modesty probably does not apply in the same way to the seraphim, the highest order of angels, although all the angels are said to have to prostrate themselves before Adam.

5 The taking of the veil by nuns in the convent symbolizes not only the withdrawal from the world but also, and more essentially, the protection of the intimacy of their relationship with Christ from profane interference—which recalls in its own way these words from the Song of Songs: "I am black but beautiful."

disrobed, in the marriage vow. The kindred symbolism of these two gifts is actually the same as seen in the Jewish idea of the *Shekhinah*, the Divine Essence—wisdom—manifested in feminine beauty. The necessity of this preliminary vow, whether initiatic or of marriage, is founded on the fact that before wedding the Absolute, man is summoned to commit his immortal soul sacrificially and unconditionally, for such a depth of oath is the only one to accord with the wondrous nature of the gift which, in its essence, is no less than the gift of divine immortality and eternal bliss.[6] Anything less is inherently sacrilegious, and the petitioner comes no better than a common thief now open to the dread retribution of the law, symbolically speaking, because to profane the sacred conjures ill fortune. For the man who is worthy, however, or who makes at least a worthy profession of faith—thus declaring sufficient rightness of intention—what he is bound to find ultimately, upon the lifting of the veil, is none other than his immortal self, for in beholding the Self—come to him through sacred beauty—he is thereby, via holy anamnesis, restored to himself, to his essence which itself is also pure beauty.[7] The veiled nakedness of the bride conceals the mystery of love and of the heart, the love—*amor* is *a-mors*, "without death"—that rescues from death, yes, but also by the same token that slays the false self; the Valkyrie's kiss brings death for it is also the kiss of life immortal.

∗   ∗   ∗

Much of what has been said about the symbolism of the veil or the screen applies naturally to that of the door. However, unlike the screen or veil, the door presupposes a passageway that can be crossed in two directions—either entering or exiting, which recalls the image of the *Janua coeli*, or celestial gate, and the *Janua inferni*, or infernal gate, found for instance in the cosmology of the zodiac.[8] Where the veil both conceals and reveals,

---

6 Thus Isis is made to say: "I am all that has been, and is, and shall be, and my veil no mortal man has yet lifted." No "mortal" man refers, implicitly, to the need for man to die first through the sacrificial consecration attendant upon his solemn oath to honor and serve the Lord—or the bride.

7 The romantic poet Novalis speaks penetratingly of this mystery in his *Lehrlinge zu Sais* ("Apprentices of Isis"): "A man succeeded in lifting the veil of Sais [Isis]. But what did he behold? He beheld—oh, miracle of miracles—himself."

8 They are depicted as separate doors; however, their symbolism (when joined into one image) can apply to the two directions implicit in a single door, and this symbolism is seen notably in the approach to the feminine sex, which can be either consecrated or profaned, because the vulva—just as the door—can lead to profane outwardness or to the sacred inwardness of the sanctuary of the heart.

the door's threshold indicates the possibility of two opposite destinations. More generally, however, the idea is that the same threshold marks the isthmus between a sacred interior and profane exterior and, as a result, the door is defended, in the lore of traditions, by fierce guardians that forbid ingress to the impure. One does not cross the threshold without appropriate obeisance, as seen in the customs of prostration, of removing one's shoes, of kissing the threshold or an amulet, and other similar marks of respect when arriving at a dwelling, which are everywhere to be found in sacred civilizations.

The image of the "forbidden door" itself is a common motif in fairy-tales and in traditional stories. In its essential symbolism it echoes, in the popular style of the folk cultures where it appears, the loss of Eden and of primordial innocence—the main character committing the punishable offense of opening the one door forbidden in an Elysian realm (which is really an earthly paradise or a realm of Edenic innocence prior to the Fall), where he is heir to every pleasure and delight he can dream of: "There they have all that they desire, and there is more with Us," we read in the Koran ("*Qaf*", 50:35). There are two main ideas at stake here: the first is that man cannot pretend to a knowledge that is only safe for God to have because this knowledge—being that of duality—can engender a fatal division; for what can serve to unite can also foster alienation. The second idea, which is essentially the reverse of the first, is that man cannot approach the Divine without suitable preparation; in other words, he cannot approach the Divine on the basis of an irredeemable duality, in the sense that he is not prepared to meet God so long as he is the dupe of egocentric separation. Just as the sun—central symbol of the Divine in the natural order—cannot be viewed directly with the naked eye without dire injury, so likewise the approach to the Divine requires both a ritual and moral preparation whereby the aspirant learns to "die" spiritually, for only the immortal is meet for the Immortal. This is as much as to say that self-naughting constitutes the preliminary basis for any sincere spiritual quest. In the motif of the Forbidden Door, the hero must vow not to open this door; in so doing, he must die to his curiosity and find contentment in the treasures and pleasures granted him in reward for his pledge—treasures and pleasures that surpass anything a mortal can know but which lose their allurement or magical essence when curiosity and its step-sister discontent creep into the soul.

* * *

The essence of the mystical experience could be summed up as the meeting between grace and faith: God's grace, free and unconstrainable, coming to meet man's faith, also free and unconstrainable.[9] This means that the subjective foundation of all spiritual endeavor comes down to intention (faith)—not techniques of concentration, not sensational trance-inducing manipulations of the soul, not a drug-induced defenestration of the physical body and its five honorable servants, the five senses.[10] And to the pillar of intention must be adjoined the pillar of ritual, that of correct method; heeding God's law—"I delight in thy law," King David says (Ps. 119:70)—is the touchstone of man's sincerity. In other words, mysticism, to be spiritually operative and blessed, depends on both a subjective guarantee[11]—intention, or *niyah* in Sufism—and on an objective guarantee—the Heaven-bestowed means. The second of the two terms, namely method of prayer (including liturgy), validates the first, intention: that is, the sincere aspirant understands that he cannot approach the Lord without availing himself first of the consecrated means that Heaven has placed at his disposal; humility forbids any alternative. This proviso is what distinguishes true mysticism from pseudo-spirituality, or also from a false esoterism discarding rituals with dangerous impunity.

Counterfeit spirituality, by contrast, will lay emphasis on impressionistic experience, exploiting the subjective pole of mystical endeavor practically to the near-total exclusion of the objective pole; and it will draw its motive force or inspiration from heightened emotionalism, intuitionism, or altered states of consciousness, thus trying to validate its doctrinal indigence with intensity of experience; it is all heat and little or no light. And by reducing consciousness to purely subjective experience—as opposed to the objective consciousness of the Real that characterizes authentic spirituality—it depreciates or even ignores petitionary prayer and supplication, which are the personal cornerstones of traditional prayer; and these cornerstones

---

9 "Also free", but not "equally free", since man's freedom is on loan from God, such as we see in the Gospel parable of the talents.

10 Frithjof Schuon, in one of his unpublished texts, explains this as follows: "The right intention excludes the personal expectation of sensible results, be it graces or spiritual degrees, or even powers or other purely profane advantages. And 'one must not tempt Heaven'" (private writings # 930).

11 The term "subjective guarantee" may seem like a contradiction in terms. But by "subjective" is meant not what is arbitrary, but the pole being, in contrast to mere conceptualization. What is more, the "intention", when correct, is far more than just a personal frame of mind. The English divine William Law admonishes: "Above all things beware of taking this desire for repentance to be the effect of thy own natural sense and reason, for in so doing thou losest the key of all the heavenly treasure that is in thee, thou shuttest the door against God" (*Selected Writings of William Law*, ed. Stephen Hobhouse [London: Rockliff, 1938-1949], p. 91).

themselves are premised on the believer's *de facto* nothingness before God and therefore on the awareness of his helplessness, which awareness in turn grants him an utter readiness to endure, if necessary, obscurity, emptiness, and aridity of soul as a test of faith that the Lord may allow or even impose on him. In other words, enlightenment is never seen as something that can be engineered, so to speak, but either as a reflux of intelligence back to its primal ground in Truth or as the meeting of a long-lost love where the believer finds again the divine Lover in an ecstatic culmination of joy, made all the sweeter from the tribulations of life and loss. In both instances— either that of enlightenment or that of faith hallowed—this return depends on forces that transcend the mechanism of effort or indeed of anything the seeker is able to muster by his own skill and merit.[12] This should seem obvious, but in fact it is not since New Age spirituality is crowded with people seeking to approach the Divine through techniques or through the manipulation of psycho-physical impressions; overlooked in all this is the fact that the essence of enlightenment means the Divinity entering and permeating our own being of its own gracious accord, for the Divinity, in its contact with man, is not an impersonal energy but an infinitely wise and loving Being. Thus, to be loved by God requires firstly our being intimately likable for God; and our likeability, in turn, is premised on our virtue and not on a virtuoso technique of concentration; this means that merit is the precondition for receiving divine graces. That said, there is a transpersonal mode of union, certainly, but this does not involve individual effort or, rather, the effort is limited to removing the obstacles in the soul preventing the free-flow of the divine stream; the rest is a question of rejoining pure Being and Consciousness.

Now, for the sake of the love of God, the sincere spiritual postulant accepts the possibility of a life of obscurity, of poverty, even of deprivation. At the very least, he closes the door to the world in order to retreat to the oratory of the virginal heart, *clauso ostia* ("the closed door") (Matt. 6:6).[13] This is spiritual poverty and this is humility. The devotee accepts this extinction (*fana* in Sufism or the *imitatio crucis* in Christianity) first because he has no other choice except to do so, man being servant and not Lord: this he accepts out of principle because the divine nature of the Object—God or the Truth—alone being absolutely real and thus immaculately precious,

---

12 Shankara, in one of his commentaries on the *Bhagavad Gita*, explains that *moksha* (spiritual liberation, or enlightenment) too, being no effect of an act, no action will be any avail to a *mumukshu* or seeker of *moksha* (introduction to the third chapter).

13 The heart is "virginal" because, as Plato explained, "it is self-existent" and thus incorruptible in its essence in that it takes nothing from outside itself.

allows no conditions to be set upon It; and secondly, it is understood that only a virginal soul is meet substance for the reception of the Holy Ghost. This is the basic meaning, in the Catholic Church, of fasting before receiving communion.[14] The sincere postulant moreover accepts this extinction as a gage of his sincerity.[15] Finally, he accepts it out reverential fear of God, whose majesty and mightiness command self-annihilation; and he accepts it out of his ardent and undiscourageable love of God, whose goodness, bounty, and beauty he trusts and longs for. To repeat, the essence of prayer is first an attitude of the soul before God—namely a combination of holy fear, love, and understanding—and, in turn, it is this attitude of soul that establishes the basis for prayerful concentration.

Again, virtuosic means without proper virtuousness of attitude can lead to supersensuous states and powers, no doubt,[16] but not thereby to God who is, in his divine Personhood, Intelligence and Love; and thus man too finds God quintessentially through intelligence and love, for the

---

14 Just how seriously medieval Christians took this preparation to heart is seen by the extreme asceticism some consented to in view of receiving the holy sacrament; some in fact feared even taking it from dread of their unworthiness.

15 In the Christian framework, this acceptance of suffering as a pre-condition for approaching the Divine is even more radical, given the fact that God in the person of Christ consented to die on the cross for the sins of man. Thus, to believe in Christ entails, for the devout Christian, a heroic willingness to share in his redemptive sufferings. To suffer for God is, in fact, to taste the joy of solidarity with Christ's tribulations: in the agony lies the ecstasy. Thus the Dutch mystic Hadewijch could write that to suffer hunger was to find replenishment: "To die of hunger [the love of God personified] is to feed and taste; her despair is assurance; her sorest wounding is all curing" ("The Paradoxes of Love", in *Passionate Spirituality: Hildegard of Bingen and Hadewijch of Brabant*, ed. Elizabeth Dreyer [New York: Paulist Press, 2005], p. 26). All of mysticism hinges on the conjunction of opposites: poverty with regard to the world leading to richness in God, death to rebirth, abasement to glory, and so on and so forth, all of which is premised on the principle of inverse analogy linking Heaven and earth. Thus, the mystic finds that the quickest way to God lies in doing the opposite of what the worldly man would do. The Sufi way of the *Malamatiyya* ("the people of blame") provides an extreme example of this, although, seen from another perspective, that of ultimate sincerity, the great Ibn Arabi considered them to be "the most perfect of the gnostics". Hujwiri, however, thought the opposite of them, considering their excesses to be a form of ostentation; both opinions showing the ambiguity or risks of resorting to such a controversial type of *karma yoga* based on the cult of doing the opposite. Assessing its spiritual usefulness depends on the degree of subtlety or crude literalness of the practice, because in its finer aspects it is very profound being based on the nothingness of all earthly vanities.

16 Even demons, it is understood, have extraordinary powers; in fact, from a purely phenomenological perspective, their powers far exceed that of ordinary mortals. No doubt techniques such as breath retention or halting circulation, extremes of asceticism, hypnotic one-pointedness of mental focus, can breach the gates of the paranormal. But what has man traded for these? His soul. And at what Faustian a price?

Divine finally will only respond to what in the soul corresponds to Its own numinous nature; in bhaktic terms, God as Love responds only to man's love. The ancient *rishis* in India acquired legendary powers (*siddhis*) that even the *asuras* (demon entities) envied, it is said, but these powers were not necessarily synonymous with sanctity. On the other hand, sanctity can open the gate to supra-normal faculties and powers: the levitation of some saints is one example that comes to mind, but also the *keramat* ("thaumaturgical gifts") of Sufis, such as bilocation, the ability to live on virtually no food—such as one finds in the accounts of medieval saints living from the sacred host alone—or the seemingly supernatural capacity of Tibetan llamas who keep their bodies warm in freezing conditions. But in that case, levitation must be understood less as a phenomenological power than as an expression of a saint's transparence of substance, of which physical lightness is an incidental byproduct; grasping the proper sequence of causality is a key in understanding the difference between paranormal powers and miraculous ones.

*   *   *

Despite all precautions to the contrary, the temptation to confuse modified states of mind with spirituality is all too easy to succumb to, especially in the case of people stalking mystical experiences. These notwithstanding, there are spiritual techniques, such as the Zen meditation on the void or the Buddhist *vipassana* meditation, which consist in elaborately objectifying all impressions, mental as well as psychic and physiological, until, through a kind of exfoliation of the ego, the heart is laid bare and restored to its pre-mundane essence; in principle such a technique does not require devotion per se as a pre-condition, let alone all the fervent religious emotionalism that can go along with it and which, in fact, can prove a real distraction for the ego. However the difficulty in implementing such techniques for Westerners—marked as they usually are with a strong individualistic psyche and who are likely to practice such a method outside of a sacred culture—lies in attempting to achieve perfect contemplation in the absence of true reverence, a reverence that normally can only be grounded in the development of virtues, starting with a sense of the sacred. Thus problems can arise from trying to assimilate the impersonality of a method such as the *vipassana* meditation, or in cultivating an understanding of Buddhism that diminishes the value of personal faith, namely of developing a technique that minimizes the relevance of personality—a sanctified personality of course—because a human being cannot bypass the personal as such, only its individualistic excesses.[17]

17 Shinshu Buddhism, with its devotional reliance on the saving mercy of Amida Buddha,

Not least, communion with the Divine is more than an experience, it is a sacrament. In the case of Ramana Maharshi, who commented on the similarity of his "method" with that of *vipassana*, we have the example of a natural contemplative, namely of a "pneumatic" who ascends to Heaven effortlessly by virtue of the purity of his substance, and therefore who cannot fall; hence, adoration was innate to Maharshi's being.[18] Adoration, however, entails the ability of forgetting oneself before the Divine, and this is the hardest thing for Westerners habituated to the cult of self-observation, or for those who have little or no idea of what a human model of spirituality looks like. Instead of converting or rechanneling personal feelings, Western Zen practice when misapplied may lead to an inhuman or mechanical blanking of feelings, an outcome which can then set the stage for a possible backlash of artificially spurned feelings seeking to reassert themselves after their inopportune banishment.

Much has also been made, be it said in passing, in pseudo-esoteric circles, of awakening the *kundalini* or lethal "serpent energy" coiled at the base of the spine, namely of lifting the ego-consciousness rapturously through the ladder-rungs of the energy vortices—or *chakras*—so as to achieve a "transcendental vision" of the cosmos. Now, all things being equal, one must grant the fact that man has a godlike intelligence and imagination that enables him to gain insights no other creature can have. And who then is to say that man cannot take advantage of such gifts? Indeed, who has the right to bar man's access to supersensuous realms if he has the power to penetrate them? Does not the very availability of such gifts qualify an individual, at least implicitly, to make use of the full panoply of means at his disposal?

One solution to this dilemma, if relevant, is to understand that these powers can be either the direct result of techniques, namely powers sought for their own sake, or they can occur as indirect results of a spiritual practice. It is obvious that man cannot help being other than what he is: if he is gifted, he cannot, out of an overzealous humility for instance, abjure these gifts, though he can learn to detach himself from them. Not least, it is easy for the soul to mistake the psychic for the spiritual. Hence, even at their peak these powers, such as telepathic insight, can be accessed independently from any intelligence or love, and yet it is precisely intelligence and love that are the marks of the Spirit; in other words, such gifts do not of themselves enhance either intelligence or love, nor, reciprocally, do intelligence and

strikes us as a path more adapted to the psychology of Westerners, who have need of a kind of holy personalism in order to meet God.

18 A key component of adoration is sweetness and infinite compassion.

love depend on them to be fully operative. Thus a Patanjali, the compiler of the *Yoga Sutras*, or, in our epoch, a Ramana Maharshi disavowed them and hence made no use of them.

One could add that the divergence between this world and the next entails the possibility of imbalance, and thus it is not always possible to draw clean lines of demarcation in this domain between the abnormal and supra-normal; in both cases the body stands as a kind of barrier—providentially so in the case of mediumistic emotionalism, burdeningly so in the case of spirituality—and this explains the recourse to trance-inducing ritual singing and drumming in the Afro-Brazilian *candomblé* or some of the frenzied rhythmic performances found in certain dervish orders, the goal being to free consciousness from the grips of the earthly body. But the flesh body is in fact the stabilizer the soul needs to protect it not only from the eruption of the supernatural but also from that of the infra-rational, because when this sheath has been compromised, there is no saying what may take possession of the soul: if it will be the higher or the lower *Maya*. There is no question that a soul touched by God can lose its equilibrium, temporarily, but one does not necessarily want to create a disequilibrium in the hopes of obtaining a divine experience; or rather this is too treacherous a possibility not to be left to the wisdom of a spiritual master; some spiritual orders, however, allow the possibility of the "fools for god". Not least, a disequilibrium of temperament can produce a fissure in the soul which may—provided there is the right spiritual substance—be a catalyst for a mystical opening, in that case: O blessed affliction! Taken in itself, however, a psychic fissure means nothing spiritually, otherwise lunatics would be mystics. By contrast, a wound of the soul can produce a disequilibrium that frees one from worldliness.[19]

* * *

The principal difficulty for the soul embarking on the spiritual journey lies in reaching the isthmus of conversion (*metanoia*): before man can know anything about the Divine he must replace, as it were, his subjective sense of self with an objective sense of Self; the Truth must displace the illusion of his importance as a person. But this Truth will likely feel at first as a death. Seen from the "narrow gate", the spiritual path appears as a desert, a barren land where the soul feels deprived of everything that it finds naturally pleasurable; the aspirant now feels doomed to die because compelled to

19 Schuon mentions this: "God sometimes loves to live in a wound, with the perfume of beautiful Patience" (private writings, # 260).

sacrifice its previous inclinations, opinions, and habits to the point that the soul has the impression it is being boiled to death or that it has been deserted. In alchemical terms, the substance of the soul is taken out of the world to be enclosed in a vessel (the athanor or retort of the alchemists, but metaphorically the prayer cell), which is then hermetically sealed before being committed to darkness and to the heat of fire. The soul longs to free itself and may struggle wildly to escape, but cannot do so any longer on its terms; its former substance must be "cooked" (calcinated) into itself, and the vapors of this residue purified and transmuted. If at any moment any part of this former substance ("the old Adam") escapes the vial, the transubstantiation fails; in physical terms, this means that if there is a leak, the pressure cannot swell enough to abolish itself—the alchemical image of the dragon biting its tail or that of the entwined snakes comes to mind here. Without the *nigrido*, no *albedo*: the final whitening issues from the initial blackening. The circle is now complete.

The willingness to endure even the complete absence of the Divine Presence is in fact the operative basis of all apophatic mysticism: understanding the utter and total otherness of God may stipulate as a pre-condition not being able to know or see Him at all while on earth; and, indeed, how could the fallen soul do so? In a sense, the soul's abyss is the measure of God's grandeur; that is to say, not until the soul has experienced the abyss and darkness of its utter nothingness can God's grandeur and light fully penetrate and illuminate it.

Yet there is not only the negative aspect of mortification, there is also the positive aspect,[20] and it consists in this: when the soul does encounter the Divine, or gleans a taste of Heaven, the sheer wonder of the Object itself compels extinction. At that moment of supreme entrancement there is no sense of one's importance, no ambition, no selfish desire, utterly none. In the alchemy of love, for instance—which can serve as a symbol of the blissful meeting with the Divine—the soul is emptied of itself: it is stripped, cleansed, and laid bare in poverty before the ineffable wonder of the beloved (whether groom or bride) who, by contrast, possesses all riches.

Be that as it may, the above considerations allow one to understand how it is not only foolhardy, but actually impossible—according to the law of "spiritual physics"—to seek to experience the Divine on terms not set by the Divine Itself because the very nature of an individualistic ambition precludes divine grace. For instance, to desire to realize identity with God

---

20 And these phases do not necessarily follow in this order: the sequence can be reversed to begin with a positive or elating grace, which then serves as a prelude for the spiritual death to come.

constitutes instant disqualification;[21] and without grace, no salvation and, *a fortiori*, no spiritual realization. Hence, a return to God entails, first, a return to the Center away from the peripheral individuality the ego represents. And this return depends not least on the slaying of the *moi haïssable* (the loathsome self): "He that humbleth himself shall be exalted" (Luke 18:14).[22] In second instance—having now parted with the flawed self—the return to God depends upon entering the mold of perfect man, such as is found in the imitation of Christ or that of the Buddha, or any one of the major *avataras* who appeared historically on earth as the living personification of the divine Self. And finally in third instance, following this exchange of egos from imperfect man to perfect man, the spiritual return entails self-transcendence. The possibility of holy immanence, wherein the Divine wells up from one's innermost heart, is premised on at least the initial adoption of these three steps, otherwise there is the risk of the spiritual life turning into self-exaltation.

Single-minded focus on putting God first, based on a veridical sense of certainty—Saint Bernard's *vehemente cogitatio* (intense meditative concentration)—along with fierceness of commitment to the divine, compels the world to actually serve us—or, to be more exact, to serve God in us. The soul which is thus heaven-dedicated becomes like a blazing funeral pyre where everything the world feeds it ends up feeding the flames of its sacrifice; every previous contrivance of desire is now smelted in a roaring furnace of love[23] which, at the same time and through the grace of detachment (what Saint Francis calls purity of heart) is as serene as a lighted devotional lamp in a prayer niche.

Thus, for the God-centered man, solicitations, either from the soul or from the outside world, are no longer like riptides that threaten to pull the soul out in subjective musings and daydreams; rather, these solicitations are converted into fountains praising God. This is why Saint Augustine can say: "Love God and do what thou wilt". For the pure, everything is pure— *omnia munda mundis.*

*   *   *

Perhaps the most dangerous thing in the spiritual life is the cult of singularity. And the next most dangerous thing? Sheep-like conformity.

---

21 Such a desire proves a complete misunderstanding of the grounds for *theosis*.

22 Which Nietzsche cynically recasts as: "He that humbleth himself wishes to be exalted." But pietism is not piety.

23 Examples of such fervor abound in Christian mysticism. See for instance Richard Rolle's *incendium amoris* (the conflagration of love).

That is to say: to cultivate our individual uniqueness is to emphasize what is the most accidental, and hence least real in us. But, at the reverse end, a mindless conformity is like the shadow opposite of singularity because it can amount to fleeing the divine uniqueness that the soul needs to realize inasmuch as God created it and wanted it to be, to be a unique possibility. In that respect, to rely on the falsely reassuring comfort of letting the blind lead the blind is a manner of not fully assuming one's destiny as a noble individual in our own right; the challenge of existing is to become a real person and not just a pale shadow of someone else's dictate. That said, egocentrically speaking, singularity corresponds to the active pole of individualism and mindless conformity to the passive pole; strangely, the non-individualism of inertia rejoins the egotistic tendency of individualism, for both are a form of selfishness, one in passive and heavy mode, the other in dynamic and passionate mode. In order to escape both pitfalls, the ego must learn self-effacement, neither flaunting itself but neither just fitting in with dull conformity or blind obedientialism; the soul is called to espouse a kind of anonymous independence, neither grandly rejecting the crowd, nor joining it mindlessly. And here is the great paradox for the ego, because in effacing itself, it actually finds itself: in other words, in effacing itself before the Real—or the sole Unique—it finds itself through its root identity with the Self. The less conspicuously individualistic we become the more inspiredly real. Put differently, uniqueness is not bestowed by dint of our mere existence, because no distinction lasts forever. Rather, our personal uniqueness grows in proportion to our awareness of the Unique itself, whence the irreplaceable value of the imitation of a divine model—the "singular nature" (*al-fardaniyah*) which is the supreme exemplar.[24] Thus we wish to mention once more that what characterizes a normal traditional civilization is the same prophetic stamp imprinting the countenance and attitude of a majority of its members, but each time in a specific personal mode. This seal derives first from a central divine figure of the stature of a prophet, and secondly from the great saints who reflect and re-echo across generations the nature of such a seminal figure; and it is re-echoed again by the priests and pious faithful. Ancestor worship—at its best—is also based on the idea of such a divine paternity or fertile exemplar.

Does all this then mean that the principle of "experience" is to be discarded as useless, as something purely subjective and therefore to be

---

24 Strictly speaking, Sufism reserves the idea of *fardaniyah* to God alone—it is an equivalent of the Vedantic *kaivalya* ("solitude" or "solitariness")—and quite understandably so given Islam's insistence on the Unicity of the Supreme Divine Principle. However, one nonetheless finds an Ibn al-Arabi speaking in his *Futuhat al-Makkiyah* of the "*fardaniyah* of our Lord Jesus".

distrusted or rejected? It has been alleged that a religion cannot live long with the loss of experience—that is, without "experience" religion soon loses its vital raison d'être. But in that case the notion of experience must be carefully sifted from that of sensationalism, because there is what might be termed "objective subjectivity" and "subjective subjectivity" inasmuch as a distinction can be made between objective and subjective experience, both being personal obviously, since we are talking about "experience", but not in the same manner. In other words, one can distinguish between "subjective experience", which is inherently unstable, arbitrary, and unreliable, and "objective experience" which may sound like a contradiction in terms[25] unless one understands that the soul is made to partake of the Real through the mirror-like capacity of the intelligence for perfect personal adequation. In that sense, the personal experience a person can have of reverence, awe, and love becomes an "emotional" adequation for the soul's knowledge of the True, the Beautiful, and the Noble because, in themselves, feelings, sentiments, emotions, and instincts are all delegate faculties of intelligence itself. In Vedantic Hinduism, emphasis is placed on the concept of *anubhava*, namely the certitude occurring as a direct result from experience, be it ontological (inward) or merely occasional (outward). Now if it is obviously true that until knowledge descends into the heart, there can be no effective certitude (which is "objective subjectivity"), at the same time, there can be a certitude of the Spirit reflected in the mind as Truth, and this can be the prelude to the actualization of certitude in the heart; in other words, even though the first certitude occurs in the mind, it is nonetheless not purely mental but pre-existential as it were, or the harbinger of the full heart-certitude to come, which will fuse pure consciousness and pure existence as one.[26] But for this intellectual certitude to become fully operative—existentially and morally—it needs to free itself from the mesh of subjective or individualistic experience; hence the necessity first of cleansing the soul of its profane otherness, although truth also facilitates this cleansing. Only

25 For those who insist that all experience has to be subjective, we will say that an objective person's experience cannot be qualitatively the same as that of a subjective person whose experience of things will be influenced or even distorted by his interests, passions, or sentiments. Moreover, several people can have the same objectively subjective experience of seeing a sunrise, just as they can of any other phenomenon that is objectively verifiable, spiritual or otherwise.

26 Schuon even speaks of "truths which present themselves as axioms because they fall within the realm of the five senses and that, as a result, can be proven *ab extra* [from the outside]; and there are others that are axiomatic owing to the fact that they are to be found in the very substance of intelligence and therefore, by that fact, can only be seized as evidence *ab intra* [from the inside]" (*The Transfiguration of Man* [Bloomington, IN: World Wisdom, 1995], p. 63).

then is the mirror made spotless or the vessel transparent enough for the self to experience the Self.

This process is illustrated by the liquefaction of the alchemists in which a formerly base substance is transfigured back into its eternal essence according to the formula that the soul must become disembodied so that the Spirit can become embodied: "The body must become spirit and the spirit body", we read in an alchemical manuscript.[27] Be that as it may, in these considerations regarding "graces experienced", what matters is not what the soul *feels* but what it *does* upon receiving the graces—operatively, concretely, objectively; and this belongs to the realm of character, not of experience,[28] and then what matters is what the soul becomes, in the wake of these graces. Not least, some of the greatest changes in a soul often take place beneath (or outside) the threshold of consciousness—that is to say outside the realm of experience as such—somewhat in the fashion of a solution becoming progressively and invisibly saturated, remaining completely liquid the whole while, until, at the decisive point, it undergoes instant crystallization. Many men have become saints wholly unawares, which proves the irrelevance of the cult of experiences that "New Age" spirituality cultivates.

*　*　*

The advent of the machine age, with its cold, brutal pragmatism, and the inexorable science of numbers connected to it—for instance the monomaniacal reliance on measurements and the scientific rationalism they buttress—was bound to provoke a counter reaction from a life force— the primal *eros*, for one, but also the *affectus*, the feeling or affective soul— that cannot fit into the rigid strictures of pure rationalism or of an overly mental culture that misprizes instinct as primitivism.[29] The legacy of a

27 *The Glory of the World*, or *Table of Paradise*, which is part of *The Hermetic Museum* collection of alchemical writings (London: John M. Watkins, 1953), vol. I, p. 182.

28 Once again Frithjof Schuon: ". . . instead of being governed by phenomena and following inspirations," one should "submit to principles and accomplish actions" for "what counts in the eyes of God is not what we experience, but what we do. Doubtless we may feel graces, but we may not base ourselves upon them. God will not ask us what we have experienced, but He will ask us what we have done" (private writings, # 982).

29 Tribalism has many forms, and its complete and unnatural suppression in the modern world has led, it seems, to a kind of backlash in the form of a substitute primitivism seen, among other things, in the epidemic of tattoos people graft on their skin. Man is not just a brain but a being, and he needs an existential outlet for his values and beliefs—or what passes for these—through ornaments and symbols worn on his body. However, modern man, ignorant of traditionalism, ends up disfiguring his body with the talismanic debris of his Götterdämmerung civilization.

metrically Cartesian mind not only outlaws supra-rational intuition, but misunderstands how the physical body can be a form of intelligence as well as a means of consciousness (and of vital wisdom) in its own right. In turn, this hypertrophy of the mind produces an excessively cerebral type of human being who lives in a sterile cocoon of plastified, metallic, and chemical substances whose molecular inflexibility are alien to the natural rhythms of the soul because they do not "breathe and feel" and thus are dead to the influx of the Spirit. A scientist might object that even artificial substances have some kind of porosity and therefore are not absolutely stable (or inert). This may be true, but only up to a certain point because one of the characteristics of an unnatural substance is the fact that it is not organically dissolvable (bio-degradable) except at temperatures that exceed the normal parameters of our biosphere. Traditional metallurgy—whether of the gold-casters, wheel and rim makers, or the sword smiths—probably constitutes the outer limits of what is still normally possible in the domain of manufacture without alienating the soul. However, even as natural a substance as wood, when not literally pulverized and re-compressed, is now readily processed and trimmed according to the "heartless" symmetries of the most mathematically mental of rectilinear angles, before being finished off with sterilizing seals or paints that deal the final death blow to what is left of its organic soul. In contrast, we remember entering homes in Morocco where the scent of cedar still exuded fragrantly from the wood panels and beams or posts; these, their craftsmen contended, had "still not finished growing", their aromatic aura reverberating in the atmosphere. This is what Shintoists know as *ke*, the "mysterious force of nature", a supreme architectural example of which is the Grand Shrine at Ise.

To criticize rationalism, however, should not grant one license to castigate reason itself, or even less to revert to animalism. Reason, in itself, is a divine faculty whose justification lies in *recta ratio*, namely on a rectitude of logic premised on an impartial sense of the truth. However, reason—and the mind—is often singled out as the culprit for our hyper-cerebral civilization and, as a result, a counter-culture has arisen dedicated to the spontaneous impulse of primal feeling, or pure spontaneity, or of an animal-like naturalness. Man must beware here: there is a seemingly very fine line—seen from the human vantage point—between the supra-rational and the infra-rational, when in fact the distance between them is incommensurable. But tampering with the mind or mistreating it can lead the unwary to cross this line in one short step down, for the "corruption of the best is the worst" (*corruptio optimi pessima*). Falling into the infra-rational is really the result of the failure of having been adopted by Grace, hell being in that sense the price of our Heaven-born *dharma* forfeited. Now, between these two levels of consciousness there is a door, and this door is normally closed for average man. We have termed this door as being "forbidden" because it cannot be opened with impunity by man; the realms it bars at its threshold are near infinite, both up and down, both in bliss and in woe.

*   *   *

The suggestive and possibly over-quaint use of the term "forbidden door" may recall the imagery of fairy tales; or it may bring to mind imagery one finds in mythic tales such as the "forbidden fruit", images meant for children, some will opine, though they have their meaning for adults too. Now to be born a man is to be born enclosed in the protective lock of the five senses, which both allow him to relate with his surroundings while at the same time keeping him insulated from a dizzying consciousness of the immensity of the cosmos, whose infinite amalgam of energy vortices and boundless processes no human being could behold and still preserve his sanity. Thus to attempt to pierce the envelope of the five senses—which function normally as a merciful womb—can compromise the whole basis of our humans state; to seek to pierce or violate this mode of perception is to play with fire. "Moralistic prudery!", some will contend, eager to speak in terms of exotic notions such as the *chakras*, or energy centers in the body, which they seek to awaken; or they will refer to notions such as the *koshas*, the doctrine describing the five sheaths enveloping the *atman* or individual soul; these sheaths, it is assumed, must be transcended to reach the great cosmic mind or *Mahat*. The fundamental error in this viewpoint lies less in the theoretical conception than in its practical realization, because no *chakra*-kindling or *kosha*-breaching experiment will bring the soul one iota closer to Divinity. One cannot approach the Divine except through the Logos, that is to say either through the Word of God become man (the *avatara*) or through the heart-intellect which is the microcosmic Logos and of which the God-man is the macrocosmic or outward paragon. For the sake of emphasis, we want to repeat what we stressed earlier, namely that without homage and reverence of the Divine in its manifestation as the Logos, there is no rebirth in blessed immortality. Even in Islam, which radically minimizes the human, the imitation of the Prophet constitutes the indispensable basis upon which man approaches God. In fact, there is no religious tradition in which veneration is not the basis for communion with the Divine because man cannot return to the Absolute by bypassing man, who is, after all, the quintessential creation of God. Even the worship of God Himself presupposes some human adequation reflecting the "personality" of God, otherwise worship would not only be meaningless, it would be impossible.[30] What we are saying is that one cannot *love* a purely abstract principle: one loves God because He—to use a personal pronoun—is lovable, and supremely so in virtue of the fact that He is a being and not just an axiom or some ethereally blank luminescence.[31] Strange to say, the ecstasy that can be unleashed through the awakening of the *chakras*, marvelous as it can be, does not in itself lead to virtue, otherwise any mortal who had found bliss in sexual consummation, or in hallucinogenic stimulants, would *ispo facto* be sanctified, when such is obviously not the case: the joy felt—the rapture, the ecstasy—no matter how blissful, only enhances the nature an individual person happens to possess; although such a bliss should, in principle, lead to a melting of the heart, the reality is that it can just as easily worsen character, and lead to vice, not to mention crime. Spirituality, as we feel obliged to emphasize once again, is all about moral character and not about experiencing states. And without such moral character, paradise is not only unattainable, but unendurable should one have a taste of it.

How should one describe the attitude of a trespasser into the Mysteries, who has the temerity to want to manipulate what is inherently a divine energy, whether the *kundalini* or otherwise, as if it were a scientific experiment or an exotic pastime? How could he want to awaken these sacred energies without wondering whether he is worthy of the Divine in the first place—to think to steal the king's daughter, as it were, for his own pleasure, she who is destined solely for the hero? Bluntly stated, God will far prefer a cranky bungler who fears Him reverentially, rather than a conceited "samadhist" who smiles condescendingly at the world's folly, but who has no fear of Him.

The dynamic ratio of our five senses is built on universal laws of order and harmony that correspond physically, and symbolically, to the material realm man dwells in while on earth; the heart-intellect is, as it were, divided into these five faculties while remaining a unified and governing agency above (and within) them. If it is objected that our bodily consciousness is an inferior mode of being—"For now we see through a glass, darkly" (1 Cor. 13:12)—with which the heavenly state of the blessed is as the difference between sight and blindness, one will concede that it is thus more because of the contents of consciousness than because of the mode. In other words, for consciousness to be divine, it need not

---

30 *Zazen* meditation is an obvious exception but it is still premised on the idea of rejoining the original Buddha nature through the quieting of the individual mind, and this quieting is analogous to the Christian or Muslim doctrines of abasement, mortification, and extinction, minus the emphasis on the affective concomitants.

31 And, to repeat a point made earlier, God's supra-personality is not impersonality.

be visionary in the sensationalistic or empirical sense of the term, but simply noble. That is enough—for man—while on earth, otherwise God would have created a human being with operatively supra-mundane faculties; but then, this man would be elsewhere than on earth; at which point, creation would lose its basis for existing—and so on and so forth in a kind of reductionism *ad absurdum*. That said, to affirm that earth-bound consciousness corresponds to a norm is not to affirm that it is ideal, hardly so; nor is it to affirm that the consciousness of human beings has always been as exclusively sense-bound as it is at the end of the *Kali Yuga*. Although one cannot describe in empirical terms what the heavenly vision of the blessed is, one can assume—metaphysically—that all phenomena in Heaven are transparent in the sense that the divine Unity—and Love—is never obscured by antagonistic dualities such as they are on earth. Thus, the difference between the mystic's otherworldliness and profane man's awareness is really more an issue of depth of understanding (or intuition) than of being open to supra-sensual phenomena, or spirits, auras, and the like. This is what Schuon has termed "the metaphysical transparency of phenomena" and this is what constitutes the sage's vision.

*   *   *

We must now address a particularly controversial if not vexing issue, that of ingesting psychogenic substances in view of enlightenment. It is vexing because it should be obvious that drugs and true spirituality belong to altogether different realms. At the same time, it is undeniable that psychogenic substances can open the gates of the soul, allowing a human being access to supra-sensory domains normally closed to ordinary mortals. False spiritualists dream of transcending, not themselves—for that would defeat the purpose—but states of consciousness, namely to pierce through the envelope layers (*koshas*) enclosing our daily consciousness in order to gain access to the immortal vistas within. There is an assumption that this can be done at will, without first "seeking permission from the gods". Psychogenic substances are probably the easiest way to jump in one leap over this divide, although the destination point is unlikely to be spiritual if the starting point is profane; nonetheless, part of this outcome may depend on an individual's substance, not to mention also the nature and context of the means which can be part of a ritual process.

It has also been assumed that ingesting such substances was a normal mode of relationship between man and the Divine[32] prior to the advent

---

32 An argument has been made that the *Upanishads* were revealed to priests through the ingestion of *soma*, "the sacred food of the Gods", and there is in fact mention in the *Vedas*

of religious moralism which then proscribed them, as if it were moralism that had created the notion of sin when in fact it was responding to a pre-existing state of affairs. And it is even supposed that the "supreme state" of absolute consciousness (*turiya* in the Vedanta) can be accessed by such psychogenic substances or, at least, that they serve to open the way to it. But such endeavors overlook whether or not our "waking state" (*vaishnavara*) does not in fact correspond to a necessary or divinely willed state of existence, and therefore dodges the question of why our waking state should be overcome in the first place instead of being perfected; that is to say, why meeting God in our "waking state" itself is not a legitimate goal, since this state was given to us by Him and that, furthermore, He made Himself known to us in this fashion.

What is also overlooked is the fact that this "waking state", on its level—and unlike the "dream state" (*taijasa*)—is analogically connected to the "supreme state" (*turiya*), in the sense that it is the reflection of the supreme state (*turiya*) in the "name and form" (*nama-rupa*) level of our created world. Therefore, this waking state's main function is that of objectivity, even if this objectivity is calibrated to the material world, as well as to the phenomena—both inner and outer—which are part of *Maya*'s weaving, namely the impressions, emotions, and thoughts arising from existence on earth. Thus for a human being to be awake—as a psychosomatic creature—is to be a witness on earth of the manifested (or outward) forms of the Divine Self, no less. Consequently, to live effectively in the "here and now", as opposed to living in some half-dream state of subjective musings, experiences, or fantasies, corresponds to a true victory over the soul, which is otherwise prey to ever-shifting currents. The soul, we will remember, when not under the aegis of the Spirit, wants to act as a solvent seeking to weaken or emasculate the Spirit's influence. However, to return to *turiya* or the supreme state: in the *Mandukya Upanishad*, this final state of consciousness is defined as "neither subjective nor objective experience" (sometimes translated as: "neither consciousness nor unconsciousness"), which does not mean that it is neither subjective nor objective but, on the contrary, that it is both subjective and objective together—or objectively subjective and subjectively objective. In other words, it is

---

of this *soma*; and the same argument has been made for the Eleusinian Mysteries. One also knows of the peyote and mescaline that are part of Mezo-American rituals, as well as accounts of the ingestion of the *agaricus* mushroom by the Celts and ancient Germanic tribes, meant to drive them into a bellicose frenzy. And some even believe the legendary apple in the Garden of Eden was really *amarita muscaria* (or the *agaricus* mushroom). We are not in a position to confirm or refute any of this, only to explore the general issue, which raises a number of logical questions.

both awareness and non-awareness, in the sense that deeper awareness beholds Reality inwardly in its non-differentiated substance while at the same time beholding it outwardly in differentiated modes, understanding both relationships—impersonally and personally—simultaneously.[33] This perception, being inherently non-phenomenological, can be grasped both in its outward or flesh-and-body mode and in its principial essence, in virtue of the fact that creation is finally not other than a materialization of Spirit, or *Prakriti* reflecting *Purusha*.

No doubt, from a certain perspective, the world is *Maya* or illusion; but it is only illusion when misperceived by man or when the "metaphysical transparency of phenomena" is no longer understood by him. Put differently, one could say that man's limitation—or sin—resides not in the fact of his outward existence as such—which, to repeat, is necessary and willed by God—but in seeing his existence as separate from God, and therefore in considering himself *de facto* independent; hence, it is the "independence" or "separateness" that is the illusion, not the fact of existence. Moreover, if from the point of view of the Fall fleshly existence entails a stigma, this scourge really has less to do with the possibility of the flesh—which is completely innocent in itself—than with man's passionally carnal will; otherwise one could not encounter the possibility of some saints whose bodies were exhumed incorrupt, nor *a fortiori* miraculous possibilities such as the Dormition or the Assumption, or that of levitation.

We feel compelled to pursue this vein of thinking a little further because the issue of transcending the self and that of the illusion of existence is often defined in too black and white terms. The crux of the problem, it seems to us, is that because of his outwardness (or individualism) man idolatrously divorces the effect from its cause: "They know only an outward appearance of this lower life" (Koran, "The Romans", 30:7). Fallen man is fragmented and therefore he not only fragments what he sees but, on top of this, he is also prone to then idolize the fragments in an effort to regain the Absolute or Unity he has lost. Thus, through the "waking state" (*vaishnavara*), he mistakenly superimposes—Shankara terms this *adhyasa*[34]—his own limited awareness, desires, and fears on objects and on

---

33 As Schuon has pertinently remarked: "The difference between ordinary vision and that enjoyed by the sage or the gnostic is quite clearly not of the sensorial order. The sage sees things in their total context, therefore in their relativity, and at the same time in their metaphysical transparency" (*Light on the Ancient Worlds*, p. 98). This is to see Unity within multiplicity and multiplicity within Unity, or God in all things and all things in God.

34 Superimposition (*adhyasa*) is the placing on top of something the image of something else: such as mistaking a rope for a snake so that one sees only the snake, and not the fact that the rope is a rope. This is the classic metaphor found in the Vedanta.

the universe, and thus creates a series of illusions or half-truths; whereas, for the egoless contemplative this same universe and its symbols presents itself both as objective factualness and as a unified tapestry of inspiring beauty and grandeur; he thus sees the changing play of phenomena with a dispassionate eye while also detecting in creation's creatures and symbols a kind of formal liturgy of the Divine. Profane man, for his part, tends to vampirize phenomena: unable to recognize the Creator in the living signs, he takes what he can of their energy unaware of the possibility of Eucharistic communion latent in earthly delights. To paraphrase Saint Paul, he may in fact be eating his own perdition because, in exchange for His gifts, God requires our soul: to enjoy the pleasures of the gods one has to be divine oneself, or the pleasures will consume us.

*　*　*

Returning to the issue of gaining divine states by human means, our assumption throughout this chapter has been that truly mystical states are not obtainable without the intervention of divine Grace—namely a state achieved *ex beneficio*; conversely, Grace presupposes a virtuous predisposition. If such is the case, what then are we to make of claims by people using psychogenic substances, be it mescal mushrooms—not inappropriately termed "flesh of the gods"—and other plants such as *ayahuasca* ("vine of the soul"), or through chemical means, who maintain that ingestion of such substances has led them to a beatific vision of Reality? First of all, one will want to note that what others have termed "beatific or visionary experience" is most likely not so by any objective standard; indeed, the dreary banality of these experiences themselves, which are often nothing more than a deformation of consciousness, comes from the fact that they are similar to the fluid permeability and plasticity one finds in ordinary dreams, except that in this case it is magnified to a psychedelic extreme; to term this "mystical" is an abuse of language.[35]

---

35 To discover, through a psychedelic experience, canyons in the crease of one's pants or to see paved highways turn into flowing streams, or colors change into one another or into musical notes, or to behold forms and figures metamorphose into other forms like one can perceive in thunder-clouds has no value in itself and, in fact, it is rather alarming because a derangement of the senses is no light matter. Some of these experiences are akin to undergoing an enhanced Rorschach test, except in this case the inkblots are everyday people and objects seen through a psychedelic deformation, which brings us to make this point: to dismantle reality, which is basically the premise of modern art, is not the same as to decipher its underlying symbolism. Barriers can be ruptured in two ways: by transcending them from above, or by falling beneath them; decomposition is not transfiguration. That is why we can speak of a "forbidden door".

Moreover, ecstasy in itself, divine as it is, is of no value unless it serves as the leaven for a permanent change of character for the better. Of course the reverse is not necessarily true: if a mystical experience does not change a person's character, this does not necessarily prove it is not genuine, because a person may not live up to a grace received. The issue should be easy to adjudicate, but not everyone disposes of the right criteria: for example, some of the criteria are to be found in the quality of experience itself, that is to say what matters is not only the beauty of the experience but also the absence of trivial or ugly details which might compromise this beauty and that in fact would betray the non-divine origin of the experience. Then, we have the criteria of the effect on the person's soul itself: does the bliss experienced improve or worsen their character?

These subjective considerations notwithstanding, one will note that in every realm of creation, there are specific creatures or substances— an archetypal one being Soma, "the King of Plants", said to have been grown in Indra's heaven—that directly embody or symbolize the Divine.[36] Thus, in the vegetal realm, one finds psychogenic substances, also known as "entheogens" (*en-theo-gen*, the inspired etymology of which means "putting the god within"), that open onto the supra-formal realm and that, in principle and when placed in the "right hands", can serve as catalysts towards the Divine; this, however, presupposes a ritual context and a psychic substance predisposed to Heaven, one might say. Now, if the stage is set correctly, then the "entheogen" may reveal a person to itself, or may at least deliver a clue—perhaps a message from the spirit (or angelic) world—to help a person on their path, but it will do so more in the way of a medicine of the soul—presumably under the expert doctoring of the shaman—than as revelation proper, for such a grace transcends the psychic realm, and may be inversely proportional to all sensationalism, coming without fanfare in the form of a discrete insight.[37]

Indeed, there are cultures, the Amazonian Indian tribes notably, in which ritualized drug use is a normal mode of communion with the Divine. However this fact calls for two comments that apply to all similar cultures. First, due to their destiny, the psychic homogeneity of such peoples, especially when combined with the consistency of their shamanic cosmology, cannot be compared with the porous psychic heterogeneity of

---

36 As was noted in the chapter, "Individuality Is Not Individualism".

37 Once again Schuon: "There is in metaphysics no empiricism: principial knowledge cannot derive from any experience, though," he adds, "experiences—scientific or otherwise— can be the occasional causes for intuitions of the intellect" (*Roots of the Human Condition* [Bloomington, IN: World Wisdom, 2002], p. vii).

Westerners. Thus, if under the guidance of a shaman, an Amazonian Indian can enter into communication—in a predictably consistent manner!—with a spirit helper animal which acts as a teacher and guide, the same result can hardly be expected for a Westerner intent on duplicating such an experience, unless he undergoes some form of initiation by the shaman; but then the latter point entails a kind of providential need to do so in the first place; idle curiosity would not meet this proviso. Secondly, the prevalence of such ritualized psychism does not necessarily constitute a spiritual superiority per se over great traditions such as the Vedanta or Taoism or Buddhism, to say the least; it may in fact even be a degeneracy.[38] In the Golden Age, where every man was a prophet and carried Heaven's Law naturally within himself, he had direct access through his heart-intellect to all divine and earthly wisdom; the immanence of divine wisdom was the human norm. Once access to the door of this inward wisdom was closed, man had to rely henceforth on priestly intermediaries and on outward means, whence the need for rituals previously superfluous. Therefore, to assume that primordial man communed with Heaven through psychogenic plants is to misunderstand the very nature of the heart-intellect, which is independently prophetic and omniscient and therefore not dependent on any psychosomatic catalysts. But even in a period as late as the Middle Ages, it was still possible to find mystics who communed with Christ directly through the sacrament of the host; some of them shunned all material nourishment, even subsisting entirely on the host alone, their bodies meanwhile exuding fragrant oils, while they carried the taste of honey in their mouths in keeping with the sweetness of their heart.[39]

One last point: mention was made above that a psychogenic substance, by producing a disruption of the normally fixed parameters of

38 Mircea Eliade has been derided, wrongfully in our opinion, as an academic ignoramus for alleging a similar thing in his book, *Shamanism*, where he mentions that drug-induced ecstasy is a degenerate practice and therefore a latter day phenomenon. Karl Kéreny in his book, *Dionysos*, avers the same. To understand this is to understand the epidemic nature of magic, sorcery, and spiritism where things are not done in "God's Name" but for the sake of harnessing powers, perhaps beneficent, perhaps not. The difference between a truly spiritual perspective and a psychic one is well illustrated by the difference between the Plains Indians' Sun Dance and the practices of the Peyote cult of the so-called Native American Indian Church. One is reminded here of the story of the Shoshone medicine man, John Trehero, whose vision of two trails, one that stopped after a short distance near the hills and one that went over the hills "into the horizon", going on and on without end. Seven Arrows, his spirit helper, explains that the first one is the way of Peyote and the second that of the Sun Dance religion (see *Yellowtail: Crow Medicine Man and Sun Dance Chief*, ed. Michael Oren Fitzgerald [Norman: University of Oklahoma Press, 1991], p. 57).

39 See Caroline Walker Bynum, *Holy Feast and Holy Fast* (Berkeley: University of California Press, 1987).

consciousness, can dislocate an individual's perception of reality and open the imagination to a much vaster frame of reference. We shall add that, all things being equal, this is not necessarily bad, because conventions and habits can have a deadening effect on the mind; thus—in the very best of cases—the psychogenic experience can sometimes loosen the grip of material illusion holding the soul prisoner in a suffocatingly small cocoon and free it for flight in an immense universe previously undreamt of, in which objects that once appeared totally disconnected now share intelligent relationships formerly unsuspected; in some respects, this in fact corresponds to a posthumous or out-of-body experience. But this is yet another reason why it should be left alone and never be approached on an experimental basis. Indeed, and even assuming the best of circumstances, the question still remains: once the imagination is opened, what then? Who has the mental and characterial fortitude to recover from the shock of such an opening? What will the person now do with his life? Furthermore, as if the above were not risky enough, a psychedelic experience can either weaken the will, making it limply passive for the rest of an individual's life, or fissure the psyche, perhaps permanently, or in extreme cases even lead to a diabolic delirium of cascading horrors ending in madness.[40] It is also noteworthy that psychogenic mushrooms are fungi that feed and grow on the decomposition of life; this feature gives them the role of "gatekeeper" in the natural order, opening the channels between earthly life and the supernatural realms. Therefore, they should only be manipulated with the greatest of caution because they can precipitate the user into realms which he may be mentally unfit to handle. Indeed, it is much easier to open the "forbidden door" than to close it once opened.[41] Once again, right intention

40 This point is of such crucial importance that we want to quote from the Swiss astrologer, Charles Vouga, who mentions the traditional association of the planet Saturn with the function of Saint Peter, "guardian of the gates of Heaven, who forbids entry to those who have not fulfilled the requirements that he alone knows" (*Une astrologie pour l'ère du verseau* [Monaco: Editions de Rocher, 1979], p. 130). To quote him further: "It [Saturn] ensures that we have the necessary solidity, that we are changed into marble or, to be more exact, into a diamond. . . . One finds many experiences of ecstasy which are made while ignoring the order Saturn represents, and these are those produced by drugs. Out of ignorance for the Laws, one wishes to force one's way through and there are terrible repercussions in the individual. One must not go into the 'Transfinite' without Saturn having said: 'Now you are ready. . .'" (p. 131). It will be recalled that in sacred tradition Saturn fulfills the role of the cosmic intellect.

41 In an Arabian version of the tale, the hero, young Shaykh Hakim, after opening the door out of greed and curiosity, having lost everything he loved, is condemned to a life of poverty. Oddly enough, however, the bargain can be reversed, allowing us to choose either this world now or Heaven later; in the Faustian bargain, man can have his best wishes granted

may make the difference between success and disaster. *In vino veritas* ("in wine truth"): wine brings out the truth of the soul; so let none presume who they are in this respect. Wine and intoxication, which have always been symbols of mystical union, may only serve to increase stupefaction of the senses or brutishness when in vulgar hands. Hence in Isaiah: "I have trodden the winepress alone; and of the people there was none with me.... And I will tread down the people in mine anger, and make them drunk in my fury, and I will bring down their strength to the earth" (63:3-6).

*   *   *

The sin of curiosity which prompts a seeker to open the "forbidden door", comes all too often at the price of the loss of wonderment, or the sense of the heavenly. And this loss is also that of innocence. If man could take pleasure in life's beauties, as God intended him to, no restless urge would goad him to pierce the veil of the five senses to seek out extra-sensorial states. He would find contentment in the plenitude of his spiritual possibility here on earth. It may seem simplistic—or boring—to affirm that one of the goals of the spiritual life is to rediscover a state of perfect simplicity which goes hand in hand with a sense of childlike gratitude wherein man finds blissful sufficiency in the blessings of the day vouchsafed to him by a beneficent Creator: love of kith and kin, the shelter of a beautiful home and garden, victual bounties, and a measure of wealth to shelter him from indigence. To have any of these on earth is a rich blessing and a joy. Wanting more is begging for trouble.

More profoundly, man must understand that his relationship with the Divine is determined by faith—as well as faith's extension as *ratio fidei*, or Saint Anselm's "intelligence operating through faith"—because, on earth, the Divine is ordinarily hidden, or is only perceivable through the symbols and gifts of the outward world. Thus "blessed are they who have not seen and yet have believed" (John 20:29). It is faith, namely the degree of one's personal faith, that makes this earth both bearable and enjoyable—bearable with regard to its trials and enjoyable with regard to its benefits. And faith leads to gratitude, and conversely; hence a King David can declare: "I will wash mine hands in innocency, that I may publish with the voice of thanksgiving, and tell of all thy wondrous works" (Ps. 26: 6-7).

It is piety, in its profoundest sense, which opens the gates of Heaven. The soul whose heart has not leapt for joy at the mention of the Name of

on earth but at the cost of eternity. Confirmation of this possibility can be found in the Koran: "Whoso desireth the harvest of the Hereafter, We give him increase in its harvest. And whoso desireth the harvest of the world, We give him thereof, and he hath no portion in the Hereafter" ("Counsel", 42:20). Everything has its price.

God, or who has not shuddered in awe before God, is unfit to meet the Lord. What we want to say is that God does not just want our mind, or our awareness: He wants our hearts so that we can say, echoing Hannah's canticle: "My heart rejoiceth in the Lord" (1 Sam. 2:1). And deeper and fuller still, He wants our own divine likeness born of sanctifying virtue so that, to quote from William of Thierry's "Golden Letter" (*Epistola aurea*), we can declare: "O Lord, our God, who created us to thy image and likeness, that is, to contemplate Thee and to enjoy Thee whom no one contemplates to the level of enjoyment save insofar as he is made like unto Thee".[42] It is only then, only on this holy basis—to rejoin this chapter's opening theme—that the soul can aspire to the longed-for "face to face meeting" with the Divine.

When the heart melts in love, then the mind, like the full moon rising, reflects the solar Truth and the Beauty of the Lord, and it is all that it is meant to be, not just a cold, impersonal meditative witness, nor a dizzied plaything of whirling phenomena, but a serene and luminous mirror of the radiant heart-intellect, or of the "Divine within".

---

42 "Exposition on the Song of Songs 1", in *Sources chrétiennes* (Paris: Cerf, 1940).

CHAPTER 12

Hieros Gamos or the Sacred Marriage

I love them that love me; and those that seek me early shall find me.
(Prov. 8:17)

The mystery of individuality must include an image of it seen through the prism of the masculine and female duality which divides the individual into two incomplete halves, as it were. The universe is ruled by polarities, the essential one being the masculine and feminine polarity—positive and negative, man and woman, themselves personifications of the metacosmic polarity Absolute-Infinite found at the heart of Reality. Though divided, these polarities presuppose an underlying unity without which they could not oppose each other; without this unifying factor, they would be complete strangers instead of completing each other. This common unity for man and woman is the fact of their being *anthropos* (human beings), a fact taking precedence—in certain decisive respects—over their being either male or female.

The universe, in order to radiate and expand, depends on the attracting complementarity as well as on the feuding opposition[1] between the masculine and feminine. Without polarity the universe would collapse and be reabsorbed into Non-being, or the formlessness of the Essence; and yet without unity this polarity would lead to chaos. Another expression of the underlying unity is found in the oppositional but magnetic attraction between these two poles; it is in this synthesis of mutual repulsion and attraction that the dynamic radiance stimulating all creatures and forms of life originates, so much so that it is the perfection of absolute masculinity, in its purest intensity as Truth and Strength, and the perfection of absolute femininity, in its purest intensity as Love and Beauty, that determines the vital vibrancy of the universe. If these poles are diminished or confused to any degree, then to that very measure the universe loses the dynamic tension sustaining its vitality.

What woman loves in man is essentially his strength and intelligence, or his liberating objectivity, and in this respect man is equated with the motionless center or the static or axial principle, as reflected by the inherent verticality and hardness of his body and the morphology of his sexual

---

1 "He [God] said: Go down from hence [the Garden of Eden] one of you a foe unto the other" (Koran, "The Heights", 7:24).

anatomy, his phallus being a symbol of the vertical axis—the sacred lingam in Hinduism symbolizing the male creative energy of the Divinity. And what man loves in woman is essentially her beauty and her love, her kindness and mercy, or the mystery of her liberating subjectivity, and in this respect woman is equated with the dynamic circle of life, as reflected in the inherent roundness and softness of her body and the morphology of her sexual anatomy, her vulva recalling both the mystery of a flower and that of inwardness, or in fact the heart.[2] If man is the tree trunk and sap, woman is the branches and fruits; if man is the stabilizing center, woman is the liberating fullness; if man is the solitary numeral "one" or unicity, then woman is the numeral two and by extension gregarious multiplicity—or if man is related to the odd numbers which hold together and unify the even numbers, then woman is related to the even numbers whereby unity is divided and fructified. Their mutual fascination is procreative and reviving for the whole cosmos, but the cosmic power of this erotic attraction requires the kind of magnification that only opposites provide: hence the universe thrives when each pole holds a paragon status in the full glory of its possibility: man as solar hero king and woman as goddess of gracious love, but also as seductive enchantress that lures the male pole out from sterile solitariness. As mentioned, this interplay of qualities all stem from the Absolute-Infinite polarity which, translated into human terms, are Truth and Love. Now in being Truth man is also discernment, and in being Love woman is also redemption; in other words, and counter to the symbolism of even and odd numbers just depicted, where man divides woman unifies.

As to the question of the specifically masculine and feminine attributes of each sex, yes both man and woman are human beings first of all, but certain traits can be rightfully termed "masculine" or, vice versa, "feminine" without abuse or prejudice inasmuch as a man and a woman are visibly different, that is to say, inasmuch as they have different archetypes. At the same time, one can take some qualities, such as "courage", and simply say there is a masculine version and there is a feminine version of it. And similarly for "tenderness", there is a masculine type of tenderness and a feminine one. Nonetheless, it is not wrong to generalize and thus to say that courage falls roughly speaking on the masculine side of the equation and tenderness on the feminine, but never exclusively so because, to repeat, both man and woman are *anthropos* first and foremost. To formulate things in another manner: it is not necessarily a weakness if a woman is

---

2 However, even if woman is more directly associated with the heart, the sexual anatomy of both sexes represents the heart, in exteriorized mode for man and in interiorized mode for woman, whence in fact the directness of the analogy of the heart with woman since the heart is inward before it is "outward", if one may say.

lacking in courage—or, to be more exact, is lacking in confrontational or combative courage—or if she must work harder at it than a man, but for a man it is certainly unmasculine to lack courage. Conversely, it is unnatural for a woman to be lacking in tenderness, but less so for a man; or, at least, a man has to be more careful (depending on the circumstances) in show-ing tenderness than a woman, because she can identify heart and soul with tenderness in a way not possible for a man, except in intimate circumstanc-es. But finally, in all of these matters, it is a question more of degree than of absolute differences since man and woman contain both *yin* and *yang*. Be that as it may, these two poles have become harder to differentiate in modern times and this is part of the cyclical situation mankind finds itself in, in a civilization that is forswearing its spiritual heritage.

Given that we have two poles, their deterioration is a harbinger of the deterioration of the universe itself. The deterioration of these two poles starts with their confusion, namely when man becomes unduly feminized and woman unduly masculinized; we say "unduly" in recognition of the fact that no pole can be totally absolute otherwise it would dominate every-thing and cease thereby to be a pole; hence a pole always contains an ele-ment of its opposite which is the basis of their common axis. In this sense man and woman share, as mentioned above, a mutual quality as human beings and, in this manner, encompass in a *yin-yang* fashion an element of each other so that perfect man contains some "feminine" or gentle element or he would become pure hardness, were that possible, just as woman con-tains some "masculine" element or she would dissolve entirely into soft-ness, were that possible. In their complementarity, man and woman both seek to regain their lost unity, through the erotic embrace notably, while projecting this unity through their dueling duality; and this rhythmic join-ing and parting constitutes the dynamic pattern of all of creation. In this sense, the cosmos can be likened to a tantric mystery.

*   *   *

Man—considered now as a masculine-feminine entity, or as *anthropos*—is composed of both soul and Spirit, or one changeable and one changeless part, or one mutable and one immutable portion. One could say that man is both mortal and immortal, but his soul is not mortal in the same way that his body is; yet, at the same time, the soul is not immortal in the way the Spirit only can be. The Spirit, despite its being the realest—or only truly real—part of an individual, is paradoxically the most invisible because being of a supra-material (and supra-psychic) substance it cannot be directly apprehended through sensory means the way the soul can be. Its presence therefore is unfelt, empirically speaking, because transcending the five senses. At the same time, not being inexistent—though non-existent materially and psychically—it is graspable through intelligence, or rather through spiritual intelligence, because reason can only infer of its existence but not detect it directly, this role belonging to the heart-intellect. Similarly, the soul too is supra-material with respect to the body, though not so with respect to the Spirit because, in contrast to the Spirit, the soul is also composed of a perishable substance, although it is customary to speak of its immortality, which is true enough; but only the Spirit can be said to be unconditionally deathless because of its immutability.[3] That said, it is important to understand that the dividing line between the Spirit, soul, and physical body is only semi-absolute: from outside it is practically absolute, but immanently there is continuity of substance between the three, although Spirit can be defined as belonging to the pole essence and the soul (or the soul-body complex) as belonging to the pole substance.

There is nothing the soul loves more than the Spirit and therefore nothing it longs for more than the Spirit. In the spiritually realized individual, the soul is at first betrothed and then united to the Spirit in a sacred union of luminous beatitude—or in the classic image taken from Tibetan Buddhism, that of the *yab-yum* icon depicting the interlacing of Wisdom and Compassion. In a profound sense, the Spirit and the soul correspond to the male and female polarity, although strictly speaking the Spirit is neither masculine nor feminine while being both in their essence.

Now, even though human beings are composed of both soul and Spirit, our habitual consciousness is that of the soul, while the Spirit remains in the background, undetected—although truth and logic, and the understanding of first principles, provide a gateway to the Spirit. Be that as it may, the Spirit, in the experience of most men, remains inherently latent, mysteriously present but hidden behind the veil of the soul, which is woven of the phenomena of endless thoughts, impressions, sensations, emotions, desires, aspirations—all of whom press for the individual ego's attention. And these phenomena—the soul's everyday experiences—are what the soul considers to be habitually true or real and thus meaningful. Yet all of these impressions amount to illusions inasmuch as they are finally but ephemeral images, no sooner arising than dissolving, crowded out by

---

3 The ultimate perishability of the soul is not similar to that of the body: instead of being decomposed and eliminated, as the physical body must be, the soul is recomposed ascentionally into the Spirit, the transition being somewhat like the reabsorption brought about by a laying down to sleep (a dormition), as it were, which is the profounder meaning of the idea of resting in God or of recovering divine peace. In very rare cases, however, there is the possibility of an assumption in which a physical body is transfigured and swept heavenward, as in the case of Elias and of the Blessed Virgin.

newer ones, as if life were a waking dream: the homes and the streets where people meet, the tables where they sit, and the beds they lie in, all of these will be empty one new day, or filled by other people. Now these settings are the habitat of the soul, not of the Spirit which can never be of this world. At the same time, it is thanks to the Spirit that all of these experiences can have a meaningful order and connection and therefore can be marshaled to serve a goal instead of falling apart into so much empty fretting and forgetting. Or, seen from another viewpoint, the soul's experiences are like the multicolored threads of a tapestry held together by the Spirit: according to this image, the Spirit is then the warp and the soul and its experiences the woof.

The soul in itself, when free from the turmoil of individual preoccupations, is a feminine fertile substance, the role of which is to convert and transmit the Spirit's light into all four corners of creation, much like the moon, in its twenty-eight stations as it circumscribes the heavens, refracts the light of the sun.[4] In the science of alchemy the soul is normally defined as feminine and corresponds therefore to the moon, the dynamic or mutable pole, whereas the Spirit is defined as masculine and corresponds to the sun, the static or immutable pole. Man's journey through the earth—and through the *samsara*—is transcribed symbolically by the journey of the moon across the heavens: joined at first to the sun, then leaving it to circle the earth, before returning to the sun. The profound symbolic meaning of this relationship is that the moon/soul "lies with the sun", before waxing, pregnant now with the sun's light, in order to give birth to a sacred infant at the moment of the full moon, before waning and rejoining the sun in what is a monthly perennial rhythm, transcribing the cycle of birth, growth, decay, and death of the cosmos. More profoundly yet, the symbolism of "lying with the sun" corresponds to spiritual initiation, in which case the full moon corresponds to the fruition or spiritual realization (*samadhi*) of this sacred spark. In this way, metaphor, symbolism, and mythology present synthetic teachings that go beyond mental analysis.[5]

---

4 The Sioux medicine man Black Elk recounted that the sun-dance lodge, image of the cosmos, was made up of twenty-eight poles, and that the buffalo, also an image of the cosmos, had twenty-eight ribs (*The Sacred Pipe* [Norman: University of Oklahoma Press, 1989], p. 80).

5 The ancient people who built the temple of Stonehenge to enshrine the sacred moments of the summer and winter solstices understood more of the nature of the sun than do modern astronomers, if the latter ignore the analogy between the central luminary and the Self. Of what avail is it to know the sun's size and position in our nebula if its meaning as symbol of the Spirit, as well as of the macrocosmic heart of the universe (and the microcosmic heart of man), is overlooked?

Transposing these analogies, it can be said that while the essential role of woman is to bring the Spirit's offspring to life in creation, she is at the same time the veil of universal illusion, both seducing and dispersing, for the same veil that refracts the Light also veils it. Thus woman, in spite of herself, can pull man away from the Spirit and therefore needs man's strength to reconvert her energy heavenward; but man himself, depending on his degree of virile self-domination, can be dissipated by her beauty instead of re-centered before Heaven. As soul, woman is unfixed substance: volatile, protean, unstable, and deceiving,[6] mirroring the moon's unstable (or "unreliable" or "faithless") orbit around the earth, and therefore, like the moon, in need of the centering and stabilization that only the Sun-Spirit can provide. And this is where man's role intervenes: even though an individual man can be just as much in bondage to the ego, and therefore, like her, is also identified with the soul, nonetheless his gender's archetype is the Spirit. And, conversely, woman is not just soul in all respects: in her sacred mystery, and as holy inwardness, she is an incarnation of the Essence and in this manner she too rejoins the Spirit.

However, when dealing with man and woman in the abstract—as opposed to their individual substance—it is not incorrect, symbolically speaking, to say that man embodies Spirit as such and woman soul as such—or respectively the Absolute and the Infinite—or to affirm that man represents the vertical and determinative axis and woman the horizontal or receptive axis. And it is in this sense that one can speak of the relative superiority of man over woman as regards social functions,[7] for the symbolism outlined establishes that man as center and principle has a creative force

---

6 According to this relationship, if man is "truth" woman is "illusion" or "cosmic lie", and, in this sense, one can say that man is normally dispassionately logical and rational—or more so—whereas woman is more opportunistically self-interested. By "opportunistic" we mean to say that for woman "truth" considered purely as principle is something cold and abstract, and thus unnatural; therefore, for her, the "existential end justifies the means" while "truth" is found above all in tangible results and not in abstract principles. If she has to resort to "lies" for an outcome she considers to be existentially true, so be it, because for her it is life above all that is truth, not the Principle (or not the Principle if it "contradicts" life); whereas man, by contrast, may sacrifice life for Principle, for an idea, or an ideal. For woman, man can seem heartlessly theoretical, while for man, woman can seem to be too sentimental or even irrational. These are generalizations, of course; however they outline differences in emphasis between man and woman, and can explain some of their misunderstandings.

7 The Infinite is really an inner dimension of the Absolute; but to speak of the Absolute is to speak of Totality, which is the role of the Infinite to radiate. To clarify further, one could say that man embodies the vertical warp in the loom and woman the horizontal weft. Now the weft cannot stand on its own, whereas the warp can; however, the warp would be desolate without the weft, and would therefore lose its purpose.

that finds its fulfillment in both strength and objectivity—a strength suited both for building and destroying, incidentally, and an objectivity that divides and analyzes—whereas woman as enveloping periphery (in contrast to the exclusivity of the male center)[8] and as warmth-giving life, embodies a compassionate force that finds its fulfillment in unifying and healing, and not in separating and opposing as with her male counterpart. From another viewpoint, however, man is outwardness, objectivity, and discernment whereas woman is inwardness, subjectivity, and union; in that sense, man is identified with the pole transcendence and woman with that of immanence. Transposing these attributes once more onto the social plane allows us to define "man as discernment" and therefore explain his directive and legislative role, his capacity to lead and to govern, just as they allow us to define "woman as union" and therefore explain her role to nurture, heal, and sustain. Be that as it may, man's superiority on the social plane cannot be absolute and therefore is often more functional than substantial since everything depends finally on the quality of the individuals, and in this domain—that of the personality—all questions of decisive superiority derive from the human merit and giftedness of each person;[9] thus there are women who rule as queens, with passive prince consorts, or even women "statesmen"—the prophetess Deborah's counsel, for instance, was sought by everyone—but these will always be more the exception confirming the rule.[10] And in religion, where traditionally a woman cannot hold a priestly function,[11] she can, in exceptional circumstances, hold the role of a spiritual

---

8 Geometrically speaking, if man is the central dot, woman is the whole circle. Or, if man is the hard angle that breaks, woman is the curve that bonds. Without the angle, no foundational square; without the circle, no unity.

9 However, it is a fact that the great creative geniuses of mankind have all been of the masculine sex, an observation that accords with man's procreative power. That said, without woman, man would have no inspiration to create in the first place.

10 Nonetheless, even if in a monotheistic framework, and others, a woman cannot have a function *ex officio* (that is, officially), she can privately be a spiritual teacher *ex beneficio* (that is according to special privilege, benefit, or gifts) because then the question centers on the spiritual qualification of the individual and not on their sex. There are, after all, women Church doctors, such as Saint Catherine of Siena and Saint Teresa of Avila. (For some of this issue, see *Medieval Theology and the Natural Body*, chap. "Medieval Impediments to Female Ordination", compiled by Peter Biller and A. J. Minnis [York Medieval Press, 1997]). In Hinduism, we have the example of the sage woman, Maitreyi, who was called a *brahmavadini*, namely "an expounder of the *Veda*".

11 Some semi-exceptions come to mind here, the women priestesses in Shintoism and that of the Roman vestals, examples that we cannot detail here, except to say that the prominence of their roles was due to an emphasis in these religions respectively on nature and on the hearth, which are naturally female provinces.

guide in the esoteric domain, a domain, precisely, where essence overrules form, inwardness outwardness, which means also that the sexual polarity is either transcended or both poles serve equally as symbols of the Spirit.

Adopting for now this symmetry in which man is equated with the Spirit and woman with the soul, man as strength provides security for woman without which she cannot blossom; by strength, we mean not merely physical strength but moral strength, the essence of which is self-domination complemented by equanimity and, intellectually, serene objectivity, otherwise it is not really self-domination but repression. The essence of self-domination derives from the fact that it is the Spirit's nature to rule the soul, which means that man, to the measure that he is identified with the Spirit, manages not to be overcome or seduced by the soul, or—in psychological terms—does not succumb to subjectivity, irrationality, caprice, or all other arbitrary inclinations; in a word, manhood is the impetus to transcend oneself, and man succeeds in this by not succumbing to impulse, emotions, and petty temptation.[12] Conversely, when man yields to passional impulses or allows moods to determine his opinions and choices, or when he loses his self-control, patience, or temper, he risks becoming the slave of chaotic desires, forfeiting his role as embodiment of the divine Center or Axis.[13] Now all of this is profoundly disquieting for woman, who then finds herself either defenseless before the male's arbitrariness or possible irrationality—two of her main weaknesses—or else is forced to herself assume the archetypal male virtue of objectivity, impassivity, and imperturbability—she whose fundamental nature is that of deep empathy and emotion (not dispassionate and apparently "sterile" *ratio*), for feeling and emotion are part of woman's genius; these traits stem of course from her archetype as the embodiment of love and healing mercy. Indeed, woman is feeling because she is love; man, by compensation, is reason because he embodies truth and justice. In other words, it is in woman's nature to yield and to submit—which means also to adapt and to welcome—and not to confront or oppose, just as we have mentioned it is in man's nature to lead, to conquer, and to rule, and thus to confront and oppose and, if necessary, to defeat and possibly to slay.[14] Needless to say, it is a question here of ar-

---

12 In counter distinction, due to his very outwardness, man is likely to be less self-controlled sexually.

13 "He that hath no rule over his own spirit is like a city that is broken down, and without walls" (Prov. 25:28).

14 Even if a modern sensitivity—affecting to be politically correct—recoils at the aspects of "yielding" and "submitting" being assigned to a woman's archetypal role, there should be agreement about "slaying" being fundamentally unsuitable to her gender. But in fact, what

chetypal attributes, that is to say of cosmic qualities found in the nature of the universe, and not strictly of their social applications. Hence, to argue about social suitability is an altogether secondary question that should not cloud the archetypal meaning.

Now if woman, in her intimate nature, is soul longing to surrender to Spirit, it goes without saying that she is not willing to surrender to just any man, however real the cosmic archetypes, but to a god or, in fact, to God himself. Therefore this "submission" cannot be a purely social question; rather it is a state of nature, like that of a stream following the contours of the land or that of the splendor of an open field lying before the sun in a "submission" that is regenerative and not the result of a rigid abasement. Transposed onto a cosmic plane, it is the "submission" of the earth circling the sun, of night welcoming day, of the planets "obeying" their courses, of *Prakriti* honoring *Purusha*.[15] And man, in turn, eased in his severe duty of upholding Principle or Truth, can find deliverance in woman's welcoming gentleness and kindness and will then, in a reversal of polarities, now do her bidding, effortlessly. But when the nature of these poles is damaged or inverted in the case of each sex, then woman's inherent sweetness can turn to bitterness, changing her into a fury who, in revenge for man's weakness or arbitrariness, will harass him mercilessly. And yet, she weeps to do so because, whether she knows it or not, her harassment is really a lame attempt to have him become the man she would have him be. Thus, by attacking man, woman is secretly hoping that he may yet rise to the challenge and not fall for the shrill bait of her badgering; that he will stand in impervious strength before her assault, while displaying magnanimous and loving generosity, thus rescuing her from her own restless and potentially chaotic nature. Man, for his part, perhaps bewildered by woman's invectives, risks everything if he allows himself to be dragged into a tangle of recriminations that woman herself dearly hopes to be delivered from; but only a hero can rescue her from herself, not a petty, arbitrary, unmanly impostor. And thus the drama of the sexes unfolds.[16]

is missed here is that the "yielding" and "submitting" is the normative opposite of the "slaying", precisely; hence one cannot logically agree with the part of the equation that suits our personal interests (or social prejudices) only and not the rest.

15 "He [God] covereth the night with the day, which is in haste to follow it, and hath made the sun and the moon and the stars subservient by His command" (Koran, "The Heights", 7:54).

16 These situations obviously presuppose a conflict between essentially good-willed partners and therefore do not apply to selfish, malicious, hard-hearted individuals whom nothing will placate.

In establishing such distinctions, it may seem that we are opposing Truth to Love—or Intelligence to Being—when in fact these poles cannot be truly opposed since in essence love, when deep, is a form of intelligence just as intelligence, when integral, is a form of love; however, in creation ruled by outwardness and division, Truth and Love are not only polarized but can enter into opposition, so that it is not wrong to equate them with the masculine-female polarity: in such an opposition, Truth becomes reason and Love becomes sentiment; or we have the rivalry of mind versus heart, cerebralism versus life, or the dichotomy of the objective and the subjective. Needless to say, such a schematization is not intended to suggest that woman cannot know the Truth or, conversely, that man is unfit for Love, for as mentioned both man and woman intimately combine the reciprocal attributes of Spirit and soul in their respective essences. Yet, inasmuch as a man is not a woman, and vice versa, this manner of contrasting their specific virtues is not inappropriate. Therefore, when a man displays commanding self-domination and lucid reason this normally has an irresistible and deeply liberating effect on woman, for she is now free to be totally feminine and thus to blossom without fear of exposing her vulnerability—this vulnerability or sensitivity being a necessary dimension of her nature. In Heaven, of course, woman can manifest such "weaknesses" as kindness, mercy, and sensitivity without the risk of vulnerability, but not on earth, whence her need for man's strength and protection—and his clear-headedness—barring which she is forced, very unnaturally so, to herself become strong and even tough, if not dryly rational; but such an effort comes at the price of a certain masculinization. It should be obvious that if circumstances force a woman to embody the Absolute, she does so to the detriment of her embodiment as the Infinite, from whence her love and beauty ensue. Finally, however, both man and woman represent *Atma*, he as Absolute and she as Infinite—the prototype of *Atma* being in the end superior to either of its two poles.

*   *   *

Woman, by cosmic decree so to speak, does not carry her center within herself, and she therefore needs man in order to find herself; she cannot be fully herself without man. Man on the other hand, owing to his identification with the pole Absolute, carries his center within himself, and therefore does not, strictly speaking, need woman to be himself; in other words, man has a certain affinity or need for solitude. But this is not a natural state for woman, who by innate temperament thrives best in companionship, for she is substance and totality.[17] But even if for man this root identity with

---

17 There are women hermits, of course, such as (in India) Lalla Yogishwari, Mirabai, and

the solitariness of the pole Absolute grants him a certain capacity for self-sufficiency,[18] this is so more in principle than in actual fact for every man has an individual soul and in this respect he is similar to woman, psychologically speaking; he therefore also needs woman as a companion.

Mention was made that from a social standpoint, man holds some functional superiority due to his "outwardness"; from a spiritual standpoint, however, the symmetry just outlined is reversible or open to several combinations: woman, as inwardness, is intimately associated with the mystery of what the Sufis term the *sirr*, the "divine secret", whence the symbolism of both veiling and unveiling that plays such a central role in the contemplation of feminine beauty, the deeper aspect involving the sacredness of beholding the essence. An excessive emphasis on veiling, and on guarding woman from the predatory passions of men, while necessary in a world populated by brutes, can overshadow the deeper function of veiling which—all questions of man's sinfulness aside—has to do with protecting man from beholding the Divine Essence unworthily. "No mortal hath yet raised my veil", Plutarch annotated on one of the statues of Isis, meaning that only what is immortal in man is fit to behold the supreme goddess. In that respect, man—fallen man—is identified with the profane in need of conversion before being allowed the sight of immortal beauty. Dante confirms this: "While any who endures to gaze on her must either be made noble, or else die (*Vita Nuova*, 19, 1.35-36)." In this respect, the divine Essence that woman embodies has an annihilating effect on form as outwardness—or as profaneness—which must be purified and transfigured into the ineffable. Yet, humanly, this ineffable aspect of woman, not suited for mortal eyes, is compensated by the extraordinary sweetness she embodies, a sweetness healing all fissures, all inadequacies, and answering all needs.

More prosaically, the average man, obscurely attracted as he is to the mystery of "essence-made-woman", needs the virtue of love to overcome the potential destructiveness of lust, in which case sexual bliss, instead of fostering graciousness, can have a paradoxically hardening effect on the soul, even inciting a meanness of spirit depending on a person's individual substance; or the gentleness of a woman, instead of inspiring chivalrousness, can invite brutality from the haste-driven male. This is one of the reasons why there are so many religious strictures placed on the wanton indulgence of sexual passion: the same force for life and ecstasy that can be an inspiring support for spiritual union, can also be the cause of man's undoing as well as of woman's downfall, whence the need to sacralize and

---

more recently Ananda Moyi.

18 See Patanjali's *Yoga Sutra*, chap. 4, "*Kaivalya Pada*" or "Isolation Sutra". Also, man is inherently identified with the changelessness of *Purusha*, the transcendental state of absolute independence.

channel that force, or at least to neutralize it. Left unconverted, passion's savage need, once sated, can quickly turn to mortal indifference, or even to revulsion. So many intimate trysts, born in passion end in post-coital disgust, because man and woman are more than physical bodies; therefore, to woo in lust is to part in disgust, for love cannot survive the absence of romance which alone does justice to the soul's heavenly substance. There is an analogy here between wine and love: the cup that maketh merry and lifteth the spirit can also unshackle a beast. *Duo sunt in homine* ("Man is made of two natures").

*   *   *

Because woman is identified with the divine Essence, it is important that her sacred mystery be preserved, sheltered, even hidden. Now, paradoxically, this dimension is part of the deeper cause accounting for the subordinate role assigned woman in traditional societies, whether implemented fairly or unfairly. Inevitably, in a world of hyper-virility, social subordination leads too easily to a depreciation of woman and this accounts for her oppression and abuse; in that respect, woman's fate is parallel to that of the sacred which is readily profaned, by men in particular. Because she embodies inwardness, or heavenly mystery, woman can suffer from men who have no notion of inwardness and therefore who exploit her relative defenselessness; but in denigrating woman, man ends up denigrating his own substance and loses thereby all graciousness. Manhood, it should be obvious, is not proven by the cult of brute strength: the measure of man's strength is proven by his courtesy to woman, by his chivalrousness. Now for woman, the solution to such an abuse cannot lie in so-called "woman's liberation", which does nothing for her archetype as feminine mystery and holiness, but on the contrary risks damaging everything that constitutes her cosmic genius; in other words, the oppression of woman cannot be solved on a purely political plane.

Moreover, the irony is that in wanting to liberate herself outwardly from man, woman pays indirect and grudging homage to him by wishing to emulate him, be it only by opposition, when in fact her integral liberation can only lie in the espousal of true femininity and not in a rejection of her archetype; all the more so as the kind of man she is seeking to challenge is either a brute or an emasculated version of virility, otherwise she would feel no need to revolt against him in the first place, since her intimate fulfillment as woman lies precisely in her adoration of true man. That is why all the sociological and political compensations obtained by modern woman do nothing, in the end, to correct her fundamental problem, because in becoming "man-like" woman ceases being woman in certain vital respects,

THE MYSTERY OF INDIVIDUALITY

and is therefore trading one injustice for another. It will be asserted that both man and woman are *anthropos*—or human beings—before being polarized by gender, and thus a woman can excel in virtually any activity that man excels in, even—exceptionally—in such a traditional male bastion as warfare; but that is not the point, otherwise sexual polarity would have no human or cosmic significance.[19] Our assumption, therefore, has to be that the cosmos depends on the fullness of this polarity and not on its diminishment, let alone its cancellation, for this latter result could be the ultimate outcome of the modern social experiment that seeks to uniformize sexual similarities until both men and women—cross-dressing and borrowing bizarrely from each other—start looking and behaving like a hybrid sex, or non-sex, a trend which is an utterly unnatural state of affairs that can only de-magnetize the universe, if this is the right term.

On a related note, mention should also be made here on the so-called liberation of both sexes from the strictures of "prudery" and the complete loss of public discretion about formerly taboo dimensions of sexuality—note the contemptuous use of the term "prudery" to mock the dignity of privacy.

Not least, part of the need for mystery in sexual matters pertains to the nakedness of the human body and its sacred symbolism. Alone among creatures man and woman are "dressed" as it were in their flesh; animals do not have this possibility. Human nakedness is an existential manifestation of the Spirit itself: in the case of the male it is the perfection of the Absolute made flesh and in that of the female the perfection of the Infinite made flesh. The fur coats of animals, because of their variety precisely, are peripheral expressions with respect to the sacred Center man and woman represent in their disrobed glory. Moreover, the theophanic beauty of man and woman's nakedness is further proof of the non-utilitarian nature of their soul, namely of the contemplative centrality of their being, which is also why it must, on earth, be clothed, just as the Divine Principle itself takes on manifold disguises within creation, otherwise creation could not bear to hold it.[20] In other words, man and woman's nakedness foreshadows paradise. Primitivism, or physical crudeness, does nothing to undermine this affirmation, because the physical body in its material opacity as the outermost projection point of the Spirit opposes the Spirit while still be-

---

19 Yet clearly, a woman, taken collectively in her female gender, cannot match a male in virile physical strength.

20 By that token, nudism is a complete aberration, unless it is part of a tribal culture, in which case the absence of clothing is compensated by the symbolism of ornaments and designs such people "cover" their body with, not to mention the primordial innocence found in such tribes.

ing a direct witness to It by the nobility of its anatomical forms; in this sense extremes meet. Such a paradox, in which the flesh reveals and yet opposes the Spirit, results from the law of inverse analogy ruling manifestation wherein what is greatest in Heaven is least on earth and what is greatest on earth is least in Heaven. In this sense, the naked human body as divine form is identified with the Spirit, but as flesh it is corruptible and perishable.

* * *

In the warfare pitting Mars against Venus—which has its cosmic purpose—women, of course, know well enough how to fight back.[21] But in the conflict between a man and a woman, it may be surprising for some to note that it is essentially the man who bears the ultimate responsibility for the strife because being strength itself, by virtue of his cosmic archetype, man is the pillar not only of any social structure but also of the order in creation. Therefore, if he is weak, or does not fully endorse his duties and prerogatives, chaos is bound to ensue and in that situation nature unleashes forces that vie for supremacy in the void left by man's dereliction, indolence, or even feminization. If, in the unfolding of creation, it is Eve who plays the necessary role of temptress, it is nonetheless Adam's weakness that brings about the Fall; this scenario is echoed, *mutatis mutandis*, across time. Because of man's centrality in outward creation, his erectness and his uprightness guarantee both the strength of a civilization and the preservation of the moral order; in that respect, woman cannot fall as far as man, and consequently her fall is nowhere as profoundly disruptive as that of man. In fact, woman cannot fall unless man falls first,[22] whereas the reverse is not true, in the same way that a house cannot fall unless its pillars crumble; this is simply a law of nature: indeed, the almighty vault of Heaven itself rests foundationally on the male's virtue. This then is the reason why the feminization of man is such a calamity; and this is also why it is an end-of-civilization occurrence.

And here we must open a parenthesis, much as we would prefer to avoid the subject: it is partly in view of this calamity that the traditional opprobrium against male homosexuality must be understood, in the radical

---

21 King Solomon knew something of this in the several occasions he wrote about it, such as: "It is better to dwell in the wilderness, than with a contentious and angry woman" (Prov. 21:19).

22 We are referring of course to woman in a generic or cosmic sense, not woman as an individual, in which case her sex plays no role in her morality or salvation.

violation of cosmic norms that it involves. The entire sub-trend of modern society is moving concurrently with the emasculation of man, as well as in the direction of erasing the distinctions between the sexes. What is disguised as tolerance in people's eagerness to accept a polymorphous sexuality, heedless of gender, is really an augury for the complete and utter ruin of the cosmos: as man's virility goes so goes nature. Not surprisingly, one of the first targets of this social upheaval is the institution of marriage which, forever and everywhere, has only been between a man and a woman whatever the singular or plural forms it can take, monogamous or polygamous or even, in some very select exceptions, polyandrous. Society from time immemorial has been built upon a sacralized doctrine of the marriage between a man and a woman, but never between two creatures of the same sex.[23]

It is a truism to mention that in nature a positive can only be joined to a negative, which is the physical trace of what *in profundis* is the tantric relationship between Mars and Venus or between Shiva and Parvati. Transposed to the human plane, this principle means that a man can only be truly wedded to a woman and vice-versa, confirmation of which is the child, who is otherwise unobtainable. And this has a symbolism that extends beyond the mere material fact of procreation because the fruit of a union can just as well be inward as outward: this fruit is always a restoration of an original unity that has been sundered; hence, just as the child embodies—outwardly, in his physical oneness—the reunification of the parents' divided sexuality, so too the tantric (or esoteric) fruit of love is—inwardly—the restoration of the oneness of the heart-intellect.[24] Consequently, the same axis, or current, ruling erotic pleasure and procreation opens out either earthward or heavenward, or towards both simultane-

---

23 To our knowledge, no society in history has ever consecrated a union between same-sex partners; hence, the modern initiative for doing so is one more indication of an end-of-time event. Indeed, one criterion of an apocalyptic situation is the terminal inversion of timeless norms, or rather the institutionalization of such an inversion. However, there may be a historical precedent to what is no doubt a cultural exception, namely in the *Midrash*, where one reads: "Rabbi Huna said in the name of Rabbi Joseph, 'The generation of the Flood was not wiped out until they wrote marriage documents for the union of a man to a male or to an animal.'" (It is mentioned twice: Genesis Rabbah 26:5; Leviticus Rabbah 23:9). The extreme gravity of this initiative can be seen in the fact that it provided the tipping point for God's wrath. Not least, in the case of males, there are no means for consummating their erotic urge without incurring disease, whereas, in heterosexual unions, the risk of disease is essentially confined to excess promiscuity, which is nature's proof of the unnaturalness of the former mode of union.

24 We are not saying, as Catholics do, that the *sole* spiritual justification for sexual relations is children.

ously; and, as such, these two dimensions cannot be dissociated; in other words, one cannot simply take the erotic force that leads to creaturely birth and transpose it arbitrarily to a non-heterosexual situation and expect the same psychic or spiritual benefits, or at least expect no psychic repercussions—because nothing, for man, is ever neutral. Also, in alchemical terms now, the procreative force's spiritual magic depends on the fusion between what in Tantrism is known as the man's *virya* and the woman's *rajas*—the material supports of which correspond respectively to the semen and the menstrual fluid—or, in alchemy, it depends on the supra-physical fusion of sulfur and mercury leading to the restoration of the androgynous or immortal essence now freed from the division of earthly duality. It is important to note, however, that we are speaking here of an androgynous "essence" (in Hinduism, Shiva as Ardhanrishvara when joined to Parvati) but not of an actual androgyne—which does not exist as a creature; this androgynous essence must be understood in a spiritual sense where mind and heart are reunified.

At the base of a homo-erotic attraction, one cannot exclude the possibility of a potentially noble attraction to perfect man—or, in the case of woman, perfect woman—but at the cost of actually ever realizing it since in itself the homosexual part of the attraction presupposes an inability (or unwillingness) to go beyond one's sexual otherness, and that is finally the bane of such an affinity. However, seen from the perspective of the *fitrah*, or the sacred primordial norm, the immorality of homosexuality has to do with the sterility—whether spiritual or genesiacal—of what finally can only amount to an aborted union. In other words, to sequester the procreative force of *eros* and thus to divert it from its fulfillment in the alchemical otherness of a true opposite—be it an earthly spouse or, by delegation, the Divine—is to subvert its magic for an inherently unnatural end, whence the unavoidable narcissism of a homoerotic union, this narcissism which entails loving oneself, via a same-sex proxy, and thus failing to transcend oneself. Even if a love between same-sex partners mimics and can even replicate some of the psychological states or emotions of the love between a man and a woman, perhaps exceptionally even of the nobler kind, it can never achieve the extinction—and thus redemption—of surrendering to the otherness of one's alchemical opposite, and it is this potential for utterness of surrender to the "Sacred Other"—male or female, but both divine—that sets the stage for the transfiguration of love from ego to God, and hence to immortality.[25]

---

25 In the ecstasy of erotic consummation, the fullness of bliss cannot be achieved without the sacrifice of one's petty joy and without, it should be added, the extinction of each gender's limitation as a strictly polarized sex. In other words, the fullness of ecstasy is premised

Be that as it may, these considerations require mentioning another aspect of the "feminization" of man, but positive this time: there is an archetype, in mysticism, for the masculine soul becoming spiritually "feminine" with regard to the Divine. An example of this is found in the inspired devotionalism stemming from the Hindu cult of Radha and Krishna, the archetypal lovers in Indian mysticism: Krishna, as the perfect male divinity and as the *avatara* of Vishnu, is so lovable that devotion to him can induce a male worshiper to identify himself vicariously with Radha, whose intense love of Krishna is the model of the soul's love for God—or of God made man. In terms of spiritual polarities, such a vocation inspires in a male soul a state of pure receptivity and tenderness and ecstatic longing for Krishna as a result of which he becomes wholly soul with respect to Spirit. We mention this only to point out the possible polyvalence of the human psyche, and not to propose, needless to say, that there could be a true model for the feminization of man, which would be a contradiction in terms. Moreover, the mystical feminization of a man's soul does not entail in the slightest that the man will become otherwise effeminate or emasculated as regards his daily behavior because such an outcome would amount in fact to narcissism and therefore not constitute an egoless surrender to the Divinity; in fact, the divine nature of the object—namely God as Krishna—excludes any perversion, precisely. Such a mystical possibility is a question of vocation, in which a spiritual love can so seize and consume a soul that it succumbs to God in tearful adoration through an intensity of pure feelings and emotions, and does so to the exclusion of the typically intellective attributes of male spirituality such as reason and logic and sobriety, or those of heroic combativeness. However, it should also be specified that such an ecstatic vocation of liquefying love and tears can also have—for a man—a female object, namely the *Shakti* or Divine Mother, as in the case of Ramakrishna.[26]

---

on the resolution of the "cosmic" separation, something which cannot occur—or cannot do so to the same degree—in a monosexual situation, for in the resolution, the heavenly male-female androgynous prototype (symbol of the Spirit) is restored, however briefly. Images of this abound in the lore of alchemical drawings. In the yogic doctrine of the body-soul's subtle channels, this resolution corresponds to the merging of the *ida* and *pingala* channels in the *sushumna* axis.

26 The "gift of tears" is, of course, a mystical feature found in all the great religions. For instance, the prophet of Islam said: "Weep, and if ye weep not, then try to weep" (Ibn Majah, *Iqamah*, 176). This recalls the Jews at the Wailing Wall, and also the custom of the American Indians to "lament" in a solitary retreat in nature. In answering the question, "What is the greatest strength of a devotee?", Ramakrishna said: "He is the child of God and his greatest strength is tears" (Quoted in *Sri Ramakrishna, Dichos y Sentencias* [Palma de Mallorca: José J. de Olañeta, 2006).

Beyond the obvious distinctions of man as active and woman as passive, or of their emblematic sun versus moon polarity, the qualities of each sex are also reversible, so that although man is *a priori* operatively active and therefore dynamic or forceful and woman *a priori* operatively passive and therefore static or receptive, there is another aspect in which the male seduced by the female becomes passive and the female active, as depicted in the Hindu iconography of the goddess Kali dancing on Shiva's inert body; the same iconography is seen in the Egyptian sky goddess Nut arching over the earth god Geb in amorous prelude to their embrace; and here the normal symbolism equating earth with mother and Heaven with father is completely reversed.[27] In other words, once man sets woman into motion— or when the solitary One unleashes the dynamism of multiplicity—then motion takes over and man, as center or axis, becomes identified with the "passivity" or apparent "inertness" of the motionless center; whereas woman, now awakened out of her passivity and made active by man's impetus, becomes like a devouring fire that takes over while man's initial (or principial) instrumentality that aroused her is rendered useless.[28] This reversal of poles derives, no doubt, from the penetration of *Purusha* into *Prakriti*, so that what is principially static and inactive (*Purusha*) becomes dynamic and active (*Prakriti*) when projected onto the plane of duality or nature; this is the law of inverse analogy where the Principle moves from inward to outward in its manifested form, while, of course, remaining motionless beneath (or within) its cosmic exteriorization. Likewise, in the sacrum of intercourse, the male principle once spent dies, as it were, whereas woman becomes active, especially in receiving the seed that is engendered in her. It is this reciprocity that prevents one from saying that the male principle is hierarchically superior and at the same time allows one to affirm that it is indeed superior, for if the female (or the goddess

---

27 This embrace is featured in Tantrism by the *viparita-maithuna* coupling.

28 In Taoist cosmology, woman is considered to have near infinite *yin* (the primordial energy) whereas man's *yang* is limited: once he expends it, he loses his virility. These aspects, moreover, may explain the Germanic attribution of a male gender to the moon and a female one to the sun: "*der Mond*" (masculine) and "*die Sonne*" (feminine). In fact, a number of ancient languages and traditions adhere to these attributions: in Sanskrit the names of the moon such as Kandra, Soma, Indu, and Vidhu are all masculine. The Lithuanians also associate the moon with the masculine gender and the sun with the feminine. In Japan, it is the sun goddess, Amaterasu, that holds the central role, whereas her brother, the moon god, is relatively insignificant. The Druids observed the same attributions. Finally, the divine act of manifestation itself entails a reversal of poles, giving soul *de facto* predominance over Spirit, time over eternity, motion over motionlessness.

Nut or Kali), by assuming the dynamic principle becomes superior to man it is finally only because of male's primordial initiative, precisely. In fact, in some formulations the female becomes symbolically "masculinized"— as in Buddhism, which teaches that before a woman can enter *Nirvana* she has to become a "man"; Saint Augustine asserts the very same thing. Such a teaching however—leaving aside its appearance of misogynous dialectics—is really alluding to the fact that only identity with the Spirit saves, so that for the soul to gain salvation it must unite with the Spirit to the point of total identity, even forsaking its former soul-personality and, in the case of woman, its soul-gender, at least symbolically. We mention this only to situate some of the subtle play of switching identities that the Spirit undertakes upon entering creation; and these alternations moreover help situate with what respectful consideration woman must be treated by man, for her "inferiority" cannot be understood without also understanding her "superiority".

True superiority, however, derives purely from the Spirit, which transcends duality, and not from any sexual duality per se; hence, so long as man and woman are seen as incomplete halves of a polarity, both can assume interchangeable positions of superiority inasmuch as each can play the role of Spirit or of Divine Essence with regard to the other. Examples of such interchangeability of the roles of the sexes were standard in medieval Christian spirituality where Christ was seen as mother; we even have images of a nursing Christ, for instance in the mystical experience of Saint Catherine of Siena, or in the example of Saint Francis of Assisi suckling his flock.

On the plane of creation itself, while the male has certain decisive advantages, he is still born of a woman, "dies" in woman in the coital embrace, and at the end of life is buried in "mother earth"; in that sense, everything that man is—in creation—derives directly from woman. In this earthly respect, then, woman holds a sacred superiority to man because she is identified not only with the home—or the origin—but in fact with all of nature, the *Prakriti*. And yet, precisely as *natura naturans* or *Prakriti*, woman longs for the Spirit; and even if the Spirit—or man— is born through her, he as son, is ineffably father too, in the sense—to borrow again from Christianity—that Christ has been defined medievally as the "Virgin Mary's father", which fact grants us an insight into the real meaning of the designation of Mary being the "Mother of God". These considerations would seem to contradict the Bible's account of woman being drawn from man's side, but this is not so, for we are dealing here with two different levels: woman being taken from Adam's side, post-creation, refers symbolically to the completeness and centrality of the Adamic prototype as such in pre-creation.

Each sex represents finally for the other a wondrous totality, their individuation as man and woman being secondary to their capacity to embody the Spirit itself, albeit in two different modes, so that depending on the relationship man can sometimes be seen as moon relative to woman now become the sun and vice versa, of course.[29] In fact, when deep, the love between a man and a woman can lead to the medieval "exchange of hearts" where "each becomes the other's mine" and where, as a result, they are powerless to take their heart back[30] so that they henceforth live for the sake of the other in a sacrifice combining intense bliss and pain at the same time; the joy of union enhances the pain of separation since so long as they walk on earth they cannot taste the permanent fulfillment of their mutual completeness.[31]

Now to resume with our earlier topic. On the individual plane, it is the search and need for the restoration of a lost totality that is celebrated in marriage; whence also its sacredness, for it can enable the alchemical transfiguration leading to this primordial unity that each partner carries in his or her intimate selfhood. The Latin word for "love" is *amor* (*a-mor*) meaning either "without-death" or "to-the-death", for man, in loving, dies to his ego, just as the bliss of conjugal consummation entails a momentary death of the ego, briefly immersed as the partners are in the stream of immortality flashing through their loins. Procreation is the act by which the earth is peopled and its seed carries the potential of an infinite number of descendants to mirror the stars in the firmament, as God told Abraham.

Woman's beauty, as personified in the noble bounty of her anatomy and further enhanced by her softness, makes of her a palpable symbol of

29 Quoting from Frithjof Schuon: "Man, in his lunar and receptive aspect, 'withers away' without the woman-sun that infuses into the virile genius the life it needs in order to blossom; inversely, man-sun confers on woman the light that permits her to realize her identity by prolonging the function of the sun" (*Esoterism as Principle and as Way*, p. p. 139).

30 As an example of this, we have the story of Saint Catherine of Siena who recounts how Christ, in a special vision, came to her in 1370. According to her contemporary biographer, Raymond of Capua, Christ appeared to her while she was in prayer and removed her heart. Upon recounting this to her confessor, he merely laughed, but she held to her version. A few days passed and then, upon completing her prayers one day, Christ appeared to her again holding a shining heart in his hands; he opened her left side once again and inserted the heart, telling her that he was giving her his own heart in answer to her praying to have it. Christ then closed the opening and healed her wound, but she bore afterward a lifelong visible scar, which was apparently seen by many, as a token of this experience. See Pierre Debongnie, "Commencement et recommencements de la dévotion du cœur de Jésus", in *Le Cœur: Les Etudes carmélitaines*, 29, 1950, 147-192.

31 Cosmologically speaking, the force of *eros* is actually one energy divided into two aspects; its nature therefore is to be always one and not two, whence the irresistible attraction between the sexes.

the Sovereign Good (the *Summum Bonum*) destined for the melting of the heart and liberation. But, if craved as a thief craves a treasure, her blinding charms can lead to a soul's harm because one cannot hope to capture immortality on a plane where all is perishable and without giving of oneself in return; nature avenges herself on those who wish to enjoy her without respecting her power or who profane her sacredness.[32] These basic points account, once again, for the importance of the sacrament of marriage, or at least of a ritual blessing for the enamored couple, not forgetting that, in truth, a marriage always involves three agents: the spouses and God, for it is really through God that the partners can meet and be joined as one, whether they know it or not. Each partner is receiving the rare and extraordinary gift of the other, for each is finally the son or daughter of God, and this is what the sacred ceremony of marriage is meant to evoke and to preserve.

*   *   *

We have mentioned that each soul, in seeking the beloved, is seeking the Spirit; and in this respect both man and woman play the part of soul, each seeing in their opposite a delegate of the Spirit, for in seeking for love the mortal soul is really yearning for immortality; in the same manner, the bliss of love derives entirely from its heavenly essence. But this search for love is made arduous by the fact that the soul is unlikely to recognize the Spirit when it first meets It, the reason being that to truly become wedded and reunited forevermore to the Spirit involves for the soul a dying to the world and to the mortal self one has become accustomed to calling "myself". For the Spirit is not of this world; nor therefore is the happiness it promises of this world, except by distant reflection. Furthermore, the Spirit can prove a stern taskmaster, and therefore upon first encounter It will not always be recognized as the prince (or the princess) of one's dreams, all the more as the soul wants to appropriate the Spirit for her earthly desires, seeking to mold It into her mortal fancies, something the Spirit cannot acquiesce to. Hence, to taste deeply of this happiness requires a dying, a transition the soul is loath to do and does not in fact really know how to do, even though its own substance—like the Spirit—is not of the flesh either. Indeed, to speak of the Spirit is to speak of a being that has never been part of this world, but rather that belongs entirely to the heavenly realm, for it

32 The menstrual taboo, a feature of most traditional cultures, derives its precautionary impetus from the power of this force that is wasted, as it were, each time the ovum matures without conception; as such, woman in this state must be confined to isolation so that the force of conception peaking dangerously for naught, as it were, can be neutralized.

is incorrupt, deathless, invincibly strong, and ravishingly beautiful. And, unbeknownst to the soul, It is actually dedicated to helping the soul find It once again.

However, the soul for its part, wandering on earth, is inclined to betray the Spirit over and over again while fancying to have found perfect happiness in this or that mundane creature or pastime; and it will lavishly invest in this or that person a love that is really meant for the Spirit, and this is why there are so many disappointments in love, either because the sentiment is misplaced or because the person invested with such love cannot rise to the occasion. This drama of the wandering soul and of the Spirit-in-disguise conjuring the soul finds echoes in popular legends such as that of the "loathsome bride" or of "beauty and the beast": in each case, the Spirit, appearing under some mortal mask, seems like a repelling entity that the soul recoils from and yet must somehow learn to love; the moment of truth comes when the soul must accept to love this seeming "beast" or accept to kiss this "loathsome bride"—such as the legends of the "*fier baiser*" (or "noble kiss on the mouth") of some outwardly unappealing figure— and lo and behold the soul, to its astonishment, discovers a maiden or a prince of unearthly beauty[33]. It is then discovered that the Spirit's former repellence is entirely a matter of the soul's subjective perception; in other words, for fear of dying, the soul is affrighted by the personage serving as the instrument of that death which therefore takes on, in the soul's eyes, a foul or loathsome appearance. "I am black but beautiful", the bride says in the Song of Songs; and "the kingdom of God is only for the thoroughly dead", we hear Meister Eckhart admonish.

The Spirit, for its part, was once of one substance with the soul and only, with great trepidation and sore misgivings allowed the soul to part from It to enter into the realm of time and the great Wheel of Existence, of birth and rebirth; It weeps to be parted from the soul, but knows that the soul (moon), if it is to project the Spirit's radiance (sun) into the remote realms of darkness must be allowed to forget its original nature, for this forgetting is the preliminary seeding ground for the harvest of recollection, as it were, through which creation is eventually redeemed and restored back to its divine archetype. Without this phase of forgetting the origin, there would be no creational egress, no projection to the remotest ends of manifestation and time; in fact, this projection-forgetting is the Spirit's sacrifice, whereby It gives up its own life-substance—now become the soul as creaturely individuation—for the benefit of the fructification of creation,

---

33 The Spirit, of course, can wear the disguise of either a male or a female figure depending on whether the seeking soul is that of a man or of a woman.

but a fructification coming at the price of separation, death, and loss, all of which must transpire before the transfiguration of the great return. And the Spirit, for all its heavenly power, is helpless at first to rescue the soul once it enters the individual *comedia* of existence. Finally, after many a tribulation, the soul remembers its heavenly spouse and, repenting from its multiple betrayals, atones and returns, wiser and sanctified from its odyssey.

Such a depiction of the relationship between the soul and the Spirit begs the question: can the Spirit have "feelings"? The answer really is yes and no, because in one respect the Spirit transcends all dualities, and is also of a transpersonal substance. But in another respect all dualities are a divided expression of the one Spirit or, formulated differently, all dualities borrow their reflected reality from the Spirit, including consciousness, love, and will—human attributes only in appearance—or Intelligence-Bliss-Power which were the three attributes mentioned at the beginning of this book as defining Divinity: *Sat-Chit-Ananda*. Thus the question becomes rather: what is the origin of feelings, do they derive from Spirit? Insofar as the essence of consciousness (*Chit*) is Spirit then the answer speaks for itself. Put differently, it is not that the Spirit is human but that the human is fashioned after the Spirit.

*   *   *

A popular refrain asserts that "love is blind", which is true for what it is worth, because love is a subjective experience; but a profounder saying captures the essence of love's gift: "If thou fallest in love thou shalt see", and this points to love's possibility of leading to a rebirth of the soul; this is why Dante could describe his ecstatic meeting with Beatrice as a *vita nuova*, or a "new life". In that sense, love comes into the soul like the sun in a darkened cave and illuminates it and brings it warmth; it is then an awakening that offers the lovers a foretaste of the bliss of immortality while on earth. Truly, it is not love that is blind, but infatuation, for love in itself is a form of knowing—of God reclaiming himself through the theatrical duality of two beings—and is therefore anything but blind. Indeed, love transfigures the ordinary back into the extraordinary or the human back into the Divine.

However, we are entitled to speak loosely of infatuation on the human plane as "love" even if it is born from a mixture of true insight and illusion. If it is true that love—especially if one-sided—can be merely a fervent wish in which one person confers on the beloved all of his or her longing for an ideal figure, it is also true that if such a love is nobly deluded, then who would dare call it entirely an illusion? A noble sentiment is never an error in itself; only in its misapplication, namely when it is bestowed on someone who either is undeserving of the honor or who is essentially an unwitting prop for another person's dreams; but this does not lessen the love's quality. On the other hand, love can reveal the celestial essence of another person's soul and in that sense it can serve as a means of spiritual transfiguration in which each partner is then inspired to revere the other in worshipful admiration as well as in tenderness, love then becoming an earthly intuition of heavenly archetypes.

And the aspects of tenderness and admiration are themselves premised on the twin aspects of sweetness and majesty, or of childlikeness and royalty, which constitute the essence of the sanctified soul. Transposing now these twin principles onto the human plane, they account for each partner's need to find in romance a balance between intimacy and distance—or of ecstasy and sobriety—with the other: the aspect of intimacy expresses the mystery of Immanence, of shared spiritual identity in which "each has become the other's mine"; this is the relationship of equals, of ecstatic oneness, of deep mutual devotion; but at the same time the aspect of intimacy must be balanced by the mystery of separateness which expresses the dimension of Transcendence in which "each has become the other's god", because if love requires sameness of essence in order for the partners to meet, it also requires sacred otherness in order for the partners to fully complete each other. In this worshipful reverence of the other, any risk of idolatry is offset by the humility and self-effacement that true respect entails: awe for the other has an extinguishing effect on the ego who learns the gift of self-effacement, enduring patience, meekness, and sacrifice, for in loving the other there is a loss of self and—in the greatest of loves—a death.[34] In other words, spouses must find some balance between closeness and apartness because life on earth cannot be a permanent union—except in the heart—and also because without this sobering mystery of apartness, intimacy can degenerate into casualness and triviality, which is the surest manner to destroy the magic of romance. Indeed, love cannot endure without respect, which is like a form of "objective love", if one will. Love thrives as much on the distance of mystery as it does on the closeness of intimacy; or, one might say, ecstasy must be punctuated by refreshing pauses to retain its vibrancy.

Hence, to recapitulate: Immanence and Transcendence, mystery of oneness and mystery of otherness, love and respect, tenderness and admiration, warmth and coolness, or closeness and distance, each of these poles must be actively present for the sacred marriage (*hieros gamos*) to be

---

34 This is why those who die of a broken heart are considered martyrs and gain instant beatification in Heaven.

properly consummated and preserved. Of course, in Heaven, the elements of distance, coolness, and separateness lose their privative or purifying necessity, but not, quite obviously, their quality of worshipful respect.

Not least, loving and honoring each other amounts also to honoring God, who brought both spouses together, and without whom they would not be able to be united.

*   *   *

Man, as expressed earlier, embodies Truth. Now Truth—which is another term for the Absolute, or the Principle—has an immanent, formless essence that can be termed "feminine" and this is Wisdom. In Hinduism one would say that Wisdom is the *shakti* or the feminine energy of Truth; indeed, none can claim to have understood the Truth until it descends into the heart and is changed from cold and objective ideation to warm and subjective being. This alchemy of Truth transfigured into Wisdom is the essence of the sacred marriage and the deeper meaning of the love between man and woman: she attaches—or fixes—herself to him so that he may melt into her: mystery of pure focusing or exclusive centering, on the one hand, and mystery of all-encompassing radiation, on the other; mystery of surrender and mystery of exaltation, of contractive extinction and of blissful expansion, of death and life. In the union of masculine and feminine the universe is re-centered in the Eternal Principle (Truth) and at the same time reborn in joyous life (Love). And through woman become divine *Sophia*, man finds his spiritual realization, for she as holy Essence delivers man from outwardness and separation, as we have said, and restores him to union with the immanent Divine. And reciprocally, through man as embodiment of Truth, woman is reawakened to her own divine substance that allows her to mother the birth of the Spirit in her heart, thus enabling her to pass from passive substance to active essence, enlightened by the Spirit through the support of man as holy Truth. In this alchemy of love and consciousness, both man and woman are reborn, as it were, from each other and through each other and in each other.

In the immortal words of the Sufi poet Ibn al-Farid: "I had been enamored of her, but when I renounced my desire, she desired me for herself and loved me. And I became a beloved, nay, one loving himself. Through her I went forth from myself to her and came not back to myself. In the sobriety after self-effacement I was none other than she, and when she unveiled herself my attributes became hers and we are one" (*Ta'iyyatu'l-kubra*).

GLOSSARY OF TERMS

Adi-Buddha (Sanskrit): in Tibetan or Vajrayana Buddhism, the "Primordial Buddha" or the self-emanating Buddha, the antecedent and therefore self-originating being from whom all Buddhas are born. Assimilable to the Eckhartian notion of *Gottheit* or Godhead and the *Brahma Nirguna* of the Vedanta.

Adam Kadmon (Hebrew): in the *Kabbalah*, "Primordial Man".

Advaita Vedanta (Sanskrit): essential Hindu doctrine of the non-duality of the Self, and the Oneness of Reality.

Agape (Greek): in Christianity, the highest or most selfless form of love and charity.

Agnosia (Latin): in the "negative theology" or "apophatic mysticism" of a John Scotus Eriugena and a Dionysius the Areopagite, this term refers to the "unlearning" of worldly knowledge required as a preliminary foundation for learning in God.

Aham Brahmasmi (Sanskrit): "I am *Brahma*"; the Vedantic doctrine of ontological identity between God (*Brahma*) and man in the supra-individual core of the human soul (the *aham*, "self" or "I am").

Ahamkara or *ahankara* (Sanskrit): in Vedantic philosophy, the principle of individuation.

Anatma (Sanskrit): Buddhist and Hindu doctrine of "no self"; *atman* (derived from *Atma*) being the individual self, whence the term *an-atma* or "without self".

Aql al-Awwal (Arabic): in Islamic philosophy, the first or primordial intelligence; according to Al-Farabi and Avicenna (Ibn Sina), the first intellective emanation of Godhead, belonging to "Necessary Being" (*al-wajib al-wujud*) or that which cannot not be.

Arhat (Sanskrit): in Theravada Buddhism, one who has reached total Awakening; also a perfected saint.

Ativarnashrami (Sanskrit): in Hinduism, a person who is beyond caste.

Atma (Sanskrit): in Hinduism, the supreme Divine Principle.

Avatara (Sanskrit): in Hinduism, a salvific descent and personification of God on earth.

Avidya Maya (Sanskrit): in Hinduism, the *Maya* that darkens and leads away from *Atma*, causing ignorance and illusion. See *Maya*

Bodhisattva (Sanskrit): in Mahayana Buddhism, an enlightened being who, out of universal compassion and wisdom, foregoes his or her entry into *Nirvana* in order to help earthly souls to attain salvation.

Brahma Nirguna (Sanskrit): in Vedanta, the Supreme Being without qualities (*nirguna*), about which nothing can be posited.

Brahma Saguna (Sanskrit): in Vedanta, the Supreme Being "with qualities" (*saguna*); corresponds to the creator God of monotheism or the *Ishvara* of Hinduism.

Brahmana (Sanskrit): in India, the priestly caste.

Buddhi (Sanskrit): the "higher intellect"; the first degree of the manifestation of *Atma*; also known as the "great principle" (*Mahat*). It is created yet still divine, and corresponds to the projection of God's universal consciousness in creation.

Budo (Japanese): in Japan, a method or way of martial arts.

Chen Jen (Chinese): in Taoism, "True Man"; analogous to the *Adam Kadmon* of the *Kabbalah* or the *Purusha* of the Hindu *Sankhya* philosophy.

Chi (Chinese): in Chinese cosmology, the life force or energy, the *élan vital* inherent in all of creation and in its creatures; similar to the Hindu notion of *prana*.

Creatio ex nihilo (Latin): in Christianity, the doctrine of creation coming "out of nothing" (*ex nihilo*), namely positing a mysterious or indescribable origin.

Deus absconditus (Latin): in the thought of Saint Thomas Aquinas, the idea of the "God hidden" behind His revelation and therefore as not perceptible by human means.

Deus revelatus (Latin): God in His self-revelation to man.

Dharma (Sanskrit): in Indian philosophy, the Law and Order of the Universe; also the individual duty and therefore destiny of a human being according to caste. In Buddhism, the body of doctrinal teachings of the Buddha relating to the supreme Truth.

Diksha (Sanskrit): in Hinduism, spiritual initiation.

Ein Sof (Hebrew): lit. "no end" or "infinite"; in the *Kabbalah*, God as He was before Self-manifesting in creation.

Ex cathedra (Latin): lit. "speaking from the chair"; the Catholic doctrine of papal infallibility promulgated in 1870. According to this dogma, the pontiff, while not error-free in his person, can make an infallible pronouncement when speaking *ex cathedra*, or with the full authority of the Catholic Church's sacred *magisterium* inspired by the Holy Spirit.

Fana (Arabic): the Sufi doctrine of extinction before God and therefore of supra-personal union with the Divine. Analogous to the Christian doctrine of *mortificatio*, or self-annihilation.

Fitrah (Arabic): "innate human nature", which Islamic theology considers to be man's innate predisposition for the Divine. Man before the Fall, or man as created directly and gloriously in the primordial image of God.

Gottheit (German): "Godhead"; "Beyond-Being" or the unknowable God—"unknowable" by man as man, but knowable through the heart-intellect. In the thought of Meister Eckhart, Supra-Being (*Gottheit*), in contrast to the creator or personal God (*Gott*) of theology.

Guna (Sanskrit): in Hinduism, the three constituents qualities of creation: *sattva* or the intelligent, luminous, ascending principle; *rajas* or the active, expanding, fiery, and passional principle; and *tamas* or the descending, dull, inertia-bound, and tenebrous principle.

Ida and *Pingala* (Sanskrit): in the yogic doctrine derived from the *Shiva Samhita*, the body-soul's subtle channels, with *ida* corresponding to the lunar, cool, or feminine principle and *pingala* to the solar, hot, or masculine principle. They merge in the central axis known as the *sushumna*. They correspond to the Chinese *yin* and *yang* energies, as well as the principles of mercury and sulfur in the Western alchemical tradition.

In mutua funera (Latin): "in a mutual funeral".

Jalwah (Arabic): in Sufism, "going forth" into the world to manifest the Divine received in the sanctum of the *khalwah*, or prayerful retreat; also, recognizing the reflection of the Divine in the world.

Kabbalah (Hebrew): a body of esoteric wisdom concerned with the mystical aspect of Judaism.

Kali Yuga (Sanskrit): "the Dark Age"; according to Hindu scripture, the last of the four ages characterized by a maximum of remoteness from the Divine Principle, and reflected humanly by the degeneracy of doctrines and customs.

Ke (Chinese): in China, the mysterious force of nature, or the animic essence found in natural materials (such as wood, stone, silk, etc.) and which a craftsman needs to understand in order not to violate the material or to "kill" it as he processes it.

Kenosis (Greek): in Christian theology, the doctrine of "emptying" or rendering oneself void of the individual self in order to become an open vessel for divine grace.

Khalwah (Arabic): in Sufism, "prayerful retreat"; withdrawal from the world for the sake of God; by symbolic extension, spiritual interiorization.

Kosha (Sanskrit): in Vedantic philosophy, the five sheaths or envelopes covering the individual self: 1. the food or gross body (*annamaya kosha*); 2. the air or emotional body (*pranamaya kosha*); 3. the nerve or mental body (*manomaya kosha*); 4. the discerning or intelligent body (*vijnanamaya kosha*); and 5. the supreme body of bliss (*anandamaya kosha*). This delineation shows in what manner *Atma* (or the Divine Self) is, reversing the scheme, immanent in the *atman* (the individual self).

Krita Yuga (Sanskrit): the period of the Golden Age in the Vedantic doctrine of the *yugas*.

Kshatriya (Sanskrit): in India, the warrior caste.

Logos (Greek): lit. "the Word" and also "Reason"; understood as the conscious divine agency in creation. For the Greeks, this principle is equated with *Nous*. In Judaism, it is "the word of God" that can address man, via the "Burning Bush" for instance. For the Jewish Hellenist philosopher, Philo, it was "the first born of God". In Christianity it is equated directly with Jesus, if not with God the Father himself. Universally, it is both the archetypal personification of *buddhi*, equatable with the cosmic intellect, and also the direct human manifestation of this on earth in the form of the *avatara* as embodiment of divinity and wisdom.

Maha Pralaya (Sanskrit): in Hinduism, the doctrine of the final dissolution of creation.

Materia prima (Latin): "first or prime matter"; in Platonic cosmology, the undifferentiated and primordial substance that serves as "receptacle" for the shaping force of the divine Forms or Ideas; universal potentiality.

Maya (Sanskrit): the Hindu doctrine of universal illusion, of the unreality of the cosmos, or of *Brahma* taking on the veil of earthly existence.

Mudra (Sanskrit): symbolic or ritual gestures in Hinduism and Buddhism performed with the hands as well as with the body.

Mutatis mutandis (Latin): lit. "the necessary changes having been made", which can be paraphrased as: "all things being equal" or "each in their fashion" or "with the respective differences having been considered".

Nama-rupa (Sanskrit): "name-form"; in Buddhist psychology, corresponds to the constituents of "intelligence and being" in creatures. More narrowly defined, *nama* refers to the psychological faculties of a human being and *rupa* to his body.

Natura naturans and *natura naturata* (Latin): terms coined in the Middle Ages to describe nature considered in her twin roles as active (*natura naturans*, or "nature creating") and passive or inert (*natura naturata*, or "nature created").

Nivritti Marga (Sanskrit): in Hinduism, the path of extinction or of return to the divine Principle.

Noesis (Greek): See *Nous*

Nous (Greek): intellect (or heart-intellect); the highest faculty in man, by which the truth can be directly known. The process of intellective (or divine) consciousness is known as *noesis*.

Paramahamsa (Sanskrit): lit. "supreme swan"; in Hinduism, a designation applying to a very gifted spiritual master or to a sage who has attained a supreme yogic state (*nirvikalpa samadhi*), in which he can discern Truth from illusion, or the Real from the unreal.

Paramatma (Sanskrit): in Vedantic metaphysics, the Absolute Self or Supreme Soul, also the Oversoul. In *Advaita Vedanta* the term refers to *Nirguna Brahma*, or *Brahma* "without attributes".

Parousia (Greek): lit. "presence"; the Second Coming of Christ, marking the time "when the stars shall fall from heaven" (Matt. 24:29), bringing the "end of the world".

Philosophia Perennis (Latin): the "perennial philosophy"; the universal and eternal spiritual and metaphysical wisdom underlying all the particular systems of philosophy.

Pleroma (Greek): God in his infinite totality. A term found both in the New Testament and in Gnosticism. For Saint Paul, it is God in the fullness of his Godhead (Col. 2).

Pontiff (Latin): lit. "bridge-maker", a term designing the twofold nature of man as the link between Heaven and earth; also a term for the pope.

Prana (Sanskrit): in Hinduism, the sustaining life force or vital energy that is the essence of life. Considered to be in the air, it enters living bodies through the breath.

Pratyeka Buddha (Sanskrit): a "solitary Buddha"; a Buddha-realized being who, contrary to the *bodhisattva*, does not teach and therefore does not have disciples. Centered entirely on *Nirvana* at the expense of the *samsara*, he still possesses in this fashion a spiritual influence on the world.

Pravritti Marga (Sanskrit): in Hinduism, the the unfolding of creation.

Prakriti (Sanskrit): lit. "making first"; the fundamental, "feminine" substance or pre-material cause of all things occurring in manifestation; in the *Bhagavad Gita*, described as the "primal motive force" composing the three *gunas*.

Purusha (Sanskrit): lit. "cosmic man"; the divine Self projected into human form at the archetypal or universal level of manifestation; the informing or shaping principle of Creation; the "masculine" demiurge or fashioner of the universe.

Quod absit (Latin): lit. "which thing, let it be absent"; a phrase commonly used by the medieval Scholastics to call attention to an idea that is absurdly inconsistent with accepted principles.

Rajas (Sanskrit): See *Guna*

Religio Perennis (Latin): the "perennial religion"; a term denoting the supraformal religion underlying all formal religions and which is by definition timeless; the essence of all religions.

Resignation ad infernum (Latin): "resignation to hell"; a term occurring more particularly in a perspective of "passional mysticism" in which the agony of separation from God combined with a spiritual sincerity so overpowering, leads to the soul's despair, suffering as it does from the contrast between its individual imperfection and God's perfection.

Ruach Hakodesh (Hebrew): in Judaism, the "Holy Spirit"; the presence of God Most High (YHVH).

Samadhi (Sanskrit): in Hinduism and Buddhism, a state of consciousness equated either with enlightenment or with a blessed state of oneness with the Divine and correlatively of detachment from egoic individuality.

Samkhya (Sanskrit): one of the six philosophical schools of India; focused on cosmological doctrines involving the principles *Purusha* and *Prakriti*.

Sanatana Dharma (Sanskrit): in Hinduism, the "eternal law"; the term has become synonymous with Hinduism, although strictly speaking it transcends all religious forms, these forms being essentially expressions of its nature.

Sat-Chit-Ananda (Sanskrit): respectively "Being", "Consciousness", and "Bliss"; in Vedantic philosophy a description of the nature of *Brahma*.

Satsanga (Sanskrit): the term combines *sat*, referring to God's absolute "being", and *sanga*, "company" or "union", hence: "to be in the presence of God's being", and by extension, holy company.

Sattva (Sanskrit): See *Guna*

Satya Yuga (Sanskrit): in Hinduism, the "Age of Truth", the first of the four ages of creation, namely, the one situated closest to the primordial paradise, if not overlapping it.

Sensum fidelium (Latin): in Christianity, the "sense of the faithful" or the ability for the whole body of Christian believers to "sense" the doctrinal truth and to recognize it, the assumption being that the flock will be inspired and led by the Holy Spirit; the counterpart to the clergy's authority as interpreters of the *magisterium*, or the Church's doctrinal authority embodied in the episcopacy, or reigning bishops.

Shekhinah (Hebrew): in Judaism, the "presence of God" as manifest in the Tabernacle and the Temple in Jerusalem. Esoterically, the Divine Essence as feminine in its substance and mystery.

Sirr (Arabic): in Islam, the "secret" or essence of man's soul; the divine root of man.

Shudra (Sanskrit): in Hinduism, the fourth or worker and laborer caste.

Skandhas (Sanskrit): in Buddhism, the aggregate of sensation, feeling, and perception, as well as mental formations (volition, impulses), and consciousness, which constitute the existence of a creature on earth.

Sub specie aeternitatis (Latin): "under the aspect [seal] of Eternity".

Sunnah (Arabic): in Islam, the religious and social imitation of the example of the prophet Muhammad.

Tajalli (Arabic): in Sufism, the aspect of God's splendor shining in creation.

Tamas (Sanskrit): See *Guna*

Terribilità (Italian): a sense for awe-inspiring grandeur born from the fearsome side of the Divine majesty.

Theosis (Greek): a term designating the process of spiritual realization in which the soul becomes holy, or divine, and attains to knowledge of Godhead.

Upaya (Sanskrit): in Buddhism, a "heavenly stratagem" designed to save the largest number of souls as possible.

Vacare Deo (Latin): lit. "to be empty for God", to be receptive to God; by extension, spiritual poverty.

Vaishya (Sanskrit): in Hinduism, the third caste, that of artisans, craftsmen, and merchants.

Vidya Maya (Sanskrit): the *Maya* that enlightens and leads to *Atma*.

Viparita-maithuna (Sanskrit): in Tantrism, ritual sexual intercourse in which the woman assumes the superior position.

Virya (Sanskrit): in Hinduism, the male essence, energy, force, willpower.

Viveka (Sanskrit): "discrimination"; in Vedantic philosophy, the faculty in man that discriminates between Reality and unreality.

Wei wu wei (Chinese): in Taoism, "effortless doing" or "acting without acting"; a key precept explaining the art of egoless action, as well as the attitude of "letting be".

Yab-yum (Sanskrit): lit. "father-mother"; in Tibetan Buddhism, depicted iconographically as the male deity in sexual union with the female deity.

Yuga (Sanskrit): "epoch", "age"; according to Hindu philosophy, a cycle of creation is composed of four ages: the *Satya Yuga* or Golden Age, the *Treta Yuga*, the *Dvapara Yuga*, and finally the *Kali Yuga*, or Dark Age, in which mankind presently finds itself.

For a glossary of all key foreign words used in books published by World Wisdom, including metaphysical terms in English, consult: www.DictionaryofSpiritualTerms.org.
This on-line Dictionary of Spiritual Terms provides extensive definitions, examples, and related terms in other languages.

INDEX

Absolute, the, xi, 3, 4, 13, 25, 34, 42, 44, 51, 55-56, 67, 100, 103-107, 111, 116-119, 121, 123, 130, 141, 147, 153-155, 180, 189, 210, 212, 227-228, 231, 242-243, 247, 261, 265, 274, 278, 282, 285, 297, 303

accident, the, 55, 74, 146, 161, 204, 228

Adam, 25, 51, 84, 107, 110, 125, 149, 169, 246, 255, 286, 291, 299-300

Adamic prototype, 138, 291

Adi-Buddha, 6, 299

alchemy, 23, 118, 119, 121, 225, 228, 255, 277, 288, 297

American Indian(s), 30, 33,46, 80, 114, 268, 289

Amida Buddha, 175, 252

Ananda, 1, 161, 283, 295, 304

Anandamayi Ma, 10

animalism, 260

Aquinas, St. Thomas, 4, 19, 35, 110, 116-117, 145, 191, 300

archetype, ix, 13, 44, 46, 47, 48, 51, 61-65, 74, 98, 105, 108, 119, 120, 205, 213, 222-223, 240, 274, 278, 280, 281, 284, 286, 289

aristocracy, 62, 197, 212

Arjuna, 56, 137, 140, 142, 177, 185, 234

atheism, 14, 1501, 154, 155, 156, 157, 183

Atma, 14, 43, 51-57, 106-107, 119, 122, 146, 199, 220, 236, 282, 299, 300, 302, 305

Augustine, St., 1, 35, 89, 142, 256, 291

Avatara(s), 6, 38, 57, 62, 77, 139, 146, 203, 213-214, 227, 246, 261, 289, 302

barakah, 46, 62, 208, 214

Beatitude, 1

Beauty, 52, 64, 97, 120, 135, 136, 161, 169, 224, 225, 242, 245, 247, 271-274, 278, 282, 283, 285, 292

Bhagavad Gita, xii, 56, 58, 106, 112, 140-142, 146-147, 177, 185, 190, 209, 222, 234, 245, 250, 303

Black Elk, 58, 277

Blessed Virgin (Mary), the, 36-37, 63, 276

bodhisattva(s), 6, 25, 53, 57, 73, 77, 139, 174, 300, 303

Bolshevik, 72

Brahma, 14, 103, 119, 127, 233, 299, 300, 302-304

brahmana, 240-242, 300

Buddha, 6, 39, 53, 57, 62, 68, 95, 121, 123, 154, 160, 175, 206, 214, 252, 256, 262, 299-300, 303

Buddhahood, 14, 16, 57

Buddhism, 14, 16, 40, 44, 53, 56-58, 63, 77, 91, 109-110, 122-123, 137, 147, 154, 165, 174-175, 206-207, 214, 223, 227, 252, 268, 276, 291, 299-306

Burckhardt, Titus, ix, xi, 49, 79, 109, 232, 307

capitalism, 204

Catherine of Siena, St., 49, 79, 279, 291, 292

Catholic Church, 22, 67, 92, 135, 181, 207, 209, 211, 251, 301

Catholicism, 135, 205

Cause, divine, 55, 106

Center, divine, 7-9, 29, 58, 64, 94, 99, 104, 114, 126, 162, 166, 193, 199, 203, 223, 228, 232, 241, 256, 273-274, 278-280, 282, 285, 290

chakras, 32, 253, 261, 262

Chit, 1, 161, 295, 304

Christianity, 28, 36, 37, 40, 56-57, 61-64, 73, 77, 110, 111, 121-124, 134, 137, 158, 162, 164, 180, 182, 223, 239, 250, 291, 299-300, 302, 304 clergy, 73, 199, 305

collectivism, 54

Confucianism, 238

Consciousness, 1, 4, 26, 103, 107, 126, 229, 236, 250, 304

Coomaraswamy, Ananda, ix, 124

creation, 4, 5, 15, 27, 30, 32, 36, 37, 39, 43, 51, 53, 54, 55, 56, 72, 73, 75, 89, 93, 94, 98, 99, 103, 104, 105, 106, 107, 108, 109, 111, 112, 113, 114, 115, 117, 118, 119, 122, 124, 126, 136, 145, 150, 151, 152, 161, 162, 163, 166, 167, 168, 169, 170, 171, 172, 174, 175, 200, 206, 226, 227, 230, 231, 233, 235, 236, 238, 246, 261, 263, 265, 266, 267, 275, 277, 278, 282, 285, 286, 291, 294, 300, 301, 302, 303, 304, 305

Creator, the, 5, 8, 25-28, 30, 34, 43, 46, 51, 56, 67, 75, 80, 110, 151, 161, 166, 203, 232, 238, 266, 270

criminals, 179, 187, 189, 191

Crisis of the Modern World, xi

cyber-age, 29

democracy, 68-69, 71, 74-75, 83, 90, 100, 197, 201-203, 212, 217

Desert Fathers, the, 28, 35, 207, 217

despotism, 225

Dharma, 68, 130, 241, 300, 304

Divine, the, xii, 1-5, 9, 11, 14, 19-22, 25, 31, 34-35, 37, 49, 51, 52, 55-59, 65, 69, 73, 91, 93, 99, 103-111, 114, 121, 124-128, 130, 136, 139-144, 146, 149-155, 158, 160, 171, 174, 183, 197, 221-223, 228-229, 233, 245-256, 261-264, 266-267, 270-271, 283, 285, 288-289, 295, 301-305

divorce, 76, 156, 179, 181

Dwapara Yuga, 163

Eckhart, Meister, 5, 13-14, 26, 37, 48-49, 108, 111-112, 124-125, 133, 144-145, 156, 160, 214, 223, 294, 301

economics, 31

egalitarianism, 68-71, 211, 216

ego, 3-4, 19-20, 23, 26, 39, 42, 46, 48-49, 58, 78, 109, 120-125, 127, 139-140, 144, 146, 147, 150, 159, 252-253, 256-257, 276-278, 288, 292, 296

Elysian Fields, the, 127, 128

emptiness, 15, 24, 221, 238, 250

eros, 6, 226, 259, 288, 292

essence, the, 4, 55, 62, 64, 74, 84, 105, 107, 108, 115, 117, 125-126, 128, 132, 136, 139, 144, 146, 151, 154, 171, 210, 216, 247, 259, 273, 276, 278, 283-284, 288, 291, 297

Eternal, the, xii, 37, 102, 297

Eternity, 3, 6, 20, 27-29, 91, 98, 100, 156, 175, 179, 185, 305

ether, 221, 230, 234, 241

evolutionism, 12, 36, 43, 70, 104, 118, 119

Fall, the, 19, 25-26, 125, 138, 166, 168, 193, 206, 221, 248, 265, 286, 301

faith, ix, 1, 7, 9, 10, 11, 17, 24, 34-36, 52, 57, 66, 91, 113, 122, 125, 134, 140-141, 146, 150-157, 175, 184, 186, 190, 199, 201, 205, 220, 224-225, 229, 235, 239, 247-250, 252, 270

feudalism, 213

First Principles, xi

fitrah, 14, 50, 80, 159, 235, 288

Four (Cardinal) Directions, the, 230-235, 238

Four Elements, the, 230-238, 241

Francis of Assisi, St., 137, 256, 291

freedom, 4-5, 19, 23, 45, 71, 80, 83-84, 126-127, 132, 134, 137, 142, 166-167, 187-188, 202, 222, 249

free-will, 2, 5, 127

Fusus al-Hikam, 57

Ganges, River, 2, 80, 119

Garden of Eden, 160, 165, 169, 200, 248, 264, 273

Genesis, Book of, 30, 95, 116, 236, 287

gnosis, xi, 13, 32, 111, 215

Godhead, xii, 1, 4, 11, 14, 24, 30, 38, 54-56, 124, 128, 144-145, 240, 299, 301,

303, 305
Good, the, 2, 4, 5, 19, 21, 127, 128, 129,
    132, 140-141, 147, 152, 161, 165, 168,
    170, 171-174, 215, 220, 293. See also
    Summum Bonum
goodness, 129-133, 142, 145, 157, 158, 161,
    169, 174-175, 191, 220, 222, 246, 251
Great Spirit, the, 30, 34, 58
Guénon, René, ix-xi, 54, 105-106, 212
gunas, 22, 106, 142, 163, 233, 303

Heaven, xii, 1, 5, 10, 12, 16-17, 22, 26-37,
    41, 51-52, 54, 57-58, 61, 64, 68, 71-
    78, 91-94, 96-101, 112-114, 120-121,
    123, 125, 127, 136-137, 139, 142-145,
    151-156, 164, 167-168, 175, 177, 182-
    183, 188, 193-194, 205-210, 223-224,
    227, 233, 249, 251, 253, 255, 260,
    263, 267-270, 278, 282, 286, 290,
    296-297, 303
hell, 22, 50, 58, 73, 75, 95, 111-112, 121,
    131-132, 143-146, 158, 165, 172, 194,
    224, 260, 304
hermitages, 91
Hinduism, 6, 14, 24, 27, 40-44, 58, 62-
    63, 75, 93, 106, 111, 122, 134-137, 165,
    166, 168, 174, 206, 211, 220, 233-236,
    239-241, 258, 274, 279, 288, 297,
    299-307
Holy Name, the, 131
Holy Spirit (Ghost), the, 4, 48, 62, 81,
    206, 251, 301, 304, 305
human genius, 32
humanism, 74, 75, 85, 134, 183, 208
humility, 8, 12, 20, 35, 48, 53, 91, 95, 97,
    122, 157, 213, 217-218, 220, 238-239,
    249-250, 253, 296

Ibn Arabi, 42, 57, 114, 251
iconography, 61, 64, 135, 214, 290
idealism, 12, 69, 73, 135-136, 153, 181-182,
    223-224
ignorance, xii, 1, 19, 29, 38, 40, 51-52,
    58, 92, 106, 123, 130-133, 140, 154,
    156, 163, 165, 201-203, 208, 217, 225,

233, 269, 300
image, divine, 42, 67
iman, al-, 17
immortality, 4-5, 26, 45, 64, 79, 120,
    127, 155, 164, 226, 247, 261, 276, 288,
    292-293, 295
individualism, 7-8, 19, 20, 22,43, 46, 48,
    54, 103, 122, 125, 155, 166, 224, 228-
    229, 257, 265, 267
intellectus purus, x
Isis, 246-247, 283
Islam, 21, 37, 40, 56-57, 61-64, 67, 73, 84,
    87, 89, 93, 110, 116-117, 123, 134-137,
    145, 164, 180, 182, 202, 206, 210,
    215, 235, 239, 245-246, 257, 261, 289,
    305

japa, 27
Jesus Christ, 25, 31, 36, 40, 42, 45,48-49,
    57, 61-63, 66, 77-78, 92-93, 101, 110-
    113, 120, 124, 127, 130-133, 137-138,
    143, 150-151, 154, 164, 178-183, 194,
    214-215, 220, 222, 229, 246, 251,
    256-257, 268, 291-292, 302-303
Judaism, 56-57, 62, 73, 134, 137, 301, 302,
    304-305
Judas, 224
Judgment Day, 8, 151, 157
Jung, Carl, 47-48
Justice, 132, 167, 180, 192

Kabbalah, 110, 299, 300, 301
Kali, 73, 77, 80, 135, 137, 143, 163, 174,
    182, 203, 212, 263, 290, 291, 301, 306
Kali Yuga, 73, 77, 80, 135, 137, 143, 163,
    182, 203, 212, 263, 301, 306
karma, 19, 27, 44-45, 97, 129, 188, 190,
    222-223, 251
kingship, 67, 71, 74, 85, 90, 100, 102,
    205, 213, 223
Knights Templars, the, 220
koan, 39, 55, 105
Koran, the, 16, 34, 46, 51, 65, 69, 73, 76,
    96, 101, 103, 105, 108, 110, 115, 126,
    139, 140, 143, 149, 151-152, 161, 168-

169, 171, 174, 177, 188, 205, 211, 236, 245, 248, 265, 270, 273, 281

Krishna, xii, 22, 56, 62, 137, 140, 142, 177, 185, 234, 289

kshatriya, 71, 90, 205, 240-242, 302

Lakota, 37

Law, 50, 68, 178, 180, 268, 300

Logos, 6, 37, 49, 61, 184, 206, 261, 302

Love, 1, 4, 13, 23, 25, 39, 142, 234, 236, 238, 242, 251-252, 256, 263, 273-274, 282, 296, 297

marriage, 114, 155, 156, 181, 246-247, 287, 292-293, 296-297

Mars, 286-287

martyr, 47, 212

Mary Magdalene, 63

materialism, 115, 150, 198

Maya, 43, 51-52, 54-55, 106-107, 199, 254, 264-265, 300, 302, 305

Mecca, 119

mercy, 7, 9, 54, 68, 73, 98, 132, 146, 156, 175, 190-191, 195-196, 220, 224, 229, 246, 252, 274, 280, 282

metaphysics, ix, 39, 50, 55, 160, 200, 209, 232, 267, 303

Middle Ages, the, 37, 67, 69, 75, 81, 93, 94, 117, 161, 213, 230, 268, 302

mitakuye oyasin, 37

modern science, xi, 12, 32, 100, 173, 198

monks, 28, 62, 64, 73, 90, 158, 207

morality, 80, 129, 130-137, 142, 155, 181-182, 187, 226, 237-240, 286

Moses, 93, 103, 160, 161, 180, 246

Muhammad, the Prophet, 8, 37, 41, 57, 62-63, 84, 110, 140, 177, 215, 229, 305

Muslims, 80, 85, 136

mysticism, 50, 113, 215, 224, 249, 251, 255-256, 289, 299, 304

nakedness, 6, 246-247, 285

nationalism, 88-89, 235

Neoplatonism, 4, 110, 111, 164

New Age mysticism, 50

New Age spirituality, 11, 20-21, 250

New Testament, the, 180, 303

Nietzsche, Friedrich, 186, 220, 256

Nirvana, 54, 291, 300, 303

nobility, 7, 16, 17, 28, 33, 65, 68, 90, 122, 136, 215, 221, 223, 286

nomadism, 28, 54, 76, 86

objectivity, 7,8, 16, 23, 33, 92, 130, 178, 197, 217, 218, 221- 222, 238, 264, 273, 279, 280

Old Testament, the, 180

oligarchy, 197

omniscience, 200, 206

Origin, divine, xii, 6-9, 13, 29, 34, 44, 71, 72, 100, 104, 111, 131, 138, 150, 199,-200, 203, 241, 291, 294

orthodoxy, ix, xi, 11, 50

Ottoman Empire, 37, 87, 88, 89, 90

Paradise, 3, 109, 143, 144, 145, 164, 224, 259

Philosophia Perennis, ix, 2, 303

Plains Indians, 28, 40, 207, 223, 232, 238, 268

Plato, x, 6, 84, 85, 104, 114-115, 153, 161, 197, 203, 212, 228, 250

Plotinus, 19, 111

pneumatology, 2, 5-8, 10, 226.

pontifex, 1, 27, 56, 61, 206, 233

populism, 201

prajna, 103, 108

Prakriti, 22, 105-109, 114-115, 163, 167, 229-233, 236, 238-239, 265, 281, 290-291, 303-304

prayer, 27, 37, 53, 75, 113, 173, 217, 229, 249, 251, 255-256, 292

priests, 61, 64, 90, 92, 257, 263

primordial innocence, 17, 248, 285

primordial man, 25, 29, 42, 80, 99, 125, 232-233, 234, 236, 239, 241, 268

Primordial Qualities, 230, 231

primordial wisdom, 17

Principle, the, 55-56, 66, 107, 109, 119,

161-162, 204, 278, 290, 297

progressivism, 27, 64, 97, 101, 164, 180, 193, 199-200, 215

prophecy, 12

prophet(s), 6, 37, 38, 62, 64, 73, 75, 81, 84, 125, 140, 146, 211, 215-216, 223, 229, 257, 268, 289, 305

Protestantism, 67, 135, 205

prototype, divine, 69, 76, 120

psychoanalysis, 28, 47, 48, 172, 173

psychologism, 187

psychology, 2, 5, 8-11, 17, 21, 27, 29, 31, 33, 46-47, 58, 187, 226, 253, 302

psychotherapy, 10, 11

Purusha, 22, 105-109, 114, 229-233, 236, 240-241, 246, 265, 281, 283, 290, 300, 304

Pythagoras, x

quantum physics, 48, 115, 164, 227

Ramakrishna, 52, 289

Ramana Maharshi, 58, 103, 241, 253, 254

Ramdas, Swami, 241

Real, the, 3, 20, 24, 36, 38, 54, 55, 57, 63, 107, 123, 147, 161, 172, 184, 199, 225, 249, 257, 258, 303

Reality, 14, 23, 32-33, 35, 38-39, 47, 56, 128, 149, 153, 159-161, 179, 192, 198, 215, 225, 233, 241, 265-266, 273, 299, 305

reason, 260, 302

religio perennis, ix, 159

Renaissance, the, 35, 65-67, 89, 94, 99, 101, 135, 160

Revelation, 11, 59, 73, 97, 101, 130, 210, 211, 245

Rumi, 40, 105

sacred, the, xi-xii, 16, 46, 61, 80-81, 91-92, 94, 114, 138, 147, 154, 214, 252

sacred art, ix, 64, 66-67, 92, 93

sacred pipe (of the Lakota), the, 30, 36

sainthood, 68

saint(s), 3, 6, 21, 35, 40-41, 44, 47-49, 61, 63, 65, 67, 72, 74, 77-78, 90-92, 113, 121-123, 130, 134, 139, 140, 143, 146, 156, 159, 160, 186, 214, 222-223, 241, 252, 259, 265, 299

samadhi, 15, 56, 123, 141-142, 277, 303

samsara, 9, 12, 17, 19, 44, 54, 55, 58, 112, 115, 127, 132, 157, 184, 277, 303

samskaras, 44, 122

sanatana dharma, 50, 159, 235

sannyasa, 24

Sat, 1, 161, 295, 304

Satan, 7, 49, 149, 152, 164-165, 168-171, 174

sattva, 22, 106, 120, 142, 163, 233, 301

Satya Yuga, 2, 98, 143, 163, 304, 306

Schuon, Frithjof, ix-xi, 2, 4, 9, 21, 29, 43, 50-51, 53, 58, 72, 84, 92, 100, 105, 109, 113, 116, 138, 143, 147, 151, 166, 181-183, 232, 235, 249, 254, 258-259, 263, 265, 267, 292, 307

scriptures, 10, 12, 54, 73, 103, 143, 167-169, 172, 174

secularism, 202

Self, 1, 3, 7, 8, 10, 20, 26, 41-45, 50-51, 54-59, 103-112, 119-126, 140, 142, 144-147, 160-161, 236, 247, 254, 256-257, 259, 264, 277, 299, 300-304

self-domination, 23, 136, 173, 225, 278, 280, 282

Selfhood, 7, 58, 144, 246

Sermon on the Mount, the, 180

Shakespeare, William, 20, 211

Shankaracharya, 103, 106

shudra, 71, 135, 240, 305

Shunyata, 14

sin, 50, 73, 80, 132, 134, 136, 140-142, 156, 165, 172, 183, 190, 240, 264, 265, 270

Sioux Indians, 30, 245

Smith, Huston, xi

socialism, 71, 202

sociology, 27-28, 31, 54, 215

Song of Songs, 53, 107, 126, 246, 271, 294

sophia perennis, ix

Sovereign Good, 2, 4, 128-129, 141, 152, 220, 293

spiritualism, 50

spirituality, ix, xii, 8, 11-12, 17, 20-23, 30-33, 36, 40, 49, 53, 91-92, 98-99, 139, 143, 155, 163, 212, 214, 226, 249, 250, 252-254, 259, 263, 289, 291

stoicism, 122

Stoddart, William, xi, 87,

Stonehenge, 233, 277

submission, 281

Substance, divine, 55, 103, 105-106, 110, 146, 161, 204

Sufi(s), 24, 40, 43, 46, 50, 54, 57, 75, 80, 109, 113, 115, 117, 124, 140, 143, 145, 169, 208, 251-252, 283, 297, 301

Sufism, 14, 23, 49, 106, 108, 110, 114, 117, 139, 206-207, 229, 235, 249-250, 257, 301-302, 305, 307

Summum Bonum, 128-130, 141, 220, 293

superstition, 35, 150

Supreme Being, 1, 4, 300

Supreme Principle, 4, 5, 55

symbolism, ix, 17, 64-66, 79, 93, 94, 101, 118, 135, 138, 139, 143, 150, 162, 165, 193, 204, 227, 232-233, 247, 248, 266, 274, 277-278, 283, 285, 287, 290

Taj Mahal, the, 93, 94

Taoism, 110, 165, 174, 184, 238, 239, 268, 300, 306

Ten Commandments, the, 180, 181

theocracy, 154, 197, 201, 203

Third Eye, 58

Tibet, 62

timocracy, 197

tradition, sacred, ix, xi-xii, 11-12, 30-31, 41-42, 58, 90, 92-93, 97, 99-101, 114, 154-155, 199-200, 205-206, 208, 215, 222

traditionalism, 92, 97, 259

Treta Yuga, 163, 306

Trinity, the, 56

True, the, 2, 147, 161, 215, 258

Truth, 1, ix, xi, 5, 12, 14-15, 19-21, 23, 25, 26, 45, 50, 66, 97, 98, 160, 163, 198, 199-201, 209, 215, 218, 225, 234, 238, 241-242, 250, 254, 258, 271-274, 281-282, 297, 300, 303-304

tyranny, 70, 88, 198, 208, 212, 219

universality, ix, 53

Upanishad(s), 41, 73, 93, 103, 106, 140-142, 233, 241, 263-264

upaya, 137

utilitarianism, 118, 179

vaishya, 90, 240, 305

Vedanta, 1, 43, 50, 55, 103, 106, 161, 199, 222, 264-265, 268, 299-300, 303

Vedas, 77, 155, 165, 169, 233, 236, 263

Venus, 286, 287

virgin birth, 36, 110

Virgin Mary, 62, 63, 291. *See also* Blessed Virgin

Virgin nature, 3

virtue, 7, 76, 97, 240

Vishnu, 62, 77, 289

Void, the, 14, 121, 123, 139, 147, 170, 228, 252

Wakan Tanka, 58

White Buffalo Maiden (Woman), 30, 245

Wisdom, 4, 11, 13, 21, 29, 40, 43, 49, 53, 57-58, 68, 73, 87, 100, 109, 116, 124, 142, 151, 161, 182, 183, 232, 235-236, 258, 267, 276, 297, 307

yang, 226, 227, 230, 275, 290, 301

yin, 226, 227, 230, 275, 290, 301

yugas, 28, 71, 162, 163, 302

Zen Buddhism, 15, 16, 55, 126, 161, 206, 252-253

Zoroastrianism, 164

BIOGRAPHICAL NOTES

MARK PERRY is an author and professional translator. Although of American parents, he was born in Cairo, Egypt, in 1951 and raised in Lausanne, Switzerland close to Frithjof Schuon. He is the son of eminent American Perennialist author Whitall Perry. Mark Perry is the author of the book, *On Awakening and Remembering: To Know Is to Be*, published by Fons Vitae (2000). He is currently in the process of updating the translations of all of Frithjof Schuon's books from the original French into the English language, and has also translated a large number of Schuon's French and German letters.

WILLIAM STODDART was a close associate of both Frithjof Schuon and Titus Burckhardt during the lives of these leading Perennialists and translated several of their works into English. For many years Stoddart was assistant editor of the British journal *Studies in Comparative Religion*. Pursuing his interests in comparative religion, he has traveled widely in Europe, North Africa, India, Sri Lanka, and Japan. Stoddart's works include *Outline of Hinduism* (1993; 2007 edition titled *Hinduism and Its Spiritual Masters*), *Outline of Buddhism* (1998), and *Outline of Sufism: The Essentials of Islamic Spirituality* (2012). His essential writings were published by World Wisdom as *Remembering in a World of Forgetting: Thoughts on Tradition and Post-modernism* (2008).

Other Titles in the Perennial Philosophy Series by World Wisdom

The Betrayal of Tradition: Essays on the Spiritual Crisis of Modernity, edited by Harry Oldmeadow, 2005

Borderlands of the Spirit: Reflections on a Sacred Science of Mind, by John Herlihy, 2005

A Buddhist Spectrum: Contributions to Buddhist-Christian Dialogue, by Marco Pallis, 2003

A Christian Pilgrim in India: The Spiritual Journey of Swami Abhishiktananda (Henri Le Saux), by Harry Oldmeadow, 2008

Emir Abd el-Kader: Hero and Saint of Islam, by Ahmed Bouyerdene, 2012

The Essential Ananda K. Coomaraswamy, edited by Rama P. Coomaraswamy, 2004

The Essential René Guénon, edited by John Herlihy, 2009

The Essential Seyyed Hossein Nasr, edited by William C. Chittick, 2007

The Essential Sophia, edited by Seyyed Hossein Nasr and Katherine O'Brien, 2006

The Essential Titus Burckhardt: Reflections on Sacred Art, Faiths, and Civilizations, edited by William Stoddart, 2003

Every Branch in Me: Essays on the Meaning of Man, edited by Barry McDonald, 2002

Every Man An Artist: Readings in the Traditional Philosophy of Art, edited by Brian Keeble, 2005

Figures of Speech or Figures of Thought? The Traditional View of Art, by Ananda K. Coomaraswamy, 2007

A Guide to Hindu Spirituality, by Arvind Sharma, 2006

Introduction to Traditional Islam, Illustrated: Foundations, Art, and Spirituality, by Jean-Louis Michon, 2008

Introduction to Sufism: The Inner Path of Islam, by Éric Geoffroy, 2010

Islam, Fundamentalism, and the Betrayal of Tradition:
Essays by Western Muslim Scholars,
edited by Joseph E.B. Lumbard, 2004, 2009

Journeys East: 20th Century Western Encounters with Eastern Religious
Traditions, by Harry Oldmeadow, 2004

Light From the East: Eastern Wisdom for the Modern West,
edited by Harry Oldmeadow, 2007

Living in Amida's Universal Vow: Essays in Shin Buddhism,
edited by Alfred Bloom, 2004

Maintaining the Sacred Center: The Bosnian City of Stolac,
by Rusmir Mahmutćehajić, 2011

Of the Land and the Spirit:
The Essential Lord Northbourne on Ecology and Religion,
edited by Christopher James and Joseph A. Fitzgerald, 2008

On the Origin of Beauty:
Ecophilosophy in the Light of Traditional Wisdom,
by John Griffin, 2011

Outline of Sufism: The Essentials of Islamic Spirituality,
by William Stoddart, 2012

Paths to the Heart: Sufism and the Christian East,
edited by James S. Cutsinger, 2002

Remembering in a World of Forgetting:
Thoughts on Tradition and Postmodernism, by William Stoddart, 2008

Returning to the Essential: Selected Writings of Jean Biès,
translated by Deborah Weiss-Dutilh, 2004

Science and the Myth of Progress, edited by Mehrdad M. Zarandi, 2003

Seeing God Everywhere: Essays on Nature and the Sacred,
edited by Barry McDonald, 2003

Singing the Way: Insights in Poetry and Spiritual Transformation,
by Patrick Laude, 2005

The Spiritual Legacy of the North American Indian:
Commemorative Edition, by Joseph E. Brown, 2007

Sufism: Love & Wisdom,
edited by Jean-Louis Michon and Roger Gaetani, 2006

The Timeless Relevance of Traditional Wisdom,
by M. Ali Lakhani, 2010

Touchstones of the Spirit: Essays on Religion, Tradition & Modernity,
by Harry Oldmeadow, 2012

The Underlying Religion: An Introduction to the Perennial Philosophy,
edited by Martin Lings and Clinton Minnaar, 2007

Unveiling the Garden of Love:
Mystical Symbolism in Layla Majnun and Gita Govinda,
by Lalita Sinha, 2008

What Does Islam Mean in Today's World:
Religion, Politics, Spirituality,
by William Stoddart, 2012

The Wisdom of Ananda Coomaraswamy:
Selected Reflections on Indian Art, Life, and Religion,
edited by S. Durai Raja Singam and Joseph A. Fitzgerald, 2011

Wisdom's Journey: Living the Spirit of Islam in the Modern World,
by John Herlihy, 2009

Ye Shall Know the Truth: Christianity and the Perennial Philosophy,
edited by Mateus Soares de Azevedo, 2005